Boys Don't Lie

A History of Shoes

BOYS DON'T LIE

———————

A HISTORY OF SHOES

MARY E. DONNELLY

WITH MOIRA MCCORMICK

PurePopPress LLC, Vestal, NY

First edition published 2013 by PurePopPress LLC
Copyright © 2013 PurePopPress LLC

All rights reserved. No reproduction, copy, or transmission of this publication may be made without express written permission of the author or press.

Cover photo: Shoes, 1975. Cover design by Steven Gardner, 3rd Alternative Inc., Farmingdale, NY.

ISBN-10: 0-615-40394-8
ISBN-13: 978-0-615-40394-6

TABLE OF CONTENTS

Acknowledgements 3

Foreword by Steve Simels 5

Prologue: In the Land of Elijah the Second 9

Chapter 1: New Meat 15

Chapter 2: One in Versailles 49

Chapter 3: Move It or Lose It 77

Chapter 4: Fire for Awhile 105

Chapter 5: Jet Set 145

Chapter 6: When It Hits 177

Chapter 7: Twist and Bend It 213

Chapter 8: Under the Gun 255

Chapter 9: When Push Comes to Shove 295

Chapter 10: Never Had It Better 333

Chapter 11: Rugged Terrain 375

Chapter 12: Slipping Through Your Fingers 413

Epilogue: Sign of Life 453

Coda 463

Index 465

Acknowledgments

Many thanks to the generous people who agreed to speak with me for this book: Ted Ansani, Paul Austermehle, Cary Baker, David Bash, Moe Berg, Leroy Bocchieri, John Borack, Dan Bourgoise, Mike Braam, Tom Braam, Duncan Browne, Pat Day Cobb, Richard Dashut, Herb Eimermann, Ed Erickson, Chuck Fieldman, Michael Freeman, Mike Galassini, Stephen Gardner, Jim Girling, Lou Hinkhouse, Jamie Hoover, Jeff Hunter, Steve Hurd, Peter Jesperson (with an assist from Vern Sanden), Neville Johnson, Andy Joseph, Tim Klebe, Tom Leavens, C.K. Lendt, Bill Lloyd, Mark Malboeuf, Dorn Martell, Don McLeese, Ric Menck, Skip Meyer, Hank Neuberger, Bill Nowlin, Paul Neville, Bill Paige, Lee Popa, Paul Rebmann, Bill "Beet" Richardson, John Richardson, Ira Robbins, Hernan Rojas, Kelley Ryan, Bruce Sachs, Marty Schwartz, Marty Scott, Suzy Shaw, Barry Shumaker, Sara Haack Townsend, Jay Whitehouse, Susan Willenborg, Mike Zelenko, the Zion Historical Society.

Some subjects were unable to share their reflections with me: Ken Buttice suffered a serious stroke several years ago and has lost much of his memory; Mike Stone and Greg Shaw have both passed away. A few proved impossible to locate; others did not return requests or declined to be interviewed.

Many thanks too to those who read this in manuscript form (in whole or in part), including Cary Baker, John Borack, Lou Hinkhouse, Linda Lester, Chris Morris, Jordan Oakes, Herb Somers.

On a personal level, I wish to thank my long-suffering spouse, Andrew J. Haggerty, whose forbearance made all the work possible; Molly, Seamus, Róisín, and Sean, my beautiful family; and my sin-eater, Virginia Atkins. My brother Paul, who first played Shoes for me when I was an impressionable twelve-year-old, deserves a hearty share of the credit for this book as well.

And finally, to Gary, John, and Jeff. Without you, there would be nothing to say.

FOREWORD

By Steve Simels

If truth be told, when the lovely and talented Mary Donnelly asked me to contribute some introductory words to the book you now hold in your hand (or whatever the phrase is if you're reading it via some sort of digital device), I was more than a bit hesitant. For a couple of reasons.

The first, of course, is that I consider Mary a good friend. Secondly, if you've read any of my poor scribblings about rock music and pop culture over the last couple of years, it's almost entirely due to the fact that Mary trusted me enough to give me a spare set of keys to the car, metaphorically speaking, over at PowerPop, the website she created back in 2004, and I am thus eternally in her debt on a professional level. Both of these facts, of course, might lend a certain credence to the idea that anything nice I have to say about *Boys Don't Lie* would fall into the category of what *SPY* magazine used to refer to as "logrolling in our time." You know—a little, uh, self-serving.

Another, and probably the more important, reason I was initially reluctant to contribute to the project is that the greatest foreword to a music tome of all time has already been written, so, like, what's the point? I refer, of course, to the work of legendary Irish playwright and pub crawler Samuel Beckett, who in a prefatory note to the first (or maybe third) edition of Nick Tosches' *Unsung Heroes of Rock 'n' Roll* called it "the only book about rock 'n' roll that knows what it's talking about!", a claim (and essay) that while almost certainly actually penned by Tosches (the Great Man himself being probably dead at the time) is unlikely to be bettered any time soon, at least not by a white suburban punk like me.

All that said, however, the fact remains that *Boys Don't Lie* is an exemplary rock-band bio and then some. On the most basic level, it's brilliantly researched, to the point where one suspects its subjects learned all sorts of stuff about themselves they didn't know. It also puts Shoes' now decades-long saga into a historical/cultural/music-biz context in a way that nobody's had the wit or temerity to do before, which is to say that apart from a passionate (and convincing) critical argument for just why just these guys' music is important, it also makes clear where it came from along with the real-world strictures that led to them creating it. In other words, this band may have been hermetic and out of step with the pop mainstream on some level, but in fact none of their albums were, as Robert Christgau famously suggested, written and recorded by elves.

This is also a book about pop obsessions, by which I mean there are cult bands, there are Cult Bands, and then there's Shoes. Shoes have been a life-changer for a lot of people (Mary included, obviously) over the years, but it's not exactly news that they've never sold a lot of records (at a level, say, commensurate with their critical accolades) since their debut LP *Black Vinyl Shoes* appeared to a world in equal parts baffled and delighted by it. The subtext of *Boys Don't Lie* is how that process works, how three guys working in a sort of provincial-but-not-really isolation (their Zion, Illinois roots turn out to be far more important and interesting than I for one had realized) came up with the equivalent of a secret language that spoke first of all to themselves and then, in ways that must have surprised them, to a small subset of humanity that got the message in an instant.

Which means, now that I think of it, that Christgau's elves formulation was not completely off the mark, and that what makes Shoes unique—for those who also speak that secret language—is that they sound, simultaneously, like nothing you've exactly heard before and something you seem to have heard heretofore only in your head. Last summer, discussing the work in progress over a Japanese dinner, Mary asked me, "Have you ever turned anybody on to Shoes by playing the albums for them?" It seemed a silly question, at first, until I realized—no, in fact, I never had; the people I knew who loved the band had, to a person, discovered them on their own, without prompting from me or any other fans. And I was reminded of what Jules Feiffer said about the pop obsession of his youth—the first generation of American comic books. "When Superman at last appeared," Feiffer wrote in *The Great Comic Book Heroes*, his definitive history of the all-in-color-for-a-dime stories that changed his life, "he brought with him the deep satisfaction of all underground truths. Our reaction was less 'How original!' than 'But, of course!'"

If ever there was an "of course!" band, Shoes is it.

But enough, as it were, of my yakking; the band's story, and much, much more, awaits you. In *Boys Don't Lie*—which, despite what that probably-dead drunken Gaelic lout had to say earlier, actually *is* the only book about rock & roll that knows what it's talking about.

—PARIS 2013

Prologue

In the Land of Elijah the Second

ZION, ILLINOIS IS A SMALL TOWN built on lofty dreams.

The story of Shoes is deeply intertwined with the story of Zion, built as a haven for the followers of Joseph-Smith-come-lately John Alexander Dowie. A complex figure, Dowie's influence over this modest community is pervasive. He is its founder, its visionary, its dirty secret.

Dowie (1847-1907) was a self-professed faith healer, someone who attributed physical illness to the workings of Satan, and "divine healing" to the intervention of God through his holy servant: Dowie himself.

Born in Scotland, raised in Australia, Dowie began religious training at the prestigious University of Edinburgh. He served as chaplain at its equally renowned medical school, where he developed a hearty disdain for the potential of scientific medicine, then still a primitive, bloody business. Back in Australia, Dowie entered the ministry and practiced divine healing on the sick and lame for fifteen years, before coming to the United States in 1888. By 1893, he had landed in Chicago, undertaking a highly publicized stint at the World's Columbian Exposition.

The Exposition's organizers thought Dowie was a charlatan and denied his Divine Healing Association a place on its Avenue of Churches. So he set up shop across the street from the Exposition's front entrance, in a sprawling structure archly known as "The Little Brown Hut." There, "Doctor" Dowie (a title often given to ministers, but which perceptibly blurred the line between religion and medicine in this case) drew crowds of thousands, and even effected some "cures" of D-list celebrities like Abraham Lincoln's cousin and Buffalo Bill's niece.

But Dowie was more than just a standard-issue religious zealot: he adhered to some truly irregular doctrines. For example, he was a flat-earther, despite the fact that he himself had circumnavigated the globe, in his travels from Europe to Australia and Australia to America. Furthermore, Dowie held that that the natives of the British Isles constituted a lost tribe of Israel (much as Mormon Church founder Joseph Smith believed about the indigenous peoples of the Americas).

THROUGHOUT THE 1890S, DOWIE continued to build his flock in Chicago and elsewhere, initially extending his healing ministry through a chain of Healing Houses, and then formally establishing his own denomination, the Christian Catholic Apostolic Church, in 1896. Dowie went to some lengths to avoid antagonizing other religious figures, holding his services on Sunday afternoons, for example, so as not to compete directly with traditional churches' morning services.

But Dowie's relationship to the local and federal governments was somewhat more contentious. He refused to obey the orders of municipal politicians to register his Healing House ministries as hospitals; according to one report, he was arrested for this crime over a hundred times in 1895 alone. Dowie also clashed with postal authorities over the status of his weekly mass-mailings to his thousands of followers: he paid the higher business-postage rate, but insisted the mailings should be franked at the discount rate churches got.

Dowie was increasingly driven to create a haven where the legal distinctions between churches and hospitals and businesses disappeared. He had the followers, he had the funds, and in 1899, he began planning Zion City, forty miles north of Chicago on Lake Michigan. With a confidence bordering on arrogance, sustained by his belief that he was fulfilling God's will, Dowie determined to carve the Promised Land out of this patch of Midwestern scrub and farmland.

Dowie designed the town in every detail, taking advice from prominent surveyors and land-use managers, making Zion one of the first planned communities in America. It was laid out in a tidy grid around Shiloh Park, which also contained his Shiloh Cathedral (capacity 8,000). The original blueprint included diagonal streets as well: the map of Zion was intended to emulate the Union Jack, in honor of Dowie's British imperial lineage.

The town was also conceived as a communitarian paradise: industrial, agricultural, mercantile, and medico-religious facilities were all organized by the municipal government, which built edifices like the Zion Lace Industries, the Zion City General Stores, and the Zion Home, a massive, turreted Healing House which was, at the time, the largest wooden structure in the world.

And Zion's isolation was intentional: Dowie's flock would thus be insulated from the inevitable temptations of the big city to the south.

Building began in 1900, and though many flocked to the new utopia, Dowie himself retained ownership of all property. He leased to residents—all faithful apostles—on a 1,100-year basis. This, he reasoned, would cover the time needed for Jesus to return to earth (about a hundred years, by Dowie's estimate), plus a millennium cushion. Leasing to his followers avoided the issues raised by competing rights of multiple owners, and enabled Dowie to control who could settle in Zion—and who couldn't.

In order to make the town livable in short order, quick-and-dirty wooden structures were erected throughout the sprouting town to give the pioneers shelter while they built heaven on earth; most were eventually replaced with more permanent brick-and-mortar buildings.

To keep his flock and his sanctuary pure, Dowie the shepherd forbade a whole slew of sinful behaviors: smoking, drinking, gambling, spitting, swearing, and eating biblically proscribed foods, to name but a few. Doctors and drugstores were similarly banned, since all healing was to be done by God, via Dowie.

Zion embodied Dowie's vision of the holy city on a hill and, some said, his grandiose self-regard, since he retained such an overwhelming amount of control.

In 1906, chronicler Rolvix Harlan, in his book *John Alexander Dowie and the Christian Apostolic Church in Zion*, described the town:

> The worship of Zion is what takes up most of the spare time of the people. ... [T]hey make a business of religion. Morning, noon, and night, cottage prayer meetings are held in most of the homes, and if anyone has additional time and further inclination he may attend Bible readings or Healing Meetings at Hospice or Tabernacle, at odd hours.
>
> ....
>
> At nine a.m. the whistle at the powerhouse blows and for two minutes, Mohammedan fashion, everybody turns to prayer in whatever place and from whatever work or occupation, until the same whistle bids them turn their thoughts to secular things again.... Bill boards [sic] at the cross streets caution one that swearing or smoking or bad language of any sort are not allowed. Zion City will tolerate no breweries, no saloons, no drug or tobacco stores, no physician's or surgeon's offices, no theaters, no gambling places, no dance halls, no secret lodge rooms, no keeping or selling of swine's flesh.

It certainly appeared as if John Alexander Dowie had achieved his promised land. But as Zion developed, as Dowie's flock grew, he fell victim to his increasingly sensational ambitions—declaring himself Elijah the Second, the Restorer, the First Apostle of the Christian Catholic Church, the herald of Christ's return. He wore Old Testament-style robes, and had his portrait painted in them.

DOWIE'S FALL, WHEN IT inevitably occurred, was headlong and catastrophic.

His misfortunes started with the death of his beloved daughter Esther in May 1902 (from an unfortunate accident with a forbidden, and therefore secret, alcohol-fueled curling iron); her father publically attributed her demise to Satan. "Her beautiful body was destroyed by the enemy," Dowie said in his funeral oration, describing Esther's moving apology first to God, and then to himself, for her disobedience.

In the months and years that followed, a series of financial and ethical crises took place in quick succession. There were tales of sexual impropriety and polygamy (several current residents mention that Dowie's mansion was rumored to have underground tunnels, so he could sneak out and visit women without being seen). More substantively, Dowie's profligate spending was criticized for placing the entire project of Zion City in jeopardy.

While Zion was still in its infancy, Dowie lavished huge sums on travelling to spread his message, at the same time requesting loans from the public at large to keep Zion itself afloat. His spending, like his declaration that he was the new Elijah, was seen by some as another step in the faith healer's progression from apparent piety to overt megalomania.

In 1904, Dowie undertook a European tour to spread the gospel of his healing ministry and the miracle of Zion City. (Dowie's visit runs through James Joyce's infamous masterwork *Ulysses*.) In Dowie's absence, his trusted lieutenant Wilbur Glen Voliva administered the church for him. But with Dowie abroad, Voliva discovered the truly desperate financial straits of the church and town, and mounted a hostile takeover, suing Dowie for control of church funds. In the ensuing trial, Dowie's own wife testified against him.

Upon his return from Europe, Dowie reclaimed his power, but then suffered the one thing a faith healer simply can't afford: physical illness. One Sunday in front of his congregation, he was felled by a stroke.

That was the end; Dowie's fall was complete, and his death soon after, at the age of 59, occurred in comparative poverty and obscurity.

DOWIE'S CHALLENGER BECAME HIS successor. At heart, Wilbur Voliva was even more of a theocrat than Zion's founding father. But lacking Dowie's charisma, and faced with the task of governing a city in dire financial throes, Voliva could only grimly oversee the erosion of Dowie's utopian vision in Zion City.

Under Voliva's reign, Zion faced increasing incursions from profligate outsiders, who moved in around the city limits, selling liquor, opening drugstores, tempting the faithful. Sternly worded billboards proclaiming that the church owned all the land in town became increasingly subject to vandalism by "Independents," those who were not members of the Christian Catholic Church and resisted its role in civic affairs. In the 1930s, Zion's tenants successfully sued the church in order to own their own property; the leases were transferred to bills of sale. Churches of other denominations were also established, earning the ire of the Theocrats, as the original residents were now popularly known.

By Voliva's death in 1942, Zion's era of theocracy was over, but though the government of Zion was now officially secular, many of the moral regulations persisted. Laws banning lottery tickets and bikinis stayed on the books well into the 1960s; the liquor ban lasted into the twenty-first century. And the town remained profoundly, if not uniformly, faithful: at one point, it had more churches per capita than any other town in America.

It was into this insulated, sanctified, circumscribed world that Shoes were born.

Chapter 1

New Meat (1953-74)

THOUGH LOCATED ON THE SHORES of Lake Michigan, Zion, Illinois is not a beach town. Much of the lakefront is off-limits: the grounds of the defunct nuclear reactor are guarded, and the southern half of Illinois Beach State Park is a Superfund site. The town itself is separated from the water by a wide swath of empty land, a sand flat broken only by dunes and scrub.

The railroad tracks, which sit a good half-mile or more inland, once marked the western border of the industrial zone; now they represent the eastern edge of Zion itself. Getting to the lake requires traversing the no-man's-land between tracks and water. Once, much of that land was filled with Zion's industries, ranging from lace and candy factories to electronics plants, which took advantage of proximity to the lake for shipping.

It was an enterprising zone in the 1950s. By then, utopian Zion was superficially indistinguishable from any other small Midwestern town, its evangelical origins obscured by a veneer of *Leave It to Beaver*-style suburbanity on the one hand and industrial bustle on the other.

IN JANUARY 1953, GARY KLEBE was born into this picture-postcard small factory town.

Gary was the eldest of four children, and his childhood was a pretty typical affair: sports, school, *The Three Stooges*. His father Jerry, a court official, and his mother Arlie—a former schoolteacher who was an amateur artist and singer—raised their two boys and two girls in a state of controlled chaos in a roomy old house at the south end of Ezra Avenue, on Zion's southwest side.

The Klebe dwelling was a very old wooden construction, and as such, Gary thinks, possibly one of the "quick-and-dirty" structures built to house Zion's residents during the city's initial, Dowie-inspired development: the lot it occupied was numbered in the earliest planning maps of Zion. When the Klebe family resided there as renters, the two-house property on which it sat was owned by Mr. Shumaker, a senior citizen who lived in the front house. Gary says their landlord functioned as a sort of an honorary grandfather, since both sides of the Klebes' extended family lived all the way over in western Illinois. Fittingly, Mr. Shumaker's actual grandson, Barry, would later figure into Shoes' story.

There were occasional traumas *chez* Klebe, in particular the time in 1962 that Gary's younger brother set the house on fire while playing with a lighter, and his father had to race upstairs into the flames to rescue his sleeping baby sister. For nine-year old Gary, the most indelible imprint of that event was the lingering smell of charred wood, since the family continued to live in the house—now missing a second story—for another six months while their new home north of town was completed.

And there were familial tensions as well. Gary's father, a Navy veteran of World War II, was focused and driven, and he pushed his children—especially his eldest son—with firm expectations of success. "It was never *if* you go to college, but *when*," Gary recalls. At the same time, Jerry Klebe was often away from home, going out after dinner at night to meet with his friends and drink, something that was illegal within Zion city limits. "There was this other family in our neighborhood, their dad stayed home and went to church and mowed the lawn," Gary says. "I remember dismissing that: 'Your dad's not cool like my dad.'" Yet he was uncomfortably aware that his father's behavior caused stress, particularly for his mother, to whom he was very close. "But he was a good dad overall," Gary reflects.

SIMILAR DRAMAS WERE ENACTED IN a different key on the other side of Zion, on Elim Avenue, where the Murphy family lived.

John Murphy had a difficult debut: born a month premature in November 1953, the jaundiced infant spent time in the pure-oxygen incubators standard in the mid-fifties, and was close enough to death to be preemptively baptized in the hospital. As a child John was quiet; not athletic, but a gifted artist (who does not recall ever formally learning to draw). "I do remember being surprised that everyone couldn't," he says. Friends who offered to trade baseball lessons for drawing lessons were met with a bemused, "Don't you just pick up a pencil and go?"

Jeff, born one year and one week after John, in December 1954, was always less shy and more talkative. John (along with Jeff himself) recalls his kid brother as something of a tag-along, especially when the elder Murphy had friends over, which didn't sit well with John. This was partly due to the closeness of their ages, and partly with the peculiar point at which the school year broke, just between their birthdays. Though only a year younger, Jeff was two years behind John in school, and so the usual attraction of the younger sibling to the friends of the older was compounded by the fact that Jeff was actually closer in age to John's buddies than to his own classmates. Jeff shrugs, "I just liked John's friends better."

Their sibling rivalry was exacerbated by the fact that John's health remained relatively frail, leveling the physical differences between the older and younger boy. John remembers one particular altercation over a pick-up baseball game on the street: the brothers fought, surrounded by neighborhood youngsters egging them on. "As we swung at each other in front of our house," John recounts, "the other kids circled around us, all yelling and laughing, 'C'mon, Johnny!' 'Hit him, Jeffie!' My mom came out and broke it up. ... I was on my knees at that point and Jeff was clearly the victor." John recalls that his father, obviously worried that his older son got his butt kicked by his younger brother, later taught John how to throw punches, with a pillow as his opponent.

Their father, John Michael Murphy—known as "Mick" to everyone—worked at the Warwick Electronics factory, where the Midwest retail giant Sears, Roebuck and Co. made Sears' Silvertone televisions. The massive factory in Zion's industrial zone had originally been built by Dowie himself to house his cherished Zion Lace Industries. Mick would sometimes cram spare parts in his pants pockets, and Jeff remembers his own early interest in electronics being sparked by these mysterious objects.

"He was always bringing home odds and ends—tubes and stuff like that—and I was always drawn to that," Jeff says. "I wanted to be able to build something that would make a tube light up, because I thought it was so cool, that orange glow." He prized his two-transistor radio, and listened to it under his pillow at night. But the most inarguable evidence of Jeff's precocious fascination with electronics was a Ross Mark 400 reel-to-reel tape machine he requested and received for Christmas 1961, when he was barely seven.

Earlier that year, the Murphy brothers had gotten their first record player and started buying records: mostly kiddie fare by the likes of Uncle Remus, the Chipmunks, and the Merry Mailman, not to mention *Around the World with Donald Duck*.

But it wasn't always kiddie fare. Mick Murphy took his sons to diners and introduced them to the wonderful world of the tabletop jukebox: John remembers begging his father for dimes to hear radio hits like "Sugar Shack" by Jimmy Gilmer and the Fireballs and "Tie Me Kangaroo Down, Sport" by Rolf Harris; John says his father was particularly fond of playing him Jimmy Dean's "Big Bad John."

Family life was contentious, unfortunately. The Murphy parents were an odd match, he a blue-collar Irish-American war veteran with a penchant for other women, she a strictly-brought-up only child from a sober German family. The couple fought frequently about Mick's activities outside the house—some of which, true, were with civic organizations like the Jaycees and town bowling leagues. But there were also "lipstick-on-the-collar kind of arguments," as John puts it.

Jeff notes that his mother, Leona, had remained unusually close to her parents even after her marriage. This physical and emotional proximity possibly also created tension in the Murphys' young household. He remembers his grandparents being a lot more involved in his immediate family's affairs than is generally considered acceptable. "My grandfather was a pretty strong-willed person, and he may have overstepped his bounds," Jeff says.

But neither son initially understood just why, one day in July 1962, their father disappeared. He went to work, didn't come home, and was never seen again.

John remembers being sent by his mother, just as the midsummer dusk was falling, to find his dad at the Warwick factory. The distance, less than two miles, was nevertheless a long way for a boy of eight on a bicycle. He recalls asking a friend if he wanted to come along, and the friend's dad refusing permission because of the hour. John shrugged and went alone, only to be told by two gruff security guards at the gate that "Mr. Murphy been gone a long time."

Returning to deliver this piece of information to his mother, John recalls that she seemed distraught, but not really surprised. That night, he says, while he and Jeff were supposed to be distracted by *The Twilight Zone* in the next room, friends came to the house to comfort Leona Murphy, but she dismissed their attempts to reassure her that Mick would be back. "She knew he was really gone," John recollects. Mick had run off with a woman, they soon learned, because that woman's husband stopped by in the ensuing days to compare notes with their mother. John recalls him standing at the foot of the porch steps; Leona wouldn't let him in the house.

The boys were instructed to tell their friends that their father was on "a business trip to Chicago." They adhered to this lie—ineffectively—for nearly two years.

"Maybe Jeff and I both were too young to realize what had happened," John reflects, "or maybe we just didn't have a strong relationship with our father. But I don't remember ever being like, 'Oh, boo-hoo, Daddy's gone.'"

Their mother, however, was now faced with building a life on her own for herself and her two sons in the pre-feminist sixties. Child support and alimony were not options; Mick was just *gone*. Even his own family proclaimed ignorance of his whereabouts, and various searches by private investigators she couldn't really afford—required by law to prove desertion, and thus grounds for divorce—were fruitless.

So Leona got a job, working at the catalog desk at the Sears in Waukegan, a few miles down the road. For this, she learned to drive, a skill she'd never before needed. Even more actively involved in their lives now, the boys' grandparents came to visit at least once or twice a week: babysitting on Wednesday nights when their mother worked late, doing home repairs, showing up with homemade cookies, and making meals. "I know now they were bringing us food because we didn't have enough," John says, "but it didn't occur to me at the time."

Both brothers remember this phase of their life as seeming to last much longer than it actually did; as John puts it, "I always kind of think of a large portion of my childhood as being just the three of us."

But in fact, this "just the three of us" phase only lasted about a year and a half. It wasn't long after she'd succeeded in getting the marriage dissolved that Leona was introduced to a co-worker's brother, himself recently divorced. John recalls that Tom Scott, who worked for the electric company, came to the Murphys' house with his sister to play cards at first, but then made return trips by himself, even bringing dinner. It seemed "very natural that he'd come with buckets of chicken or fish or whatever," John relates. "He'd taken the place of our dad." The courtship lasted only a few months. By April 1964, John and Jeff had a stepfather.

OF COURSE, THE OUTSIDE WORLD was changing in important ways, too, by spring 1964. And for these boys on the brink of adolescence, the major event was the launch of the British Invasion.

Even though their hometown itself was straitlaced and pretty isolated, Jeff says, "Zion was within radio reception of Chicago. And Chicago's AM radio in the early and mid-sixties was a phenomenal influence on every red-blooded adolescent that imagined himself to be a pop star. It was a type of schooling that ingrained itself into your subconscious and fed your imagination." Particularly influential, Jeff notes, were the "new Beatles songs coming every few weeks, and two new Beatles albums a year, which groomed us on pop music."

John, however, recalls that it took him some time to warm to the Beatles. The Sunday night in February 1964 that the Fab Four debuted on *The Ed Sullivan Show*, he was torn over whether or not to watch them, since he was caught up in a multi-part Disney series—*Dr. Syn, The Scarecrow of Romney Marsh*—which conflicted with the program. In the end, he skipped everything on *Ed Sullivan* except the Beatles' performance, watching Disney until his mother called him into her room to see John, Paul, George, and Ringo on her minuscule portable television, then returning to the living room afterwards to continue viewing *Dr. Syn* on the large family set.

Despite his own childhood conflicts, John remembers the before-and-after effect of the Beatles indelibly. Before the Beatles, "I thought the radio was, more or less, a source for oddball novelty songs, where the singer was either obsessed with sinking the Bismarck, pleading with General Custer for mercy, or bragging about a Neanderthal named Alley Oop." But afterward, John says:

> It was like a five-alarm brushfire when "I Wanna Hold Your Hand," "She Loves You," and "Please Please Me" were unleashed in America. All at once, the floodgates opened and every song from every band on the radio resonated with feverishly-sung melodies and lapel-grabbing guitar licks. Talk about an embarrassment of riches—the AM airwaves were just dripping with tingly, jangly treasures, and I'm fairly certain this is where we

subconsciously learned about song structure and the mystifying appeal of aching, heart-twisting lyrics.

Gary affirms that it was clear there was something special going on: "When the British Invasion started, it was truly magic."

Gary remembers that he was a little late on the Beatles bus: his recollection of their iconic Ed Sullivan performance was the amused response of the adults around him, who mostly shook their heads at the British band's outlandishly long hair. In his new neighborhood north of town, Gary was the oldest kid around: "I had no one to learn from," he explains, "no one to play me records," and therefore a little slow to catch on to new music. But he befriended Ed Erickson, a kid in his class who *did* have older brothers. It was at the Ericksons' that eleven-year old Gary began to hear the Beatles and the other bands of the British Invasion:

> That's the age where it imprints you. I was still kind of forming my tastes, and I was impressionable, not mapped musically. The Beatles began the blueprint of what was important to me.

Gary's first real Beatles obsession came in that summer of 1964, when the record and film *A Hard Day's Night* came out. "They were hugely important to me then," he says.

Gary shifted quickly into having the yen to make music himself, requesting and receiving both a guitar and lessons for his twelfth birthday, in January 1965. It was a short-lived adolescent whim, however; these early lessons didn't last long and the guitar was soon put in a corner to gather dust. For the next several years, reports Ed Erickson, "Gary didn't play anything more complicated than a record player."

Gary fed his appetite for music with more Beatles, as well as a stack of unusual records his father had acquired from a friend who stocked jukeboxes. That pile of random singles "was like the radio, only not as popular," he notes. The stack, maybe a foot high, included some standards by adult crooners like Perry Como and Andy Williams, but also songs from the British Invasion, including the Nashville Teens' "Tobacco Road." There were also some genuinely obscure 45s, such as "Stop! Get a Ticket" by the

Clefs of Lavender Hill. "Years later," says Gary, "when I mentioned that I knew some of these weird little songs that had been cycled out of jukeboxes in the mid-sixties, Greg Shaw [founder of groundbreaking independent label Bomp! Records] was wowed. But it's just what I had available."

By the fall of '64, the Murphys, too, were acquiring new records at a steady clip, usually in pairs. "You could never buy either one of us a gift without buying one for the other as well," John says. Christmas 1963, for example, had brought John "The Little Drummer Boy" and Jeff "Jingle Bell Rock." John, who had seen Johnny Cash on television, begged for and received his "Ring of Fire" single; Jeff simultaneously got the New Christy Minstrels' "Green, Green."

But it was their grandfather who bought the Murphy brothers their first Beatles album, in the fall of 1964. He took the boys to Goldblatt's, a local department store, where they gazed so longingly at a rack of Halloween novelty records (at 99 cents apiece), that he instructed them to choose one each. John and Jeff immediately put their heads together. If Grandpa was willing to spend two bucks on them, they reasoned, they might be able to coax him to three, and then they could get a Beatles' LP!

Their grandfather bought both their argument and the record, *The Beatles' Second Album*. Jeff recalls that the first track, "Roll Over Beethoven," skipped, "which drove us crazy." He's not completely sure how he came into sole possession of it—though he and his brother "traded records with each other *a lot*"—but Jeff still has that copy of *The Beatles' Second Album*.

DURING THESE YEARS, JOHN AND Jeff were processing other major life changes. Their new dad was only the beginning. By the end of 1965, the brothers had a new house, a new school, and a new sister. First, they moved from the more industrial, working-class northeast section of Zion to the more leisurely suburban center, into a bungalow on Bethel Boulevard, one of the main arteries in the Union Jack-shaped town. Then, they were pulled out of public school as Jeff started fifth grade and John seventh, and sent to Our Savior's Evangelical Lutheran Church School, a small parochial institution on the north edge of Shiloh Park. Finally, their baby sister Tina was born the day after Christmas in 1965.

Through it all, music remained the consistent thread. What John remembers most about December '65 is not his sister's birth, but playing *Rubber Soul* nonstop.

In the mid-sixties, Our Savior's was a small school with only two instructional areas, not really classrooms. The little kids, those in kindergarten through fourth grade, were taught in the church basement. The older students, fifth- through eighth-graders, could all fit in the balcony of the church itself. Jeff says that his graduating class contained a whopping twelve students, the largest in the school's history at that point.

The Murphys' mother may have felt that a small-school experience would help John, particularly; the fact that his late birthday made him younger than his classmates concerned her. But there were drawbacks to Our Savior's size, especially in the crucial seventh and eighth grades. This is when, as preparation for high school, students typically learn about negotiating class changes, using combination-locked lockers, and navigating the increasingly complex social structures of preadolescence.

But in a school too tiny for actual classrooms, these rites of passage could not take place. And so John had a tough transition when it came time for ninth grade.

As he puts it, "High school was a cold shower. I had a classic miserable first year." Still only thirteen, John says he entered high school the way he departed eighth grade—isolated and quiet. Even the few kids who came over as a group from the parochial school didn't stick together, but scattered in that vast, more complex environment. (At the height of the baby boom, Zion-Benton High School routinely graduated classes of well over five hundred students.)

And so John kept his head down, made a few friends, and struggled through. He let his childhood crewcut grow out—but not too much, under parental threat of the punitive haircut always just around the corner. Still, by the age of fifteen, John had found a niche as a somewhat quirky misfit in the mass of teenage conformity, drawing and listening to music and coolly observing the pageant of high school.

John feared that others saw him as "a nerd, a weirdo," since he kept mostly to himself. "But I listened to cool music," he says, "and I think I was cooler than people gave me credit for." John held out hope that he'd fit in eventually, and though he "knew a guy who knew some hippies," he was not integrated into any recognized social group.

And one day, Gary Klebe reached out and identified him as a fellow traveler.

GARY'S HIGH-SCHOOL EXPERIENCE had been radically different. Pushed by the expectations of his family and, increasingly, his friends, he figured out the rules of the system quickly. He then proceeded to conform to them—apparently unquestioningly—participating in the traditional routes to school success: academics, athletics, and activities.

He was a decent, responsible student. ("I wish I could tell you that I set the cafeteria on fire, but I didn't," Gary says almost ruefully.) He was involved in student government, serving both on student council and as vice-president of his junior class.

But most of Gary's extracurricular time, and much of his public identity, was based on athletics. As John remembers Gary, "He was a jock, y'know?" He was a big kid, six-foot-two before high school even started, broad-shouldered and physically graceful. Gary played three seasons of sports every year, and held strategic positions in each: a quarterback in football, a center in basketball, and a pitcher in baseball.

The last of these was where his ambitions lay. In the summer between his sophomore and junior year, Gary was invited to a major-league try-out at Wrigley Field, drawing the attention of its home team, the Chicago Cubs. When the team's scouts learned he was headed for university, however, they simply said, "We'll keep an eye on you in college ball."

On the surface, nothing could have been more incongruous than the friendship that sprang up between these two unlikely compatriots. But John and Gary's alliance was not as peculiar as it seemed.

By high school, Gary was a subversive in conformist's clothing. He was, according to his friend (and later, briefly, a Shoes drummer) Andy Joseph, "a very quiet guy. You couldn't tell much about what he was thinking until you got pretty close to him." An insider, Gary rather longed for John's outsider status, for freedom from the expectations of family and peers. And despite his straight-arrow image, Gary was in fact at the center of a group masterminding a satirical student magazine called *Lime*—which some compared (unfavorably, John avers) to *National Lampoon* and *Mad*.

Gary laughs off these associations. *National Lampoon* was not yet widely available, he says; its first issue appeared in April 1970, nearly a year after *Lime*'s conception. And the unrelenting wackiness of the venerable *Mad*, while an inspiration, wasn't the only thing they were shooting for. Instead, *Lime* was designed to be a thorn in the sides of both the school administration and the official student paper, a goal *Lime*'s creators decidedly achieved. "It was intended to be our counterculture version of a high-school newspaper," contributor Joseph explains, adding, "But it was pretty hard to be counterculture in Zion."

One day in the spring of 1969 during sophomore English, Gary spotted his quiet classmate drawing a caricature of a teacher, and, impressed, promptly invited him to contribute to the magazine he and some other guys were planning. "John was the first person I recruited for the *Lime* team," says Gary. At the urging of his new friend, John submitted a few drawings—marked by his quirky outsider's vision of Zion-Benton High—but as the school year drew to a close and no magazine had emerged, its would-be illustrator assumed nothing had come of the plans.

But John underestimated Gary, who often quietly goes his own way without telling anyone. Unbeknownst to John, then, Gary went on to spend much of that summer between sophomore and junior year working on *Lime*. John was pleasantly stunned when, at the beginning of their junior year, Gary presented him with a copy of the magazine, with his own drawings prominently featured. "He just walked up to me in the hall and handed it to me," John marvels.

From then on, the "*Lime* boys"—Murphy and Klebe, Erickson, Joseph, and classmate Joe Higgins—formed a cohesive group.

Lime attracted a fair amount of attention. Even the superintendent of the Zion-Benton Schools noticed, calling its creators on the carpet. "He didn't want to shut us down," Joseph recalls. "He just wanted to make sure it would be acceptable"—that it wouldn't contain anything dirty, for example. The *Lime* guys assured him they weren't planning on including obscene content, and were allowed to continue, now with official blessing.

John then became a minor celebrity in his own right, since the illustrations in *Lime* were so clearly limned by an expert hand. His style uncannily mimicked the cartoonists he liked: the influence of B. Kliban, R. Crumb, and Gahan Wilson are particularly apparent in John's *Lime* drawings.

But John himself remained something of an enigma. Erickson recalls that, in advance of *Lime*'s second year, the application form for new staff members consisted of a single question: "What does John Murphy look like?" Applicants submitted written descriptions of their mysterious, gifted classmate, and John then drew a series of comic self-portraits exactly corresponding to these: among them a ninety-seven-pound weakling with an enormous mop of hair, a six-foot nine-inch pile of nearly headless muscle, and a 19th-century surgeon. (This last kid used the encyclopedia, he explained in his submission.)

Branching out, the same group of friends made a short film, a spoof of World War II movies called *Rat Patrol*—named not for the then-current television series, but rather for a childhood friend, Larry Jensen, who was nicknamed "Ratman." In it, a standard set of clichéd military characters romp in the field behind the Klebes' house, including Sergeant Block (Gary) and the euphemistically named Roosevelt "Rosie" Palmer (John), who eventually gets knifed by the Ratman. Shot on eight-millimeter film, with a separate soundtrack on reel-to-reel, the film had to be synched to an explosion at the beginning to make any sense. John notes that the soundtrack had to be re-recorded several times, since it kept getting damaged. ("Mostly, people kept spilling drinks on it," he recalls.) They charged kids to watch *Rat Patrol*, and used the money to buy identical green sweaters with patches—*Lime* uniforms—and to put on a play (Gary recalls that it was titled "A Night with the Lime Boys," but that the most prominent printing on John's poster were the words "One Thousand Naked Women," raising a few eyebrows—though a careful reader would see that the thousand naked women is what you *wouldn't* see, if you came to the play.) They also distributed a *Lime* Christmas card—featuring the all-male staff delighting in their Christmas gifts, such as the tween-girl game *Mystery Date*—to everyone at Zion-Benton High.

Lime stayed active throughout the school year, to the chagrin not only of the seniors (who saw their role as school leaders subverted by a bunch of wise-ass juniors), but also of the administration and the student newspaper itself—which, according to Gary, eventually just shut down in frustration. Midway through the following year, when its creators were seniors, *Lime* folded too; Gary shrugs, "The battle was won."

Other than his subversive print endeavors, Gary continued to play it straight at school, at least overtly. His one moment of explicit rebellion was refusing to go out for basketball his senior year, because the crewcut-wearing coach insisted that his players keep their hair short—a style Gary had already begun to leave behind. The baseball coach was more forgiving, and that was his preferred sport anyway, so Gary continued pitching in the spring.

JUST BEHIND JOHN AND GARY, Jeff's path through high school was generally smoother and less dramatic. While John had lost many of his childhood friends in the shift from Our Savior's middle school to Zion-Benton High, Jeff fared somewhat better. He'd always been more outgoing, and of course, he also preferred the company of his older brother's new friends. John thinks he paved the way for Jeff to have an easier time—"The older kid has to kind of kick in the door"—but he was still touchy about Jeff hanging around. "He's my little brother; he should get his own friends," John recalls thinking. And of course, after *Lime* took off, John's circle had more cachet, which made Jeff that much harder to shake off.

Among the *Lime* boys, John had been given the nickname "Murf." As Jeff became part of their crowd, he was inevitably designated "Little Murf." The brothers were almost always together, Andy Joseph recalls, and their home became a popular place to hang out: "They had a cave in the basement, with a stereo." The brothers' music collection was growing all the time, and friends would come to listen to records they'd never heard of. And talk. "John and Jeff *loved* to talk about music," Joseph remembers. "Their records were never mainstream stuff. They were aficionados, but they were fans, not musicians; [their interest] was all analytical."

Meanwhile, Jeff was also carving out his own space, one that was much more mechanically inclined than his brother's. In their basement on Bethel Boulevard, both Murphys had workstations; John's was full of art supplies, while Jeff's overflowed with electronic parts, an update of the old fascination he'd had with the cathode-ray tubes their dad had brought home. Jeff's grandfather had given him a watch to disassemble, which he did zestfully, trying to figure out, literally, what made it tick. "I could never really get it to work again, though," Jeff laughs. As he got older, he started tinkering with cars, too; if it had a motor that worked, Jeff wanted to know how. He took apart stereo components and eventually musical instruments. While still a student, he landed a job at Radio Shack.

At Zion-Benton High, Jeff befriended Chip Mulleman, the guy at the adjoining locker, who inspired Jeff's skills in a very specific direction: playing an instrument. Mulleman sold Jeff his first guitar, a blue Japanese Teisco Del Rey, during their sophomore year of high school. Jeff paid him $30.

THAT SAME YEAR, 1971, JOHN AND Gary graduated from high school, and both began working summer jobs: Gary did construction, pouring concrete containment walls for the nuclear reactor being built on the lakeshore, and John was in food service at a nursing home. While hanging out together in the evenings, the playful idea of forming a band started to take shape, and John named that shape: Shoes.

Much ink has been spilled debating the origin of the band's name. John absolutely insists that he was unaware of a CBS News interview from

February 10, 1964 in which John Lennon, dismissing a similar question about their moniker, quipped, "It means Beatles, doesn't it? But that's just a name, you know, like 'shoe'." Paul McCartney immediately chimed in, "The Shoes, you see? We could have been called the Shoes for all you know."

But that footage was not readily available; John never saw it until 1979. Further, if the band's name was an intentional evocation of that moment, they would certainly have included a "the," which they didn't, and never have.

Asked why they shun the definite article, John ventures, "I guess 'Shoes' just sounded right. It was like Sparks or Wings or even Big Star. The first time we heard the 'the' was from a writer; we winced and corrected him. *The* Shoes just rubbed us wrong."

Possibly, Gary says now, the name refers to the fact that, at the outset, their fantasy band was comprised solely of John and Gary, "the left and right shoes." But, he hastens to remind, "We didn't even play instruments at that time. There was no band. It was just an idea." Still, it was an idea that increased its already considerable appeal for the two as they approached college.

IN THE FALL, GARY WENT OFF TO the University of Illinois in downstate Urbana-Champaign, while John stayed home to attend the College of Lake County, a local junior college.

Gary majored in architecture, he says, because he had to study something specific; the choice of a major was mandated early at Illinois. He makes it sound like a more-or-less random choice, but that seems unlikely, given the intensive and demanding nature of the architecture program in the university's School of Fine and Applied Arts. Gary does admit he was drawn to the dual nature of architecture, which utilized both his creative and logical sides. "It's art *and* science," he points out.

Other architecture students tended to hang together, trading papers and living in common. Gary stood aloof from that social circle, preferring the company of his roommate Paul Austermehle and some other guys on his dorm floor. Austermehle recalls that they hit it off immediately, launching into a game of touch football before the first day was out. (The dorm-floor crew grew very close and got a house together later in their college years; even now, they have an annual reunion.)

His gang on the dorm floor were what Gary terms "party animals"; Austermehle tells stories of lost nights out in Champaign, drinking, getting high, playing pinball. Gary went along on these escapades, though he himself didn't drink, let alone ingest any other mind-altering substance. "I guess it was my rebellion," he reflects. "By then, *drugs* weren't rebellion; they were conformity. I wasn't going to hang out with people who made that a requirement, and these guys didn't." Austermehle notes that, despite the difference in their recreational habits, there was never any discomfort between them: "Gary didn't drink or do drugs, but there was no scorn, no judgment. He just didn't do it."

Standing with, but slightly outside of, the group was becoming a habit for Gary. "He was cool in every sense of the word," Austermehle says. Though he would never really lose the sense of team unity he had developed as a young athlete—Gary often speaks of Shoes as a team, and according to Jeff has long been particularly keen on certain ceremonial behaviors, such as doing a group shot of Jack Daniel's before every live show—Gary chafed at the pull of any group whose rules he didn't help make.

He recounts one intramural basketball final he attended almost by accident. The respective opponents were a fraternity—"big guys, six-foot-six, all wearing matching uniforms"—and an unaffiliated pick-up team. "Their biggest guy was maybe five-ten," Gary recalls, "and they were all wearing cut-off shorts and were all shaggy and stuff. I thought, 'They're gonna get massacred.' But they didn't. They took a lot of outside shots; I was rooting for them." And the little guys, the outsiders with no connection to the system, won: "They buried one long shot after another and humiliated the frat boys."

Meanwhile, John was living at home and studying art, distinguishing himself with his serious approach to his craft. Right from the first semester, Gary had started pressuring him to transfer to the university in Champaign, an idea John found appealing, so he was mostly taking prerequisites for the art program down there. But he had some decent teachers at the junior college, and they seemed to recognize his talent and vocation; John assumed he was on track to become an illustrator, capitalizing on his natural skills.

JOHN HAD ALSO BECOME A genuine music obsessive, poring over magazines, exploring in small independent record stores, and listening to obscure FM radio—then on the ascent—always on the prowl for new music. Many bands never even made it to radio, so John would also lay out two dollars for the sampler LPs of aspiring new acts that labels regularly compiled. "I was always the one among my friends who'd risk the money on something that just sounded interesting to me," he says.

As his little brother, Jeff reaped the benefits of these explorations. John remembers Jeff stumbling sleepily down the stairs while he was spinning Todd Rundgren's pop milestone *Something/Anything* in the basement late at night, griping, "Are you listening to that thing *again*?" "Hey, there's four sides!" John pointed out. "It takes a while!"

But at this point, John's main victim was Gary; if they were going to be a band, he reasoned, they had to know what was out there. Gary, too, got the Rundgren treatment; John also served up David Bowie's *Hunky Dory*. During the school year, Gary took up the challenge and went exploring on his own in Champaign. Paul Austermehle recalls Gary buying "a new record every week," sharing his obsession with his roommate.

One band Gary discovered in Champaign was Britpop progenitors the Move. He'd read a review in *Rolling Stone*, and sought out their compilation *Split Ends* just as the Move were metamorphosing into the Electric Light Orchestra. He brought *Split Ends* back to Zion at the end of his freshman year, in the summer of 1972.

Another influential group Gary picked up his first year of college was Nils Lofgren's classic band Grin. Ed Erickson was attending Illinois Wesleyan University, and that fall, he invited Gary to a campus festival to see Grin play. Gary knew of Lofgren from his work with Neil Young—"He had that certification of coolness," Gary says, "so I was predisposed to like him"—and Ed had Grin's eponymous debut album. No one else at the concert seemed to know who Lofgren was, Gary recalls. It was a good show, and soon after he acquired both the first Grin record, which had been released the previous summer, and the second, *1 + 1*, when it came out in January 1972.

Gary was excited to share the Grin records with John, but when he got back to Zion, he discovered that John already had them, and what's more, Jeff was into them, too. As Jeff relates:

> Grin was one of the first bands that I remember becoming aware of that did more "alternative" music to the mainstream stuff. I do remember hearing it on headphones and being absolutely engulfed in the acoustic guitars of "White Lies." Nils had all the elements we liked in music: acoustic and electric guitars melded together, great vocal melodies, cool instrumentation, and an "everyman's" vocal range. His guitar-playing skills were, of course, stellar—and he wasn't afraid to wear his heart on his sleeve, lyrically.

The fact that they'd all gravitated toward the same record was a promising sign. Though they were at this point a band existing only in John and Gary's heads, Shoes were developing a shared aesthetic.

John was particularly excited in the summer of '72 about the inaugural album by a new band from Memphis that he'd read about in *Rolling Stone*. "There were keywords I would look for," John recalls. "If a reviewer said a band was 'Beatlesque,' or mentioned 'pop' in a positive sense, I was in." He and Gary headed down to Waukegan, to a small independent record store called Strawberry Fields, where they each picked up a copy of the album: Big Star's *#1 Record*. "It was unusual that Gary bought it, too," John remarks. "He was usually more cautious, and waited to hear the records I bought before he'd get them, too. But we must have been really excited, because I know we bought them together."

They took their copies back to Gary's messy basement bedroom and played them, but initially neither of the guys heard whatever it was that had hooked the critics. Still, when John and Gary headed off to college separately that fall, each kept playing Big Star on his own. When they met up again at Thanksgiving, they were both full-blown devotees. "Listen to that! It's amazing!" John says now, "A lot of people discovered Big Star's debut years later as this lost record, but we actually bought it when it first came out, and it made a huge impression on us."

Gary says that listening to and parsing Big Star's music made Shoes think about how songwriting worked. "For some reason, Big Star was transparent to us," he says. "We could see some of the fragility of the music itself—see the framework, the structure of how the songs were put together—more easily than we had been able to before. It seemed like the whole thing shouldn't hang together, but it did. It was tremendous music, and tremendously influential."

Gary highlights a distinctive trait of Shoes' development at that point: the delicate balance of listening and creation, of consumption and production. They weren't listening just to listen; they wanted to know how the music accomplished what it did, achieving what Jeff calls "goosebump moments." They analyzed the music much as Jeff had once taken apart his grandfather's watch, determined, this time, to be able to reassemble the mechanism. And when they started to record themselves a couple of years later, Shoes tried to replicate those goosebumps. "Our favorite records became resource material," says Jeff, "in shaping what we thought sounded professional and what didn't."

Listening for this distinction helped develop their shared aesthetic. And through this process, their musical explorations took on added weight. Close listening gave Shoes ideas, and also confidence to try things themselves.

The letters between John and Gary when each was living at opposite ends of Illinois are fraught with fervent discussions of whom they ought to be listening to in order to hone their own skills, and what life would be like when they were, inevitably, rock stars.

Both could draw, and each provided in his letters a running series of cartoons of their imaginary band, Shoes, in increasingly comic fantasy circumstances—opening for Paul McCartney, for example, or in the guise of Alice Cooper and David Bowie, or relying on massive roadies to keep the clamoring fans at bay. Gary, assigned to create a coloring book for art class, told *The Story of Shoes* (about John and Gary, two boys from a small town where music was forbidden, finding their way to rock stardom via a talking viola and talking tuba). John designed a faux-*Rolling Stone* cover of the two of them, in color, which Gary framed and kept on his wall for many years.

AS COLLEGE STUDENTS, BOTH John and Gary had deferments from the military draft, but as it was with all young men of their generation, they had to register anyway, so the war in Vietnam was a constant threat. Gary remembers, "The war was on TV every night, and had been for as long as we could remember. I just assumed I would go. I mean, I didn't see myself fleeing to Canada. But I just wanted to get through college first."

In this era, the draft was determined by lottery, with every young male born on a particular day being assigned a random number between 1 and 365; a lower number meant one was more likely to get called up to serve.

All those born in 1953 learned their fate on the same day: February 2, 1972. Both John and Gary remember straining to hear their lottery numbers, Gary over a car radio down in Champaign and John in the college's overcrowded student union, where someone was monitoring a portable radio and writing the lottery numbers and birthdays on a big chalkboard. Listening from the back of the clamorous room, John initially thought his number was a dismayingly low twenty: a friend sent up to the front to check it out came back laughing, earning John's anger. "You son of a bitch! I got twenty and you're laughing?" As it turned out, John had misheard: his number was a much more reassuring *three hundred* twenty, with Gary's similarly, safely high. In any case, the draft was suspended the following year, and none of the young men born in 1953 were ever called up.

In the summer between freshman and sophomore years of college, Gary spotted a Kay single cutaway acoustic guitar at a rummage sale, bought it, and started trying to figure it out. Unlike his abortive stint in junior high, this time Gary was inspired: now there was an imaginary band to play for.

There were other musicians in the U of I dorm. Austermehle recalls that in the next room was a guy who went by the name of Duke and played an electric guitar. Unfortunately, he knew only one part of one song, the four-chord opening riff to Deep Purple's metal hit, "Smoke on the Water." "He played it over and over, night and day," Austermehle groans. "It drove us crazy."

In the fall, Gary learned a handful of chords from some guys in his dorm, though this could never be mistaken for formal training. Mostly, he taught himself, working through a Mel Bay guitar-instruction book he'd had since he was twelve, putting in what Austermehle calls "grueling hours" of learning his instrument: "Day after day, night after night, hour after hour, he kept practicing." When Austermehle went home for a visit, he returned with his sister's Epiphone so that Gary was able to experiment with an electric guitar for the first time. But the majority of his education took place on the garage-sale Kay acoustic.

JOHN, STILL WORKING AT THE nursing home that summer of '72, was going through another crucial phase of development he'd need for the band: he was getting his heart broken. John had dated before, but he was unprepared when a friend's sister swooped in from Canada and he fell hard—"I was *way* hooked on her."

Busy being a boyfriend, he didn't return to school in the fall of 1972. John wasn't the only one; he noticed that, though a lot of his peers had gone away to college right out of high school, by the beginning of their second year, "guys were flunking out, getting their girlfriends pregnant, stuff like that."

Around Christmas, John quit his nursing-home job, earning the ire of his mother—and the first of many exhortations to hit the road. At the same time, his love interest returned to Canada—inexplicably, for good—without telling him. "I retreated to my little corner of the basement for weeks," John relates, "listening to sad songs on albums and writing these sort of structure-less poems; getting stuff out." But his poetry shook him from his torpor and propelled him back to school: "I tagged along with our pal Ed and sat in on a creative writing class for no credit that semester, to give me something to do." John took a job as a stocker at Grant City, a local department store, and things simmered down at home.

JEFF, ON THE OTHER HAND, was following his longstanding technological inclinations. He was still in high school, he recalls, when his boss at Radio Shack told him about the TEAC 3340-S, a reel-to-reel tape recorder that automatically synched its four separate tracks, making overdubbing and combining takes much simpler. Prior to this, home recording had been a dodgy business, requiring pinpoint precision on the part of the amateur engineer, who had to line up different tracks manually in order to add instruments to an existing track—an extraordinarily exacting process. Jeff was fascinated by the potential of this new piece of equipment, one that brought together his musical and electronic proclivities.

John underlines the TEAC's importance, hailing the new machine's vital role in driving Shoes' development:

> An integral part of our inception was the onset of sound-on-sound home recording, i.e., multi-tracking; professional-level quality made affordable for the rank and file. It was hugely appealing for us. In particular, we were drawn to the idea that it wasn't really necessary for us to play all at once, or even to rehearse a song before it was committed to tape. We could take our time and methodically eke out each part of every tune. The time-saving feature that allowed us to re-record over mistakes at any point in the track, called 'punching in', saved us from having to do complete, flawless takes. We were still in the beginning stages of playing and trying to 'find' our singing voices then, so we did more punching than a Ritalin-poppin' rookie flyweight after a weeklong binge at Starbucks. One thing, though, was certain: that unassuming TEAC four-track was an imperative element in the pursuit of our humble little pipedream.

Around the time he graduated high school in spring 1973, Jeff begged his parents to co-sign a small loan with him so he could buy one of these amazing machines. They flatly refused. He then turned to a friend, Garry Holverson—who consented.

Looking to save whatever money he could, Jeff realized it would be cheaper to buy the TEAC from a discount catalog, and have it shipped to him from Washington, D.C.; it saved him about $250 over buying locally. And as Jeff phrases it, "This tape machine fathered the birth of Shoes, sometime in late 1973."

Jeff soon left Radio Shack to work at the comparatively lucrative local envelope-printing factory—first hauling boxes, but later rising to the more prestigious (and better-paid) position of pressman—a job Jeff would hold until he quit in 1979, when Shoes signed with major label Elektra Records.

But in late 1973, Jeff still had to learn how to operate the TEAC 3340-S, and there was only one way to do it.

Shoes may still have been largely a figment of their collective imagination, up to that point. But when Jeff hit the "Record" button, they were off.

THESE EARLY EXPERIMENTS WERE conducted entirely in isolation. As Gary said in a 1981 *Trouser Press* interview, "We were never in a circle of musicians when we were starting; we had a chance to teach ourselves, rather than being [taught]. There's a certain amount of intimidation about being around people that are much better than you, and we were never confronted with that."

From a traditionalist's perspective, Shoes were approaching the whole idea of being a band backwards. But with no one looking over their shoulders, they realized that they didn't *have* to do things the way they were "supposed" to be done: a freeing epiphany. As Jeff reflected in a 2008 interview, "I think in the early days of Shoes, [our driving force] was the joy of making music, any kind of music. We were just amazed that we *could* make music. And so we didn't censor ourselves at all."

John and Gary fiddled around with any musical instrument they could get their hands on, and Jeff recorded it all. He recollects that they'd pick up used instruments they (or their moms) saw at garage sales; Gary's mother owned an autoharp, and the Klebes had a piano in the living room, so both of those were taped. Then Leona Scott started giving her sons obscure instruments for birthdays and Christmas, including an African kalimba; that made the cut, too. Indeed, everything did. "There wasn't a sound we created that Jeff wasn't getting on tape," says John.

For example, John remembers the first time he played something for Gary, a tune called "Oh, My Sara." He had written to Gary about the song in fall '73, anticipating his bandmate's eye-rolling response to its frankly romantic title. "I know, I know," he said in a letter. But when Gary returned to Zion and heard what John had written, he was impressed. "That's pretty good," John recalls him saying. "That's pretty *damn* good!" It was a comforting affirmation; as John observes, at this point "it was hard to get over our embarrassment, even in front of each other."

They all recall take after take of something called "Lovely Angie." Jeff notes that no existing take of the song lasts more than fifteen seconds; John, in fact, insists it can't properly be *termed* a song. "It's a joke," he says. "We couldn't even form chords, and Gary was just trying to make me laugh." (Gary also contributed the two notes he'd managed to master on his mother's high-school clarinet.) These "musical skeletons in our closets," as John calls them, are largely buried now (though there was some debate about using sections of "Lovely Angie" on Shoes' 1996 rarities compilation, *As Is*).

But John insists that the first real Shoes song was called "You Are the Magic," which had words and chords and something like a structure. "We put all kinds of weird noises on there, like scissors snipping," he recalls. They put the song on for a handful of their friends at a party; John recalls that he sat on the floor behind a chair, hiding from everyone while it played. "I was too nervous to look at their faces." (Its title would later make its way into Jeff's "In My Arms Again": "You are the magic any boy would need.")

When Jeff speaks of these days, he generally represents himself as the engineer for the two older boys, not as an actual member of the band. But then suddenly, he was playing with them, though no one quite recalls how that happened.

It's true, John and Gary admit—Jeff was never officially asked to join Shoes. The older boys claim they saw a formal invitation as unnecessary: they'd almost never done anything without him in the room, just a few jam sessions in Gary's bedroom, with John and Gary playing both their guitars through one amp and Gary catching it on a tiny Sony two-track. But they don't consider those early ventures as anything other than rough experiments. Still, they were aware the younger Murphy was waiting for the invitation. As John acknowledges, "We knew Jeff wasn't going to be content with just pushing buttons." Whenever he and Gary considered expanding their band, Jeff was always the first person they discussed adding.

But they never asked.

IT WAS SOMETIME IN 1973 THAT John acquired what he describes as a "used, cheesy knockoff-Sunburst bass … a heavy sucker with a chrome pickguard," so cheap it didn't even have a name. For Christmas that year, he received his first new guitar, an off-brand acoustic called El Degas. "I took it with me to Champaign in January 1974," John says. "It didn't have a case, so I schlepped it around in the box. It was fine for me at the time; I only knew a few chords, but I wrote my stuff for [Shoes' homespun 1975 album] *One in Versailles* with it."

Jeff, meanwhile, had sold his first guitar, the Teisco Del Rey, to Gary, moving on to a cream-colored Fender Stratocaster. John acquired a second knockoff bass (this one mimicking a Höfner, Paul McCartney's signature instrument) from Jeff's old friend Chip Mulleman, giving Chip money to fix his own car and getting the bass in return.

Over the years, Shoes acquired a lot of gear from Mulleman; he and his bandmates liked to upgrade their equipment, and were willing to sell the used stuff to friends. Gary recalls going to see Chip's band practice, and thinking, "In six months that's going to be mine." In these years, the Murphys and Klebe played a round-robin game with their instruments, trading with each other and fellow musicians, buying guitars via the classified ads and a local paper called *Trading Times*. Gary tells of one opportunistic bargain, a Fender "whose headstock had been sawed off to look like a Rickenbacker. … We just kept swapping, moving up the ladder," Gary continues. "We'd never keep anything too long, not if we saw something we liked better." And, Jeff adds, "We usually got a good deal on it."

When it came to amplifiers, Jeff says they sometimes even shelled out for new equipment. Jeff began with "a small Gibson combo amp that I bought at the local music store." His next purchase was "a really awful-sounding (but *big*) Acoustic 270 guitar amp," bought from another friend, Don Castleberry. By 1976, Jeff was on to a Sunn Model T tube amp. "We went through a phase around 1975 and 1976 when we all played through Sunn amps," he recalls, though Gary notes that his was actually a bass amp. "It was ridiculous to play through it, really," says Gary, "but it's what I had."

After their Sunn phase, Jeff and Gary diverged. Jeff primarily favored Hiwatt 50's, and Gary went with Marshall 50's around that same time.

The amplifiers were mainly used for practice, however, when Klebe and the Murphys recorded at this point, guitars were plugged directly into the mixing board, with the player monitoring them on headphones to hear what came out.

Sometimes the guitars were run through effects first. Gary was using commercial effects, primarily a Dallas-Arbiter Fuzz Face stomp box and an MXR Distortion +. Jeff, strapped for cash, had disassembled the old Ross reel-to-reel tape machine he'd had since elementary school and built his own effect, which he called a "guitar synthesizer":

> I gutted the Ross and ran my guitar through it to get distortion, straight into the mixer, like Lennon did for his guitar on "Revolution." I mounted the electronics into a small cardboard box at the time, and later into a small metal box. It had one knob, two jacks, and a power switch—and a very noisy, compressed, unique sound. ... I often layered the sound with a harmony line or two.

Jeff employed this effects setup consistently, well through Shoes' Elektra days. Its unusual tone, he says, can be heard on "Fatal" and the "Found a Girl" demo (the latter on Shoes' 2007 retrospective disc *Double Exposure*).

The gear, they all agree, influenced Shoes' development along specific lines; they learned to use it as part of a holistic process. Who Shoes became musically depended, to a great extent, on the equipment they owned, and every part of the process happened simultaneously. "Slowly," says Jeff, "we all began learning to play instruments, sing, write, and record, all at the same time."

ONE THING SHOES DIDN'T DO WAS play live shows. This idiosyncrasy was partly an accident of location, partly a function of their natures. It's certainly true that Zion had no bars or clubs to perform in: alcohol, at this point, was still only legal in the Crossroads Diner, a restaurant that spanned the city's borderline and thus could serve liquor in the half of the room that was technically not in Zion. But Shoes were surrounded on three sides by the fertile clubland of northern Illinois and southern Wisconsin, the same circuit that would forge fellow Illinoisans Cheap Trick into a matchless live act. Chicago, Milwaukee, even Madison were within reasonable driving distances. Still, Shoes didn't perform live, at least not right away.

Why?

True, Shoes didn't have any original songs, but that in itself wasn't an issue: most bands started out doing covers; bar owners typically insisted on it. And they didn't have a drummer, but they weren't looking seriously for one, either.

The main reason for passing over live performance was Shoes' particular blend of stubbornness, shyness, and high expectations. They didn't think they could compete with the local musicians, who'd "all been taking violin lessons since they were seven or playing guitar since they were twelve or whatever," says John. "That wasn't us."

Even among their hometown friends, Shoes' musical explorations were either hidden or the subject of amused perplexity. Andy Joseph remembers, "One of them mumbled one day that they had instruments; it was the first I'd heard of it." It became a habit not even to talk about the band.

In Shoes' small, provincial town, each of them was fixed into the role he'd played in high school: the jock, the artist, the electronics whiz. Playing shows as a band was a very public statement that they were something else—a statement they didn't yet feel confident enough to make.

But avoiding the bar and club circuit came at a price. As Shoes' star ascended, they were subjected to periodic resentment from other local aspiring acts because they hadn't paid their dues in the customary (read: legitimate) way.

As John and Gary had so often depicted themselves in their letters to each other, they would privately picture themselves as rock stars in front of adoring, screaming crowds; who wouldn't want that? But they knew they weren't that fantasy: they were modest in their assessment of their own still-developing skills, and a little embarrassed about same; thus, intimidated. As Jeff points out, "The recording process gave us a chance to experiment and build confidence without the scrutiny of an audience." And the bond among the three of them was strengthened by their shared secret.

IN THE FALL OF 1973, STILL toiling in the Grant City stockroom, John fell hard again—this time for Sara Haack, a coworker he'd known from high school. She didn't remember *him* from Zion-Benton High, but he states somewhat proudly that she had a reputation as a "bad girl." "She was quiet, but she had a sultry air," he recalls. Sara worked in the juniors section, and John would regularly find excuses to wander by and talk to her.

One Friday, Sara asked him about his weekend plans, and when John said, "I think I'm going to get together with Gary," she suggested, "Why don't you get together with me instead?" John was shocked; he would never have presumed to ask her out himself. But they started dating, and things got intense very quickly: within a couple of months, John and Sara were engaged. The relationship was tempestuous, however, and its vagaries became the subject of the vast majority of John's songs in this period—at first during the five years they were on-and-off together, and then later when she had truly broken his heart.

Sara did not realize, she says now, that John was a musician when they first started dating; "I thought of him as an artist, really." But soon, she saw that the band was incredibly important to him, though she says it was "not really my kind of music." This is probably why Sara remained unaware for many years that some of the couple's most personal moments had been immortalized in Shoes' songs.

Also in the fall of 1973, John succumbed to Gary's urging and applied to the university in Champaign. Hearing nothing at first from U of I's admissions department, he continued to live his life as though he weren't going to move downstate, including formalizing his engagement to Sara at Christmas. But a scant two weeks before the semester began in January 1974, John got his acceptance letter, and hastily restructured his plans. He found a room to rent, scrambled to pack, and headed for Champaign. As John was leaving, he says his mother stopped him on the way out the door:

> "John?"
>
> I spin around. "Yeah?"
>
> She blurts out what she must've gone over and over in her mind for weeks, if not months, waiting for the right moment to delicately deliver: "Don't take drugs!"

As John and Gary went to college that January, one thing was unspoken but understood among the three of them: there was a band, the band had a name, and Shoes would all go forth together.

John's first semester away was something of an awakening. He'd decided to major in painting, because the program appeared to offer more latitude than did the more career-oriented graphic-design major. "It *seemed* to be all, 'Cut off your ear and suffer,'" he recalls. But the actual curriculum was quite regimented, and John chafed within its strictures, fuming over colleagues mired in forties and fifties Abstract Expressionism, and trying to find his own way artistically.

Socially, John fared much better. He fit in well with Gary's friends; Austermehle remembers John as "self-deprecating, humble—a funny, funny guy." Though John had his own room in a boarding house elsewhere in Champaign, he spent most of his off-hours hanging around the house Gary had rented with eleven other guys. Like Gary, he brought lots of new music, too, and was always welcome.

It was during that semester that John and Gary spoke seriously about asking Jeff to be a formal member of Shoes. But when the two returned to Zion that summer of 1974, they embarked upon *Heads or Tails,* Shoes' first real recording—and it became clear that they were too late: Jeff already was.

GENERALLY SPEAKING, WHEN Shoes record they do so with a specific project in mind; the name and concept are worked out beforehand. Not so with that inaugural effort, which they all dismiss as amateurish and crude.

The *Heads or Tails* sessions were a loosely-wound affair. After all, the three could barely play, their writing was still primitive, and their sound more heavily acoustic than it would later become.

The Murphys and Klebe would record until they messed up, stop the tape, and try it again—an arduous process. Still, as Jeff reminisced later, "It consumed us. Once we started the journey there was rarely a day when we didn't do something musical." And they liked the privacy of recording: "If we made a mistake, it could be erased forever with just the push of a button and nobody had to know it had ever happened."

According to Gary, they usually stopped after they got one decent take; there was no time for the recording-studio meticulousness Shoes would develop later. "It was a wide-open field," says Jeff, "for getting something, anything down on tape." And since the band members had no knowledge of musical notation, it wasn't possible to write any of their instrumental music down; they just had to get it recorded before they forgot it.

Despite the primitive quality of *Heads or Tails*, its songs do contain the shimmer of what Shoes would become.

Initially, John and Gary did all the writing for *Heads or Tails*. Each even submitted a tune apiece from the project to a national songwriting competition—John's "Grandpapa," an ode to the advice his mother's father had given him about girls; and Gary's "You're the Same."

Some of the compositions Gary and John brought in were "relationship songs," Jeff says, but certainly not all; the ones that weren't, he adds, were considered "safer," because they were less personally revealing. In addition to "Grandpapa," those tracks include "Clear Day," "Quarter in Nine," and "We Shouldn't've Come Here."

Shoes were experimenting with rudimentary studio tricks, too. Jeff points out that Gary's home-recorded version of a song called "So Bad" had "a cool phasing effect," achieved by "waving the microphone past the speaker to make it swirl."

And then there was the new band member. Jeff was playing guitar and singing (and contributing bass on "We Shouldn't've Come Here"). But as Gary remembers it, he and John honestly didn't realize Jeff was a full writing member of the band until *Heads or Tails* was pressed up on phonograph disc, with Jeff's "Can't You See?"—a song John calls "the best thing on the record"—as the lead-off track. "Maybe it was the fact that I played everything on it that impressed them so," Jeff theorizes. "But we had always considered John and Gary's 'Nothing Means More' to be the best track," noting that it received some airplay on nearby Kenosha, Wisconsin AM station WLIP. And the acoustic, undeveloped-sounding "Nothing Means More" was the song they chose to represent *Heads or Tails* on the aforementioned *As Is*.

Recording mostly in the Murphys' basement (optimistically dubbed "Cellar Studios" on the *Heads or Tails* sleeve) had its drawbacks. For example, they continually had to dodge the massive laundry bag hanging in the middle of the room. And Jeff remembers needing to sing in a whisper so as not to wake their stepdad; his shifts changed every couple of weeks, and he could not be disturbed during the day when he worked nights. (Under these circumstances, the direct-into-the-board recording of guitars was a distinct advantage: instead of booming amps, the recording of guitars was nearly silent outside the basement.)

In addition, they were contending with some very unprofessional interruptions. The Murphys' younger sister—now eight—would frequently invade the sessions, making animal noises and causing a general ruckus, and they were forbidden even to raise their voices to her. Gary, with three younger siblings of his own, proposed that he be allowed to "deal with the problem," but John and Jeff declined that rather ominous offer.

And of course, Shoes still didn't have a drummer. Desperate, they tapped all their friends, trying to find someone who could play, and learned that one of John's friends could, indeed, handle drumsticks, and even had his own kit. But since the Murphys' mother refused to let them install drums in their own basement, they dutifully trekked off to John's friend's house with their recording equipment, setting it up in an adjoining room because of space constraints. That first session started out okay—John's buddy wasn't bad—but at one point, noticing that his playing suddenly sounded thinner than it had been, the three went to investigate. They found their would-be stickman drumming one-handed, eating fries off the snare drum.

The next candidate was Andy Joseph, one of the *Lime* crew in high school. He had been in a band with his older brothers, and thus had more experience than the members of Shoes. And Joseph was a decent drummer—but since they had launched into recording without really thinking about the order in which things should be laid down, Joseph ended up doing the drum tracks in his attic bedroom at the end, on top of the otherwise already-completed tracks, an almost complete reversal of the customary professional recording sequence.

JEFF HAD PICKED UP A 1958 Meissner disc lathe—a home record-cutting machine—at a yard sale, and it was this novelty item as much as anything else that drove the production and structure of *Heads or Tails*. The records it cut were larger than seven-inch singles, but smaller than regular twelve-inch LPs. Jeff had a few of these blank vinyl discs, which had come as part of the lathe set; five songs, all fairly short, would fit on each side. But the actual inscribing process was tricky. One mistake and a whole disc would be ruined.

The name *Heads or Tails* was chosen to simplify Shoes' first record's graphics: instead of printing song titles on both sides of the disc's labels, the sides were simply designated "Heads" and "Tails," like a coin.

But John says Shoes were already thinking in terms of album sequencing, "of what song went on what side, of beginners and enders, that sort of thing." John designed a cover, complete with track listing, using die-cut, pre-glued Chartpak letters—and by August, Shoes had a record. It was primitive, and there were only four copies, but it was real.

By now, though, there was another problem: Shoes were about to lose a guy.

Chapter 2

One in Versailles (1974-75)

GARY HAD NEVER PLANNED ON spending his senior year abroad, but when the opportunity to pursue his major at the Ecole d'Architecture in Versailles, France presented itself, he found it impossible to resist. During the year Gary was gone, John and Jeff conceived a plan both to surprise him and to cement Shoes' relationship as a band: they wrote and recorded an album dedicated to Gary, called *One in Versailles*.

As a late applicant, Gary hadn't fulfilled all the prerequisites for the University of Illinois' international study program; his classmates, on the other hand, had been preparing for this sojourn for nearly two years. For one thing, he didn't speak a word of French. For another, though this semester abroad represented the completion of undergraduate schooling for Gary's fellow travelers, he'd still have one more semester of coursework when he returned, senior-year courses that wouldn't be offered in France.

Gary could have been on the Versailles track all along, but he hadn't really taken his education very seriously up to that point. Partly, this was due to his comparative detachment from most of the other students in his program, but mostly Gary was simply having fun being a college student in Champaign. "I'd shrugged it off," says Gary of the travel opportunity. "I just wanted to hang out with my friends." But with just a few months left of junior year, a last-minute opening sparked his interest in the overseas program. "I don't know why I applied," Gary reflects. "Maybe I needed a change." But as spring came to an end, it was settled: instead of returning to Champaign in the fall, Gary would be headed to France.

The short lead time meant that everyone in Shoes was caught a little off-guard by the upcoming trip, particularly John. After all, Gary had spent well over two years encouraging, coaxing, cajoling John to come to Champaign—and one brief semester after he arrived, Gary was leaving for a year. As John describes it, "I think I felt a little abandoned. It was like, 'Well, what the hell?' I mean," John hastens to add, "I understood and all; it was a great opportunity for him."

Gary acknowledges that the decision was both abrupt and nonchalant—the way John tells it, Gary dropped his bombshell with an offhanded, "Okay, I have this chance to see Europe, so I'm outta here." But Gary comforted himself at the time with the idea that John and Champaign and Shoes would all be there when he returned. John, however, was less convinced than Gary, particularly about what the year overseas might mean for their band. He considers this period as "our first little crossroads; it could have been the end of Shoes before it started." And John is not convinced that Gary was as unconcerned as he appeared to be about what might happen back in Illinois while he was gone. "I think," John ventures, "that Gary was actually a little nervous about putting Shoes on hold. Would the rest of us have lost interest in the band altogether in the meantime? Would one or both of us be married within the next year?" After all, John had a fiancée, Jeff a long-term girlfriend, and many of their friends had already wed, so it didn't seem that far-fetched. Jeff, too, doubted that Gary was as sanguine about departing as he claimed to be; Jeff illustrated those concerns in his title track to "One in Versailles," addressing Gary directly: "You thought that when you left, some things would pass you by."

So with some trepidation on all sides, Gary flew out in late August, after Shoes had finished *Heads or Tails*. As he departed, he hinted that they all needed to practice a lot over the next year, something John took sort of personally: after all, Gary—strictly constrained as to how much he could pack on the chartered flight—was not bringing his guitar.

LOCATED JUST TEN MILES OUTSIDE Paris, the palace of Versailles was originally a rural hunting lodge. But in the increasingly tumultuous seventeenth and eighteenth centuries, it became the center of the French court, as kings and nobles fled the potential dangers of the Paris mobs, isolating themselves at Versailles to preserve their influence (and their heads). Royal extravagances were embodied in the Baroque architecture and design of the palace and surrounding buildings; royal control was displayed by the town of Versailles' organized grid of streets, standing in stark contrast to the organic meandering of Paris's layout.

The Versailles study program had been founded at the University of Illinois in 1967, and since 1970 had been hosted by the Ecole d'Architecture de Versailles. But even though French and American students shared academic space (in the former stables of Louis XIV), they didn't see much of each other: all University of Illinois courses were taught in English, so its classes were conducted separately from those of the Ecole. "Really," says Gary, "the academic program was not so different from what we'd been doing in Champaign."

The program's participants were housed separately, as well. American students roomed, by and large, with French families; Gary and three other students lodged with a family literally "close enough to the palace that if I opened my window and threw a rock, I'd hit it." But the four Americans rarely interacted with their hosts; they had their own entrance to their rooms, and usually ate at the Ecole's cafeteria.

Still, Gary did get to experience much of Europe. The architecture program was designed with mandatory breaks for students to travel around the continent with sketchbooks in hand. About these independent trips, Gary observes, "We had assignments to study architecture, but our duties didn't limit our fun." Few restrictions were placed on where the American students could travel; they were simply expected to get out of Versailles to see as much architecture as possible.

One of these scheduled travel breaks was the first thing on the agenda upon their arrival at the Ecole. Gary did not know any of the other architecture students as well as they knew each other, so as they paired off to travel, he was left unaffiliated. "Me and the last guy in the room went to London," Gary relates, "and then hitchhiked north to England's Lake District. We had a hard time getting back, so we split up, and I returned to the city alone." In London, Gary was itching to see some live music; this was, after all, a legendary rock & roll Mecca, and so he scouted the listings for a concert to catch—any concert.

The daylong rock festival at Wembley Stadium on September 14 seemed like a good bet, so Gary hopped a commuter train to the London suburb of Brent, home of the outdoor sports arena. He remembers almost nothing about the show, even who was on the bill—"The Eagles, maybe?" Gary says with a shudder. "I know I was all excited to see English music and it turned out not to be that." The actual lineup was Crosby, Stills, Nash, & Young, Joni Mitchell, the Band, and Jesse Colin Young in a ten-hour North American folk-rock extravaganza, which didn't exactly conjure lasting memories for the disappointed Britpop seeker.

Subsequently, however, Gary got to see the now-classic heavy-metal band UFO at the storied Marquee Club in Soho, and describes being blown away less by UFO than by the sheer aura of the place, which had been home to the Who during their formative years in the mid-sixties.

Gary returned to France in time for classes to begin, and soon was working the vast majority of the time. Far from home, away from his friends, he dedicated himself to his studies. "For the first time, I lived and breathed architecture, took it really seriously," says Gary. "My grades got better, because I was around people who were also serious about it." Despite his natural shyness, he got to know some of his American colleagues— "We all spoke the language of architecture, and I was seeing it in a more positive light"—but Gary was otherwise socially isolated by his almost complete ignorance of French; his lexicon, he ruefully admits, was limited to *non* and *oui*.

Gary's solitude was exacerbated by a French postal strike that limited written contact from home for much of the year.

The election of Valéry Giscard d'Estaing as president in spring 1974 had brought in a new, conservative administration, including Minister of the Interior Jacques Chirac and Director of Telecommunications Gérard Théry. Théry was charged with making major changes to the French communications industry, like privatizing parts of the postal service. Postal employees feared for their jobs, especially in the face of statements from public officials like Pierre Lelong, who sneered at "the idiot work in the sorting centers."

The postal workers' resultant strike lasted from October to December, bringing mail delivery in France to a standstill. After three months of stalemate, Chirac and Théry backed away from their restructuring plans, the sorters returned to their "idiot work," and communications in France gradually started to return to normal. But the strike had created a backlog of mail that took months to clear up.

And so Gary remained ignorant of the fact that, across the Atlantic, a plan was hatching on his behalf.

Shoes' first "concept" record was originally John's idea. "We had gotten the recording bug after *Heads or Tails*, and we wanted to keep going," John relates. "I remember saying to Jeff, 'If we do some recording while Gary's gone, we could call it *One in Versailles*.'" Jeff, always eager to rev up the TEAC, agreed immediately. They didn't really consider Gary's potential reaction, other than wanting the recording—which they'd ship to him in France—to assure Gary the band would be there awaiting his return.

With the plan in place, John had returned alone to Champaign, a little lost without his fellow Shoe, and without the roomy crash pad that had been his second home. "I'd made friends with the guys in Gary's house that first semester, but they all splintered up in pairs or moved into their own places after that, so I saw them infrequently," John remembers. Feeling as isolated as Gary did in France, John spent his time painting, working on songs for the new record, and pining for his girlfriend Sara back in Zion.

The recording sessions for *One in Versailles* began *chez* Murphy in the same basement where much of *Heads or Tails* had been done, and with many of the same noise and time constraints. Initially, the sessions were about as informal as the previous ones had been, too: one of the first tracks, John's quirky, endearingly rudimentary "Banjo," was recorded one evening when a bunch of friends and their girlfriends did a just-for-fun recording of John's chorus before heading out to dinner and a movie.

But Jeff, growing more serious about music by the day, was chafing at the constraints of home, and looking for a way to shed them. He and John worked away from their basement whenever possible, rehearsing at the homes of other, more indulgent, parents; one practice session for *One in Versailles* was held in Jeff's girlfriend's attic bedroom, for example.

But relocating even temporarily required lugging around the TEAC 3340-S, which—though durable enough to withstand the travel—was "heavy and bulky," according to Jeff, who longed for a truly serviceable recording base.

JEFF HAD BEEN OUT OF HIGH school for a little over a year and was still living at home, and tensions were rising between him and his parents. The issues were pretty standard: chores versus freedom, the same points of contention any young adult living at home faces. One particular source of strife was Jeff's objection to babysitting his younger sister, something he didn't consider his responsibility.

When Shoes began *One in Versailles*, Jeff was working nights at Zion's envelope factory. He got paid a little more for taking the night shift, but that schedule also meant he went in to work just about the time elementary school let out. The Murphys' mother, anxious to return to working full-time now that her youngest was growing up, pressured Jeff to change his work hours in order to watch Tina; he steadfastly refused. "But when we got serious about *One in Versailles*," Jeff recalls, "and I changed my schedule for *that*, she was pretty angry that I'd do it for the band and not for her." Given

55 a "three weeks and you're out" decree, Jeff began looking for a new place to live in the midst of Zion's forbidding winter.

THAT FALL, JEFF HAD RECONNECTED with an old school friend, Barry Shumaker, grandson of the Klebe family's former landlord. (Jeff, however, had no idea that there was a childhood connection between Barry and Gary.) Shumaker was a drummer, and a good one, as far as Jeff could tell. Certainly, he reasoned, the drum drama of *Heads or Tails* wouldn't be repeated if a regular timekeeper were part of the band. Plus, they'd need one if they were ever going to play out. And Zion was a small town; it's not like there were dozens of drummers looking for a gig. Jeff knew he should enlist Shumaker quickly.

But he was still suffering from younger-brother syndrome. From Jeff's perspective, Shoes was John and Gary's band that they were *letting* him play in; he was acutely conscious that he'd never been officially asked to join, never mind deputized to find additional members. Still, with John in Champaign most of the time and Gary in France, he could hardly call a band meeting or schedule an audition. So Jeff took the leap and asked the perfectly-surnamed Barry Shumaker to drum for Shoes. Barry consented, and Jeff hauled the TEAC 3340-S over to Barry's parents' house to lay down some of *One in Versailles'* early drum tracks.

Shoes now had the drummer they needed, and due to the impending change in his living circumstances, Jeff now needed a roommate. Barry seemed like a good choice to fill that role, too. Both boys were just twenty; neither was making much money on his own. Jeff was working at the envelope factory for about a hundred dollars a week, and Barry was employed in his father's butcher shop. It happened that Shumaker *père* missed a lot of work due to a fairly serious drinking problem, according to Barry, and the business was suffering; so Jeff helped out periodically by making sausages after work—his only pay being not-quite-expired meat products. (When the shop finally went out of business, Jeff says, meals at home were "Kraft Macaroni & Cheese all the way.")

Jeff and Barry had found a place they could afford relatively quickly. The bite-sized house—a converted residential garage on a tiny, nameless alley—was maybe five hundred square feet with four rooms, including the bathroom. It was almost windowless, and the elderly man across the street kept a mob of borderline-feral dogs whose incessant barking would present a genuine recording problem come summer, as would the wasp's nest embedded in a wall. But Jeff and Barry moved in during the winter, when the chief problems were the leaky boiler and the fact that the only warmth came from an alarming open-flame space heater.

Despite its many drawbacks, the place was theirs, and they turned it into a recording studio in a way their parents would never have allowed. As Jeff details, "We'd looked for a *house* to rent so we could leave the gear set up full-time—that was our main requirement." John remembers their collective sense of relief: "Now we didn't have to ask my mom if we could bring drums down to the basement, or be quiet after our dad or sister was in bed."

Dubbed "The Cabin," because of its diminutive size and rustic, unpainted exterior, Jeff and John renamed it "La Cabane" in their Continental bandmate's honor—not a direct French translation (it actually means "hut"), but close enough. Pictures of La Cabane's interior taken during the *One in Versailles* sessions show a claustrophobic room, with people and gear crammed into every square inch.

WITH JOHN DOWN IN CHAMPAIGN, the majority of Jeff's work on *One in Versailles* was done on his own or with Barry, or—on rare occasions—with other local acquaintances. On his own songs, Jeff left room for John to come back and supply bass and backing vocals (something that remains a habit for Shoes to this day), because they weren't writing or playing together most of the time.

John did come home pretty frequently during this period—every other weekend, in fact. But that had more to do with seeing Sara than recording Shoes' new album. Thus, despite the fact that he was around Zion a lot, John wasn't really putting in much time recording. Still, he claims, he *was* thinking about and writing songs, and listening to what Jeff and Barry were laying down back in Zion inspired him: "I'm at school and I'm writing things on this acoustic guitar, and I'm coming home and hearing *electric* guitar and drums, and thinking, 'Wow, that sounds great!'"

With John away at school and his new housemate on hand, Jeff's musical tastes were diverging from their longtime diet of jangly guitar pop: he was listening to prog rock like Jethro Tull and King Crimson, hard rock like Led Zeppelin and Bad Company, and the more direct descendants of the mid-sixties British Invasion: Electric Light Orchestra (who'd evolved out of the Move), Elton John, and Fleetwood Mac. And these inspirations were pushing his own music to be more rock, less acoustic.

It wasn't long before John began getting the feeling, during his visits home, that he had to catch up with his younger brother. Jeff, with a drummer, an electric guitar, and room to stretch out, was moving fast—"He wasn't waiting around," John recalls, "and I knew I had to buckle down." John struggled to shift his "bedroom songs," which had been written on acoustic guitar in his college room, to fit this new, harder sound.

The difference between the brothers' respective title tracks for the record—John's dreamy "Un dans Versailles" and Jeff's heavier, fuzzed-out "One in Versailles"—embodies Jeff's directional shift, though both songs include hard and soft elements. John's begins with a wah-wah guitar that cedes ground to the song's acoustic body; Jeff's features an acoustic intro that lulls the listener until the song explodes, some fifty seconds in, revealing the potent rocker seething under the surface.

John's "Un dans Versailles" is sung to an imaginary girl overseas, with the second verse and chorus translated into French by "a friend or roommate of Jeff's girlfriend," says John. "I know my pronunciation is atrocious, but I think I figured if Paul McCartney could speak French in 'Michelle,' it might be cool to try."

Jeff's "One in Versailles" is aimed straight at Gary—tangible proof that their band was real, that it was happening. He brought in Tim Klebe, Gary's sixteen-year-old brother, to help him pick out the song's acoustic intro, just because he thought having a Klebe on the record would be kind of interesting. Tim, for his part, recognized his limitations; "I wasn't good," he says now. "After many recording attempts, I think Jeff realized this, too. He told me that he thought he had 'enough to make it work.' Jeff was very nice to give me credit for a few notes that he dubbed over." Jeff counters that he doubled, not dubbed over, Tim Klebe's notes; the teenager's contribution is still in the grooves.

Significantly, Jeff's "One in Versailles" ends with a spirited vow: "Now we're gonna show you what we really can do."

IF JEFF AND JOHN WERE GOING TO get this tape to Gary while he was still in France, as they planned, they had to set a schedule. In March, with the clock ticking on the remainder of the school year, John came home for spring break and laid down the vast majority of his material in a week. It was stressful for both brothers, since Jeff was still doing all the engineering, which meant that even though his own songs were finished, he had to man the board for John's tracks. This situation strained both Jeff, who wanted to have some kind of life outside recording and work; and John, who felt like he was being rushed to finish his songs too quickly, and not given the time he needed to try out his various musical options.

Laying down six songs (and parts of six others) in a little more than a week required some vocal and instrumental compromises, too, shortcuts that might not have been possible with Gary around: playful experiments like "Banjo" and "Eggroll Rock" were included alongside more fully-developed compositions. As slapdash as *Heads or Tails* had been, it was already clear that Gary was going to be Shoes' studio stickler. As John observes:

> We're all perfectionists, but for Gary *nothing* is ever quite good enough. Recording *Versailles*, Jeff and I thought, "We're just going to knock this out." It was very loose, and I remember thinking, "This wouldn't have flown if Gary were here, but what the hell."

Gary takes issue with that characterization, pointing out that at this stage, with nothing but the thrown-together *Heads or Tails* under their belts, he wasn't nearly experienced enough to be a perfectionist. But John insists, "He can't help it. It's his nature."

There are twelve tracks on *One in Versailles*—one collaboration between the brothers ("Dance in Your Sleep," on which they sing lead vocals in unison), six by John ("Do I Get So Shy," "Un dans Versailles," "Something I Can't See," "One Night," "The Sun," and "Banjo"), and five by Jeff ("Kristine," "Eggroll Rock," "Song for Her," "No I Don't," and "One in Versailles").

INSPIRED BY AN ALBUM IN BARRY'S collection that had been recorded and pressed up by their drummer's junior-high-school marching band—which had shown Jeff and John that there were ways of getting a record made without being signed to a record company—they contacted a local pressing plant. The minimum order for a twelve-inch, long-playing vinyl disc was three hundred copies, costing just over a dollar each; and so that's what Shoes got, delivered in plain white cardboard sleeves, in April.

John designed liner notes and a minimalist cover—which read simply "SHOES, ONE IN VERSAILLES" in one direction and "SOULIERS, UN DANS VERSAILLES in the other—printed in black ink on eleven-by-eleven-inch square white sheets of paper. The records came from the pressing plant already shrink-wrapped, so each cellophane skin had to be painstakingly slit along the edge in order to insert a front cover, a back cover—with track listing, brief credits, and the following line: DEDICATED TO THE ONE IN VERSAILLES—GARY KLEBE— and a stylized lyric sheet (also designed by John). Neither of the cover sheets was actually glued onto the cardboard jacket; the shrink-wrap held both in place.

John recalls that he acquired copies of *OIV* in time to bring some back to school before semester's end; Gary's roommate Paul Austermehle was one early recipient (though John thinks he might have actually charged Austermehle a princely three bucks for the honor). Strawberry Fields, the local record store, hung a promotional poster for *One in Versailles* and stocked it, though they didn't actually sell any. A few copies went to a few other friends, but mostly, the LPs sat in boxes under Jeff's bed in La Cabane. (Respected vinyl-reissue label Numero Group released *One in Versailles* in fall 2012.)

BUT THE POINT, OF COURSE, was to get it to Gary, and to do this, Jeff and John didn't need to wait for the album to be physically pressed. Gary didn't have a turntable there anyway, and even if he had, it would have been cost-prohibitive to mail a vinyl record overseas. But a cassette could just as easily be made from *One in Versailles*' reel-to-reel master tapes, and was cheaper to ship—so that's what they did. The accompanying letter is postmarked March 31, 1975; the envelope warns not to x-ray the package because it contains a magnetic tape, which is valued at two dollars.

Gary received his cassette copy of *One in Versailles* sometime in April. It was emphatically different from the primarily acoustic and comparatively roughhewn *Heads or Tails*. In fact, Gary later told John that when the guitar for the opening track—"Dance in Your Sleep"—started, he thought it was a prank, thought that they'd sent him some music by a *real* band and just *told* him it was Shoes. Not until the vocals kicked in was Gary convinced.

But he swiftly went from convinced to downright intimidated. Hearing what John and Jeff could do without him, Gary now feared that he "was just dead weight." Particularly, he felt that the Murphys had the singing well in hand, and so—even though he had sung on *Heads or Tails*—he would refuse to vocalize on *OIV*'s follow-up, 1975's *Bazooka*, and beyond. It wasn't until nearly two years later—well into the sessions that resulted in Shoes' groundbreaking self-released album, 1977's *Black Vinyl Shoes*—that Gary finally felt confident enough to commit his voice to tape. (He would not sing on stage, however, until 1979.)

DURING HIS SCHOOL YEAR ABROAD, though Gary had been consumed with schoolwork, he'd discovered almost as soon as classes began that he deeply missed playing music. He wasn't *listening* to a whole lot of music, either; European airwaves weren't terribly inspirational, Gary recalls, though Radio Luxembourg was decent, and he was acquiring some things on cassette, like the Raspberries' *Starting Over*. Mostly he just played and wrote songs on the cheap Spanish guitar he'd picked up on a sketchbook study trip to Barcelona.

Gary ended up making several of these jaunts around the continent during his semester at the Ecole d'Architecture. The Barcelona sojourn was part of a big swing through southeastern Europe—Italy, Greece, Yugoslavia. He and his fellow students returned to France through Italy, Switzerland, Austria, and Germany, and then traversed southwestern Europe into North Africa: through Spain, past Gibraltar, and on to Morocco.

Gary, who had always eschewed drinking before, now left behind his clean-living image, which inadvertently cost him an anticipated view of a fabled landmark:

> When I was on the ferry going down to Morocco, we were looking forward to seeing the Rock of Gibraltar. ... But I remember buying a bottle of Johnnie Walker Black Label and drinking the whole thing, and I passed out in the van and missed it. And then, coming back, I drank a bottle of Cinzano and I fell asleep again and missed the Rock of Gibraltar a second time.

Over Christmas, a friend from Champaign came to visit Gary, and they went to England via Amsterdam, circling back through Belgium to France; Gary sold his Spanish guitar to fund that trip. In February, there was another foray through southern France and Spain, including a stop in Madrid, were Gary bought a second guitar.

The trips accomplished their intent, both professionally and personally: they made an architect of Gary, without forcing him to abandon the musician.

BACK IN ZION, WHILE RECORDING *One in Versailles*, Jeff conceived an elaborate practical joke to play on Gary. In *Shoes: Birth of a Band*, his 2007 memoir, Jeff describes the prank:

> I was printing [envelopes] for a living at the time and my friend, Garry Holverson, worked at the offices of the local weekly newspaper. [W]e printed a fake music paper that I had conjured up and titled *Zonker*. It was about a dozen pages of photos, fake reviews, articles and fan letters documenting "Shoemania" and heralding the newest music sensation… SHOES! Gary had the [*Zion-Benton News*] delivered to him in France so [Holverson and I]

found his subscription and inserted a copy of the bogus music accolades and off to France it went.

Zonker is eight pages long, two sheets of newsprint folded into a tabloid-sized journal. On the cover it reads, "SHOES: local boys make good," with an article that includes a fabricated interview with Jeff and John's mother ("They still call once in a while to tell me they're alright [sic]. Once they came all the way home from New York just because Johnny forgot his mittens.") Inside are various photos, both of Gary—"an extraordinary shoe"—and of the early *One in Versailles* sessions, still in the Murphy basement.

Barry, whom Gary had not yet met, was introduced jokingly:

> In their never ending search for perfection in music, the two Shoes discovered [this] poor young man lying drunk in an alley, beating feverishly on an array of garbage cans. Liking his determined style, they took him in, gave him a change of clothes and, as the lad already had quite a set ... so to speak, set him to work, and immediately declared a breakthrough in tightness. Outasight!

Mock ads, a fan letter from an imaginary fourteen-year-old girl (declaring, "Even my mom thinks they're cute!"), and Gary's sole piece of overseas correspondence to them—a postcard from early October, featuring himself as a comically stereotypical Frenchman, complete with beret and striped shirt, moustache, and a pair of baguettes—made up the bulk of the rest of *Zonker*. But the most alarming part for the chronically shy Shoe was the full-page ad from the Zion Parks Department announcing a three-hour Shoes concert for the Fourth of July at Shiloh Park, right in the middle of town.

Gary remembers receiving *Zonker* late in the school year, buried in his regular hometown newspaper. He recalls his first response as confusion— "What the hell?"—followed by amusement, and then blind panic that their "goofy inside jokes," their rock-star fantasies, had been laid out for the whole community. Gary explains his credulity: "It was on the same newsprint, printed just like the other parts of the paper. I was blown away, excited—but then I was upset." Gary had quickly figured out that *Zonker* was a hoax, he says, but assumed that the flyer had gone out in every copy of the newspaper, and thus had circulated throughout Zion. "We weren't that far out of high school: Zion was our whole world. It never occurred to me for a second—and I thought about it a lot—that they could have gotten just one copy into the exact paper that came to me."

Gary immediately wrote home, in what Jeff remembers as a "mildly chiding" letter, but John recalls that Gary was genuinely peeved, tersely stating, "We are *not* ready for this." The Murphys were stung by his curt response to their joke, and John wrote back, assuring him that there really was no gig, that the joke paper and ad were sent only to him, that it was all in good fun. Gary immediately felt remorseful for flying off the handle.

By that time, however, his year in Europe was wrapping up, and Klebe was soon on his way home, with a bulging sketchbook, a budget Spanish guitar, and a notebook full of song ideas. As Jeff had stated in "One in Versailles," there was "plenty to do." It was time to get back to work.

WITH GARY BACK IN ZION, SHOES' creative process moved faster than it ever had before. Having arrived with several more-or-less complete song ideas, Gary was ready to roll. With less than three months until the school year started again, Shoes were determined to make another record, so things had to fly.

The summer of '75, Jeff recalls, was "a real scorcher," and Shoes spent it socked into the cramped, stuffy confines of Jeff and Barry's place. The four-track TEAC was moved to the kitchen, which bought a little room, but as crowded as things had been for *One in Versailles*, Gary's presence meant even more equipment and even less space.

Recording at La Cabane in the summer presented a new set of challenges. The neighbor's aforementioned dogs barked crazily all night, repeatedly ruining takes and forcing the one window La Cabane *did* have to remain closed most of the time; the phone, neighbors' lawnmowers, and the refrigerator could also ruin takes. In another effort to control extraneous noise, Shoes turned off the bulky box fan whenever they were recording.

They began with Gary's material, partly because he already had a couple of complete songs written—and a lot of ideas for more—but also because he was now the one with something to prove. After all, the Murphys had two albums under their belts, and he had barely one, *Heads or Tails*. Thus, Gary explicitly framed his contributions to the new album as responses to the songs on *One in Versailles*:

> I listened to *One in Versailles*, like, a million times, because the band had gone through the next step of its evolution, and I'd missed it. Coming back from school, I was really excited that we were recording, but anybody in that situation would feel like they'd been put in their place: "Lookit, we've shown we can do this without you, *but* we want you around, *but* ..." I had no confidence at the time; as far as I knew I was the unnecessary one. Maybe the brothers *were* where the talent was.

And so Gary was determined to make his mark, writing or co-writing six of the thirteen tracks on the new album, which they'd dubbed *Bazooka*: "Alone but Satisfied," "The Atlantic," and "Educated" (this last about a particularly insufferable and pedantic colleague in France) were his own, and "Pinheads," "I'm Brazen," and "Like I Told You" were composed with John. The relative abundance of Gary's material on *Bazooka* was due not only to his own drive, however: John and Jeff were tapped out creatively from *One in Versailles*, which was still only a few months old, and they were just getting back to songwriting.

Another shadow cast by *One in Versailles* over *Bazooka* was Gary's refusal to sing lead on his own songs. "You guys are doing fine, you just do it," he told the Murphys. John recalls repeatedly trying to talk him into it, assuring Gary, "Your voice is no worse than mine." But he was unmoved.

Deep inside, Gary did want to sing—"I knew even then that I was settling for less than I'd dreamed about," since singing was an integral part of the rock-star fantasy—but he contented himself with the backing harmonies Shoes were just starting to suss out, since that was less intimidating.

Bazooka marked the first time all the members of Shoes had specifically set out to make a full record together. They were all holding down regular day gigs: John had a summer internship at the regional planning office in Waukegan, and Gary was back working construction with a concrete contractor. (It was heavy, dangerous work; he remembers the shock of learning that one of his co-workers, a dad from his old neighborhood, had died when the Bobcat he was driving tipped over, just a few days after Gary had moved on from the same job site.) Jeff was still at the envelope factory, a job that started earlier in the day than both John's internship and Gary's construction gig, but finished earlier, too. Jeff used those couple of hours on his own every day to write and try things on tape, before the other guys clocked out, cleaned up, and came over to his place to record.

Jeff remembers "John and Gary writing together *a lot* on this album. My stuff was started by me, and the others would contribute after I got the basics down." Jeff has three solo compositions on *Bazooka*: "Move It or Lose It," "Love Took a Turn," and "My Anisette" (the last of these inspired by the licorice-flavored cordial Gary talked about discovering in France), and two songs co-written with John ("New Meat" and "Snap"). Shoes' ever-present, always-indistinct line between contributing ideas, making suggestions, or adding elements to a song that basically remained someone else's, and true co-credited collaboration, was particularly fuzzy on this record.

John recalls that, on his co-written material, he would generally compose the melody and pen the lyrics. Whichever guitarist he was collaborating with, Jeff or Gary, would handle the chord structure and instrumentation. Sometimes Gary would bring in a melody too, but, refusing to lay down even a rough vocal track, he'd sing it to John when they were alone, and they'd work it out from there. "Composition was such a messy process on that record," John admits.

On John's solo songs ("Rock Your Own" and "Along with Love"), he liked to supply more instrumentation apart from simply playing his bass, but that raised some issues as well. John cites a particular fondness for his less-than-a-minute-long tune "Along with Love," because "it didn't overstay its welcome due to some stuffy ideal of structure," offering as influential models T. Rex's compact "Beltane Walk" and "Diamond Meadows." ("Along with Love" has two verses, and no real chorus.) But especially because it was so short, John wanted to contribute more than bass; John made it known he wanted to drum, too. He promptly got a pointed phone call from Barry: "If you drum, then do I get to play bass?" Chastened, John backed down, "but I still sat behind Barry and showed him *exactly* what I wanted him to play."

For Gary, it was his first time recording with a real drummer—on *Heads or Tails*, drums had been added on at the end. Barry remembers Gary as initially pretty reticent around him because he'd forgotten their childhood friendship—indeed, thought they'd never met—until Barry reminded him that they had played together when the Klebes lived behind Mr. Shumaker's house. Barry's grandfather would crown the boys in hats made of folded newspapers, and they'd march around to patriotic songs in the old man's living room. With their longstanding acquaintance now confirmed, Barry says, "I guess Gary figured I was all right."

Once he warmed to Barry, Gary was sold on his skill. Barry's previous rock-band experience had left him with specific ideas about how and what to play—unlike the other members of Shoes, who were neophytes. Though there was head-butting now and then, they valued their new bandmate's perspective and style. "Barry was a great pop drummer," Gary declares.

Beyond their interactions with Shumaker, all three Shoes principals draw an almost total blank when trying to recall the *Bazooka* sessions. "Hot" and "fast" are the terms that most frequently pepper their recollections. But for the first time, the band members could work regularly, in privacy—and that made a huge difference in the quality of the final product. Plus, all cite their conscious decision "to make this record rock more, leaning towards distorted electric guitars rather than the acoustic-based sound we had started out with"—as expressed in the liner notes from *As Is*.

The sole ballads, Gary's "The Atlantic" and "Alone but Satisfied," were the compositions he'd brought home from France, and actually wouldn't have been out of place on the more contemplative *One in Versailles*. *Bazooka* was Gary's chance to catch up to the Murphy brothers on their more aggressive path, and as the summer got hotter and their work more intense, so did the music. Songs like the brawny "I'm Brazen" and riff-driven "Like I Told You" are transitional moments, clearly marking the evolution toward the more distorted and intricately layered rock of *Black Vinyl Shoes*—culminating in what would come to be Shoes' distinctive sound.

The title of their new record was chosen deliberately to point up the hard-soft duality they were now refining into that sound. *Bazooka* was intended to reference the iconic bubble gum—John's album-cover concept was an Associated Press photo of a kid blowing a hot-pink bubble as big as his head—but also to the power of the rocket launcher. Of course, it was also a subtle nod to the Beatles' *Revolver*.

By late August, after months of sweating and toiling, they had unofficially rechristened La Cabane "The Oven." But Shoes had accomplished exactly what they'd set out to do. John and Gary raced back downstate to continue college—Gary to complete that stray semester, John to keep plugging away at his B.F.A.—and life returned more or less to normal.

Shoes' original intention had been to press up *Bazooka* as a vinyl LP, but external constraints interfered with that plan. As explained in the liner notes on *As Is* (which includes both *Bazooka* and *One in Versailles* in their entirety), "[W]ith two guys at school and the other two barely eking out a living back home, the funds just weren't there. Hell, we still had three hundred [unsold] copies of *OIV* sitting in cartons under Jeff's bed that we didn't know what to do with." So *Bazooka* remained a reel-to-reel master tape. (In 2012, Numero Group released *Bazooka* on vinyl.)

John and Gary took their tape to the University of Illinois' campus radio station in Champaign, and tried to get it played. They didn't know anyone at the station, but reasoned that since they were students, too, the home-recorded music they were making might be of interest to other students. The station's staff promised to play it, but never did—eventually resulting in a rather contentious encounter between the station staff and John and Gary—who demanded their tape back if it wasn't going to be aired.

Outside of the college-radio incident, however, the members of Shoes were still shy about talking up their group. John remembers telling an art professor that he was in "an experimental band"—which, he later realized, made it sound like they were probably "blowing on wind chimes and tapping on empty wine bottles with swizzle sticks."

At the end of 1975, Gary finished his bachelor's degree and came home. John, who had maybe a year left to complete his own degree, put his education on what would turn out to be permanent hold, and returned to Zion as well. College had been putting a financial strain on John, so he wanted to earn some money. Plus, his longtime fiancée Sara was wearying of their long-distance relationship, and in a desperate attempt to save the engagement, John moved home to convince her of his seriousness. Once he got those two items squared away, John had intended to return to Champaign and finish school the following academic year; but by the time that semester came along, his goals had changed.

No matter what the near future would hold, the members of Shoes were committed to staying in Zion for the spring and summer of '76. As they were focusing entirely on the band now, it seemed clear that they needed to perform live. Thus, they concentrated their efforts on getting ready to play out.

SHOES' FIRST-EVER GIG TOOK PLACE in April, at a small club in Kenosha, Wisconsin called the Brat Stop. Named not for a badly behaved child but for the sobriquet of bratwurst, the pale German sausage popular throughout the Upper Midwest, the club had hosted some fairly renowned bands, including the increasingly ubiquitous Cheap Trick. Shoes prepared for the show by christening their public-address system at a pair of rehearsal sessions: one at a recreation hall in nearby Winthrop Harbor, Illinois, and the other in the warehouse of a factory that made wrestling mats. "Our friend Joe Higgins from *Lime* worked there," Gary says, explaining how Shoes came to practice in that particular venue.

"It smelled terrible," John grimaces. "I'm pretty sure we got high from the solvents." But the warehouse was spacious—and heavily padded—which is just what Shoes needed. And Higgins ended up running sound for the Brat Stop show.

Shoes played on a Thursday in front of a small house (despite the fact that, as Barry recalls, it was both amateur night *and* quarter-beer night)—with its stage dominated by an enormous photo poster of the weekend's headliners. Shoes covered the faces of the other band with their own modestly-sized placards.

Their inaugural set list was comprised mostly of songs from *Bazooka*, the source of the material that would dominate Shoes' live shows for several years. But the band also performed selections from *One in Versailles*: "Kristine," "The Sun," "Dance in Your Sleep," and Jeff's electric version of the title track.

And there were the obligatory covers; Barry remembers Harry Nilsson's jittery "Jump into the Fire," T. Rex's retro trifle "Jeepster," and Grin's garage-band raveup "Moon Tears." "We did covers because we had to," says John, referring to Shoes' dearth of enough original material to fill out a concert set, "but they were always a little 'off'—not the stuff you'd usually hear, although most people had heard of the bands." He offers as examples songs like 10cc's "Silly Love" and Paul Revere & the Raiders' "Him or Me." "And sometimes we'd do less-famous cover versions of famous songs, like Mott the Hoople's cover of Velvet Underground's 'Sweet Jane,' or David Bowie's take on the Who's "Can't Explain.'"

AMONG THE CONCERTGOERS IN THE Brat Stop's modest crowd that April evening were John and Gary's Champaign college buddies, most of them now based in Chicago, who undertook the trip to Wisconsin to see Shoes' debut. "The people who *were* there," Gary says now, "really wanted to be there."

One of the true-blue U of I pals, Paul Austermehle, started the dancing with Jeff's girlfriend, Debi. "I went to all their shows, if I could," Austermehle says now. "Our whole college crowd did. Nothing made me happier than seeing those guys play. They fuckin' *rocked*."

Someone who missed seeing Shoes perform their first-ever gig was, unfortunately, Tim Klebe, who tried to get into the eighteen-and-over show even though it took place a month before his eighteenth birthday. But security was carding at the door, and though Tim could see high-school classmates inside whom he knew were younger, the bouncers were stalwart in his case. Even the fact that his brother was in the band moved them not. Tim listened dejectedly to Shoes' stage debut from the parking lot.

More serious repercussions from that show soon followed, however. Barry's girlfriend decided that, much as she liked having a musician boyfriend, having a boyfriend in a band playing shows—shows that were attended by girls who were there to pick up band guys—was maybe a little more than she had bargained for. She began leaning on Barry to quit.

The pressure on Shoes' drummer quickly became twofold. Barry had been unemployed since the Shumakers had lost the family butcher-shop business, and in spring '76 he was hired by Camelot Music, a growing national record-store chain. Camelot offered him a place in their management-training program, but the position came with a condition: Barry would have to quit the band. "They were afraid Shoes would get discovered and I'd leave Camelot," Barry explains.

Instead, Shumaker left Shoes. It wasn't an easy decision, he says, but abetting it was Barry's certainty that Jeff, John, and Gary were "a lot more professional than I was"—that what was a hobby for him was very, very serious for them. Barry says of Shoes' reaction to his exit:

> There was some anger there, some disappointment. We had just started to build momentum, and here I was leaving them in the lurch. But I needed a job.

The drummer's departure was complicated by the fact that Barry was tied to Shoes not just by his vital band role, but also because he was Jeff's housemate. Since it would have been awkward to quit Shoes and continue living in La Cabane, Barry ended up moving out at the same time.

THE HUNT FOR A NEW DRUMMER commenced immediately. Shoes were on a roll, and didn't want to lose valuable time. As Zion wasn't a large town, their options weren't particularly plentiful, so they were able to assess them quickly. The most promising prospect was a guy who played in a cover band called Bigfoot, and who happened to be dating one of Gary's sisters. She had brought him home to the Klebes' traditional Sunday pizza night, so Gary had met him socially, but knew little about him otherwise.

Philip "Skip" Meyer had graduated from the same high school as the others, but he was several years older. He had become a drummer, he said, after being inspired by *The Mickey Mouse Club*'s talented Mouseketeer Cubby O'Brien (the only one of the kids allowed to play onscreen). That led to drum-and-bugle corps and marching band before he turned to rock & roll after high school. Skip had attended Southern Illinois University, but when he met Klebe and the Murphys, he was working construction back in Zion. They didn't travel in the same social circles; Skip's interests centered on cars and weed and girls (not necessarily in that order), and he was considered something of a playboy around Zion.

But though they weren't well acquainted with each other, Skip wasn't as ignorant of their music as Shoes figured. Gary's sister had played him a tape of her brother's band and, Skip wrote in his journal, "I liked it!"

The members of Shoes wanted to assess Skip's playing before approaching him, but not necessarily have him know they were checking him out. So they sent John, whom Skip wouldn't recognize, to scout a Bigfoot show at the Holiday Inn lounge in Kenosha. It happened that their high-school friend Jim Sinkus, who was also in Bigfoot, had approached John about designing some posters for the band, so John's presence would not appear unusual to anyone who knew him—it wouldn't be obvious that he was drummer-poaching, in any case. John paid close attention to Skip, even though he ruefully admits he wouldn't necessarily have known a good drummer from a bad one at that point, having really only worked with Barry for any length. But he came back and reported that Skip was steady and that he had "a good stage look," charismatic and self-assured.

John didn't get to meet Skip that night, and of course Skip never knew he was being scouted. The show ended early and abruptly because one of Skip's bandmates decided to set off several smoke bombs during Bigfoot's set. Smoke alarms went off, the room cleared, people scattered. The evening immediately entered the annals of local-scene lore: Skip recalls that the next day, while partying at Petrifying Springs Park in Kenosha, someone approached him and told him all about the explosive show he'd seen the night before, without realizing that Skip had been in the band.

The next Sunday, when Meyer went over to the Klebes' for pizza, Gary spoke to him about auditioning for Shoes. As it turned out, the fireworks stunt had been the swan song of a disintegrating band; Bigfoot was breaking up anyway. Since Skip was looking around for another steady gig, he agreed at least to give Shoes a shot. John, Jeff, and Gary let him believe they were trying out other drummers, but in fact, Skip was the only candidate they evaluated.

The new Shoe, accustomed to Bigfoot's repertoire of slamming tunes by arena-headlining favorites like Led Zeppelin, had to learn a lot of new music—Shoes never played more than a handful of covers, and all of the band's writers had very specific ideas about how they wanted the drums to sound on their own songs. Luckily, Skip was easygoing and basically amenable. They gave him their tapes of *One in Versailles* and *Bazooka*, and they rehearsed at least several nights a week, all summer. But there was a lot of Shoes music for him to master before they would be back to where they had been with Barry, and they were writing new material all the time. Skip, who kept the aforementioned journal during much of his time with Shoes, notes in an early entry that they were working on *Black Vinyl Shoes* material almost as soon as he joined the band, though they were not yet recording it.

DURING THIS WHOLE PROCESS, GARY continued pursuing his license in architecture. There were two paths he could follow now that he had his B.A., either returning to school to earn a master's degree, or interning at an architecture firm for a number of years to qualify for the licensing examination. Either option would take several more years to complete; Gary hedged his bets by ensuring both paths were available to him, assuaging his parents' concern over his future while buying himself a certain freedom.

He applied for and landed a paid internship, at a church-design firm that (he ruefully admits) wasn't very impressive, but had the very desirable attribute of being located in Zion, so Gary could keep moving with Shoes while he pursued his putative career. There was very little supervision in his position; Gary says he basically taught himself. "I would be handed projects and end up doing them from start to finish all on my own," he describes. "I wasn't crazy about the job, but I knew I needed it to get my license." Significantly,

Gary adds, "I wasn't truly all that gung-ho about architecture, but I don't like leaving things unfinished." He also applied to graduate school and was accepted back at Champaign, but upon autumn's arrival, a master's degree didn't seem nearly as important to him as the band.

Jeff and John both recall that ever since Shoes had begun, they'd had a sense that Gary might be out the door any day; that there was a limit to the amount of time he would be willing to spend on their project. But as John had done years earlier when working with Gary on *Lime*, they both may have confused Gary's reserved, measured demeanor with a dearth of passion. Because Gary had no such lack; he was as ardent about the band as his partners were, even if he didn't show it. In fact, he stresses, "I couldn't stand the thought of not being part of Shoes. I wanted it more than anything." Still, the dilemma over whether to forgo graduate school in favor of the band was one he agonized over all summer, finally deciding in early August not to return to Champaign. Gary calls it "the most pivotal decision of my life."

Not surprisingly, John's parents noticed that he, too, was still around the house as summer faded into fall. John is not entirely sure why he didn't return to school to finish his bachelor's degree; he ventures, "I couldn't tear myself away from everything: the band, and the relationship, and home." Though John was now back working at the Department of Regional Planning, his parents told him it was time to move out. "If I was a student and I was living at home, that was okay," he relates, "but now that I was an adult, I had to leave the nest." He was scarcely ever home anyway, going from work to Sara's, and Sara's to his brother's; and as they had done with Jeff, John's parents had now given him his own walking papers: "They said, 'Okay, buddy, we're onto you now—no more free rides!'"

John believes the band gave both Gary and him a rationale to stay in Zion in the fall of '76. "If Gary *had* gone back to Champaign, I'm sure he would have tried to get me to go as well," John observes. "But we already had our minds set on our next step: we wanted to record a new album." With both Shoes at loose ends lodging-wise, John and Gary ended up getting a house together, renting from an elderly Zion couple who wintered in Florida.

TOWARD THE END OF THAT SUMMER, Shoes and their new drummer were as ready as they'd ever be to play out in earnest. Actually, with two or three sets of material ready to go, they were getting downright antsy. So one night, says John, Shoes impulsively "loaded up the truck with our gear and sound system and drove down to play" where one of Gary's college housemates, Paul Neville, lived: Dwight, Illinois, "your garden-variety sleepy little Midwest town," nestled in the cornfields.

While Shoes hadn't lined up a place to perform, Neville recollects that the lack of organization had a larger purpose: "We all thought it would be easier to ask for forgiveness than permission."

Shoes headed to a local bar to proffer a spur-of-the-moment set, but the available space was far too small. They ended up relocating to a nearby picnic pavilion in the town's Renfrew Park, where they set up. Their only real audience members were the college buddies—in addition to Neville, Paul Austermehle and a few others had shown up—but four or five dozen local kids also materialized; not a bad crowd for a small-town pick-up gig. John thinks that their friends "took collections or maybe donations to offset our travel costs, but that money ended up being spent on free beer for attendees. The crowd—such as it was—drank up the brews and gave us a rousing response."

Rousing was one word for it; rowdy was another. As John modestly sees it, "The kids were just into having a free rock show. It didn't seem to matter that no one knew our songs." Neville recalls there being rumors of hanky-panky in the nearby bushes; Austermehle claims that the revelers in attendance probably didn't remember much at all. But the crowd raucously cheered the Zion foursome, a lift they sorely needed. After all, this was only Shoes' second show, and their first with Skip.

Intent on their performance, the band members were only vaguely aware of how trashed the crowd was—"We could see *Animal House* kinds of stuff going on," Gary recounts, "but we weren't *doing* it; we were playing." And then the Dwight constabulary showed up. And then showed up again. And again.

Neville recalls:

The police were being pretty good about [the noise], while Shoes and Shoes fans were negotiating for "ONE MORE SONG!" The crowd was definitely drunk, but the cops came [only] because the music was at 180 decibels.

At that point, the law put the lid on Shoes' unauthorized concert.

Still, a good gig is a good gig, and with that well-received performance under their belts, Shoes embarked upon their next recording project, *Black Vinyl Shoes*—politely thanking "Dwight" on its liner notes, among a list of their friends' names, as though the town were a person.

Chapter 3

Move It or Lose It (1976-77)

WHEN THE STORY OF SHOES IS told, it usually begins with *Black Vinyl Shoes*. And there's no question that the sessions resulting in this fully-realized and influential home-cooked platter of theirs represented a quantum leap in Shoes' development. Asked about their evolution—how the rough-and-ready rowdies of *Bazooka* became the noticeably polished craftsmen of *Black Vinyl Shoes*—the band members give different answers.

Jeff points to the technological innovations in Shoes' recording style, the refinement of their process of capturing specific colors and textures: "We were definitely learning a lot about what defined individual sounds, and we were buying better gear as we went along, like a new recording console"—a Peavey 1200S, which they purchased in the fall of '76. The Murphys and Klebe continued their customary practice of plugging their guitars directly into the recording console, says Jeff, "with various distortion boxes and gadgets, which produced a strange, buzzy type of effect. Coupled with our reserved vocal approach, it made for an unusual combination."

Gary thinks the increase in cohesiveness Shoes developed after their early albums, markedly evident on *Black Vinyl Shoes*, was largely due to the fact that they were playing together more as a band—at shows and rehearsals—fundamentally changing their long-held perceptions of themselves as awkward, isolated amateurs. "We were feeling like a unit," he explains. "By the time we played together and got comfortable with Skip, we thought, 'We can actually *do* this.' So we began *Black Vinyl* with a lot more confidence." In fact, says Gary, "*Black Vinyl Shoes* was the first time we knew we were a band."

And John points out that their lives had evolved enough that the commitment they'd made to the music seemed more real; no one was rushing back to school, no one was focusing his energies elsewhere. Prior to this, all Shoes projects had had external deadlines: *Heads or Tails* and *Bazooka* had been sandwiched into summer vacations, *One in Versailles* had to be completed before Gary returned from France. No more. "Let's just do it," John remembers them saying to each other.

There's no need to rank the importance of any of these technological, perceptual, and personal transitions. All contributed to the lavish creativity displayed on *Black Vinyl Shoes*.

And they had a new ambition: the desire for a recording contract became Shoes' driving force.

They'd planned, even before they began it, for *Black Vinyl Shoes* to be the record that would introduce Shoes to the world. As Jeff explains, "We knew we were going to press it up ourselves, but hoped it would serve as an elaborate demo to attract major-label interest."

All four of them were working full-time now, so recording, mixing, mastering, and pressing *Black Vinyl Shoes* was a lot more manageable financially than *One in Versailles* had been. Releasing it for sale as an income generator, however, wasn't even on their radar. "We had no idea you could make money doing things independently," says Jeff.

IT WOULD BE ONLY A SLIGHT exaggeration to say that Shoes was still almost a secret project at this point, even though they had done a few shows and were actively recording. Yet, partly because they weren't playing out a lot, partly because even now they didn't talk about Shoes much, their friends and families still had some trouble believing that the band was real; John recalls people saying, "Murf and Klebe don't do that shit." Even—at times especially—their closest friends were most skeptical.

The members of Shoes continued to leave their families largely out of the loop as well. Gary admits, "I guess I kind of hid it from my parents. I didn't feel comfortable with them knowing what I was doing at that point." After all, *they* thought he was training for a real profession.

Privacy was of paramount importance, so even though Jeff's place was "a boys' club," as Gary puts it, none of their other friends were around when Shoes were recording. "It's very nerve-wracking," says Gary of the process. "I wouldn't want to do a vocal while some idiot is sitting there drinking a beer."

In this clandestine workshop, they were formulating the changes that would solidify into the core of Shoes' distinctive sound. One clear shift was lyrical: with the exception of Jeff's commentary on greed, "Capital Gain," written and recorded first, all the songs on *Black Vinyl Shoes* deal with romantic relationships. Shoes have subsequently been tweaked for what became their particular obsession—and their generally grim view of it—but there is no question that focusing on the vicissitudes of love allowed a more cohesive record to emerge. As Gary explains, "We had come to an unspoken understanding of what good lyrics were. There was no rule that we had to write about relationships, but we started at that point and it kind of stuck; the lyrical content of *Black Vinyl* became the template for Shoes songs to follow." Further, each of the three writers started staking out specific territory within this circumscribed palette: Jeff went with wounded but hopeful romanticism on "If You'd Stay," Gary expressed bitter renunciation on "Nowhere So Fast," and John slid into good-humored raunchiness on "Boys Don't Lie."

At the same time, Shoes were creating prototypes of different musical frameworks that they would employ from then on. Gary sees his own compositions on *Black Vinyl Shoes* as each utilizing a specific musical element that propels it; he describes "Nowhere So Fast," for example, as being structured around a continuous riff rolling all the way through, with various melodic overlays. "Like a 'Day Tripper,' thing" Gary observes. "Fatal," on the other hand, pulses rather than rolls, propelled by what Gary calls a "kind of staccato, eighth-note chugging," which, he says, is "something we've done a lot through our career. ... It's one of our weapons. And 'Fatal' was one of the early songs that solidified that approach, made it the driving force of the song." In "Not Me," Gary says he was thinking of "a more percussive sound, driven by acoustic shifts," contrasting the insistent, brittle beat with the vapory vocals—particularly Jeff's soaring chorus. But overall, Gary sees *Black Vinyl Shoes* as musically "quite fragile—we were still just looking for a sound. I don't think we knew what we were yet."

YET *BLACK VINYL SHOES* WAS PROTOTYPICAL, TOO; in many noteworthy ways—for good or ill—its creation instituting a lot of the working methods and processes that Shoes would employ for many years.

Perhaps the most significant of these was the establishment of Jeff as official session engineer and mixer.

This had, of course, been the unofficial setup since the beginning. The house Shoes recorded in was Jeff's house, the TEAC 3340-S was Jeff's machine, and he naturally fell into doing all the engineering and mixing—a complicated process when limited to four tracks (professional studios typically used twenty-four). "I guess I was protective of the TEAC," Jeff says, "and probably discouraged the other guys' engineering efforts with my possessiveness. At the time, though, I didn't think they cared, and I considered running the board a serious responsibility." His eagerness to steer the recording process was obvious to his bandmates; in John's words, "You couldn't pry him away from the machine." But this meant that Jeff was doing double duty much of the time. And because the studio was in his living space, Jeff never really felt *off*-duty.

Another working method established during the making of *Black Vinyl Shoes*, however unconsciously, was the order of which writer's songs were recorded when. Jeff, who then as now tends to create in a flurry of immediate inspiration, laid down the first song, the aforementioned, atypical "Capital Gain." Gary was right on his heels, methodically ringing out all the changes he could think of before settling on a sound he was happy with. His first recorded song was the wounded warning, "Fatal." And John brought up the rear, as he has always continued to do, racing to finish his songs before the group-imposed deadline; dozens of snippets and embryonic tunes were considered and rejected before he was satisfied. His "Boys Don't Lie" slid in under the wire.

Gary and Jeff joke that John's bringing-up-the-rear method was (and is) intentional, that he's always waited until the end so he could take advantage of the new skills and equipment Shoes had acquired during the recording process—and in fact, Jeff has noted a significant improvement in production quality between his own "Capital Gain" (the first song recorded) and John's "Boys Don't Lie" (the last). John readily acknowledges his tardiness, while insisting it was anything *but* strategic. "It was much more a result of my own self-doubt," he says now. "They were bringing in songs that were more polished, much further along than my half-baked melodies and phrases. I was insecure, and it was intimidating." But when the others encouraged him to go with whatever he had, he would lay the tracks down.

BLACK VINYL SHOES, RELEASED IN summer 1977, accomplished what Shoes hoped it would and more, quickly selling out its original pressing of one thousand copies (less the three hundred or so sent out for promotional purposes), and attracting both critical and major-label attention. "If it weren't for *Black Vinyl Shoes*," says John, "we'd still be playing wet t-shirt contests." (More on that later.)

The album's shadow has been long. Critics' approbation for *BVS* has spanned decades, from *Trouser Press*'s Ira Robbins gushing in 1977 that Shoes "obliterated the competition on every level," to Noel Murray's 2009 declaration in the *Onion A.V. Club* that coming upon *Black Vinyl Shoes*—amid what he evidently considers the artistic wasteland of power pop—is "like finding a love letter in the county dump, then discovering it was written by Wordsworth." Thesauri have been wrung dry trying to identify the singular quality of the guitars, the voices, the songwriting, the production—it didn't sound quite like anything else around at the time. Robert Christgau, writing in the *Village Voice*, facetiously asserted in his glowing 1977 review that *Black Vinyl Shoes* was "produced by elves."

But one person's magic is another person's sweat, and *Black Vinyl Shoes* hadn't magically appeared overnight on these shoemakers' tables. It was the result of months of tinkering and experimentation (and sweat). Shoes were genuinely trying to create a professional-sounding product, striving to wrest fidelity and clarity from their bare-bones setup.

More than anything else, *Black Vinyl Shoes* is a chronicle of yearning. For love, partly, but not just love: the music itself reaches, reaches for something the band can almost grasp. It's rough-hewn by default, not design. As Guided by Voices' Robert Pollard stated of his own lo-fi work, in Marc Woodworth's 2006 book *Guided By Voices' Bee Thousand*, "[T]o me, it just means that you didn't have enough money so you had to record songs yourself in your own house." Woodworth notes, however, that "those initially private recordings … are the purest examples not only of doing it yourself, … but of the more fundamental self-reliance that gives the music its force and authenticity." As with Guided by Voices' work, the ephemeral allure of *Black Vinyl Shoes* is partly a function of Shoes' raw desire to make music.

In recognition of their new record-making seriousness, facetious monikers like "La Cabane" and "The Oven" were jettisoned in favor of the more professional-sounding "Short Order Studios" (though Shoes continued to use the other sobriquets among themselves). Similarly, they organized themselves as a business, Black Vinyl Records, to release the album, and instituted the numbering system they'd use from that point on: *Black Vinyl Shoes* is listed as S-51477, which means simply that it's a Shoes record, and that it was mastered on May 14, 1977.

Mistakenly believing they could copyright their songs by getting them transcribed onto sheet music and mailing them to themselves, Shoes found a sheet-music-literate friend to transcribe the compositions, and then dutifully kept the sealed, postmarked envelopes.

John has stated that "from the beginning, we thought that we were playing with the big boys," and so *Black Vinyl Shoes* came elaborately packaged for a DIY project, complete with more sophisticated cover art than either *Heads or Tails* or *One in Versailles* had sported, plus a Shoes sticker (depicting a shoelace spiraled to resemble a phonograph record), t-shirt transfer featuring a band photo, and separate sheet of album credits and pictures. It was as professional as the band knew how to make it.

ONE ADDITIONAL POINT OF INSPIRATION sparked Shoes that year: the music that they loved, which had been shoved off the airwaves by the forces of country rock, heavy metal, and disco in the mid-seventies, seemed to be experiencing something of a rebirth. Before, bands like Grin and Big Star, whose fellow travelers Shoes aspired to be, had to be hunted down in obscure record stores; you'd almost never hear them on the radio.

But in 1976, that silence lifted a little. It would be an overstatement to say that pop had become popular again, but there were signs that it was not, in fact, defunct. One sign was the Dwight Twilley Band's improbable radio hit "I'm On Fire," which had reached number sixteen the year before as a single, but was re-released on Twilley's 1976 album *Sincerely*. Gary recalls:

> Against all odds, Twilley accomplished what eluded Big Star: a hit single. The experience of routinely hearing "I'm on Fire" inappropriately sandwiched between "Disco Lady" and "Get Up and Boogie" was both depressing and invigorating. By this time, our band had developed a clear musical focus, still chugging along on the inspirational fumes of our heroes from a seemingly long-gone era. Imagine the joy of every like-minded pop band of that time in being reassured that we weren't crazy and we weren't alone.

Another inspirational force, still limited largely to the upper Midwest, were local heroes Cheap Trick. Gary continues:

> To every Midwestern pop band of the late seventies, Cheap Trick was the gold standard. If you wanted to know how to do it, you'd go see Cheap Trick. There was a time when we could see them live

on just about any given night within an hour's drive. Keep in mind that at this point Cheap Trick and Shoes were exact opposites, in a sense. We were timid beginners puttering about in the seclusion of a home studio, still learning guitar chords and almost never having faced an audience. They were polished musicians with amazing stage presence and a huge live following even before their first recording; "intimidation" was not a strong enough word. Cheap Trick were everything everyone wanted to be.

Everyone including, of course, Shoes. But these lofty aspirations were tempered by their sense of their own limitations—no member of Shoes, for example, would ever suggest that he had a voice anywhere near as spectacular as that of Robin Zander, whom Jeff considers "probably the greatest rock singer of all time"—but Cheap Trick galvanized them nonetheless. "There's no question their effect is all over *Black Vinyl Shoes*," Gary asserts. "The way they used melodies over hard, distorted guitars was definitely influential—and not just for us, but for a lot of bands."

But Gary also points to the contrast between their trajectories: "Cheap Trick played and played and played and then made a record; we recorded and recorded and recorded and then did a few shows. We wanted that piece of plastic in our hands first." Still, isolated as they were, Shoes felt just a bit less alone knowing there were others out there with a kindred musical aesthetic.

SHOES BEGAN WORKING ON *BLACK Vinyl Shoes* almost as soon as Skip was on board. His journal confirms that they started on the songs as early as May 1976, laying down the demos that constituted their writing process, but didn't start recording final versions until November.

Every weeknight and most weekend days, they would race over to Jeff's and work, work, work. They'd usually begin by six-thirty or so, and would often keep plugging away until midnight or later. And since *Black Vinyl Shoes* was recorded one song at a time, the entire band could be focused on a single track for several long weeks. Recording sessions for each song were led by its particular composer, so no single bandleader solidified; that authority shifted every couple of weeks.

The only Shoe who did not keep this schedule was Skip, who would come in at the beginning of each song, lay down his drum tracks, and take off, returning when his bandmates were ready to cut the next one. (This would remain his working pattern throughout his tenure with Shoes.) Skip showed little interest, at this point, in singing or writing for Shoes, though he would later grouse about what he viewed as his secondary band role.

While he liked the songs, Skip found the meticulous nature of Shoes' recording process frustrating. He pushed hard, repeatedly, to get them to play out more—and to record as a band, all playing together. He dismissed the technological issues that the latter studio method would raise with a simple, "That's how orchestras do it." The problem, as far as he was concerned, was that piecemeal recording required that he know the music inside-out, but never gave Skip the payoff of hitting the skins straight through a song along with his bandmates. Instead, he says, "I had to play while I was humming the song in my head." John observes, not without affection, "Skip was a typical drummer. They think recording is boring; they want to get out and play live." John adds that he thinks Skip was a little surprised by the complexity of four-track recording, the detail Shoes' singer-guitarists were putting into each song. Skip's own work was usually done quickly, according to John. "Drums were a one-take deal," says Shoes' bassist. "We could punch in anything else, but we needed a complete drum track." And Skip had more experience playing than the others, which was a distinct plus from a cohesiveness standpoint. "If you're going to have one musician in the band who's stronger than the others," John philosophizes, "make it the drummer."

And Shoes did adjust their recording style to make Skip happy, according to his journal. At first, Skip writes:

> When I would be needed to do a drum track for a new song, I would come in, whoever's song it was would show me briefly how the song would go, I would figure out a drum beat and we would do the song.

Later, they developed a more collaborative, band-based process:

> We finally modified that idea somewhat to where we would play it first all together and get a general idea of how things will be, then we record. It's much easier.

Jeff remembers Skip's graciousness when tasked to do outside-the-box rhythmic patterns, as he frequently was on *Black Vinyl Shoes*:

> It seems we were always asking Skip to play non-standard drum parts on these songs, with a lot of stops and starts and more staggered patterns than the typical 4/4-type beats that we later settled into.
>
> And we schooled him in our version of what we called 'Power Rock Drumming.' When Skip first started playing with us, he held the stick in his left hand in an underhand, marching-band style. We told him to grip both sticks overhand and *beat* them drums!

Outwardly, Skip was amenable to most directives. But his journal shows that he was sometimes disgruntled about his bandmates' insistence on certain techniques and sounds (despite his general awe at their singular focus). What was intended as creative direction from a songwriter's perspective could look like a power trip from Skip's.

But through the majority of the *Black Vinyl* sessions, Skip only occasionally chafed at his colleagues' vision of what Shoes could and should be.

About that first number Shoes recorded, "Capital Gain," Jeff recollects:

> The tempo started out slowly and then built up to a more manic pace as the song progressed. We were still experimenting with the best way to record drums because the equipment's limited fidelity mandated that the drums be recorded first, before there were any vocals or bass. It must have been a strange experience for Skip to go from drumming through cover versions of familiar hits at the local Holiday Inn, to playing drums for a song that wasn't even completely written when we started recording it. But he made his way through.

ASIDE FROM THE DRUMS, OTHER song elements were recorded under strict constraints, which required a tightly regulated process—one that Jeff managed with a flowchart in order to minimize signal degradation.

Jeff explains that Shoes generally started with the drums recorded in stereo on the first two of the four available channels, combined with a rhythm guitar or two, "panned hard to the left or right." Each channel would then be "bounced" to another (channel one going to three, and channel two to four, for example), adding instruments: extra percussion or another guitar or backing harmonies would be layered on during the bouncing process. Jeff, who'd read about pioneering guitar hero Les Paul doing something similar, improvised the process himself for *Black Vinyl Shoes*.

Where both channels had to "bounce" or "ping-pong" in order to remain in sync with each other, this necessity created extra opportunities to layer song elements, and Shoes took advantage of every bounce to do so. Gary notes that these added bits were usually played live to an existing part. "We would never have done that if we'd had twenty-four tracks," he adds. "We wouldn't have had to."

At this point, channels three and four already contained the equivalent of five or six instrumental lines, but Shoes weren't done yet. These two channels would be sent back to one and two again, Jeff explains, "as we added more instruments, voices, whatever. Typically, then, channels one and two would end up with a pre-mixed stereo instrumental song. We would then record bass on channel three and main vocals on channel four."

They'd learned through trial and error that bass and lead vocals tended to suffer the most from the effects of multiple bounces—growing muddy or indistinct after copying—so those were taped last. "The sequence in which instruments were recorded thus became very important," Jeff stresses.

Sometimes, if they didn't overlap, a lead guitar line could share the same track as the main vocal, though either one could be inserted earlier, if the vocals and guitar were likely to interfere with each other. Other percussion instruments—maracas, tambourines—could be stuck on the bass channel pretty regularly; Jeff explains that "if the level balance was off a bit, we could use EQ [equalization] to change the apparent level of the [low-end] bass-to-

[the high-end] percussion ratio, because they were on opposite ends of the frequency spectrum." But that was about all the tinkering that could be done once the commitment of instrument to channel was made.

In practice, then, Shoes were using four channels to get as many as twelve channels' worth of music.

One more complication in this process was the addition of "multing," or multi-tracking vocals. Jeff recounts, "We began doubling lead vocals early on; the Beatles were big into this," explaining that the process reveals "a natural tonal difference that creates a 'chorusing effect' between the two vocal lines or instruments or whatever, making them sound bigger, thicker and ultimately better than just one." Anything could be multed, of course—Jeff mentions that later on they liked to do it with guitars, particularly—and as the term multing indicates, it didn't necessarily stop at doubling. But for Shoes in 1976-77, operating under the strict constraints of four tracks, it was "usually only the lead vocal" getting that treatment, Jeff says, and usually only once.

Gary points out that multing vocals only required two channels, one for the pre-recorded vocal; then the vocalist would sing over himself as both tracks were recorded onto a second channel. "Most of the multing we did was on the fly," Gary says, "and of course there were mistakes. But if a singer messed up, they'd still have the original vocal track; that wouldn't be erased until they were sure the new version worked." All this bouncing meant that the process had to be pretty carefully planned. In particular, Jeff tried very hard to keep every instrument to a third-generation-or-less copy, to preserve fidelity: hence the flowchart.

ONE OF THE PRINCIPLES THAT guided the composition of a portion of *Black Vinyl Shoes* was the need to accrue more songs to fill out their live act. To that end, says John, "it was the first album we did that was really rock all the way through." While Shoes would never be the kind of band to play out two hundred nights a year, they did have a decent sense of what did and didn't work live for them, and they knew that the harder rockers connected most effectively. Skip kept steadier time when he played faster, and they were tighter as a unit.

BVS was also Shoes' first outing with seriously synthesized and distorted guitars; this gave them an opportunity to experiment with assorted effects and methods of playing. They'd already discovered that different amplifiers had different flavors, but amps were a big investment. Effects were a much more affordable method for changing the sound of a guitar. Gary and Jeff zestfully experimented with these new toys, taking the time they now had to search out the sound they wanted. Jeff details:

> We didn't have a great variety of amps to play through; we had various pedals, phase shifters, and gadgets that we would use for different degrees of distortion and effects. Gary would take great pains to get the right tone. He would often use the pedals in conjunction with a Roland Space Echo to create textures and effects.

The effects Gary was using are in evidence on songs like "Tragedy" and his solo on Jeff's "Do You Wanna Get Lucky?"

Jeff's solo in Gary's "Fatal," according to Jeff, is a combination of "synthesized" guitars, created by the little effect he'd invented from his childhood reel-to-reel recorder. "It had a unique flavor and I liked to play through it with a harmony line mixed in," says Jeff. "In those early Shoes songs, Gary's style was usually based around power chords, and my style was usually a riffy-picky style. John tended to be more of a strummer."

For Shoes, writing and recording were always parallel processes, so it wasn't until they decided to make the record that would become *Black Vinyl Shoes* that they really started composing seriously at all. As John notes, "We didn't just have a whole bunch of random songs sitting around ready to use. We thought of this [as-yet-untitled recording] as a new project like *One in Versailles*, or *Bazooka*. We said, okay, this is going to be for an album, so we just wrote things specifically *for* it."

And without the time constraints that had dogged them before, the writing members of Shoes worked independently of each other for the first time.

All the songs on *Black Vinyl Shoes* are indeed single-credited, though that indicator can be deceptive. Jeff has observed that "for some reason, John's songs seemed to be more open forums for musical collaboration; perhaps because Gary and I were more into the technical aspects of the recording and engineering, our songs tended to be more individual compositions. John's songs *required* group participation." John concurs, remarking that during the production of *Black Vinyl Shoes*, "We were more hands-off when the song came in—'This is Jeff's, this is Gary's, this is mine'—although Jeff and Gary were usually a little more hands-on when I brought something in." John thinks that, as the bass player, "my songs were always less complete. I relied more on the other two."

For example, John details, "Gary had to *drag* 'Fire for a While' out of me; I wasn't confident about anything I had." So Gary took his twelve-string Rickenbacker, and he picked at it until the song began to take shape for John. Jeff then came in and, the younger Murphy relates, "I tuned my guitar to an open chord and used a small, rusty screwdriver to bow the strings, and faded the volume up and down to make it swell. I remember laboring over the solo section, as I kept over-thinking it. So instead of an extended formal solo, John and Gary convinced me to strip things back. It ended up consisting of a few slight riffs and harmonics alternating with the slide guitar"—an unusual, almost country element. Yet the song is single-credited as John's composition, partly because he'd penned all the words.

For John and Gary particularly, writing lyrics was and is the knottiest part of composing. "It's hard to come up with something you don't feel stupid saying," John admits. Gary hates lyricizing even more: in Shoes' earliest days, Gary even proposed to John that John should take over all lyrics while he handled the music (an offer the bassist of course turned down).

Unlike the messy creative process of *Bazooka*, with *Black Vinyl Shoes* each song increasingly became the property of a single band member, and the lyric-writing process became "a little more private," John notes. Shoes' songwriters rarely, if ever, question each other about the origins of their lyrics. "If that's what he wants to say, that's what he wants to say," Gary shrugs. "It's his song." John agrees: "Even now, when somebody brings in a new song, we don't discuss the lyrics. That's like opening up your diary." This respect for each other's privacy became Shoes' unspoken rule thereafter, although John recalls a few raised-eyebrow moments when he first presented some of his bawdier outings to his bandmates (such as "Feel the Way That I Do" from 1990's *Stolen Wishes*, in which he praises his partner's bedroom style—"the way you look before you come").

But as each of the fifteen songs on *Black Vinyl Shoes* became more of a personal possession, the process gave birth to another distinctive quality of Shoes' self-produced records: a purely democratic song-selection process. *Black Vinyl Shoes*, *Boomerang*, the original vinyl release of *Silhouette*, *Stolen Wishes*, and *Propeller* all have track numbers divisible by three, with each writer equally represented. Where *Black Vinyl Shoes* was concerned, Jeff points out that this was "the first time we made the conscious effort to maintain an equal representation for each songwriter. We intentionally staggered the songs [in *BVS*'s running order] so that no one writer had two songs in a row."

THE GOAL, ALWAYS, WAS AN ALBUM with no filler. "I don't think we ever said it like this," says John, "but back then, if you bought a record and there were three or four good songs out of twelve or so, that was a good record. So the idea was, if each guy is bringing his three or four best songs, we should have a pretty good record." And "good" was defined exclusively by Shoes' own aesthetic sense, not by what they thought would sell. They were all driven by the fascination of what they could create, trying to outdo each other, surprise each other, and inspire each other, and they usually succeeded in accomplishing all three.

In terms of lyrical content, each songwriting Shoe takes a different approach—now as in the beginning.

Jeff tends to place his songs on a continuum with the music he admires, directly referencing the pop tradition. Of his *Black Vinyl Shoes* tracks, for instance, he thinks of "Capital Gain" as a response to the Beatles' "Money." Similarly, his love-struck, chiming rocker "Writing a Postcard," was inspired by the Beatles' 1963 cover of the Marvelettes' 1961 chart-topper, "Please Mr. Postman." But both "Running Start" and "Do You Wanna Get Lucky?"

started out just as titles he liked: the latter was a coy sexual euphemism that amused him, picked up from a female coworker at the envelope factory.

Gary works more through pastiche, combining details from different relationships to create a sort of imaginary Everywoman: "People will ask of a particular song, 'Who was that girl?' and I say, 'It was really about five or six girls.'" In looking over his characteristically lovelorn contributions to *Black Vinyl Shoes*, Gary jokes, "I really come off as a loser in those, don't I?" But his characteristic moodiness—his focus on the downside of romance—is a conscious choice; Gary considers introspective words to be one way of giving pop music some gravitas. "The darkness factor in our lyrics," he says, "is very important for us; the darkness collides with the lightness of the melody. That's what adds some mystery, some complexity."

John is by far the most frankly autobiographical. His romance with Sara (still chugging on throughout the recording of *Black Vinyl Shoes*) formed the underpinnings of most of his early work with Shoes, which addresses the heights, depths, and in-between altitudes of relationships, from "Someone Finer," to "Cruel You" to "Karen." John seeks the ambivalence that, he argues, makes for an effective song: "Lyric writing is like letter writing. If you have something on your mind, it's going to come out." But like Gary, John tends to focus on the uncertainty of love. "If you're going through a relationship, it's the ambiguities of it that are interesting. 'I'm happy as a pig in poop' isn't going to do it for me."

He's also willing to let chance play a role in the composition process: "Okay," John offers as example, was based on an overheard conversation:

> One night at Jeff's, Skip got a phone call; his girlfriend had hunted him down. I think they were splitting up at the time and he was trying to cut the call short, and he kept repeating, "Okay ... okay ... I will ... okay ... yeah, right ... okay ... okay." I took it from there. And I liked using a tiny, ordinary word—barely a word—for the title.

John has often observed it's when a composer thinks he's penning a specifically personal lyric—one that almost writes itself, pouring straight out of his heart—that it tends to connect most directly to the audience at large.

However, he cautions, "The easy-to-write lyrics are sometimes clichéd. You have to take a little risk. And there's always the challenge of finding something that 'feels right in your mouth': you can really want to say some word or phrase, but sometimes it will trip up your tongue. You need to formulate a whole line to make it work." John keeps a notebook at all times to collect these words and expressions as they occur to him.

AS JOHN FOUND HIS VOICE LYRICALLY, he found it literally, too: the bass player's singing style underwent a major shift after *Bazooka*. In a 1979 *Trouser Press* feature, John confessed to writer Cary Baker, "I used to hate my voice, so between *Bazooka* and *Black Vinyl* I went for that part of the voice where it gets soft and raspy." He opines that most if not all singers are "putting on a little bit. You hear Mick Jagger *sing* and he's an old blues guy; you hear him *talk*, and he's an Englishman." John considers singing to be all about "figuring out how to present yourself in a way you're comfortable with." Playing live, he says, also helped him formulate his own voice.

Sometime fairly early in the *BVS* recording process, Gary's struggle between his inherent shyness and his rock-star fantasies reached a crisis point. "Fatal," the first song he'd brought to the table, had been recorded with John singing lead, just as he had done with Gary's tracks on *Bazooka*. But the desire to sing his own songs, which John had been urging all along, was growing. Though Gary had written from France, "I've got a lousy voice," he knew that he had to sing at least the harmonies on which so much of Shoes' sound depended. "Our next big step in the studio should be perfecting our voices," Gary wrote to John then.

He primarily meant his own; one reason for Gary's reluctance to vocalize was that he was convinced John and Jeff were better. Another, he admits with a laugh, was that one part of him "wanted to be a rock star," the way the other part "still wanted to bat cleanup for the Chicago Cubs—just to see if I could." "Artist" wasn't the role he'd played most of his life: "I was an athlete; I sort of felt that doing music was going against the grain of my destiny."

It was an unrelated decision of John's that tipped the balance for Gary.

That Christmas of 1976, Shoes' bassist had the chance to spend his holiday in Florida. He'd never been out of the Midwest, so he tagged along with a friend and the friend's sister, on a road trip slated to take a couple of weeks. "I felt guilty missing Christmas with the family, and leaving in the middle of recording," he recollects.

In his absence, Jeff and Gary had three choices: they could stop recording, they could attend to some of the million little details and fills left on the unfinished tracks, or Gary could start to sing again. They chose the last of these. It was over that holiday, then, that Jeff and Gary started on "She'll Disappear," with Gary at the microphone. Though still cripplingly self-conscious about singing, he says he didn't use any more vocal effects to mask his voice than his colleagues did. And once the heretofore mic-shy Shoe started to sing, he took over all his own as-yet-unrecorded songs. "I'm not sure," Gary says now, "why we didn't go back and re-record 'Fatal,' but we were pretty happy with it as it was." He did split lead vocal duties with Jeff on his haunting track, "Not Me," which he pronounces "a pretty unusual and interesting experiment."

Both John and Gary describe being intimidated by how effortless singing seemed for Jeff. It wasn't just that he was naturally more extroverted than either of them, but he had an unusual sonic quality that translated particularly well to the recording process. "The mic loves Jeff," John says "the way the camera loves some people."

For his part, Jeff is self-deprecating about his voice, seeing his strength more as harmony than lead vocals. Jeff thinks his solo voice "lacks individual strength and definition," though he acknowledges "an unusual trait: whenever I sing with someone else, my voice sounds like theirs. Over the years I developed a pretty good ability to match phrasing with whoever else I'm singing with."

IT WAS DURING THE *BLACK VINYL SHOES* period, in which each Shoe learned to sing on his own, that the three also began developing their trademark harmonies. With zero musical training, Shoes had no formal knowledge of harmonics or intervals; they just worked out a sound they liked, which drew inspiration not just from the Beatles, but also from hallowed vocal powerhouses like the Byrds and the Mamas and Papas.

"But honestly," says John, "we just kind of felt each other out. It was a pretty instinctive process."

"It's funny," Jeff remarks. "We'll practice guitars and things, work to get *that* stuff technically correct, but the harmonies just kind of *happen*."

Working on *Black Vinyl Shoes*, the three singers began forging a little arsenal of background-vocal techniques that could be deployed when needed: countermelodies and swells ("what we call 'the ooohs and the aaahs,'" John says) and little repeated words. (Jeff reveals that the backing vocal for the refrain of "In My Arms Again," from Shoes' 1979 major-label debut *Present Tense*, consists of the word "tit," repeated percussively. "We are men, after all," he shrugs.)

For his part, Jeff thinks that he and Gary have the more similar voices, and that John's is the most distinctive, "but the blend of all three works really well." During the days when Shoes' professional studio, Short Order Recorder, was operating as a commercial venture (1984-2004), the three could sometimes be prevailed upon to provide backing vocals for an outside client's track. In one case, Jeff recalls, they did harmonies on a song for a friend who was recording there: "I remember him saying, 'It's so weird! I'm standing around talking to John, Jeff, and Gary and then when you guys start singing together, Shoes appears in the room!'"

JOHN RETURNED FROM HIS FLORIDA trip just after New Year's, in time for Sunday, January 16, 1977, when Shoes played a show on what they all describe as the worst night of their lives, in the Chicago suburb of Oak Park, Illinois. The town is no more than fifty miles from Zion, but in the pitiless winter of 1976-77, fifty miles was an arduous journey.

A *Time* magazine cover story from January 31, 1977 reports that at that point, "Milwaukee ... has had a record twenty-one days of subzero weather," and that "only a few adventurous captains steered past the treacherous floes in Lake Michigan, where ice was a foot thick eight miles from shore." Transportation and industry slowed to a crawl as fuel supplies dwindled and restocks could not get to where they were needed, with tankers literally frozen in place. Some were crushed by the swelling ice; others, "weighing some 750 tons each, were shoved atop the sturdy ice like so many giant hockey pucks." It snowed in Florida, and wind chills of fifty below and worse were recorded across the country. People hunkered down in their homes, lowered their thermostats to conserve energy, and waited for the weather to break.

Even normally stoic Midwesterners were rattled. This was no time to play an out-of-town show, but Shoes didn't have much choice. The Oak Park gig was important: there would be a woman attending who was interested in managing them, and now, deep into recording, a manager seemed to be a crucial next step toward the much-desired record contract. So six of them, the band and their stalwart roadies Garry Holverson and Joe Higgins, climbed into three vehicles—John's 1966 Barracuda, Jeff's van, and an unheated step van for the gear (which Gary and Skip drove, bricked up in snowmobile suits)—and headed for Oak Park.

While Shoes didn't play badly, they consider the show an utter letdown. There were only four people in attendance, and the potential manager didn't show.

Shoes had signed on for a grueling five fifty-minute sets, however, and the club owner held them to every second. And the worst was yet to come. The wind chill, John remembers, had plummeted to around seventy below zero, and only one of the vehicles would start on its own; the others had to be jumped. And it was only after loading out that Shoes discovered, the step van, thanks to a broken wire, now had no heat *or* lights. Girding themselves, band and crew climbed in and headed for home.

It took hours to get back to Zion, crawling up the highway in a caravan, hoping against hope that they didn't get stopped by the police. Jeff's vehicle led, followed by Gary and Skip in the forlornly darkened step van (which drove sandwiched between the two cars that *did* have lights), and John's 'Cuda was last. They finally made Zion at eight in the morning, a Monday: Jeff was already late for work, and Gary just had time to change and head out. Skip called in sick (only a slight exaggeration). John, who had prudently scheduled the day off, stayed home and watched the news, full of the execution of multiple murderer Gary Gilmore. They would unload the truck later.

Misfortune wasn't quite done with them yet, though it could also have been karma—Skip had neglected to mention he'd stashed a purloined six-pack of beer in one of the stage monitors, and by the time they unpacked their gear, the cans had frozen and exploded, ruining the monitor along with some other equipment.

Shoes had contracted for $150, and when Skip went back to Oak Park the next day to collect their money, he stopped in the men's room and glimpsed a last-straw piece of graffiti they still laugh about: "Shoes suck. Waste of money."

But Shoes shook it all off. The record was paramount, and so they returned to Jeff's tiny, frostbitten house and continued to plug away, through the rest of the winter, at what would become *Black Vinyl Shoes*.

ONE OF THE CONSEQUENCES OF recording at Jeff's was that the constrained space made standard monitoring setups impossible. Shoes had purchased a performing public-address system, the bulk of it from the same free local paper where they'd gotten most of their instruments, but there was nowhere to set up a P.A. in La Cabane. The mixing board and tape machine already filled the kitchen, and the instruments took up the living room, spilling over into Jeff's bedroom. Nor was there room for monitors. Instead, Shoes used headphones to track what they were doing. "Pioneer SE-205 headphones, to be precise," says Jeff.

John recalls the band realizing that anyone outside the tiny garage during a Shoes session that summer would have heard only disconnected fragments of music, and how peculiar it must have seemed to passers-by:

> We recorded with headphones, we sang with headphones on, we listened back in the headphones. ... It probably sounded strange from the outside, hearing one thing over and over and over, or

voices singing to no music, because everything was on headphones.

Fittingly, the liner notes for a recent vinyl reissue of *Black Vinyl Shoes* on Spain's Wah Wah Records recommend "that you *listen to this album on headphones* to truly experience how it was put together." (Italics original.)

As SPRING FINALLY SPRANG ON that miserable winter, Shoes began to see that their as-yet-unnamed project would eventually be complete, and they would have to think of something to call it. John and Gary lay in their beds at night, shouting album titles across the hallway in their rented house. *Bazooka* had delighted them with its double meaning, and they wanted to find something similarly resonant. John remembers that a number of gear- or power-based titles were considered—*Four-Track Shoes, Flanger, Electrical, Incandescent*—but that all of those seemed either too obvious or too obscure. They also considered *Note by Note*, a direct reference to their painstaking recording style. *Crewcut*, which combined their sense of teamwork (they were the crew) with the songs on the record (the cuts), was entertained for a while, and John was thinking if they ended up with that he'd ask his boss, a former Marine who still sported his jarhead 'do even in the long-haired late seventies, to pose for the cover.

Shoes liked the idea of using the names of objects around them, as ordinary and unpretentious as their band moniker, and they kept lists, scribbling prospective titles into a little book. John would then lay them out in Chartpak letters; Gary in particular liked to evaluate how the words would look on an album cover, rather than simply how they sounded when voiced aloud.

Only the most promising of these experiments made it back to Jeff and Skip, who were comparatively less involved in the naming process. When *Black Vinyl Shoes* came up—a reference to the material of the actual disc, it also played on the title of rock & roll classic "Blue Suede Shoes"—Skip recalls that it was he who said, "That's it. That's the one." Still, the search process continued, but the four did keep returning to that title, and eventually settled on it.

By the time *Black Vinyl Shoes* was in its final stages, Shoes were deservedly pleased with how far they had come. As Jeff explains, "The last song we recorded for the disc was John's 'Boys Don't Lie.' With each track we had gotten a little better at arranging and pre-mixing the instruments during the recording process, and by this time we were pretty good at it. The song seemed notably punchier than tracks recorded earlier on, and we decided to use it as the album opener." Overall fidelity, in fact, had become markedly clearer at the end—resulting, says Jeff, in "less tape hiss and a less muddy-sounding mix. We'd learned our monitoring better over time, along with how to prejudge the volumes when we premixed things together." Not only were Shoes' recording skills improving, the process was getting easier, too.

THE MONTHS OF INTENSIVE WORK, however, were starting to tell on everybody. Late in the *Black Vinyl Shoes* sessions, with John still a song or two short, the senior citizens from whom John and Gary were renting came back to Zion for the summer. John recollects that "Gary and I were talking about getting a place, but to be honest, there were some pressures from trying to finish this project, and there was some tension. Things weren't going well. And part of it might have been, again, that I didn't have all my songs done, and Jeff and Gary were kind of impatiently tapping their feet, going, 'C'mon, let's go.' I remember thinking I *might* just want to get my own place."

But that didn't happen right away. Once the homeowners returned, Gary reclaimed his basement bedroom in his parents' house for the summer. "I didn't have that option," says John, "so I stayed a couple of months at Jeff's, sleeping on a cot between the amps and the drum kit in his living room. Of course we had it folded up when we were rehearsing; then I'd pull it out again. It was really cheesy, but we knew it was a temporary thing." Eventually, John did get his own apartment.

BY MID-MAY, EVERYONE INCLUDING JOHN WAS DONE recording their songs, and Shoes began creating a final stereo mix from the four tracks. Jeff describes the process:

> About all we could really control at that point was the balance between the stereo instruments compared to the vocal and bass volume. A bit of equalization between the high and low ends overall made things sound consistent from track to track. Recording over a long period of time is bound to result in some songs sounding brighter and some songs sounding bassier; mastering helps even out the inconsistencies in volume and EQ.

Shoes borrowed a two-channel tape machine for this step. The process of mixing four channels down to two was complicated, mostly because of their lack of experience. Jeff explains:

> Not yet having learned the art of tape editing, we would carefully park the tape at the precise spot that we wanted the next song to start, and then start both tape machines together to record the mix of the next song. Oftentimes, there would be a click or pop on the final mix, due to the refrigerator turning on or the tape machine leaving a thump from starting to record. This would force us to rewind the two machines and re-record the song until there were no electronic hiccups. It was very tedious and time-consuming.

But the process did give Shoes a chance to hear their now fully-mixed record the way regular listeners would. They opened up the windows, cranked up the volume—and went outside, to monitor their creation in the balmy weather. "It was the first time we'd heard it through speakers," Jeff recalls. "The sun was shining and we were out of the kitchen at last." They fiddled with spacing between the songs, but as they listened to the record, they started to get excited about it. "We'd changed our lives for this, and here was the result," Gary muses. "It was significant, legitimate. We needed something to tell ourselves that all the bridges we had burned were worth it, and here it was, and we were really happy with it."

ALL EYES NOW TURNED TO JOHN, the visual artist, for the album graphics. He'd been procrastinating, but time was up. So John spent some time thinking about what look he wanted for the cover, settling upon a favorite doodling style from college in which the elements of the letters were treated as geometric shapes, each being shaded individually. He hand-drew the original design in sepia-tone, "sort of watercolor-y," John says, but it was reproduced in black and white, for financial reasons—brown counted as a color for printing purposes, black didn't—and also to stick with the "black" theme. John ended up so pressed for time that he took a sick day from work to complete the design. "It was all pen and brush, so there was no going back if you made a mistake," he stresses. "I had to be pretty careful."

The insert was even more complicated. They'd only been able to turn up one picture of all four Shoes where someone wasn't making a weird face, or just didn't like how he looked; they'd designated that one for a band t-shirt. In desperation, they gathered one evening at a friend's apartment, where John's and Jeff's respective girlfriends, Sara and Debi, shot photo after photo of the band: separately, together, posed, candid. Garry Holverson had made a Black Vinyl Shoes t-shirt, and they took a picture of his then-wife pointing at it. But there were scant performance shots, and even fewer of production. "We didn't have a lot to choose from," John acknowledges, "but we were trying to create the illusion that we were a real band, with fans and stuff." John carefully tore up the photo session's resultant prints—the originals, he notes, in their original sizes. "There was no room for error," he says. He then built a photo collage—inspired by Todd Rundgren's *Something/Anything*—sticking the pictures down with rubber cement. The collage formed one side of the *BVS* insert; credits comprised the other.

Then there were the sticker and t-shirt transfer to round out the package. The sticker was no problem: in those days, graphics businesses had rolls and rolls of border in tape form. The sticker was a square of adhesive border adorned with the aforementioned spiraled-shoelace-cum-phonograph-record. The t-shirt transfer was based on the one rare band picture they could all agree on. Both were easy enough to design, and simple to produce: "We used some Insty-Print shop for those," John recalls.

While John was monkeying with the album graphics, the record's post-production process was in full swing. At the end of it, Shoes found a plant in Chicago that would press their masters onto disc, and they had to race to get all the materials—stickers, t-shirt transfers, inserts, and covers—to the plant on time for everything to be assembled properly. When they received the first boxes back from the plant in early summer, they were awed. Here it was, the "piece of plastic" they'd worked so hard for. "This was our proof that we were a real band," as John puts it. "We were really proud that we'd pulled it off. It was a fat package; you could feel there was stuff inside." Still struggling for legitimacy, even in their own minds, John says that *"Black Vinyl Shoes* gave us an edge. It proved we were serious, that Shoes was not just an extracurricular activity."

THAT SUMMER, THE BAND continued to gather regularly at Jeff's, sometimes rehearsing for and then playing the occasional show, but most often just checking on the progress of *Black Vinyl Shoes* as each finished product exited the garage, addressed and adorned with postage. There were always questions to answer. Who had they sent it to? Had there been a response? Who should get it next? Jeff describes the band members as perpetually "living on pins and needles that summer."

Never having launched a record before, Shoes did the best they could to get *Black Vinyl Shoes* into sympathetic hands. Scouring local publications, they'd jotted down a list of critics who seemed partial to their kind of music. If a writer reviewed an album they liked, that person made the list. If a radio station played music they liked, that station made the list.

As Jeff tells it, Shoes "began sending promo copies of *Black Vinyl Shoes* to anyone that we thought might be interested in hearing it. We gave away over three hundred copies to press and radio folks—but it was well worth it." Jeff would come home from work every day and hand-write cover letters to the targeted critics and radio stations, explaining who Shoes were and what they were doing—then package them with the records and proceed to send them out into the ether. And Shoes would wait. They weren't even really sure what exactly they were waiting for.

One recipient was Bill Paige, a young writer at the *Illinois Entertainer*, a free monthly newsprint magazine widely read in the Chicago-area music community. Paige, who regularly tracked the city's new-music scene, wrote the first review of *Black Vinyl Shoes*. In it, he took note of the professionalism of Shoes' package and the "British feel" of Shoes' music, observing that "each writer has a particular style that carries with it a score of not easily identifiable influences. This combination makes for a fresh rock sound with some imaginative arrangements, and gives Shoes a reasonable chance at establishing a new pop criteria [sic]."

But Paige hastened to assure his readers that, though he liked the album, Shoes were not "destined to be the Next Big Thing," and observed that "John and Jeff are clearly the better writers … while Gary sticks to a basic, conservative format that makes it hard for him to shine." Gary was devastated, convinced that he had been revealed as the impostor he'd feared he was since the day he heard *One in Versailles*. "It was the first review," Gary says, "and I got panned." Years later, when Paige was visiting a recording session for Shoes' 1982 Elektra release *Boomerang*, he remarked that he'd always liked Gary's writing. Gary shot back, "No, you didn't"—still stinging from that bygone review.

Another *Illinois Entertainer* contributor, the aforementioned Cary Baker, was a journalism major at Northern Illinois University in DeKalb when *Black Vinyl Shoes* showed up in his mailbox, complete with one of Jeff's handwritten missives. He was intrigued enough to put it on the turntable.

In the accompanying letter dated August 16, 1977, Baker read:

Mr. Baker,

My name is Jeff Murphy. I'm with a band called Shoes and we, through our own resources, released an album. Here is a copy. Let me explain a little bit about how it was done. We did most of the work involved: writing, performing, recording, album design, mixing and graphics. The recording was done on a four-channel machine, so it obviously won't sound like a major production out of New York or LA, but we're hoping people can overlook this and concentrate on the songs. In other words, this is what we can do under trying circumstances. Also, I would like to point out that we've had very little live experience since we've decided to attack from the recording standpoint first. I know that seems a bit unorthodox, but we think we stand a better chance this way. Please give a listen and if it sounds interesting, call or drop a line.

Thanks,

Jeff Murphy,

Shoes,

Zion, Illinois

Chapter 4

Fire for Awhile (1977-79)

IN AN APARTMENT IN DEKALB, Illinois, Cary Baker put *Black Vinyl Shoes* on the turntable, openly skeptical. "All I knew about Zion, a small exurb on Illinois' northeastern border, was that the streets had religious names and the no-nukes perennially protested the ComEd reactor which lay amid the sand dunes of Illinois State Beach," he would recollect in *Trouser Press* two years later. Baker now admits he had a Chicagoan's attitude toward these small-town rockers—"I couldn't believe this band from Zion, a little town full of churches, could make a record like this"—but "the moment I heard 'Boys Don't Lie,' I was *finished*." Baker's *Trouser Press* piece then details the question he promptly asked himself: "Could the Great American Pop Album of the 1970s really have fallen into *my* hands ahead of almost anyone else's?" In a recent interview, Baker enthused:

> The whole album had this sound I'd never heard before. How could they be so new at their instruments and get *this* sound? It wasn't even power pop; it was a sound of its own. The sound they had for those guitars ... wow! I heard this, and I thought,

"Somebody gets it!" And those harmonies! It could only have been a couple of brothers and a close friend who all grew up together.

Baker was a convert.

He was also no ordinary rock & roll fan; he'd been writing about music since adolescence, even founding a blues fanzine called *Blue Flame*. By college Baker was a working rock journalist, writing for nationally circulated magazines *Creem* and *Bomp!*, as well as local and regional publications including the *Illinois Entertainer*, the *Prairie Sun*, and the *Chicago Reader*.

He had also launched his own independent rock label, Fiction Records, which he ran out of his DeKalb apartment. "I'm not completely sure why I didn't rush Shoes' record out right away," Baker muses. "I think I saw them with the potential to go farther than my label could take an artist." Instead, he says, "I spread the gospel."

Spreading the gospel, for Baker, meant sharing *Black Vinyl Shoes* with "everyone I knew." And he wasted no time in taking up the cover letter's invitation to contact Jeff Murphy. "Jeff was my first conduit into the band," Baker says, "though I got to know all of them, eventually." Once he had befriended Shoes, he recommended to Jeff a number of like-minded journalists who, he thought, would be receptive to *Black Vinyl Shoes*.

One of the people Baker told the band to contact was Don McLeese, the pop music critic for the alternative weekly paper *Chicago Reader*. McLeese recalls receiving a long, handwritten letter from John, whose penmanship, he says "was like calligraphy—almost unreadable." At John's invitation, the critic came up to Zion to meet Shoes, and to attend a show at the Night Gallery in Waukegan, where they were a last-minute replacement act. The result was a long piece in the *Reader* about Shoes, their first major profile.

McLeese says now that the feature was an unusual piece for several reasons. "It was something of an anomaly for the *Reader* to run stories about any band from outside the city limits," McLeese observes. And while the writer had been given a larger-than-customary number of column inches to fill, the *Reader* wasn't fully behind Shoes: though the assignment was a cover-story-length piece, Shoes were not, in fact, getting the cover. Indeed, as McLeese confirms, Shoes were the proverbial prophets without honor in their own country, not to mention city: "They were much better known by record collectors—and even overseas—than they were at home."

In the piece, McLeese draws both parallels and distinctions between Shoes and Chicago's then-current punk scene:

> Make no mistake about it, despite all the technical difficulties, *Black Vinyl Shoes* is a homegrown tour de force. Although the New Wave has made homemade recordings a commonplace, most of the records do little to mask their garage origins. ... While others emulated the trash-can ambience of [Television's raw first single] "Little Johnny Jewel" under the banner of "minimalism," Shoes set their sights on Queen or Fleetwood Mac standards of quality. [And in fact, Shoes would go on to work with the producers associated with both of these bands, respectively—and in that order—Mike Stone and Richard Dashut.]

McLeese sent a clipping of his article to the East Coast alternative paper *New York Rocker* to see if they'd want to pick it up as a reprint; an editor there responded with a terse note saying they weren't interested in bands who wanted to be Queen or Fleetwood Mac, missing the point (about high-quality production, not musical style) entirely.

Other names Baker passed along to the band included a pair of tastemaking fanzine moguls: Ira Robbins (editor and publisher of *Trouser Press*) and the now-deceased Greg Shaw (editor and publisher of *Who Put the Bomp!* magazine). As *Trouser Press* was published out of New York and *Bomp!* from southern California, Shoes suddenly had an editorial presence on each coast; Robbins reviewed the record himself for his magazine, while Baker did the writeup for *Bomp!*

It's hard to overstate how important these connections were for Shoes.

Prior to this juncture, they had been working in all-but-complete isolation, aware of only a few sympathetic bands and a handful of regional music journals; as far as they knew, there was no real underground scene at all. Their live shows at this time were amateurish and rarely memorable for

Shoes' performances themselves: one featured the aforementioned wet t-shirt contest between sets (Skip proudly informed his journal that he took the winner home); at another, a political fundraiser, the entire audience moved to the bar in another room when Shoes began to play, leaving them entertaining an echoing hall. Yet another, celebrating the opening of a local watering hole, was shut down by the police when it turned out the establishment hadn't bothered to get a cabaret license—rendering Shoes' performance illegal.

And so Shoes languished in this small-town milieu, continually striving for something better.

As Jeff puts it, "We'd really been operating in a vacuum. Zion had (and still has) no clubs or bars to play at, and Chicago and Milwaukee seemed a world away." Geographically cut off in this remote Bible-thumping hamlet, Shoes' sole feedback on their music had been from each other. "We were receiving nothing from the outside that told us we were worth a damn," Gary says flatly—before adding, "But the early press reviews of *Black Vinyl Shoes* were stunning." The awed reactions of bona-fide music cognoscenti changed everything for them.

Except in Zion.

This conflict between cosmopolitan respect and provincial indifference would hound Shoes throughout their career. "We never drew any attention in Zion," Gary says. "We weren't celebrities there." And so Shoes were caught in the frustrating position of having released a highly regarded critical gem, but with nothing to show for it on a day-to-day basis.

As they became aware of the larger musical movement that would be called power pop (and then modern rock and indie, and eventually, alternative rock), Shoes learned that they already played a part in it. It wasn't just the Dwight Twilley Band on the radio and Cheap Trick in the clubs—there was an entire underground pop scene, having sprung out of, but now distinct from, the punk movement of the seventies.

Bomp!'s Greg Shaw was committed to resuscitating for these bands the term "power pop": a mid-sixties Pete Townshend coinage. But Shoes didn't utilize that descriptive themselves—at least not at the time of *Black Vinyl Shoes*. "I still find myself somewhat reluctant to use the phrase in reference to artists of the seventies," Gary says, "only because at the time, none of us were unaware of belonging to any 'power-pop movement.'"

Still, as Shoes continued sending out *Black Vinyl Shoes* to critics and editors, the movement recognized *them* as long-lost brothers, gathering them up in a warm welcome-home embrace.

OUT IN CALIFORNIA, GREG SHAW had begun scouting the rock & roll standard-bearers of the day, offering them valuable press coverage and, for a lucky few, the chance to make a record. He first located rock's raw, rebellious essence in punk, but as punk gave way to monochromatic hardcore, he increasingly saw the future of music in a fusion of punk energy and three-chord melodicism: power pop.

In a March 1978 editorial in *Bomp!*, Shaw argued:

> Punk rock as we know it today … was a form of shock treatment, a necessary therapeutic stage between the lobotomized atrophy of the early '70s and the kind of healthy organism pop will hopefully be by the early '80s. …. The qualities we loved it for—loudness, deliberate stupidity, calculated offensiveness, violent rejection of everything passé and boring—helped it make the dramatic break with early '70s rock culture that was so necessary, brought the media coverage that spread the rhetoric that recruited more and more kids to the movement, all that and more.

Punk, Shaw argued, was a form of pure, if limited, rock. He proposed that punk rock was at one end of a pendulum swing, and pop at its opposing position, personifying those points with the bad boys of the Detroit proto-punk scene, the MC5, as the former extreme and the Britpop-turned-disco Bee Gees as the latter:

> My feeling has always been that the best music comes toward the center of the pendulum's swing, when rock contains strong elements of pop; and pop of rock.

Thus, Shaw argued, that center position was represented by the Beatles, the Raspberries, Badfinger, Dwight Twilley: power pop.

Shaw took the reins into his own hands, funding occasional releases from the new artists he considered to be mining this vein, including the Flamin' Groovies, 20/20, and many other, more obscure, acts. Shaw gave these bands a chance to make records for his independent Bomp! label, though no one (including Shaw) ever made any money at it.

Shaw saw in Shoes, unschooled geniuses from nowhere—or nowhere that mattered from a coastal perspective—the pure embodiment of his deeply-held belief: rock & roll was alive and vibrant, even vital, outside the corporate boardrooms that, by the mid-seventies, controlled much of its distribution and determined much of what got airplay.

Bomp!'s founder had formulated this theory years earlier, first with partner David Harris in their mimeographed music-and-culture fanzine *Mojo Navigator*, a sort of history-as-it-happened chronicle of the rise of San Francisco's Haight-Ashbury-centered hippie movement (1966-67). But *Mojo Navigator* was more than that; one early reader described it as containing "gnostic apocrypha from a forgotten bible without a name." The fan continued:

> Behind every page there seemed to be a theory, an incantation disguised as a question: this music is a secret. It is born in secret and makes itself public as a secret a few initiates can tell—and once they have told enough people that the music is no longer a secret, will it still be music at all? There wasn't the hint of an answer, just the affirmation of the irreducible thrill of hearing the secret before everybody else did, and the irresistible thrill of passing it on.

That reader was future venerated rock scribe Greil Marcus (*Mystery Train, Lipstick Traces, Dead Elvis*), who would do some of his earliest writing for Shaw at *Bomp!*

Mojo Navigator existed for less than two years; Shaw and Harris dropped the project when the mainstream press, personified by *Rolling Stone*'s founder and publisher Jann Wenner, moved into San Francisco. Once *everybody* knew about the Haight, Shaw lost interest.

A few years later, Shaw, an inveterate fan of both the popular and lesser-known purveyors of British Invasion sounds, put his fascination to work in *Who Put the Bomp?*—its title nicked from Barry Mann's 1961 hit single, and eventually shortened to *Bomp!*. Here, Shaw chronicled rock history in a critical way—still as apocrypha for the initiated, but also as the continuing development of various rock subgenres (surf, psychedelia), taking both the art form and the history quite seriously.

As Shaw related in his retrospective of the magazine—written as liner notes for the 1995 *Destination: Bomp!* compilation—"For its first five years, *Bomp!* was about this kind of revisionist rock history, and a clubhouse for those who dreamed of breathing some of the fire of the '60s back into rock's wimped-out veins." He also gave space to a new generation of serious rock writers: Marcus, Dave Marsh, Lester Bangs, and Ken Tucker all wrote for *Bomp!* at some point.

But *Bomp!*'s real strength was its ability to be backward- and forward-looking at the same time.

WHEN JEFF, AT CARY BAKER'S encouragement, contacted Greg Shaw, Shaw was immediately enchanted by Shoes. They had taken in all the influences that Shaw thought were important—absorbing the lessons of the British Invasion and the Byrds—and processed them through their own lens, creating a style whose "purity" Shaw would later praise. And Shoes had done it alone, without any self-conscious response to a scene or a critical community; they hadn't even known either entity existed.

As Baker marveled in his *Bomp!* review of *Black Vinyl Shoes*, "Shoes had never heard of BOMP magazine, the Sneakers or [Chicago's definitive punk nightclub] *La Mère Vipère*. Fueled by their own intuition that it was 'all coming back,' they simply recorded the great Midwestern pop album in their spare time at home." Shaw concurred, and he was energized.

The West Coast pop connoisseur acted quickly, immediately contacting the band and offering all kinds of advice and support to help push them to the next level professionally. One of Shaw's first suggestions was that they set up a Shoes fan club, which would need its own post-office box to serve as return address. Pursuant to this first order of business, Shoes had postcards printed up to hand out at shows. The front sported a rare photo of the band members laughing hysterically, with the caption, "I will do absolutely anything to be in the 'Shoes Fan Club!'" and a space for the applicant's mailing information. The first issue of ShoeNews (later changed to the precisely-rhyming ShoesNews) soon followed.

THE INDIE-RECORD MOGUL ALSO proposed releasing a newly-recorded Shoes single on his Bomp! label. One song could be drawn from *Black Vinyl Shoes*, Shaw said, but he wanted a new Shoes tune for the flipside. John tells of long band meetings spent parsing every song on the album, weighing the pros and cons of each until they eventually chose John's upbeat "Okay" to be re-recorded in a professional studio.

With "Okay" in the hopper as side A, the single's B-side needed to be something co-written by the other two guys in order to preserve Shoes' democratic songwriting structure.

But since "Okay" was John's song alone, this presented something of a problem. Jeff had written with John, and Gary had written with John, but Jeff and Gary had never written together, and their working styles were very different—each more intense, in his own way, than the relatively easygoing bassist. Jeff wrote rapidly, usually happy with what his inspiration provided him; Gary insisted on trying out every possible option before deciding where his songs would go. But they were determined to proceed with the collaboration; it wouldn't be the last time Shoes struggled to see their way through a self-imposed problem.

Jeff had been working on a riff that he called "Wonderwax," which he played for Gary at La Cabane. Gary listened and then created a complementary riff, composed of power chords, to layer over the top.

This account makes the process sound easier than it was, however. John stopped by while they were writing one Saturday, and found that things didn't seem to be going well at all. Gary and Jeff were taciturn, clearly not happy; says John, "They were moping." Gary shrugs off this characterization as just part of the writing process: "Tension is inevitable when two people come up with different ideas concurrently." Still, doggedly determined to hammer the song out, "Gary and I hashed out the rest of the chords and stuff," says Jeff.

The new fan-club postcards had arrived, but these full sheets had not yet been cut into separate cards. Appropriating one page of them, Jeff scribbled rudimentary lyrics to hang on the "Wonderwax" framework: future Shoes classic "Tomorrow Night." Gary confirms that "Jeff did the lion's share of the work on the singing melody and lyrics; I might have had a couple of words in there." Glad to offload that particular responsibility, Gary concentrated mainly on the musical structure.

Though they weren't completely comfortable, Gary and Jeff's partnership worked. "In the end, we always find a compromise and arrive at a workable solution, despite a few bruises along the way," Gary muses. When they played "Tomorrow Night" for John, he immediately responded, "Really cool B-side!"—a comment he now cringes at, realizing how backhanded it sounds. But he didn't mean it negatively, and after all, *something* had to be the flipside of "Okay."

As it turned out, Bomp! designated "Tomorrow Night" side A and "Okay" side B, though it's not clear who made that decision (nor on what basis). "Tomorrow Night" went on, of course, to become one of Shoes' two or three most recognizable songs. But Jeff and Gary would not collaborate again, at least not without John in the mix.

As Shoes' deal with Shaw developed, they began to see that there were additional legal decisions to make, such as who would be administering publishing rights—that is, tracking radio play and other uses ("performances") of Shoes' songs, collecting royalties from permissions services BMI and ASCAP, and paying the band a small fee per performance. Shaw offered the band two options: either they could arrange a standard publishing-rights deal with Bomp!, in which the label handled publishing in exchange for half the collected fees; or they could try a relatively new publishing company, Bug Music, which was run by a friend of Shaw's named Dan Bourgoise.

Bug did not make or sell records; they focused solely on publishing administration, and thus could afford to take a much smaller cut of the performance royalties than a label could, leaving more for the artists. That sounded good to Shoes, and so they hired Tom Leavens, a Chicago-based entertainment lawyer who had been recommended by Bill Paige, to negotiate the deal with Bug. During this same period, Shoes met and befriended Bug's chief.

Dan Bourgoise was a record-industry veteran originally from the Midwest, who had worked with Shaw and his wife Suzy at United Artists Records in Los Angeles, where Shaw published an in-house music magazine. In 1975 Bourgoise, who had been early-sixties hitmaker Del Shannon's road manager, agreed to recover publishing rights for the veteran rocker, who'd hit #1 in 1961 with "Runaway." ("If you can do it, I'll split it with you, fifty-fifty," Shannon had proposed.) Bourgoise was successful, eventually becoming Shannon's manager before founding Bug Music that same year.

Bourgoise also represented most of the Bomp! catalog through Bug. So when Shaw sent him a copy of *BVS*, Bourgoise put it on his turntable. "I heard *Black Vinyl Shoes* and just went crazy," Bourgoise recounts. "Where did this come from? I had to keep playing it, thinking, 'This just doesn't exist! This music, this sound!'" Shoes' new publisher became another unofficial advisor for the band.

THE SECOND WEEKEND OF NOVEMBER, Shoes headed for the Chicago suburb of Schaumburg to record the Bomp! single, in a 24-track recording studio called Hedden West. They laid down Jeff and Gary's new song, "Tomorrow Night," along with a noticeably punchier version of "Okay," trading out some of the acoustic guitars for a more intricately instrumental electric version.

Shoes were ready for the session, if a bit apprehensive; after all, this wouldn't be like messing up in front of each other, nor was it like a live show, where a mistake could be passed by and forgotten. But they had rehearsed and rehearsed and rehearsed, and were as prepared as they could possibly be. They were sure the staffers at Hedden West knew what they were doing, and Shoes were dead-set on being first-take perfect for this session.

But as it turned out, nearly everyone involved was as green as they were in 24-track recording.

Aside from Shoes, five people were present at the sessions. Journalists Bill Paige and Cary Baker had come aboard as observers and advisors. Hedden West's studio manager Michael Freeman, a British transplant—who would go on to be a 2011 Grammy winner—stopped in briefly; the session was primarily handled by one of his junior studio engineers.

Also in attendance was local scenester Steve Meyers, who had presented himself to the band as a potential manager, though they hadn't hired him yet. Nevertheless, Meyers had attended a few of Shoes' infrequent shows and offered them advice. "He saw something in us, I guess," Gary says. "We listened to him, and he started acting as kind of an unofficial manager." At the time, Meyers was in the process of forming a booking agency with Jim Girling, Cheap Trick's live sound engineer and the fifth person on hand at Hedden West for the Bomp! session.

The band members were confident they couldn't do better than having an engineer as accomplished as Girling, whose work had awed them for years; per Meyers' advice, they'd hired him to engineer the Bomp! single. At that point, Girling had run sound for Cheap Trick for about three years, he says: "I'm from Rockford [Cheap Trick's hometown], and I went to school with Jim Peterson, [the band's bassist] Tom Petersson's brother. He was a roadie for his brother's band, and I got roped in through him." But Girling was just leaving that job, and looking to expand his horizons. And like Shoes, he was a neophyte at professional recording.

When Shoes arrived in Studio B and started setting up, the problems became obvious pretty quickly. Shoes had assumed that in a professional studio, they could refine their sound to perfection, and were frustrated to discover that that wasn't necessarily the case. "We knew exactly what we wanted," Gary relates. "We were rehearsed and all raring to go. But the engineering was slowing it down." No matter how Girling tweaked the dials, they simply couldn't get the drum sound they wanted.

The main issue seems to have been Skip Meyer's drum kit. "I'd seen them live; I knew Skip could play," Girling says. "And he had a fine kit for live playing. But it was a bad studio kit." The sound Shoes heard in their heads, which they assumed would be easy to capture in a real studio, simply didn't happen. "The band wanted Fleetwood Mac-type drum production," Girling details, referencing the painstaking, costly collaboration of drummer Mick Fleetwood and future Shoes producer Richard Dashut, something far beyond the scope of a local 24-track studio doing a weekend session with an amateur band. "We had a terrible time with it," Girling remembers.

Girling was a gifted sound technician and he had been in the studio with Cheap Trick when they cut their first two widely-acclaimed albums. But he hadn't been behind the board engineering those sessions; he wasn't even familiar with the recording process, except in a very general way. If there were secrets to getting the drum sound Shoes were after, Girling didn't have them. And Shoes were pushing to get the job done quickly so as to keep it affordable. Gary says now, "It was a bad time for him to be learning. Nice guy, talented guy, but it just was the wrong setting for him."

"Eventually I had to tell them we just weren't going to get it," says Girling. The band was frustrated and disappointed at this news.

Hedden West's junior engineer, who knew the studio and equipment well, stepped in. He was only supposed to be on hand as a staff representative (essentially, to keep clients from breaking the equipment), but ended up overseeing the majority of the engineering and production.

Over the course of the weekend, Shoes soured on Steve Meyers, who wandered around with a clipboard much of the time; no one remembers what he actually did. "He sure *looked* like a manager, though," John says dryly. Moreover, in anticipation of their first professional recording, Shoes had allowed Meyers to steer them toward a photographer who'd shot Cheap Trick, to take their own band photos. The proofs happened to arrive for inspection while they were at Hedden West, and Shoes weren't happy with them—or with the suddenly inflated price tag they bore. They expected Meyers to settle the issue, but he declined. The band, upset that Meyers was letting them down—especially on this important weekend—stopped considering him for manager.

Two solid days of recording at Hedden West were followed by a few days' worth of mixing; the final versions of both songs were completed on November 17, 1977, a week before Thanksgiving. "Tomorrow Night"/"Okay" is credited on its Bomp! Records label as being co-produced by Meyers and Shoes. Girling is listed as engineer; special thanks are given to Cary Baker and Bill Paige.

As always, John designed the record's cover, this time utilizing a technical solution to an aesthetic problem. The issue was Skip's facial hair, which, despite repeated urging, he refused to shave. In early pictures of the band, the difference between Skip's appearance and the others' is striking: not only did he sport a Fu Manchu moustache, but he also favored the flashy disco shirts, dashikis, and Mexican pullovers popular in the mid- to late seventies. His style contrasted sharply with the solid colors and clean-shaven appearance favored by his colleagues.

For "Tomorrow Night"/"Okay," John killed two birds with one stone. First, he rendered a picture of the band in high-contrast black and white, effectively muting Skip's loud shirt. Then, since their faces were now stark white on a black background, John took white-out and carefully, carefully, erased Skip's 'stache. The effect was striking, leaving nothing but each Shoe's eyes, nose and mouth, and creating a more uniform band appearance. Jeff notes, "Skip took the hint and shaved shortly after."

MEANWHILE, *BLACK VINYL SHOES* WAS still making waves. Another crucial review came from Ira Robbins of *Trouser Press*. In many ways a more traditional rock journalist than Shaw, Robbins was concerned not with writing an underground history or a codex for the initiated, but with spotlighting what he considered to be interesting music—much of which, when Robbins founded his essential fanzine in 1973 as *Trans-Oceanic Trouser Press*, was coming out of England. Robbins points out that "a few issues in, although we had written about a few American artists, we declared ourselves 'America's Only British Rock Magazine' and made that a focus; not exclusively, but predominantly." Still, with an emphasis on bands like the Who, the Kinks, and the Rolling Stones, *Trouser Press* (as its name was abbreviated in 1976) was somewhat more mainstream and less arcane-wonky than *Bomp!*.

But like *Bomp!*, *Trouser Press* was also committed to supporting non-corporate music, "so writing about Shoes was no stretch for me," Robbins says now.

At that point in the late seventies, Robbins notes, the independent movement was just forming in earnest. "A parallel music business grew up," says Robbins, "unbeholden to the first one." He continues:

> What happened was that all the needed elements of a music industry sprang up in parallel to the existing one—labels, media, clubs, tour agents, lawyers, and PR firms that did not request acceptance by the existing structure.

The components of this shadow industry enabled each other to grow interdependently: the labels needed the bands, the bands needed the media, the media needed the clubs and the tours. So together, these forces made possible a path around the major labels. As Robbins says, "My attitude always was that making music was the achievement, and how it was sold was insignificant. I'm an old political radical." And so a band who had taken it upon itself to create a record and share it with the world was exactly the kind of thing that would draw his attention.

In his review of *Black Vinyl Shoes*, Robbins cited the same handwritten letter that had struck Cary Baker, explaining that it was this, as much as anything else, that moved Shoes' LP to the front of his must-listen pile. Robbins' *Trouser Press* review reads:

> The production techniques employed are so debonair and witty that the lack of real studio facilities seems not to have slowed them down appreciably. ... [T]he inventiveness and resource shown here beats the hell out of lots of discs that cost $40-50 thou to produce. If any band ever deserved a year of free studio time, Shoes do. What they might be able to produce under ideal conditions might be astonishing.

While Robbins favorably compared the band to a slew of the usual respectable suspects, including *Help!*-era Beatles, *Sell Out*-era Who, the Raspberries, and the ever-present Cheap Trick, he also came up with some fairly unusual comparisons: Robbins heard in Shoes the disparate echoes of Gary Glitter, Boston, Tommy James and the Shondells, and Bachman-Turner Overdrive.

And like many of the early critics, he predicted major-label success for the band, identifying as one of Shoes' strong points their variety of voices and styles—the very diversity that would later pose a problem for those in the mainstream music business who were tasked with selling Shoes. For Robbins—as for the band itself—the three front men presented:

> ... the kind of multifariousness necessary to prevent singleness of direction. When Shoes start releasing records via a major label (shouldn't be too far off), they won't have any trouble coming up with a string of singles that will sound similar but different enough to stay creative. When a group combines an individual sound with a broad ability to write interesting songs, they're in business.

Little could any of them have predicted the difficulties the conventional, corporate music industry would have selling a band with that seemingly ideal dynamic.

BUT SHOES' APPROACHING THE LIKES of Greg Shaw and Ira Robbins at the outset was much like their forgoing live performance in favor of recording.

Instead of first building up a local fan base and critical following through coverage in their hometown press, Shoes were reaching past Zion while barely out of the gate.

Shoes also leapfrogged over Chicago, which fostered some frustration and mistrust among their fellow travelers. Much as Cary Baker had initially, briefly done, Chicago music scenesters cast a skeptical eye on these small-town rockers who, improbably enough, had done an end run around the very press and club system they themselves were trying to master. "Chicago is a club-based music scene," Don McLeese points out, and anyone who hailed from—or first made a name for themselves—outside the city limits violated the unspoken rules: "In those days, even Cheap Trick were not considered a *real* Chicago band in that sense." And while hailing from far-flung Rockford, Illinois, Cheap Trick played the Chicago area often. Shoes—though closer to the city—were much further off its radar: Zion defined itself explicitly as not-Chicago, and Shoes didn't play Chicago clubs.

Of course, Shoes did have staunch supporters in the Chicago press: Baker, McLeese, and Paige. But the Zion quartet's relationship to the Chicago music scene—as opposed to the Chicago press—was always vexed. They had thought that it would be easy to make friends in the city, but instead saw themselves dismissed as poor country cousins, as uncool, as not having earned the attention they'd received from outside; also, as a goody-two-shoes band. "We were never as squeaky clean as our image," Gary insists. "But that didn't matter."

Gary remembers finding the whole music-scene dynamic to be small-minded and "so stupid. Bands would come to see us play and they wouldn't talk to us; or we'd go to see them play, and then there would be a party and they wouldn't talk to us. Later you'd get to know them, and you'd realize that was just what the scene was. We'd wanted to be part of it and talk to like-minded people, but we obviously didn't fit in at all."

McLeese tells of seeing Shoes at the Night Gallery in Waukegan one evening, just as the buzz from *Black Vinyl Shoes* was starting to draw local attention. Standing in the back of the room, he noticed two members of Pezband, another Chicago power-pop outfit championed by Greg Shaw. "They didn't watch for more than a song," McLeese relates. "Then one turned to the other and said, 'We don't have anything to worry about,' and they left."

In that sense, the Chicago scene was not the cosmopolitan-world-within-an-hour's-drive that Shoes had hoped it would be; it was the petty politics of Zion writ large, the same mindset that Chicago exports Urge Overkill and Liz Phair would later decry as "Guyville."

But Shoes continued to forge ahead, even without Chicago's blessing. Over that Christmas (of 1977), Greg Shaw visited the Windy City. On New Year's Eve, Shoes welcomed 1978 by playing Night Gallery in a blinding snowstorm; lifelong Californian Shaw was reportedly terrified, but braved the weather to see them. A few weeks later, Shaw wrote to Jeff, proposing a one-year, one-album Bomp! deal. The advance was modest, and support was minimal—just a few thousand dollars—but it *was* an offer.

However, the "Tomorrow Night" single had just been released, and it was already obvious to Shoes that, for all his big ideas and visionary fervor, Shaw wasn't much of a businessman. The band had been paid a small advance for "Tomorrow Night"/"Okay," but if it was selling, they didn't know about it. And though Shaw's album offer made it clear he wanted to work with Shoes again, they weren't clear on the specifics of his proposition. "He never told us what he wanted," Gary states. Was Shaw talking about the re-release of *Black Vinyl Shoes* through the independent distributors Bomp! used? Did he want a new record, based on the unnamed demos they were currently making? Shoes weren't sure, and they were too polite to ask. He didn't offer them anything like a time frame, either. And did Shaw even have the money to make *any* kind of deal with them? They certainly hadn't seen anything from "Okay"/"Tomorrow Night."

Nevertheless, as late as May 1978, Shoes were still stating in their fan-club announcements that they expected to reissue *Black Vinyl Shoes* through Bomp!, while politely sending replies to fans who wrote requesting *BVS*, explaining (not entirely truthfully) that all the original copies of *Black Vinyl Shoes* had sold out.

And so Shoes held off on making any decision, hoping a better offer would come along.

A CRUCIAL DEVELOPMENT IN THE spring of '78 was Shoes' rental of the basement of Field's—a dress shop on Zion's main drag, Sheridan Road—for recording purposes. For the first time, Shoes operated a studio that was not part of a band member's home. They had external access from a rear door, and each Shoe had a key; they could all come and go as they pleased. They impishly christened the place BFD Studios.

There was nothing much to said basement—an open space, all cement, with low ceilings and no windows. Shoes' section accounted for about two-thirds of the room; the rest was rented to a local Weight Watchers chapter. "When you walked in, there was a little area with these chairs and weight charts and stuff, which had to be kept clear for their meetings a couple of nights a week," Gary recalls. "We couldn't make music when they were there." At the other end of the basement was Shoes' studio, partitioned off with the cases used for transporting their sound equipment. They hung blankets and cheesy old curtains, both for privacy and to deaden the sound somewhat, leaving just a small passageway from the meeting space to their private area.

Even with the new space, Shoes' recording and rehearsal schedules didn't change much, since those were structured around their day jobs; as before, when they weren't at work, they were at the studio. "It was every weekday night," John says, "and then usually Saturday and sometimes Sunday during the day. We were always there."

Saturdays after seven p.m. were held open as potential date nights. And there was the occasional Friday evening off, if there was a show they wanted to see, but Shoes maintained a very steady schedule of rehearsing and recording. "We tried to do quieter things, like vocals and maracas, when the dress shop was open," Jeff recalls, "but I don't see how they could not have heard us up there sometimes." Periodically Gary or Jeff would stay alone after the evening's session to work on his own material in private.

BFD was of course a much better production space than La Cabane had been—and especially for Jeff, the change of venue was remarkable. "It was a *huge* relief," he says, explaining that his bandmates "had free access to the gear without me having to be there, too. We became more efficient as a result, and we could work in shifts, allowing each of us the occasional day off." Not that the band didn't have misgivings about this new freedom—"You have to remember that this was our *life*, and any time spent away from the studio felt like we were slacking off." Still, Jeff acknowledges, "We did consider it a bit of a respite to have some 'forced' days off."

These included many Weight Watchers nights, though the meetings were only held once or twice a week, and only for an hour or so. Some nights, the band would work around the dieters, breaking for dinner during the meeting. But it wasn't always a smooth cohabitation, according to Gary: "One time, we could tell they'd been over on our side—we could see that they'd been touching our instruments." John thinks the ladies "might have moved things looking for additional folding chairs or something." But Gary recalls Shoes' defensive response: "We hung a sign, a skull and crossbones saying, 'Do Not Enter.' Zion's a very Christian community, obviously, and one of the ladies wrote on it, 'God loves you'—they'd taken it as a threat. But we weren't trying to be scary or anything, despite the skull and crossbones. This was our *business*, and we didn't have any way of securing it."

The security issue *was* a genuine concern, as Shoes' move into the dress-shop basement had been accompanied by some serious economic investment. They had taken out a band loan and bought some new equipment; most notably, a Tascam eight-track recorder and Tascam mixing board, finally retiring Jeff's old TEAC 3340-S. In addition, they all kept most of their instruments and gear down there, including multiple guitars, amps, and drums; plus, there were Shoes' speakers and monitors for live shows. (Before the band was able to move out of Field's, there *was* a robbery, but the Weight Watchers group wasn't the culprit.)

It's hard to overstate how much the new space and new equipment transformed Shoes' working conditions. The Tascam system and its extra tracks, Jeff details, "gave us more freedom to record without having to commit to the early premixes the four-track had required. We now had the luxury of keeping the drums on their own two stereo tracks, leaving the remaining six for other instruments and vocals." After a few experiments—recording their concert staple "Ever Again,", and re-recording "Like I Told You," which had been on *Bazooka*—Shoes set out on what would become the demos for their next record fairly quickly.

ANOTHER MAJOR IMPROVEMENT in their modus operandi was the addition of a second recording engineer: Gary. This development took place as Jeff and Gary together learned how to implement their new gear.

Gary wasn't a complete neophyte, Jeff stresses. "Even though he may not have been directly involved in the four-track 'hocus-pocus' of premixing and ping-ponging tracks, he was acutely aware of the engineering process." Gary agrees:

> I'd done little things even on the four-track, punching things in while Jeff was playing or whatever. But it was during that time at BFD that I got to a point where I *could* do the whole thing.

For Gary, learning to engineer was a liberating experience. "I could see the advantage of it," he says, "the freedom it would give me." Part of that was simply more time to work:

> John and I, when we did *Black Vinyl*, had to be further along in our writing process than Jeff, because La Cabane was Jeff's place, and we didn't have unlimited time to experiment and write there. Since you didn't have time by yourself with the tape player, you had to be more prepared when you came to each session.

Now, in a neutral space where no one was being inconvenienced, it seemed silly to be continually roping Jeff in. Gary says, "Every time I wanted to do something, I didn't want to have to say, 'Oh Jeff, do you want to come over so I can record?' I just thought, I want to get going here, so I'd better figure it out." Both confirm that Jeff never sat down and showed Gary the ropes; having private access to the equipment allowed him to teach himself.

Learning to engineer also helped Gary's writing process evolve, simplifying it significantly. Before the studio at Field's, he describes:

> I had my little setup: two cassette players. I would record on one, and then play it back and record on the other, just using the ambient speakers in the room. I did this only to put a vocal over a guitar; it was the crudest thing imaginable, but it worked. At least I had something when I woke up the next day. And I could play it for those guys and at least give them an idea of what I was doing.

But after the move to BFD, "I would actually go down to the studio and write songs. I'd just run the tape loops and jam." Gary's songwriting noticeably flowered in 1978, partly because of this new freedom. "That was an incredibly productive year," he says.

The privacy afforded by Field's basement helped Gary develop as a vocalist, too; his guardedness and perfectionist tendencies had always made recording vocals difficult for him. Singing in front of an audience, even one comprised of his bandmates, was a daunting prospect. But underneath the dress shop, all alone, Gary was more comfortable experimenting with and refining his vocal skills—knowing no one would ever hear his mistakes.

Shoes also set up a proper monitoring system, something the dinkiness of La Cabane had prevented. This meant that it was now possible for Shoes to practice as a band, all together, and have some rough idea of how things would sound in concert. "This was the time we started getting better at the whole live thing," Gary recalls. "We had the band and our P.A. set up all the time, and we'd go straight through the songs with Skip, running them together like it was a real show. We knew we were going to have to face this, and the basement down there was our opportunity to prepare for it."

The increased size of their facility also meant that Shoes could record guitars more traditionally—by miking the sound as it came out of the amp and adding effects before the recording process, rather than after. They still plugged directly into the board sometimes, but now, Shoes had a choice. With more arrows in their quiver, they began to achieve something closer to the polished sound they sought, as made clear by the aural distinction between *Black Vinyl Shoes* and *Double Exposure*. (Released in 2007, the latter is comprised of the demos for *Present Tense* and *Tongue Twister*, Shoes' first two major-label albums, recorded between 1978 and 1980.)

Shoes threw parties in Field's basement as well, serving as their own house band in their own space. As Gary describes, "We actually had our P.A. set up in Field's like it was a little nightclub. We put together a little stage with monitors and stuff, and we even had these old couches and lamps." They sometimes invited people in to socialize, and hear them play, in this low-key environment.

It was at one of these parties that Shoes met guitar maker Jol Dantzig, who crafted custom instruments with his partner, Paul Hamer, at suburban-Chicago-based Hamer Guitars, which was currently benefiting from the endorsement of Cheap Trick's flamboyant axeman Rick Nielsen. Hamer had been a boutique company, creating one-of-kind instruments since 1973, but at that point in 1978, Hamer was just making the move to a more standard —and less customized—production process. The factory's output was still modest, however, only about ten guitars a week. Hamer's publicity strategy was to get its guitars into the hands of rising musicians, gaining exposure by having the Hamer name attached to specific artists. (Jethro Tull and Bad Company were among the first to endorse Hamers.) All three Shoes began patronizing Hamer Guitars in this period.

The move down to the basement, then, had been a significant step upward for Shoes' professionalization.

Soon after La Cabane lost its studio status, Jeff moved out of the garage altogether. He settled just north of Zion in the even smaller town of Winthrop Harbor, where Gary already lived. Gary had spent the winter of 1977-78 in the snowbirds' house again, alone this time; he found his own apartment when the homeowners returned in the spring. Jeff soon took another unit in the same building. They joked that John could get one, too, and they'd just treat it like a big dormitory, but John resisted; he liked his own place, living above the family of one of their old *Lime* buddies in central Zion.

For Jeff, the Winthrop Harbor move made a tangible difference in his quality of life. La Cabane had never had a real heating system, just the primitive open-flame space heater, which—despite its downright intrepid pioneer vibe—"was really inefficient during those incredibly cold winters," Jeff remembers. The house was never truly comfortable; it was sweltering in the summer and freezing in the winter. What had appeared colorfully rustic when he had moved in at twenty seemed a lot less appealing at twenty-four.

Jeff's new place, despite being a third-floor walkup, was a significant improvement. And since Jeff's dwelling was no longer the nerve center of

Shoes, he actually had some time to himself. "The newly-found free time allowed me to see my then-girlfriend more," Jeff says, adding wryly, "But by then the relationship was already tragically damaged."

So by the summer of 1978, Shoes were in possession of a better studio, better equipment, and better living circumstances. *Black Vinyl Shoes* had critics abuzz, and had all but sold out its original pressing. They'd released a single on a respected underground music label. But Shoes were still waiting for something bigger, though as John remembers, they didn't know precisely what form it would take.

JOHN IN PARTICULAR WAS FEELING stalled for much of 1978. He and Sara had called it quits, more or less for good, but he was stung by the loss; his songwriting from this period, much of which ended up on *Present Tense* and *Tongue Twister*, betrays his keen sense of having been wronged. John's nostalgia was given full voice in "Karen" (originally demoed for *Present Tense*), his feeling of powerlessness in "Your Very Eyes," his jealousy in "Somebody Has What I Had," and his exasperation with the state of the affair in "Cruel You."

The fact that '77 had been so eventful for the band, says John, made '78 seem pale to him by comparison:

> We'd gotten favorable press from *Black Vinyl Shoes*, and had this involvement with Greg Shaw and Bomp! And that started opening up the scene; I remember having arguments—'Should we play out? Should we not play out?' We were recording again, too, and we'd been expanding beyond the local thing. But in '78, we were stuck.

Shoes didn't know how to move ahead; they could not agree on even the most basic issues, like playing out.

Gary was usually the sticking point on that one.

For one thing, Klebe was self-conscious about his stage presence: at six-foot-five, with a football player's broad build, he thought he looked nothing like what rock stars were supposed to. "I wanted to be Mick Jagger or David Bowie," he says now. "They didn't even *make* cool clothes in my size." John, though only slightly shorter, had a lithe build and could pull off the look more successfully, and Jeff had an almond-eyed, teen-idol dreaminess.

Fighting his persistent case of stage fright, Gary still refused to sing live for much of this year. He had no desire to slog it out in the bars, like Cheap Trick or the myriad other hopeful bands that crowded the northern Illinois club scene, dismissing the pay-your-dues approach with a curt, "That's a waste of time." Gary didn't mind playing small clubs if it was a stepping stone to something bigger—say, a decent showcase for a good crowd or a potential label—but if there wasn't a clear, career-advancing reason to play out, he simply didn't want to. And the Murphy brothers, though generally more eager to do live shows, largely respected their bandmate's resistance.

Instead, Shoes adhered to a focus they *could* agree on: seeking the elusive record contract. They didn't even consider what might follow the attainment of that goal; the goal itself consumed them. They wrote and recorded and re-recorded and practiced. They had begun putting together simple press kits with band photos and clips of *Black Vinyl Shoes*' reviews, which they sent out to any label representatives in charge of A&R (Artists & Repertoire), the people who scouted and signed new acts, whose names they could find, but received no response, and a record deal seemed as beyond their grasp as ever. "We kept wondering," John relates, "how to parlay these nuggets of success —*Black Vinyl Shoes*, the Bomp! single, the press—into something better. How should we apply our energies? All we could think about was getting a record contract."

ENTER MARTY SCOTT. SCOTT HAD founded New Jersey-based Jem Imports in 1971, when he was still a university student, distributing hard-to-find British records on college campuses along with a couple of friends. By 1978, Scott's company had grown significantly; not only did Jem now administer several subsidiary labels, including the jazz imprint Passport and the rock-oriented PVC, but also handled distribution for other labels—including Bomp!.

Jem's PVC imprint was designed to license and release debut albums by artists Scott believed were destined to make a splash—a roster Scott called "the FARM team," for First Album Release and Manufacture. These were one-offs for Jem, bands Scott knew he would never be able to afford to keep in the long run. Shoes were about to become one of these acts.

The band members had mailed Scott a copy of *Black Vinyl Shoes* back in '77, and he was taken with its hard-edged, haunting sonic quality. For Scott's part, he didn't connect Shoes with the "Tomorrow Night"/"Okay" single he already distributed, he says now, adding that he has no real recollection of "Tomorrow Night"/"Okay" doing very much; thus, Scott's interest in Shoes was not based on the single's tepid sales. They'd sent him *Black Vinyl Shoes*, and it was *Black Vinyl Shoes* that wowed him.

Scott approached Shoes directly, offering to relicense the album on Jem/PVC. (In a neat bit of synergy, PVC stood for polyvinyl chloride, the *actual* black vinyl Shoes referenced in their album title.) Gary maintains that he didn't see anything odd about the offer, though clearly it cut out Shaw as a middleman—after all, if Bomp! had released *Black Vinyl Shoes*, Jem would have distributed it anyway. Still, says Gary, "I never regarded signing with Jem/PVC as doing an end run around Greg. I saw them as two completely separate entities." Clearly, Scott wanted to take advantage of the opportunity Shoes offered, so he wouldn't share it with Shaw if he didn't have to. But Jeff thought maybe Jem was "trying to starve Greg out," making sure Bomp! had no claim on *Black Vinyl Shoes*.

In early 1978, Scott came to Zion, flying into Chicago and driving two and a half hours through a snowstorm to meet them. They talked about making future records for Jem, but instead of Jem paying for Shoes' studio time, Scott offered to buy them some additional recording equipment. "I don't think he was doing it for the sake of our art form; he was doing it to save himself some money," Gary theorizes. Buying them gear would be considerably more economical than purchasing studio time, and Scott could tell from *Black Vinyl Shoes* that they would use it effectively. (Scott notes that this equipment-in-lieu-of-advance deal was an arrangement he'd made with other bands.) After some negotiation, Shoes agreed to the *BVS* reissue, but not to making a new album for Jem, at least not yet. They earned $1,000 for the reissue, licensing Jem to print and release *Black Vinyl Shoes* for five years.

Even that limited agreement with Scott, according to Jeff, "really upset Greg Shaw." In a letter to Shoes' attorney, Tom Leavens, Shaw expressed regret that the band was dealing with "people whose disinterest [sic] in themselves and their music they are well aware of." But Shoes' main concern had to be their own careers, and in the absence of a concrete offer from Shaw, they felt compelled to take the Jem deal.

With new cover art (a band picture), redesigned inserts (the collage was integrated onto an inner sleeve, with lyrics included on the sleeve's flipside), and a wider potential audience, *Black Vinyl Shoes* was released on Jem/PVC in summer 1978. "As a result of the PVC reissue," says Jeff, "there was a new wave of press"—including a radio interview on WLUP in Chicago along with a raft of print—that finally garnered major-label attention for Shoes.

WHILE THESE NEGOTIATIONS WERE still going on, Shoes were contacted by the office of Chicago's mayor, Michael Bilandic. Gary took the call. Would the band be interested in playing a set for a new city-sponsored music festival set to launch in late summer? Called ChicagoFest, it would be held on the lakefront's Navy Pier over almost two weeks in August. Gary figured that the mayor's office was looking for local acts, "pulling from a pretty small pond"—and Shoes, as a homegrown Illinois band with a heightening profile, probably seemed like a good bet. They took the gig.

Gradually, Gary was beginning to buy his bandmates' arguments in favor of more live performances, despite Zion's logistical limitations. So when Shoes got a call from a guy in Minneapolis named Peter Jesperson, asking them to play a Twin Cities club called Jay's Longhorn, they accepted, even though they'd never heard of either entity.

It was a fortuitous phone call. Though ringing on behalf of the Longhorn, Jesperson actually represented multiple concerns: he also managed legend-in-the-making Minneapolis record retailer Oar Folkjokeopus. Owner Vern Sanden had founded the store in 1973, and in 1974, he hired Jesperson. Oar Folk made its way in the early days, Jesperson recalls, mostly by selling Beatles 45s: "At that time, you had to buy the singles to get the B-sides you couldn't get anywhere else," Jesperson points out. The store did a lot of business with independent distributors like Jem, too, purchasing imports and hard-to-find records from Marty Scott's company. Oar Folk's employees freely recommended music to their clientele, offering a money-back guarantee if the customer didn't like the purchase.

Shortly after Jesperson started at the record store, he began deejaying at the Longhorn seven nights a week. By 1977, Jesperson had expanded his ambitions even more, co-founding influential indie label Twin/Tone Records (which would nurture locally-grown, future post-punk idols the Replacements, among other notables). Musicians moved into the neighborhood around the store, making Oar Folk the physical as well as spiritual nucleus of the Twin Cities' burgeoning indie rock scene. "We wanted people to hang out, and to buy records," Jesperson says.

Vern Sanden had read about *Black Vinyl Shoes* in *Trouser Press* and written to the P.O. box in Zion to order copies for Oar Folkjokeopus. "We played it in the store and everyone loved it," Jesperson recounts. "We sold a lot of that record. Shoes were totally up our alley." Oar Folk had moved a lot of the "Tomorrow Night"/"Okay" single as well, and overall sales convinced Jesperson that Shoes would draw a good crowd in Minneapolis.

So in July 1978, Shoes traveled north to the Twin Cities.

Jesperson thinks the audience numbered maybe two hundred; not full capacity for the Longhorn, but respectable. Still, according to Jesperson, "It was the highlight of the season for us."

And it was indelibly memorable for the band—at the Longhorn, Shoes faced the first out-of-control audience of their career. These were not the T&A-obsessed partiers impatient for Shoes to get off the stage so the wet t-shirt contest could get started. Minneapolis was a serious music town, and the crowd was a punk crowd, accustomed to responding energetically to music they liked. They liked Shoes, though John modestly allows, "It may not have been *us* so much as the fact that that's just what they did at every show."

Shoes' set was crushingly loud, Jesperson recalls, which surprised him—at least some of *Black Vinyl Shoes*, after all, was relatively restrained and acoustic-guitar-based. And though, as Jesperson puts it, "You could tell they were kind of inexperienced [in live performance], and stronger instrumentally than vocally," the Longhorn audience didn't care. Says Jeff, "They went *crazy*."

When Shoes finished performing and started making their exit, the crowd rushed the stage. Skip lost his sweaty shirt in the melee, and when they finally made it backstage, a friend serving as a roadie had to hold the dressing-room door shut against the throng long enough for Shoes to get changed. The fans followed them back to their hotel, where the party raved on until the police broke it up.

It was the first time Shoes ever felt like rock stars.

"As far as we were concerned, they *were* rock stars," Jesperson says. "But they didn't have a rock-star-sized chip on their shoulder; they just looked like they loved their music."

SHOES WERE READY FOR CHICAGOFEST.

In a contemporary news account of the festival's 1978 debut, David Novick, writing in the neighborhood newspaper *Hyde Park Herald*, stated that it was extremely well-organized, pointing out that "the majority of the professional staff at ChicagoFest had been hired away from Milwaukee's [longstanding music festival] Summerfest. ... Up to ten years' experience in the sticks helped make second city's [sic] festival slick." Novick reported that "over 250 different acts performed on six major stages over a ten-day period. Five smaller stages, including a comedy showcase, disco dancing, and a children's area hosted additional entertainers. A circus, giant midway, cinema and craft area featuring the shlockiest [sic] collection of junk ever assembled completed the package." Novick opined, however, that the size of the festival interfered with its success, simultaneously complaining that it needed "a more human scale" and that it lacked a folk-music stage, and calling it a "cult of personality" celebration for Mayor Bilandic himself. But ChicagoFest drew SRO crowds, and for Shoes, kicking off the Saturday lineup at the capacious, floating Rock around the Dock stage, it was the biggest show they'd played yet.

A few hundred people were in attendance, despite the early hour, when Shoes took the stage at noon. Jeff's memory of the day is a blur: "We had no idea what to expect. We were just flying blind." Gary remembers that "as a band, we were nervous—but *I* was terrified." Though Shoes would never really develop the passion for live performance that drives other bands, they did eventually learn to enjoy themselves playing the first-ever ChicagoFest, and it ended up being a triumphant show. In fact, Gary describes the gig as "the highlight of our careers at that point."

Shoes weren't the only ones having a life-changing experience at ChicagoFest. A suburban adolescent was making his virgin foray into the big city, and Shoes were the draw:

> One of the first times I ever trekked into Chicago was at the tender age of fifteen to attend a huge lakefront music and cultural festival called ChicagoFest. I still wasn't able to drive at that point (obviously), so my buddies and I rode the commuter train from our sleepy little town in the northwest suburbs, and to this day I still retain a palpable sense of how thrilling it was to get out of the suburbs and explore the big, mysterious inner city for the first time.
>
> Our first destination upon arrival was Rolling Stone[s] Records to paw through the vinyl. ... To an impressionable dork just getting started collecting vinyl it seemed like Mecca. Our visit to Rolling Stone[s] was just a side trip, though. The real reason my friends and I made the journey was to hit the "rock barge" at ChicagoFest to see a little known power pop combo from Zion, Illinois called Shoes (not *The* Shoes, just Shoes). We'd been primed by rave reviews of their new album, *Black Vinyl Shoes*, in the local press, and we were more than impressed that the band had written, recorded and released it on their very own "independent" record label.

The teen was an aspiring drummer named Ric Menck, who would go on to found the acclaimed alternative pop bands Choo Choo Train and Velvet Crush with his fellow Illinoisan, bassist and vocalist Paul Chastain; Menck would also drum for Matthew Sweet and, briefly, for Shoes themselves. In a recent article in the fanzine *Ugly Things*, Menck reminisced about Shoes' effect on him:

> I tell you honestly, the day my friends and I saw Shoes perform at ChicagoFest was the day I decided to dedicate my life to rock and roll. Watching them slink onstage in their dark-blue corduroy jeans, plug into a series of buzzing Marshall amps, then crank through a set of tunes that sounded like a cross between the Raspberries, the Byrds and the Ramones was all it took to do my head in completely. What made it more special was that Shoes were hometown boys, and they had started their group from the ground up. I figured if they could do it, so could I, and from that day forward they became one of my principal sources of inspiration. Less than a year later my teenage group Drats (not *The* Drats, just Drats) entered the studio to begin work on our own debut vinyl effort.

One other relationship was formed during this period that would have later repercussions for Shoes. Ever since their *Lime* days, John and Gary had remained friends with high-school buddy Ed Erickson. Now Ed introduced them to his cousin, Doug, who was living in Madison, Wisconsin and also loved music.

Doug was a guitarist, and he and his friend, drummer Bryan "Butch" Vig, had founded a rootsy power-pop band called Spooner. Ed thought that his musician cousin and his musician friends might get along. Doug would later adopt the nickname Duke and simplify the spelling of his surname to Erikson, as Spooner evolved into critical favorites Fire Town and Fire Town into mega-sellers Garbage. But at this point, Erickson and Vig were just looking for like-minded people to hang out with, and a fair amount of correspondence transpired between the two young bands.

SHOES WERE STILL JUGGLING the Bomp! and Jem offers when they were contacted by Seymour Stein, the legendary founder of Sire Records, home of the Ramones, Talking Heads, and other paradigmatic acts. The band met one of Stein's representatives at a Talking Heads concert at swanky Chicago showcase club Park West in late August, and Stein himself traveled to Zion sometime that fall.

John remembers the music mogul coming to their basement studio to talk, bringing what appeared at first to be an offer better than anything they'd heard so far. Stein proposed giving Shoes $30,000 to record an album, a pretty respectable amount in the late seventies. But that fee was for recording alone; there was no advance, as they recall, and when they asked Stein, "What are we supposed to live on?" he replied, "You have girlfriends, don't you?" It was a distinctly unsatisfactory answer (and even if Shoes were the kind of guys who lived off girlfriends, only Jeff actually *had* one at that juncture).

Another sticking point was that Stein expected a heavy concert schedule from Shoes. Touring would mean quitting their day jobs, which, in the absence of financial support from Sire, simply wasn't an option. Gary says that Stein treated Shoes "like he was doing us a favor" by dangling this bare-bones deal. And he emphasized the negative aspects of the contract, the weighty load of expectation and responsibility that would fall on their shoulders should he sign them. "Seymour didn't make it sound inviting," Gary says.

To top it off, Stein never actually made Shoes a concrete offer. Numbers and terms were thrown around in conversation, but nothing was ever actually presented to them on paper.

This may have been because Stein himself was in something of a transition. Sire had made its name as a visionary major label by signing electrifying new bands like the Ramones and Talking Heads, leading lights of the CBGB's punk scene in New York—but at that time (1976-77) Sire's distribution was being handled by an ailing ABC Records. Stein was reportedly dismayed by the spotty distribution that the Ramones had received from ABC; Talking Heads had even delayed signing with Sire because they were concerned about the same issue. (ABC eventually folded, after being purchased by MCA Records in 1979.) Stein had switched Sire's distribution to Warner Bros. in 1977, selling the label to Warner outright in 1978. Thus, in the summer of '78, Stein may not have been in much of a position to make a solid offer to anyone. But the Sire chief, always in the vanguard of new trends, clearly wanted to let Shoes know he was interested.

However, once *Black Vinyl Shoes* was reissued on Jem/PVC in the fall, the clock was ticking on Stein and Sire. Jem's Marty Scott tells of how he and the Sire chief often competed for new bands in this period; in one meeting with future synth-pop hit machine Depeche Mode, for example, the band told Scott that Stein was scheduled right after him. It may have seemed to Stein, in August 1978, as though he had almost unlimited time to court Shoes. But all that changed when *BVS* was released on Jem/PVC, which provided actual distribution to actual record stores, so consumer access to *Black Vinyl Shoes* was no longer predicated on handwritten letters or personal contact with the band. And once the album was widely available in record stores, things happened quickly.

MARTY SCHWARTZ WAS AN up-and-coming radio promotion man from Buffalo, New York, by way of Miami, Florida. He had grown up around Buffalo radio, and then after college went to work in a Florida record store across from the University of Miami. While there, Schwartz befriended a promotion guy from Viscount Records in Miami, who eventually offered the young music fan a job. Soon after, Schwartz was hired away from Viscount by Elektra Records' promotion department, and they moved him to New York City in 1975. "New York was hopping," recalls Schwartz, who became enamored of downtown, underground music culture, particularly the punk scene.

Schwartz soon ascended to the position of Elektra's vice president for rock promotion in New York, a role with a lot of clout—and an equal amount of responsibility. It was Schwartz's job to break bands: to get them on the radio with proper retail support. This meant making sure the stations' program directors were rewarded for adding Elektra songs to their playlists, making sure Elektra's publicity department geared up simultaneously to secure press coverage for the bands people heard on the radio, and just generally making sure that all the label machinery worked together to spur record sales.

Schwartz also genuinely loved music, even outside his job: he frequented the hipper music retail stores in New York, and it was in the landmark Greenwich Village record shop Bleecker Bob's that he'd first heard *BVS* over the sound system. "I listened to the whole of *Black Vinyl Shoes*, and I just flipped out," Schwartz says. "I thought it was an amazing record." He'd already heard of Shoes and their audacious living-room creation through the rock press, and Schwartz was impressed enough at what he heard to take the record to his own label.

But back on the West Coast, Schwartz says, his colleagues at Elektra Los Angeles weren't exactly blown away by Shoes, and he had to do a major sell job to label brass. "They didn't have a clue about the underground scene," says Schwartz. Instead, they were mired in mainstream California mellowness: "Linda Ronstadt, Jackson Browne stuff. They really didn't get the underbelly of rock." Frustrated, Schwartz took *Black Vinyl Shoes* to his own boss, the national head of rock promotion for Elektra, a tough young street kid from Detroit named Ken Buttice.

Still in his twenties, Buttice had swiftly ascended because he was a natural at radio promotion. At that time, promo was a person-to-person business; promo guys courted the radio program directors who had the ultimate say on which new records got added to their station's playlists, showing them a good time, getting them wasted, getting them laid. Some labels were jobbing out this work, contracting to independent promoters—who were presumed to have a better feel for the pulse of their local scene, since they were not allied to any particular label. (Fredric Dannen's groundbreaking 1990 exposé of independent promotion—*Hit Men: Power Brokers and Fast Money Inside the Music Business*—explains this phenomenon in detail.) But Buttice reportedly had no interest in giving up that part of the job; he liked doing the nuts and bolts of promotion himself, schmoozing and boozing and whatever else it took to get his records on the radio.

Buttice was also ambitious. Promo was fun, and he was good at it, but everyone understood that the prestige record-biz department was A&R, which had been without a head at Elektra since George Daly left the position in late 1978. Buttice had set his sights on that department; he'd cultivated the current president of Elektra, Steve Wax, as a mentor, and knew the key to that transition was signing a band. And not just any band. They had to become huge: gold records, platinum records, Grammys. Everything—including Buttice's coveted position of vice-president for A&R—depended on that ideal signing.

Schwartz was unofficially deputized by Buttice and started, as he puts it, "sniffing around on the East Coast" in late '78. That made sense as a locale to scout new talent: Elektra had already had tremendous success earlier that year with the Cars. This Boston-based new-wave quintet had recorded a demo single, "Just What I Needed." But the Cars had had the good fortune to get theirs into the hands of another aspiring A&R rep, Maxanne Sartori, then a disc jockey at Boston's progressive-rock powerhouse WBCN-FM—where their demo became a local hit.

Previously, Sartori had worked in A&R at groundbreaking independent label Island Records, with its venerated founder Chris Blackwell —but Island was struggling in the late 1970s, and she was looking for something more stable, at a bigger label. So it was that Sartori brought the Cars to Ken Buttice at Elektra; they were signed by the end of 1977, and their self-titled first album came out the following summer, producing a string of hit singles and selling over six million copies—sextuple platinum. Buttice was confident, then, that Sartori had the ear for hit bands, and got her hired as an A&R representative in Elektra's New York office.

But it was Marty Schwartz who was Buttice's right hand on the East Coast. When Schwartz brought Shoes to Buttice, he immediately vetted them through Sartori, who said that yes, she *had* heard of Shoes; in fact, the buzz around them was nigh-deafening.

However, in late 1978, Shoes were in the aforementioned lull that so frustrated John. *Black Vinyl Shoes* was out there doing whatever it was doing (Jem never sent them sales reports, and after their initial advance, Shoes never saw any remuneration from the record), but for the band, there were no new developments. They'd had a quiet fall and winter.

Adding to Shoes' distress, work was interrupted that fall by the previously-mentioned robbery at the studio. The dress shop was being painted, members of the painting crew had keys to the building, and one night when Shoes arrived to lay down some tracks, they discovered four guitars missing. Nothing else was taken; no amps, no speakers, no production equipment, no effects, just the guitars in their cases. "We assumed it was two guys who each took one in each hand," says Jeff. "Definitely not professionals"—since the equipment the thieves ignored was much more valuable than the instruments they took. Still, Gary lost a Gibson Explorer, Jeff a Gibson Firebird and a 1973 Fender Stratocaster, and John his Fender Precision bass. "It was a pretty depressing time," says John.

But they tried not to let the theft slow them down. Shoes settled back into the studio and continued to crank away at their demos. When these were finished, they sent them out to major labels, hoping to capitalize on the reissue of *Black Vinyl Shoes* and the promise of their new work, which, abetted by the eight-track recorder and Shoes' development as songwriters, they truly felt was the strongest they'd done to date.

The focus started to return to their live playing, now that Shoes had a more-or-less full set of demos for another record. They began working these demos into their live act; John remembers playing a local club called Green Briar and bluffing his way through Gary's new song, "Too Late." Gary still refused to sing it live, and John is not even sure the lyrics were complete, but says, "I know I knew the melody well enough to make up something that fit the space." Gary *had* started to sing, just a little—in the basement in front of friendly faces—but continued to shy away from it in club performance.

As THE YEAR ENDED, SHOES came full circle, returning to Dwight, Illinois for another show: they played the local American Legion hall on New Year's Eve as 1978 gave way to 1979. It was not quite as slapdash as the last time Shoes had performed in town—this time, they had an actual venue—but major elements were still missing; most notably, a stage. According to host Paul Neville, their old Champaign buddy who had instigated the first Dwight show (and this one, too), "We had to borrow the stage from the Catholic Church." They didn't have roadies, either, so Shoes hauled the risers themselves, lugging them through the bitter-cold night down the main street of Dwight. Neville recalls being terrified that "one of them would smash their fingers and not be able to play." But it was a good show; Shoes were unquestionably improving as a live act.

Mostly, this is because the band had made a conscious decision to do so, regularly running their sets over and over and over back at the studio. "We were as well-practiced as we could have been at that point," says Gary. Still, as John remarks, they were just recording and rehearsing for some theoretical gig that might come up some day. There was no particular sense of urgency; Shoes were mostly unaware of the sequence of events at Elektra that the reissue of *Black Vinyl Shoes* had set in motion.

As Shoes sent their demos out, nothing but rejections came in—a situation that was disappointing, but not panic-inducing. For one thing, they were prepared to release these as-yet-untitled demos themselves, as they had done with the original *Black Vinyl Shoes*, if everything else fell through. But the band members also knew that they had more options now. Jem's Marty Scott might be willing to do something, once the demos were finished. Greg Shaw, too, would probably want to release what they had, assuming he could afford to. Just after the first of the year, Shoes sent Shaw eight songs from the new set: "Too Late," "Hangin' Around with You," "I Don't Wanna Hear It," "Karen," "Jet Set," "Hate to Run," and a re-recorded "Tomorrow Night." Shoes told Shaw that they had seven more songs ready to go, and that if he had any interest at all, he should contact them.

Seymour Stein met with the band again during a layover in Chicago in January 1979, while the city was shouldering through what would be its toughest winter on record. His appearance was testament to the clout he now had: Stein was sporting a Warner Bros. jacket, in honor of Sire's new role as a member of the Warner entertainment family. By this time, however, Shoes had done some research, and had a sense of what other unsigned hopefuls were being offered in the way of recording contracts. They'd also learned that Sire had a reputation for offering relatively modest funding, and would expect to own half the publishing rights to their songs; having already consulted with Bug, they knew they didn't have to settle for that arrangement. While this time, as before, Stein put nothing definitive on the table, Sire's chief did restate his interest in working with Shoes; had an acceptable concrete offer been made, the band very likely might have taken it.

"But then," John says, "in the middle of fucking fourteen-foot snowdrifts, this knight came riding in on a white horse. His name was Kenny Buttice."

KEN BUTTICE WAS IN NEW YORK on a Friday night in January 1979 when he saw a new ABC-TV documentary called *Heroes of Rock and Roll*. It featured the rare footage of Lennon and McCartney declaring that the Beatles could have been called the Shoes.

Back in Zion that same night, several members of Shoes were at a party with *Heroes of Rock and Roll* on in the background. "We caught it for just a nanosecond," John recalls, "but that was enough. It was one of those weird moments where the whole room goes quiet, and every neck in the room turned at the same time."

Partygoers ribbed them good-naturedly about the clip, the existence of which they'd previously been unaware; Shoes were surprised and, understandably, rather delighted. "But it really was a complete coincidence," John emphasizes, adding that Gary approached him with the caveat, "This could come back to haunt us, you know."

Buttice, though, claimed to see it as nothing less than a sign from God, as he said when he immediately contacted Jeff Murphy.

Heroes of Rock and Roll had aired on a Friday. Buttice and Marty Schwartz were in Zion by Tuesday.

JEFF SAYS THAT WHEN BUTTICE initially called him, he'd offered to fly Jeff alone to New York for negotiations. No, Jeff had replied, that wasn't quite how Shoes operated: if one of them came to New York, they'd all have to come. Instead, Buttice and Schwartz came to them.

During another blinding snowstorm in early February, the Elektra execs arrived in Zion in a limousine, an unusual sight for the town's mostly working-class residents. The snowdrifts may not have been *quite* fourteen feet high, but they certainly overtopped ten; even Buffalo native Schwartz was awed.

Shoes met at the basement studio to play for Buttice and Schwartz. In what they would come to learn was remarkably commonplace in this new-to-them business, the Elektra reps each disappeared for a bit before Shoes began to play; the band didn't ask why. While Schwartz was out of the room, before they had played a note, Buttice assured Shoes, "We'll work something out."

All their meticulous practicing had paid off, as Gary remembers:

> When Kenny came, we actually did a show, just cranking through the songs one after another. One song stopped, and we had a transition, and then the next song started. We'd been rehearsing this long before we'd even heard of Kenny, so when he came out here, we were more than ready.

John remembers seeing the label honchos silhouetted in the back of the basement, heads together, conferring during their set. Afterwards, Shoes cranked up the tape deck and played the two men some of the new demos they were working on (the ones that would become *Present Tense*). Then they headed to dinner at the most upscale restaurant they could think of, Ray Radigan's, over the Wisconsin state line in Kenosha. "It was the only place we knew that had white tablecloths, where you could get something other than pizza," John says. There, Buttice convinced Shoes of his faith in them and their talent.

When they returned to Jeff's apartment in Winthrop Harbor, Buttice turned his considerable salesman's skills on them. Shoes may have thought that they were there to sell themselves to him, but Buttice was already sold. His job was to sell Elektra to *them*. And the things Buttice promised made their heads spin. They were, quite simply, going to be the Biggest Band in the World, he assured them. "Are you guys ready for success?" he asked. "I mean, *big* success?"

Wowed, even awestruck, and scarcely daring to believe it, they answered, "Sure!"

Gary recalls that, compared to Seymour Stein's grim predictions of nonstop touring and comparative poverty, "Kenny made it sound like we were going to the Land of Oz." No specific dollar amounts were mentioned, but the Elektra rep assured the band, "We're going to take care of you. You'll never have to worry about money again."

And, as Jeff recounts in *Birth of a Band*, the meeting ended with a plan. He quotes Buttice as saying, "Meet me in L.A. on Thursday; there'll be tickets at the Chicago airport. Bring a lawyer."

Chapter 5

Jet Set (1979)

Neither Jeff nor John Murphy had ever been on a plane before, and Jeff had never even traveled beyond the upper Midwest. But within a week, all four members of Shoes met with attorney Tom Leavens at Chicago's O'Hare Airport, to board a flight for Los Angeles. Leavens had helped Shoes set up both their publishing deal with Bug Music and the *Black Vinyl Shoes* reissue with Jem.

Less starry-eyed, more seasoned artists than Shoes might have been a little wary of the rush they were being given by Buttice. But Shoes were keyed up; *this* was the dream. What had they been working for, given up their nights and weekends for, neglected their girlfriends for, taken ribbing from their friends for, if not a major-label record contract?

Part of the band members' excitement was their sense of being in a whole new world. Jeff remembers the disjunction of leaving the frigid, snow-caked Midwestern February and arriving "less than four hours later, 2,000 miles away, in balmy, sun-splashed Hollywood, California. I can't emphasize enough the contrast of not only the climate, but our entire lives, between Zion and Los Angeles." John, in discussing Shoes' first SoCal sojourn, comes back again and again to the word "surreal," and indeed, that's how it seemed to the band.

When Shoes arrived at Los Angeles International Airport (LAX), they were picked up by Maxanne Sartori, who had flown in from New York to meet them. She showed them around L.A. that first evening, and tried to get Shoes to hang out with her on subsequent nights, sometimes phoning long after they'd gone to bed. Each time, they politely declined. "These were some of the most important days of our lives; we knew that," John says now. "We didn't want to spend them hung over." For Gary's part, he says that they *were* perfectly willing to go out, but that they wanted to meet girls, something Sartori's presence would've interfered with.

It seemed to Shoes that Sartori was anxious to make sure that both they and Elektra witnessed her interest in the band, presumably so that she could be named Shoes' A&R representative—their creative and career advisor within Elektra—when the time came. Her apparent goal was no secret to Marty Schwartz, certainly: "Maxanne really wanted to A&R them; I didn't give a shit. All I cared about was *breaking* the band."

But Sartori was caught in a bind. Technically, Elektra was half of Elektra/Asylum Records: one company with dual headquarters on the East and West Coasts. But practically speaking, there were significant corporate and cultural differences between the New York office, which mostly handled Elektra, and the Los Angeles office, which mostly oversaw Asylum. New York was closely following the punk and new-wave movements; L.A. was still stuck on seventies easy-listening, countrified soft rock.

Sartori worked out of the New York office, and despite—or perhaps because of—her East Coast cachet, was something of a fish out of water among her L.A. colleagues. Shoes recognized that, as Skip Meyer puts it, "We should have been managed out of New York," but now, for better or worse, they were seen as "Kenny's band," and Kenny wanted to handle them out of Los Angeles. It wasn't all bad—Buttice's star was ascending, and Shoes' wagon was hitched to it—but there *were* repercussions. According to Marty Schwartz, "Maxanne was pushed aside by Kenny," who would eventually give the band to a new, completely inexperienced A&R rep in L.A.: Carol Thompson, whose primary qualifications, says Schwartz, seemed to be her residence in Los Angeles and her loyalty to Buttice. But Thompson's role, at this point, was mostly titular: in actuality, Buttice handled most of Shoes' A&R details himself, according to the band members.

Still, before *anyone* could be designated Shoes' A&R rep at Elektra, there was a lot of negotiating to do. The band didn't yet have a manager, but they did have Tom Leavens, and they had developed good relations with a few key people out on the West Coast.

ONE OF THESE WAS BUG MUSIC'S Dan Bourgoise. Cognizant of his experience in the industry, Shoes asked Bourgoise to negotiate with Elektra on their behalf, and he agreed. After the first day of talks, Bourgoise asked permission to bring aboard another lawyer with more music-business experience than Leavens: Neville Johnson, an entertainment attorney of his acquaintance.

Bourgoise called Johnson in because the preliminary contract Elektra had drafted considerably exceeded the band's goals. They'd only been expecting a little more production money than the $30,000 Seymour Stein had mentioned, and hopefully an advance to live on until records started selling. When Elektra came in with much larger offers, Shoes and their team realized that they needed to reassess their position quickly.

The Cars had sold six million copies of their debut album the previous year, and Elektra's offer indicated their expectation that Shoes would do comparably well. According to Gary, "I think the first time we understood what was expected of us was when Dan came out of those meetings. He was just *flying*." Great things indeed were predicted, and money seemed to be no object for Elektra. Given that, Bourgoise wanted some backup in the negotiating room—someone with more field experience than Leavens— and Shoes green-lighted Neville Johnson.

ELEKTRA'S FUNDS WERE FLOWING for a reason: 1978 had been a banner year for the music industry in general. Record sales, which had risen steadily since 1955 regardless of the prevailing economic climate, were at an all-time high. As Frederic Dannen details in *Hit Men*:

1978 was an *annus mirabilis*—a year of miracles. RSO's *Saturday Night Fever* and *Grease* each grossed over $100 million at the box office; the latter film became the biggest movie musical of all time. The soundtrack albums of the two movies sold about 30 million copies apiece worldwide, an all-time record that would not be surpassed until Michael Jackson's *Thriller*.

Gold (500,000 units sold) and platinum (one million units sold) records abounded; in 1978 nearly three hundred albums were so designated, and more than seventy singles. Disco was at its peak. The music industry was flush with cash, awash with drugs, and euphoric.

In such an atmosphere, big-money deals rained down. "Those were some of the excesses of the times," Bourgoise says. Shoes' negotiations went on for several weeks, mostly concerning production financing, but in the end, the band signed a deal for up to ten albums over seven years, with a $60,000 advance plus a generous recording budget for their first record. And the funds available for production were set to increase with each record: the album that would become *Present Tense* was budgeted at $125,000, but the next budget promised was $150,000, and so on. As Bourgoise recalls, "They felt at Elektra that 'this was our next Cars.' ... All these doors opened up monetarily—at the beginning, anyway. It was amazing."

THERE WERE SEVERAL UNUSUAL clauses in Shoes' contract. One was that Shoes were signed not as recording artists, but as a production company. Jeff professed in his memoir that "this allowed for much more control of song selection, production, and creative control." But Gary and John disagree. Tom Leavens confirms that, whatever the language of the Elektra contract, it was structured far more like a recording-artist deal than a production-company deal: Shoes may have had final say over the production of their records, but they weren't paying directly for studio time and a producer; Elektra was. Had they been given a proper production-company deal, Elektra would have been out of the picture entirely until Shoes delivered the final product. In actuality, Elektra was intimately involved in all of Shoes' major decisions leading up to the production of *Present Tense*. Gary comments that the contract terms "forced us to spend extravagant sums we wouldn't have spent," on promotion, travel, and publicity.

Another atypical but actually favorable clause in Shoes' contract specified that if Elektra picked up their option to make an odd-numbered album, the even one would also be picked up. In other words, funding the first album meant that the second was automatically funded as well; funding the third guaranteed funding the fourth, and so on. This "in for one, in for two" clause would have significant repercussions down the line for Shoes. Though California law limited the term of the agreement to seven years, according to Neville Johnson, the contract included four separate options: Shoes could have made as many as ten albums for Elektra if all the options had been picked up over that seven-year period. That seems like an implausible output, but the Beatles had done it, and the members of Shoes welcomed such parallels between themselves and their idols.

Another non-standard clause in the contract stated that, should the band ever get dropped and Elektra allow their music to go out of print, rights to the masters of their Elektra recordings would revert to Shoes after five years. This "reversion clause" was at the time a very unusual piece of legal maneuvering, and Bourgoise is proud of it. "I've never known anyone to get that from a major label," he states, noting that labels almost always retain in perpetuity the rights to the music they release. "It delights me when I think that Shoes have all those records back." (Some artists have actually been sued by their former labels for writing songs that simply *resemble* their previous work. Veteran roots-rocker John Fogerty won a 1985 lawsuit brought by Fantasy Records—alleging that a Fogerty solo song had plagiarized a Fogerty-penned hit by his previous band, Creedence Clearwater Revival, whose catalog Fantasy owned—and it drew widespread public attention to the problem of creative artists losing control of their own compositions.)

Bourgoise says he insisted on the mold-breaking reversion clause for Shoes in "the heat of that whole artist-owned ethic." After having fought to retrieve Del Shannon's rights for him, Bourgoise was only too aware that it behooved him to ensure that his artists would own their own rights in the long run. He also points out that he may not have been a standard negotiator, nor Neville Johnson a standard entertainment lawyer: "Traditional music attorneys are about money upfront. So much of [their process] is trading off future stability for the short-term buck." But Bourgoise and Johnson were thinking in the long term.

Bourgoise also makes note of his belief that Elektra didn't take the reversion clause very seriously. There was no comment when it was inserted, he says, "and as negotiations went on, that little part of it stayed in, almost unnoticed." The only way the clause could be activated would be if Elektra lost interest in Shoes. (Bourgoise supposes Elektra's position was, "'If we've dropped them from the label and taken [their records] out of print, what do we care who has the rights?'") And in the heady days of February 1979, Elektra's ever dropping Shoes appeared highly unlikely.

Contract negotiations continued past that long weekend in California, after the members of Shoes returned to Zion. "We had day jobs," Gary shrugs. "We weren't ready to leave those until we had something solid."

AND SHOES WERE ALREADY embroiled in Elektra politics they didn't understand. With no real head of A&R in early 1979, everybody at the label was looking for acts to sign; clearly, that was the key to moving up in the company. The tantalizingly empty position of VP of A&R was a plum ripe for the picking, and a prestigious position: its greater proximity to the label's power centers certainly made it the next logical stepping stone for an ambitious young executive like Ken Buttice—but not only for him.

Shortly after Buttice first made contact earlier in the month, Jeff had received a strikingly similar Elektra call—this one from George Steele, the VP of marketing. He, too, wanted to talk to Jeff about signing with Elektra. Shoes would later theorize that Steele had gotten wind of Buttice being poised to sign a monster band—and having figured out that Shoes were the potential monster; sought to have his name attached to them, too. As John figures it, Steele "wanted his fingerprints on the deal." But when he received Steele's call, Jeff was unfamiliar with this particular marketing exec, and when Steele told Jeff that Elektra was interested in Shoes, Jeff replied with a nonchalant, "Yeah, we know."

Instead of making Shoes wary of Elektra's internal workings—the likely power play in which they were the pawns—the call convinced them that they were indeed a very hot commodity: a thrilling prospect for Shoes.

This perception of themselves as desirable was confirmed by a direct approach from Capitol Records as well. One afternoon while still in California, Shoes were visited at their hotel by a representative of Bruce Garfield, Capitol's president, who extended an offer on Garfield's behalf: "Capitol is going to beat anything Elektra offers you."

This was impressive. Capitol, after all, had been the Beatles' label in America, and its iconic stack-of-records skyscraper was a Hollywood landmark. Shoes figured Capitol was simply responding to the buzz, and didn't actually know anything about them and their music. As John puts it, "Whoever proposed signing us must have been in a panic: 'We gotta get these guys!' It's kinda scary that a major label would make that offer out of the blue, but when you're a desired commodity, and we were, there they are." Says Gary, "Our market value had gone up."

Though Shoes had no legal commitment to Elektra at this point, in the wake of the Capitol news, they did not play off Capitol against Elektra for more money (which they were allowed, perhaps even expected, to do). Far from being tactical, their response was personal: Shoes felt they owed Ken Buttice their loyalty, and they called to tell him they were going home to think.

Buttice immediately announced, "I'm comin' over!" True to his word, he was at their hotel within minutes in his chocolate-brown Rolls-Royce, and proceeded to take Shoes out to Fatburger for what he assured them were the best burgers in L.A. Afterward, as they all stood outside in the spring night, Gary remembers that Buttice seemed hurt. When he queried, "Are you guys still with us?" Shoes admitted that they were getting what they tactfully called "outside pressure." Still, the band members assured Buttice that they were happy with Elektra, and he assured them the label's intentions were pure.

This latest turn of events had Shoes seeing nothing less than supernatural forces at work. "We thought we were being tested," remembers John. "We thought it would be bad karma not to go with Elektra at that point."

Still, Shoes were eager to get out of L.A. "We were burned out," Gary says. "It was a lot different from working our day jobs; we weren't used to networking with people all day and all night, knowing so much was on the line. And then it was complicated by this other offer. We just wanted to go home."

Nothing more was said about the other offer, although ironically, when Shoes returned to Zion, it was to find a letter from *another* A&R rep at Capitol—rejecting the demos they'd sent earlier that year. (After the ink was dry on Shoes' Elektra deal, Capitol president Bruce Garfield sent Bourgoise a congratulatory letter, along with a bottle of champagne.)

SHOES MADE ANOTHER TRIP west at the end of February to check in again on the ongoing negotiations. During this visit, Buttice offered them studio time, pressuring country producer David Molloy (fresh off his success with Eddie Rabbitt's "I Love a Rainy Night") into running a session for them. "Okay, Buttice," Molloy reportedly sighed. "I'll make your demo."

Unfortunately, the sessions with the incongruous Molloy weren't very productive, according to Shoes. Initially, recording was done at a place called The Annex, a decades-old Hollywood studio in a converted house. In his memoir, Jeff describes the atmosphere there as being "a little too casual." He recalls now: "The Annex felt more like a hangout, flophouse, than a studio. Too much hippie vibe, man. Lots of people hanging around, doing—well, I don't know what." John remembers laying down the vocal for "Now and Then" in a bedroom there, and thinking, "This is the big leagues? This is what we did at Jeff's."

Convinced that this scene wasn't quite for them, the band asked for time at the more upscale Village Recorder in Santa Monica; things didn't go much better there, however, due to constraints of both time and technology. Jeff explains:

> Two days [Shoes' entire allotment] was hardly enough time to do what we would normally take a week or more to do in our home studio. In addition, we had very bad luck with the gear. During the sessions, the mixing console started having problems with some of the channels, and two Pultec EQ units died. Finally, the 24-track tape machine lost its mind while rewinding the tape for "Every Girl," and the master tape was destroyed as the ... tape operator slapped at the reel that was spinning out of control, wrinkling and spilling the master tape onto the floor.

Shoes only managed to rough out one salvageable demo, John and Gary's "Now and Then." While the fault lay with an unlikely series of mishaps, it was a less than auspicious beginning for the nervous young band.

But producer Molloy seems to have thought he had something. In summer 2011, a set of his studio monitors appeared on eBay with an explanatory note: when Molloy had a good session, he would ask the artists to sign the monitors. Shoes' signatures are right up front, their first names clustered around the inscribed date: February 26, 1979.

Negotiations with Elektra took another month, and on April 5, Shoes signed their record contract at Tom Leavens' office in Chicago. They received their advance in one large lump sum, and Jeff took the check home to display to his and John's mother, Leona Scott. "But when I showed it to her, and I was so proud, she said, '[Elektra] is going to want that back, you know.'" Jeff notes that his mother was a great believer that the good and bad always travel in pairs, often citing the German adage, "After laughter comes tears." As it turned out, she would be right—but at the time, Mrs. Scott's response seemed unnecessarily dour.

Now Shoes launched two search processes: they would need a producer for their debut album (Molloy wasn't being considered), and they would need a manager.

Accustomed to managing themselves, Shoes were seeking a professional who could run interference with the label, but leave them to their own devices musically. Elektra suggested many candidates for the position, but none of these prospective handlers seemed to understand or appreciate Shoes' democratic dynamic: each, for instance, tried to suss out which Shoe was the leader of the band—not understanding that there wasn't one.

Shoes were relieved, then, when Dan Bourgoise announced, "I'd like to throw my hat in the ring for management." Though primarily a publisher, Bourgoise had been steering Del Shannon's career since 1975; plus, Shoes knew and trusted him. And Bourgoise liked Shoes. "The thing that impressed me," he says, "was that they had a lot of street smarts as far as who they were and where their career was headed." In his 1978 *Chicago Reader* interview, for example, Don McLeese had noted that Shoes were eyeing the big picture. "We would be as leery of someone coming up and saying, 'Here's a million dollars, go make an album,' as we would be of someone saying, 'Here's a thousand,'" Jeff told the writer. McLeese stated, "Shoes are in it for the long haul; they are planning on making pop music a career, and they are willing to wait for a backer who shares their confidence and their commitment." Bourgoise was unquestionably their man. That was one search ended: their publisher signed a management contract with Shoes the first week of May.

MEANWHILE, THE PRODUCER hunt continued. This decision would have to be finely calibrated; Shoes were studio rats, utterly fascinated by what technology allowed them to do with their music, and eager to get started on this new phase of their career. They were also cautious, preferring to find a producer who would help them refine and sharpen what they were already doing, not one who would overwhelm their sound with his own signature stamp. But Shoes weren't just a band now, they were an investment—and everyone invested in them had an opinion about what they ought to do next.

The band members often felt, during this period, that they were being wedged into a mold shaped by the conventional wisdom of the record business. As Bourgoise recounts:

> Once the label had Shoes, there was a lot of strong-arming; they were protecting their investment. Most people at labels didn't really

have a clue how to make a successful record, but they knew that if they paid a producer who had [a track record of] hits, that was the way to go. You get your big-name producer and sound your best.

In spite of themselves, Shoes were intrigued and thrilled by, if a little apprehensive of, this allegedly foolproof strategy. And Bourgoise remarks that it wasn't like Shoes were champing at the bit to get back to the dress shop, either. Indeed, he observes, "They were enamored of the idea of recording at a bigger studio and having a big budget. They reasoned that since *Black Vinyl Shoes* had sounded good, imagine what they could do in a studio! Use a big studio for big sound; that supposedly produces the big hits. And do it in a place that's competitive, with somebody competitive as producer." But Shoes still didn't know who should guide them through this process. Add to that the band's impatience just to get moving, and their tension levels continued to rise.

Throughout April and May, production candidates flew into Zion to meet with the band. As Gary stresses, Elektra was insisting on someone with a name. Jeff recalls meeting several such VIPs: Martin Rushent, a British producer who'd helmed discs for his countrymen, including glam-rock titans T. Rex and Baroque punk act the Stranglers; Keith Olsen, who'd produced Fleetwood Mac's self-titled 1975 megahit; Craig Leon, whose credits included iconic New York trailblazers Blondie, the Ramones, and Suicide; and even Barry Mraz, producer of arena rockers (and fellow Chicagoans) Styx.

The band also took phone meetings with other potential collaborators, including one memorable confab with veteran producer and rock eccentric Kim Fowley. "Get everyone together, because I'm only gonna say this once," Fowley proclaimed. In the ensuing discussion, Jeff recounts, Fowley expressed annoyance at Shoes' refusal to move to L.A. (which he strongly advocated), at their reclusive natures, and at their hesitance to cede control, calling the band members "the Greta Garbos of rock." Fowley didn't get a callback.

As time went on, the list of rejected candidates grew longer, and the options narrower: prospective producers' summer schedules were starting to fill up.

The final candidate Elektra sent to Zion was Mike Stone. The label knew him from his work with Queen—Stone had steered their biggest hit album to date, *News of the World*—but he had also been an engineer for super-producer Roy Thomas Baker, and thus was connected to the Cars—an important link that encouraged Shoes' advisors at Elektra.

Shoes liked Stone. He appeared to be mainly interested in engineering, rather than imposing his style on them, and he seemed to be pretty low-key personally, with a compatible sense of humor; they bonded over *Saturday Night Live* and Monty Python jokes. There were a few potential pitfalls to be cautious about—"We didn't want to go into Queen-land," John specifies, "and we didn't want the label to treat us like the poor man's Cars"—but by the time Stone left Zion, Shoes were confident enough that they could be themselves with him at the board.

Shoes' choice of Stone also helped determine their recording venue. He wanted to work at The Manor, a renowned studio owned by Virgin Records mogul Richard Branson, which was located in an historic hunting lodge in rural Oxfordshire, England. John recalls Stone (who passed away in 2003) telling them he liked it, because he had worked there before, with Queen; it was a familiar space for him, in his homeland. John thought Stone was also anxious to be near his wife: "I think he wanted a bit of a working vacation."

It might seem at first glance that for Shoes, The Manor itself, and the glamour of recording there, were the primary draws. "It was the rock-star thing to do," Dan Bourgoise explains. "It's very seductive, this kind of stuff: here's someone at Elektra, and they're saying, 'Do you guys want to go to a castle in England to record?'" It looks like you're getting the serious treatment—you're in the high echelon immediately."

But in actuality, band members say The Manor's main appeal was its isolation. "When this was described to us by Mike Stone as complete privacy," recalls Gary, "an ocean away from the record label—and even quite a distance from the Elektra people in London—we said, 'We're there; that's the place for us.'" John confirms, "We wanted to sequester ourselves and get it done."

In that sense, Shoes went across an ocean and moved into a foreign mansion to duplicate the privacy of their Midwestern dress-shop basement.

WITH THE PRODUCER AND RECORDING venue now decided, things moved quickly. The plan was to fly to California one last time, do a photo shoot for the album cover and make some final preparations, return to Zion, and then leave for England during the last week of June.

Shoes were scheduled to fly from Chicago to Los Angeles on May 25, 1979, the Friday afternoon before Memorial Day weekend. Candidly, they were looking forward not only to getting started on the record, but also to spending a couple of days on the California beach beforehand.

But on Thursday, May 24, Carol Thompson, the Elektra bean-counter who was just coming on as the band's A&R rep, figured out that the company would be paying for four unnecessary days of hotel rooms, since business would not resume until after the holiday weekend. Hastily, Elektra changed the band's departure from Friday to the following Tuesday, earning a fair amount of grumbling back in Zion.

The flight Shoes were supposed to take was American Airlines 191 from O'Hare to LAX. Writer David Young reported in the *Chicago Tribune* on May 26, 1979:

> As an American Airlines DC-10 jet roared into the sky over O'Hare International Airport on this Friday afternoon, its left engine fell off. Flight 191, bound for Los Angeles at the beginning of the Memorial Day weekend, rolled over in the air and plunged to the earth less than a mile from the runway. The plane "burst into a pillar of flame and smoke that could be seen up to eight miles away," the Tribune reported. ...
>
> All 271 people on board and two people on the ground were killed. ... The death toll could have been higher, but the plane just missed hitting a trailer park north of the airport.

"We read later that the DC-10, which had been unknowingly damaged in January, had been used as the regular afternoon plane between Chicago and L.A. on a daily basis," Gary says soberly. "That means we were probably on that same piece of equipment at least twice before it crashed."

The band members were deeply shaken by their close call. "It was hard to take in," John reflects. "It's still hard to take in. I have many times imagined that moment, what it must have been like on that plane."

A significant number of people didn't realize that the band *hadn't* been on that plane. As Jeff recounts:

> The New York office of Elektra was unaware that our schedule had been changed and thought we were among the casualties on Flight 191. So the phones started ringing, and we spent Friday calling friends and relatives and explaining that we were okay and we would be flying out on Tuesday.

For Shoes, it is still difficult to process the fact that "we had been so close to being on that plane," Gary says. "It came down to one person, one phone call." "Even now," says John, "we don't like to talk about it."

At the time, try as they might, Shoes couldn't help but see the near-miss as a harbinger of their fate. (They weren't alone: Jeff remembers that "Elektra interpreted this close call as just another sign that Shoes were destined for greatness.") "Subconsciously," says Gary, "I think we all thought our survival was part of the plan, something that was meant to be."

"We never took it lightly," John emphasizes, "but we pressed on."

ON TUESDAY, MAY 29, SHOES flew to Los Angeles to finalize preparations for their record, and begin the publicity process. This included taking part in two photo shoots: one for publicity pictures, and one for the cover of the freshly-baptized *Present Tense*. The album's title—repurposed from an unused song title of John's—was chosen to indicate that the band, semi-famous for something they'd done nearly two years earlier, had started afresh. "We wanted people to see us in the present," John explains.

At the cover's photo session, shot by photographer Elliot Gilbert and overseen by Elektra art director Ron Coro, each band member had his picture taken separately. They enthusiastically supported this decision: no one knew better than Shoes themselves how tough it was to get a good picture of the four of them together. The block color-removal process utilized in the finished product was first described to them; it sounded kind of interesting, so they agreed to it. For the front cover, Shoes were told to look tense, fixed; on the back, like they were in motion.

There was a second photo shoot as well, this one with Randee St. Nicholas. A former fashion model, she was now a hot rock photographer, the artful eye behind the Beatlesque cover of just-being-released blockbuster *Get the Knack*. Shoes arrived at her studio and prepped for the shoot, but they were so uptight, Skip notes in his journal, that St. Nicholas first plied them with vodka to loosen them up.

Shoes also met again with Mike Stone in L.A., and finalized plans for England.

Then they went home to pack up equipment and wait. Shoes were bringing as little gear as possible—just their instruments, including a new set of drums they'd purchased for Skip. They left behind their array of effects and production equipment, eager to avail themselves of a professional studio's arsenal—which Shoes were sure would be better than anything they owned.

They departed Chicago in late June. Preflight at O'Hare Airport, Shoes were shown mockups of the *Present Tense* cover—and were dismayed at the results. "None of us were crazy about our individual shots," John remembers. Art Director Ron Coro had hyped them up on the stylized cover concept that purported to depict Shoes in "the present tense," but they didn't perceive that result. "It just looked, well, normal," John says. "I think we expected it to be blurred, to indicate motion or something, but it wasn't." And the "block color removal" process that had been touted so highly "*sounded* much cooler than it turned out," in Jeff's view. But it was too late now to do anything about it, so Shoes shelved their objections.

UPON THEIR ARRIVAL in London, the band had a full week of free time scheduled. It was designed partly to let Shoes adjust to the six-hour time change, but it also gave them the opportunity to be tourists, to give a few interviews, and to meet the staff of the London Elektra office. The planned scheduling gap turned out to be not just helpful, but necessary: once on the ground, Shoes were distressed to learn that, because they had not submitted a full manifest listing all their gear before they left Chicago, their instruments were hung up in British Customs. "We almost didn't get [the instruments into the country] at all," Skip journaled. Fortunately, the snafu was cleared up within a week (the length of free time they'd been scheduled to spend in London anyway). But Shoes already had the jitters, and the uncertain fate of their instruments hadn't helped calm their nerves.

It was during this week that, browsing in a London record store, they were stunned to come across a copy of *Black Vinyl Shoes* with the Jem/PVC artwork (a band picture, rather than John's ink drawing)—but sporting a Sire Records imprint. Says Jeff, "Only two parties had access to the masters: us and Marty Scott. And we knew *we* hadn't authorized a Sire version." He bought a copy, having no idea how this had transpired.

Elektra had booked Shoes into a stodgy, old-world-British hotel near Trafalgar Square called the Royal Horseguards. "It had probably been pretty swanky in the 1940s or '50s, but by the time we were there, it was kind of old-fashioned," John recalls. Jeff concurs: "The Royal Horseguards was small and dingy-feeling."

They coped with the mustiness, says Jeff, by getting out of their hotel as much as possible, despite the traditionally gray, sodden weather. "Hey, it was London, England! We were jazzed!" John was struck again by the sense that this whole experience was real and surreal at the same time: "This was our new life. *Everything* was different."

One moment that brought that fact home, John recounts with a self-deprecating laugh, was when he walked out into Trafalgar Square on the fourth of July—and wondered briefly why there didn't seem to be any recognition of the holiday. "Oh, *right*," he reminded himself.

Later that day, Shoes left for Oxfordshire. It was an infrequent sunny afternoon, and they rode the hour and a half or so in a chauffeur-driven Bentley through the bucolic British countryside, quaffing ale and marveling at the change in their fortunes. "It was truly like a dream," Gary says, "on every level imaginable."

As they drove alfresco, however, Gary became aware that his throat and sinuses were swelling up; he was "coming down with the worst cold of my life," at the one time he couldn't afford to. "I thought, holy shit, I'm in trouble here," he says. Everyone except John caught the cold, but Gary's was worst, and hung on longest. The scratch vocal tracks he recorded at the beginning of the sessions were literally scratchy: Gary could scarcely talk.

But The Manor itself was sublime. Strolling around the property just after their arrival, John recalls stripping off his shirt in the sunshine. They surveyed the grounds—tennis courts, basketball hoop, go-kart track, and two swimming pools. Rounding one corner, they spotted a beautiful, bikini-clad young Anglo-Indian woman luxuriating on the lawn, and Jeff remembers thinking, "We're gonna like this place!" The sunbather was a Manor employee; part of the studio's appeal—for Shoes as for a lot of other bands—was that it was staffed almost exclusively by attractive young females.

Inside the manor house itself, they were undeniably impressed by its air of historic elegance, even though they couldn't ignore the difference in scale. Shoes are a tall band—their average height well over six feet—and they didn't exactly *fit* in the sixteenth-century building. Gary remembers always having to duck to get through doorways.

The house was brimming with curiosities: an eight-foot model ship their globetrotting landlord Branson had picked up in some exotic locale; an enormous dining table crafted from a massive oak tree, halved; tapestries, including one with The Manor depicted as Heaven; and a multitude of paintings. Says Gary, "It was like being in a museum; we were awestruck by it." "That place was *nice*," says Skip.

Mike Stone, who was familiar with The Manor's layout, had already laid claim to the biggest and most posh bedroom. The others quickly called dibs on their own digs, says John, leaving Shoes' bassist as the last to choose, but he landed the most exclusive bedchamber of all. Isolated at the far end of the hall, facing the pool, it was the same one Mick Jagger had used when he came to visit his songbird paramour Marianne Faithfull.

Recording, Jeff notes, was delayed by one more day: since Shoes had arrived hot on the heels of Public Image, Ltd. (who were making their second album, *Metal Box*); John Lydon's characteristically expectorant vocals had left some of the mics clogged with spit, and "they had to be disassembled, cleaned, and disinfected" before Shoes could use them. They killed time by experimenting with acoustics in different rooms of The Manor, since the entire complex, from studio proper to each room in the house, was wired for sound.

Sessions finally began late that evening, though as Skip records in his journal, not much got done that first day. "We'll give it hell tomorrow," he assures himself. And indeed, the next several weeks were focused and intense.

AFTER ALL THE NEGOTIATION AND struggling to set their own direction, when the moment came, Shoes largely put themselves in Mike Stone's hands, deferring to his musical judgment almost entirely. They were ready, as John put it, "to do what the big boys—the professionals—do."

It wasn't the way they had worked before; in every other project, the writing and recording were parallel endeavors. But now, Shoes were working from completed demos. "We knew those songs like the back of our hands," Gary says. "We could have cut them live [i.e., played them straight through, as though on stage], if we'd had to."

But what the "big boys" did was like neither live performance nor Shoes' usual process. Professional recording artists, it turned out, broke songs down into their constituent instrumental parts, and recorded one instrument at a time, playing each song on an album project start to finish.

Stone got them started by doing the drum tracks. Skip was set up in the game room of the main house rather than the studio itself, which was located in a separate wing. The game room was cavernous and acoustically "live," a good drum space. Skip wasn't recording alone; he had John playing with him and usually one of the others as well.

The early rhythm tracks went "pretty smoothly until we came to [Gary's percussive bump-and-grind] 'I Don't Miss You,'" Jeff relates. Skip himself terms these sessions "disastrous": "The timing was all off—after one whole day of working on it, we had to scrap it. And the next day it was the same thing."

Shoes' problem was the lack of one small commercial effect—which they'd purposely left back in Zion so they wouldn't look like rookies. Jeff and Gary elaborate: "For the original demo, we relied heavily on our Roland RE-201 Space Echo," Jeff says, "which we recorded along with the drums to provide a very crucial, rhythmic slap-back echo to the drum track." But the Space Echo had stayed behind—because, according to Gary, the effect "wasn't considered professional. It was more of an ordinary consumer kind of thing, something a bar band would use when playing live." But without the visceral sense of the slap-echo, Gary says, "Skip couldn't feel the pace as he was playing—which was the problem." It took two extra days to get the complete drum track for "I Don't Miss You" on tape.

It was an important lesson for Shoes: sometimes their own cheap gear could provide something that a gleaming professional studio couldn't.

But this was no time to ruminate on lessons learned; Shoes needed this track. In order to compensate for the missing rhythmic cues, Skip and John would have to play to a virtual beat, leaving room for the studio to insert a specialized echo effect during post-production. In later years, the use of a click track (a metronome beat fed through a drummer's headphones) would become common during recording sessions—but not in the seventies. "Using click tracks was a relatively new (and controversial) approach at the time," says Jeff. "There was a rudimentary timer built into the console, as I recall, but it only made this sharp, annoying clicking sound." Jeff continues:

> One of the girls from the staff was sent into town to the local music store to buy [an actual] metronome. Its [more manageable electronic tone] was then pumped at tremendously amplified volume

to Skip and John's headphones so they could stay on the beat. It took several hours to get a solid drum track, and John and Skip were pleading for mercy at the end of every attempt, due to the mammoth headaches that they both developed from that metronome in their ears.

Even with all that effort, the finished album is paced differently from the demo version: slightly slower, with a thicker, bassier drum sound.

SHOES BEGAN RECORDING *Present Tense* on July 5, and after four days had four drum tracks finished. By July 12, Skip's task was complete. The others would not finish until August 5, three and a half weeks later; granted, this was fast work, but not fast enough to allay Skip's tedium.

Since Skip didn't play guitars or sing, and wasn't involved in the technology of recording, he had a lot more free time than did the other band members, aggravating an already-existing three-versus-one dynamic (one that would eventually have serious repercussions). Back in Zion, Skip had seen this as a plus: he'd come in when he was needed and go home when he was done, to work on his cars or hang out with his friends.

Here in England, though, he was stuck for the duration. While his bandmates were continuing their work in the studio, Skip was just sitting around. His journal was now filled with the minutiae of marking time—backgammon with John, tennis with Jeff (scores are fastidiously recorded), swimming, going drinking with the brother of one of the Manor maids. One morning after a well-fueled night, bleary with hangover, Skip bumped the light over his bedroom sink. It fell out of the wall, and in lunging to grab it, Skip dislocated his shoulder.

In one memorable passage (July 14, the same day he dislocated his shoulder), he complains that recording of guitars has started, absorbing everyone else's attention and making Skip's search for a tennis opponent that much more difficult:

> Nobody plays around here. So I played against myself and won. Now I'm challenging myself to a game of backgammon. I'll probably lose. The hardest part for me is coming up, and that is trying to keep myself busy.

Skip's boredom was alleviated somewhat when it turned out that he needed to redo two songs—"Now and Then" and the persistently troublesome "I Don't Miss You." In his journal, the drummer writes, "They could hear a slight variation in the drum beat. ... I hope my bum shoulder holds out." "Now and Then" came together quickly—though Gary maintains, "I can still hear the slight timing variation at the beginning of the song"—yet Skip still couldn't nail "I Don't Miss You." He says they talked seriously about cutting the song from *Present Tense* altogether, but then Stone came up with a save: "I got off the hook. They ended up splicing [a serviceable] outtake to the beginning of the song."

STILL, WHILE STONE WAS supremely capable in a technical sense, Shoes increasingly got the feeling that, as John puts it, "he just wasn't a fan of our music. I don't think he understood quite what we were going for."

One bone of contention was the demos.

Shoes had labored over these demos. Like many of their peers, they couldn't read or write musical notation, so they didn't have paper scores of the songs. Instead, Shoes used the demos as the models for their studio creation. It had taken nearly a year to record these templates that the band had thought would be used as a constant reference in the studio.

Stone, however, was uninterested in the tapes. "Mike didn't want to listen to our demos," says Gary. "He saw them as being inherently inferior."

The band members recall Stone as visibly annoyed and impatient when, for their own reference, they played the tapes in the studio. "It was necessary for us to remember parts and illustrate the effects we were going for," says Jeff. "But I think it just really bored Mike." Shoes did what they had to do, "but we knew he wasn't happy."

Stone's utter disregard of Shoes' demos highlights a troubling aspect of the band dynamic in this period. Throughout their tenure at Elektra, they were far more willing to blame themselves if something seemed out of place than to identify a problem with the system. Any qualms they had *must* be due to their own ignorance, they generally assumed. In this particular case, the big producer in the big studio was telling them that their own work was insufficient, and of course they believed him.

ONCE THE RHYTHM TRACKS were done, guitar tracks started: an arduous process. "There's one drum track, and one bass," says Gary "but there are all sorts of guitar tracks to be done: electric, acoustic, leads, rhythms, more leads, fills." The meticulous layering of the guitars gives Shoes' records their distinctive sound, but it's inarguably time-consuming, typically locking the three guitar-playing Shoes in the studio for weeks.

Jeff's memoir of *Present Tense*'s recording process is filled with specifics of chasing down certain guitar sounds. For example, in order to capture the guitar solos for his fed-up rave-up, "I Don't Wanna Hear It":

> We set up a 1x12" Boogie amp in a small bathroom under the stairs in the main house. We wanted a reflective room so the guitar would echo and sustain. Because the bathroom was very small and there wasn't much space, we positioned the amp on top of the toilet and I sat on a small chair next to the amp and proceeded to record the guitar solos for the song. We wanted to record the guitar at the very brink of feeding back so the volume in that tiny bathroom was incredibly loud. I used the same set-up to record the guitar solo in "Cruel You."

John helped out with the guitar parts, but says his efforts just irritated Mike Stone. The first time Stone saw John playing an acoustic six-string, Stone queried bluntly, "Why are you doing that? You're not the guitarist." John was surprised, never having considered himself as solely a bassist; he always played a regular guitar too, especially on his own songs. But Stone "liked to keep everyone in their stalls," says John. Eventually, he got Stone to let him play guitar on several songs—"Every Girl," "Your Very Eyes," "Somebody

Has What I Had," and "Three Times"—which he considers something of a victory.

And Stone was impatient with Shoes' attempts to monitor the production and mixing process, once the recording of *Present Tense*'s planned thirteen tracks was complete. At The Manor, he was relatively indulgent of their hovering over the board, but when they moved operations to London for mixing, the tension ramped up. "In the mixing phase, we got pretty adamant about what we wanted," says Jeff. At issue was drum sound, a recurring Shoes obsession: "I remember Mike saying, 'Listen, there's *one way* to mix drums and *this* is it!' We disagreed, pushing for a sharper, cleaner snare-drum sound."

One more source of discord with their producer was Shoes' lack of formal musical training. Certainly, in comparison to Stone's previous clients, Queen in particular, Shoes were green in that respect. "He'd been used to dealing with the operatic [lead singer Freddie] Mercury, with the technician [guitarist Brian] May," John explains. "We threw him for a loop." At one point, Stone suggested that Shoes change the key of a song, something none of them knew how to do. "We replied, 'Uh, what?'" John laughs. On the other hand, Shoes harbored concerns that Stone's Queen-honed production style was overly bombastic, that he was missing some of the subtleties of what they were trying to capture.

Still, working with Mike Stone was a worthwhile experience, and Shoes learned much in the process. One striking development was the way Stone transformed their vocals. Prior to *Present Tense*, Shoes didn't think of themselves as a band of vocalists, being modest, even self-deprecating, about their singing skills; all agree their voices are too weak, too light. To remedy this, Shoes had learned on their own to punch them up some, through multi-tracking. "But this," says Gary, "was different." Stone "multed the hell out of us," says John, and showed Shoes what serious stacking of vocals could accomplish.

Stone's vocal-stacking process was awe-inspiring to them from the first time they employed it. John recalls that during the recording of Gary's haunting, indelible rocker "Too Late," which would become the first single off *Present*

Tense, Stone suggested that there was room for a bigger chorus. As John relates:

> Mike had us sing the chorus all in unison. "Do it again," he said. "Again." And every time, he would go and talk with Marlys [Duncklau, the tape operator], and come back. "Again." "Again." Finally, he said, "Not bad!" That was high praise coming from him. He called us into the control room to hear it—and we were blown away.

Three voices had become six, twelve, twenty-four. "Too Late" was a revelation, and it is probably no overstatement to say that Stone thus redefined Shoes' sound and their self-conception. As Jeff says, "We became known for our backing vocal harmonies. We'd thought we were a guitar band, but the label started to refer to us as a vocal band."

During the mixing process, Stone taught Shoes another trick. "Too Late" was shaping up to be one of *Present Tense*'s stellar tracks—"That one really kind of snuck up on us," Jeff says. But Stone thought its ending was kind of abrupt. Wouldn't it be cool, he proposed, to repeat the chorus once more before the coda? Well, sure, the band said. But left with only limited time to do overdubs, how were they to re-record the instruments and multi-track the vocals to match? No problem, Stone assured them, copying the final chorus and smoothly splicing it in, pre-coda, as though it had always been there. Shoes were awed. "It seems silly now," Gary says, "but splicing like that had honestly never occurred to us."

LIFE AT THE MANOR WAS conducted on a completely different scale from what the band members were used to in their apartments back in Zion. With its on-site lodging, The Manor was designed to free up recording artists to focus on their work when they wanted to work—and when they needed to relax, opportunities for leisure activities were everywhere. The studio was available twenty-four hours a day, requests for wake-up times and breakfast needed merely to be jotted down on a chalkboard to be fulfilled, and the resident Cordon Bleu chef prepared a lavish dinner nightly.

For Shoes, this last point was a particular plus. "Our band is so into food," Gary admits. "To some bands it probably wouldn't have made any difference that they had this great chef there, but for us it was a big deal." Jeff agrees wholeheartedly, weaving tales of Japanese meals with five kinds of seaweed, and the wonders of crème caramel. John waxes poetic about bacon and chutney sandwiches brought to the studio in mid-afternoon by girls on staff, regretting only that "you really didn't want to eat too much, because dinner was coming."

But aside from relishing the cuisine, studio rats Klebe and the Murphys weren't able to take advantage of all The Manor's amenities—though thanks to his lighter schedule, Skip took to playing tennis and riding the go-karts. (Jeff reports once watching Skip steer his kart into a patch of stinging nettles and then learn the miraculous healing power of aloe.) As for John, who spent more time in the studio than Skip but still marginally less than the gearheads, Jeff and Gary, he struck up a relationship with one of the girls on staff.

But mostly, Shoes' complete concentration on *Present Tense* precluded their getting caught up in the distractions of their surroundings. Dan Bourgoise, who visited The Manor during recording, describes them as "so focused on their music that they could have been on Pluto, and it wouldn't have made any difference."

To the extent that they did notice their surroundings, Bourgoise says, Shoes remained largely unspoiled by the lavish milieu; indeed, "they were able to see the humor in it." Once, Bourgoise remembers Gary leading him into the kitchen and throwing open a cabinet to reveal row upon row of the British cookies known as Jaffa Cakes, while Gary just smiled and shrugged at the extravagance of it all.

Jeff's greatest regret from this period, he says, is being unable to attend the July 18 birthday party for their landlord, Richard Branson. "We were on a time crunch because we had already booked time to do the mixing at Trident Studios," he says, "and Gary and I had more guitar work to do." Gary elaborates:

That's how Jeff and I missed Richard Branson's party. We would keep a close eye on the production part of it, so even when we weren't engineering ourselves, we'd say, "Add a little more bite to it," "Let's compress that or add a little more flange to it," or something like that. We were much more locked in the studio.

By all accounts, Jeff and Gary missed quite a bash.

The guitarists encouraged John and Skip to attend, though, which they did, accompanied by two of the Manor maids. Branson's small group of merrymakers sailed along the canals of London, on a low barge, that was "like a houseboat," according to John.

Onboard, bottles of wine were plentiful, but when they found that corkscrews weren't, the guests improvised. Skip explains that there was a not entirely sober rumor going around that, if you banged the bottom of a wine bottle on the edge of the boat, pressure would force the cork out. He claims he saw a fellow guest do it, and was convinced that he could, too, if he tried. Enthusiastically, Skip tried.

In good shape from drumming, Skip put considerable muscle into his attempt to expel the cork. It was not, however, the first bottle he'd helped the revelers consume, and he may have used a tad more force than necessary; in any case, Skip lost his balance, tumbling backward into the foul water of the canal. John, who'd been looking the other direction when he heard the splash, turned to share a man-overboard laugh with his bandmate—and instead, saw it was Skip himself who'd taken the plunge.

"There he was," John recounts, "fully dressed, dog-paddling toward the quay wall. He had trouble climbing it because it was so slimy, but eventually he got up there." At John's behest, the boat turned back to fetch its lost passenger in the gathering gloom. Skip leaned as far out toward the boat as he could, preparing to jump from quay wall to deck, when the fence he was clutching gave way and he fell into the water again. To the riotous laughter of his fellow partygoers, Skip finally managed to clamber back on the boat, wrapping himself in a blanket someone had located. (Skip was not, incidentally, the only landlubber in the drink at Branson's floating fête, as he took pains to point out in his journal: "Three other people fell in when the boat docked.") The next day's music press, Jeff recalls with a laugh, featured a news item about Branson trying to kill Shoes' drummer. Twice.)

The party continued with Skip back aboard, and by the end of the night, John was the only one in any shape at all to convey them back to The Manor. And, as Jeff notes:

> John taking the wheel meant that something weird had happened. John doesn't have the greatest eyesight, so for him to drive at night, for over an hour, on unlit country roads, in a foreign country, on the opposite side of the road, in a car with a stick shift and the steering wheel on the opposite side, in the wee hours of the morning, after having partied with Richard Branson and his guests, was an incredible accomplishment.

John shrugs, "I was the least drunk."

Another time, Shoes took a night off with Stone and spent it in London, visiting various private clubs. At one, John recalls, they met the widow of Marc Bolan, the late, legendary lead singer of T. Rex. (Skip journaled that the club "had some nice women, but it was filled with puffs"—presumably "poofs," British slang for homosexuals.) And they all remember sleeping on the floor of Stone's flat, with a recent Miss Europe traipsing around in her nightie.

Still, evenings out like these were relatively rare; Shoes were unaware of most of what went on in the world that summer. And one major event that they missed was the birth and death of the movement that came to define them: power pop.

OVER THE FIRST HALF OF 1979, disco had dominated the American charts, with acts such as the repurposed Bee Gees and Rod Stewart (both having been rock hitmakers in the sixties and seventies), Chic, Gloria Gaynor, Donna Summer, and Amii Stewart taking turns holding the number-one chart position.

Even when new-wave stalwart Blondie topped the charts briefly, as April led to May, it was with a single that throbbed to the unmistakable disco beat: "Heart of Glass." On June 28, the day Shoes had left for England, Donna Summer's "Hot Stuff" was ceding position to Amii Stewart's "Ring My Bell." Thus, it seemed to Shoes that disco was what they had to battle.

But tastes were changing. In the summer of 1979, with Shoes ensconced in idyllic isolation at The Manor, a new song was climbing the charts—not quickly, but inexorably—and it would change the math completely: the Knack's lascivious, riff-driven "My Sharona."

There's a somewhat bitter irony in the way Shoes discovered the Knack. As Jeff writes in his memoir, at the end of the *Present Tense* sessions and as a prelude to their playback party, Stone invited the band and some of the Manor staff to a celebratory dinner at a London restaurant called the Opium Den.

It was a long evening of drinking contests and debauchery. As Jeff relates, "Many bottles of warm sake were consumed and we must have been getting loud, because the restaurant staff ended up putting up partitions to wall off our little corner of the dining area." Things *were* getting a bit out of hand, at least for a public place: breasts were being exposed, people were hooking up.

And Jeff remembers this being "the first time we heard the Knack's 'My Sharona.'" "The restaurant only had one record," Gary says, "one rock record, I mean. They played it over and over and over." "And everyone bounced around to the new American single," says Jeff. He didn't fare too well in the drinking contests, passing out once they got back to The Manor and sleeping through the *Present Tense* playback party; Jeff heard more Knack that evening than Shoes.

MUCH INK HAS BEEN spilled excoriating the Knack for their role in what is often seen as the too-fast rise of power pop, and its attendant precipitous decline. Pop historian Carl Cafarelli, for example, observes in his essay "A History of Power Pop" in John Borack's 2007 volume *Shake Some Action*, that for many bands classed under the general umbrella of power pop, "their chances for retail success were mercilessly overshadowed by the blockbuster sales of ... the Knack." Other critics disparaged the L.A. band's attitude—all smirking and sneering and refusing to grant interviews—keyed by the overweening arrogance of lead singer Doug Fieger. In the 2004 film documentary *Getting the Knack*, critic David Wild states, "Something about this band exploding that big, and seeming to take it only half-seriously, rubbed people the wrong way."

Fieger (who died of cancer in 2010) once insisted that "if the Knack hadn't hit big, if *Get the Knack* had sold only as many units as, say, [Big Star's critically lauded but commercially inert] *Radio City*, they would have been revered today as a visionary cult act." Possibly, but that isn't what happened, and by the end of the summer of 1979, critics and listeners alike were decidedly weary of the Knack Attack.

Capitol hadn't expected *Get the Knack* to be a monster record; Fieger recalled in *Getting the Knack* being told by the label that "we'll be lucky if we sell 50,000 copies." Instead, *Get the Knack* blew through almost six million units in 1979, giving the Cars a run for their money. Capitol had even overlooked the obvious single; nothing was chosen until several weeks after the album came out, when it became clear that "My Sharona" was the song deejays were gravitating toward.

As Wild says in the documentary, "The Knack went from zero to ninety and basically became a car wreck very, very quickly. And I think it was mostly because of the media. We went from 'Gotta hear the Knack!' to 'Get the fuck outta here, Knack!'" San Francisco visual artist David Hughes launched a "Knuke the Knack" campaign that amused Fieger and company (until they issued a cease-and-desist order), but the backlash—or, in the ubiquitous pun-laden jargon of the day, the Knacklash—was much larger than that.

HAVING LEFT AMERICA IN JUNE and spent the summer closeted away from the world, Shoes had been blissfully unaware of the sheer, steamrolling dominance of *Get the Knack*. When Elektra signed Shoes, they were looking for the next Cars, but by the time *Present Tense* was released a scant three months later, the Knack was the new standard. And as radio would make painfully apparent, Shoes were not the Knack.

There were material differences in the way both groups worked, which may have had some effect on the way their respective 1979 albums were received. The Knack essentially recorded live; they used very few overdubs and thus were able to get their debut record done in eleven days, for less than $20,000. That was the cost of a week and a half at the Manor. In the long run, timing was probably more important than cost, however. By the time *Present Tense* was released in the United States at the beginning of September, it was seen as being of a piece with what the Knack were doing—and amid the ferocity of the Knack backlash that fall, that would prove a serious handicap.

BUT THAT REALIZATION WAS STILL a month away at the beginning of August, when Shoes returned to London for mixing. They stayed at the Townhouse, another residence and studio owned by Virgin, and mixed at the venerable Trident Studios. Also staying at the Townhouse were British mod-rockers the Jam, working on what would become their 1979 album *Setting Sons*. According to Jeff, both bands developed a friendly rivalry over the new video game Space Invaders.

Soon after mixing began, bad news came from America: Gary's dad was facing life-threatening surgery for pancreatitis. Though it was an acute attack and came as a complete surprise to Gary, it was not really news to either of his parents; Jerry Klebe hadn't really been well for a while. "They concealed it from me," Gary says now. The Klebes had discussed visiting England during the *Present Tense* sessions, but his father's ill health prevented that. And now the illness had become critical, very quickly. Gary's songs were moved up to be mixed first, and he caught the earliest possible flight home to be at his father's bedside.

The elder Klebe weathered the surgery, but not well. "We still thought we were going to lose him," Gary says. Doctors hastily deployed different medications in an attempt to save him, and finally managed to stabilize Gary's father with the steroid Prednisone. It worked, to a point: Jerry Klebe lived, but he faced a long recuperation, and, according to Gary, he was "never really the same after that."

Away from England, apart from his colleagues, embroiled in this family crisis, Gary listened to the mixes of his songs over and over, and came to a decision. "Jet Set," one of his harder-edged songs, just didn't fit with the rest of *Present Tense*. Gary called England to tell them to drop it from the track list.

Surprised, John and Jeff attempted to convince him to include "Jet Set," as planned. It may be, Gary admits now, that that's what he was really looking for: reassurance from his bandmates that the song was good enough. "And I probably could have been talked into it," he says.

But as the phone was passed around the control room at Trident to discuss the status of "Jet Set," it came in turn to Mike Stone, who listened to Gary's panicked arguments about why the song should go. "I know what you mean," Stone affirmed, and that was the end of the debate; if a professional agreed that it didn't belong, it didn't belong. "Jet Set" would not see the light of day for another seventeen years, on Shoes' outtakes and rarities compilation *As Is*.

Mixing *Present Tense* was completed on August 22, and Jeff and Skip were anxious to get home to their sweethearts. But John was still seeing the girl from The Manor, and so all three of them headed back to Oxfordshire for one more night. Jeff and Skip left the next day, but John stayed on as long as possible, wringing every precious hour out of his sixty-day work permit.

When John got to the London airport, he checked his luggage, and then somehow missed the boarding call for his flight to Chicago. Sometime later he casually inquired when it was due to depart, only to be told it was long gone. In a panic, John demanded to know how he could get back to the States, and ended up dashing through the airport to catch a flight to Boston, with no time to call anyone at home.

Back in Chicago, Jeff waited patiently at O'Hare for his brother to deplane, still shaken by his own homecoming: he had returned to find himself unceremoniously dumped by his girlfriend of five years.

But John hadn't gotten off the plane, a distracted Jeff finally realized. He checked baggage claim; John's suitcases had arrived, and were still circling the carousel, but there was no sign of his brother. Jeff hung out long enough to merit a parking ticket, but he had no way of knowing John had taken the connecting flight from Boston.

When John finally arrived in Chicago, he was closer to home, but now stuck at the airport. He made a flurry of calls; no one answered. Finally, in desperation, John phoned his landlord, their old *Lime* friend and sound guy, Joe Higgins. By pure coincidence, the call caught Gary, who'd stopped by Higgins' place to see John, having assumed he was already back in Zion. Gary immediately set off for O'Hare to retrieve his exhausted bandmate.

A week or so later, Shoes made a hasty one-day trip to New York City for mastering. After an improbably lengthy taxi ride from the airport to the West Village ("We got played," by the cab driver, Jeff says), they met Mike Stone and George Marino, the mastering engineer, at Sterling Sound. In one long, intense day, they mastered all twelve songs, flying back to Chicago that same evening. *Present Tense* was done.

IN THEIR PAST, WHEN SHOES had finished their home recordings—all of them—they'd had a moment to consider the final product before thinking about who should hear it. But they were about to learn a hard lesson: the professional music business didn't work that way at all. It was driven by deadlines and motivations that had nothing at all to do with the process of making music.

Present Tense was advertised, that September, as a "rush release," though no one in Shoes is sure what drove the frantic pace—Buttice's excitement? An attempt to qualify for a 1980 Grammy award? But for whatever reason, after that summer of intense work, *Present Tense* hit the streets almost as soon as it was finished: the test pressing is dated August 31, 1979—two days *after* its official release date.

Chapter 6

When It Hits

1979-80

KEN BUTTICE, THEY HEARD, LOVED *Present Tense*. He locked himself in his office and listened to the masters over and over and over. "I don't know what he thought he heard," John says self-effacingly, "but obviously it was something." When Shoes did finally head out to L.A. to see Buttice in September, the Elektra executive was effusive, telling Skip Meyer, "Listen to that! These songs are gonna make a star out of you, kid!"

But what he didn't hear, apparently, was a single, because Elektra released the record the first week of September without a seven-inch, without even designating a particular track to push on radio. Elektra promo man Marty Schwartz recalls, "We had a hard time coming up with a single. There was no clear-cut consensus song. The songs on *Present Tense* were more about a feel and a vibe, not about the Top Forty." Valuable promotional time was lost casting about for The One.

According to Dan Bourgoise, Buttice was only interested in marketing Shoes "as a hit singles band." It wasn't an inevitable designation: in the late 1970s, bands frequently would release an album without a single and let the program directors and deejays of AOR (album-oriented rock) stations decide which song they thought deserved the most airplay. Such an approach had served artists like Fleetwood Mac well: with the greater freedom of FM radio and the relative autonomy of individual deejays, a band could theoretically have several songs being played by different stations and sell albums based on any one of those songs.

By definition, AOR stations were less constrained by label-designated singles, but that didn't mean they didn't focus on specific tracks; after all, a station could only air one song at a time. And waiting for an album to become a hit took longer than deciding on a single and pushing that.

Buttice didn't want to wait. He wanted a hit single off *Present Tense*.

As Elektra Records' VP of radio promotion, Buttice gauged success by radio play. Given that orientation, the choice of the single ought to have been a matter for serious thought by everyone involved—by the band, by their management, by A&R. Shoes had asked Mike Stone what he thought the single should be: "He came back with 'Somebody Has What I Had,' which really surprised me," John, the song's ever-modest composer, recalls.

Shoes themselves hesitated to choose a song, for two reasons. First, they didn't know how this new, big-league world worked. If there was a formula for success at this level, obviously the pros had it and Shoes didn't. Second, though the success of the band was obviously a group project—they would sink or swim together—no one wanted to come off like he was pushing himself forward as the leader of the band. A writer or singer suggesting his own song for the single would be a presumption of egotism none of them wanted to display.

But the crucial choice of *Present Tense*'s first single was not made by the band or their label. It doesn't even seem to have been made by radio program directors, though the input of PDs was becoming an increasingly common part of the selection process industry-wide. Instead, the single was chosen by Chicago radio listeners.

John tells of sitting in Gary's apartment with his bandmates early that fall, listening to afternoon-drive deejay Sky Daniels running a Shoes-based phone-in contest on WLUP-FM, Chicago's growing AOR tastemaker. Daniels was asking his listening audience to choose which of two tracks they wanted to hear in rotation on "The Loop."

The first two songs on side one were the contenders—"Tomorrow Night," sung by Jeff, and "Too Late," sung by Gary—and Daniels invited his callers to phone in their preference. "It was like a Battle of the Bands within the band," John recalls.

When the results were tabulated, with "Too Late" on top, "Jeff's jaw just dropped," says John. "I don't think he thought that's how it was going to end up." In fact, says John, the surprise was band-wide: because "Tomorrow Night" had already been road-tested via the Bomp! single, they were all confident about it. They'd designated it as side one, track one, a traditional placement for expected singles. "Too Late" had been more of a late bloomer, coming into its own only in the mixing room in London.

Soon after the WLUP listeners voted, Elektra contacted Shoes to say that "Too Late" would indeed be the first single. "Is that really how they made the decision?" John still wonders.

RADIO PROGRAM DIRECTORS OFTEN did have an influence on choosing singles during this period. Just a few months before the release of *Present Tense*, *Billboard* ran a story titled, "Labels Let Radio Pick Out Singles from LPs." In it, reporter Ed Harrison cites the growing—though by no means novel—trend of record companies releasing an album without choosing a particular track to emphasize. "The decision to go with a consensus cut determined by radio programmers is happening more frequently and is found usually in the case of a new or not yet established artist," Harrison writes. He offers as an example Rickie Lee Jones's playful, jazz-flecked 1979 hit "Chuck E's in Love," the first single off her self-titled debut album, which was not released until a full seven weeks after the LP.

Harrison also interviews Ken Buttice, then still vice-president of promotion, who notes that Elektra's "single choices sometimes depend on radio and in other instances there is an obvious single that stands out without giving anyone a choice." Coming out of promotion, rather than A&R, Buttice obviously had faith in this particular method of finding the right song to launch an album, since it privileged program directors: his preferred population, the one he knew best.

But Harrison's article does not mention scenarios like the one Shoes experienced. A phone-in vote may have been strikingly democratic, but it handed this all-important decision down to an inarguably nonprofessional audience: not necessarily a bad thing, but hardly standard record-company practice.

BUTTICE'S INCLINATION TOWARD RADIO did pay off: *Present Tense* started getting airplay almost immediately. Skip noted in his journal entry of September 13 that WLUP was airing "Too Late." *Billboard* listed *Present Tense* as a national "most added" album for the week ending September 19, 1979, in all regions except the Southeast.

Now Elektra's promotion machine began cranking in earnest. Record retailers across the country received in-store display materials including Shoes posters, dummy album covers, banners, and life-sized orange footprint stickers designed to lead customers straight to the bin holding *Present Tense*. The West Coast record-retail chain Licorice Pizza ran a "Shoe Off" contest in which fans wore funny shoes to in-store band appearances; the funniest-shod contestant won Shoes flair, including custom shoehorns and enamel shoe pins and various other pieces of footwear-themed swag. In the lagging Southeast, *Billboard*'s "Talent Talk" column reported, "Elektra/Asylum sent retailers in the south pairs of old shoes without explanation as a way of breaking Shoes, a new act, in the area."

Marty Schwartz, Elektra's regional promotion director for New York, reflects on the label's largesse (apart from the "pairs of old shoes"): "Kenny signed the band and allowed me to spend a ton of money trying to break them." What was the money spent on? "Promotional tours, wining and dining program directors all over the country," Schwartz details. "Luxury travel to convince radio people that Shoes were the next big thing." Instead of touring, the band members flew out several times to the East Coast, where *Present Tense* was particularly strong, and a few times back to L.A. as well: making appearances in record stores, doing interviews, whatever Elektra asked.

In his memoir *Shoes: Birth of a Band*, Jeff reports that "the label kept us busy with in-person and phone interviews whenever we were available." He reprints a page of notes from one three-day period, November 26-28, during which a band member did a radio phoner literally every half-hour, every afternoon. They assigned responsibility democratically, of course, dividing the calls among the four of them: a total of twenty-six interviews in three days.

As the fall gathered momentum, independent promotion people—the new trend in the industry—were hired to work the single. "We would never have gotten that mention in *Billboard* if they hadn't," Bourgoise says. Schwartz confirms the use of independents, though he says "indies" were not employed to the extent that they later would be—because Elektra promo guys were exceedingly fond of doing everything themselves. "E/A was among the all-time great labels, but bad choices were made all the way around," says Schwartz. "We got caught up in a whirlwind of too much fun and *way* too much money to spend."

THE MONEY-IS-NO-OBJECT PROMOTION of *Present Tense* is a vivid illustration of the major shift that had occurred in the record industry in the 1970s. As Frederic Dannen observes in *Hit Men*, that decade marked a transition—from labels run by aficionados and even artists to labels run by deal makers and salesmen. Of course, those elements had always been present in the industry, but now, they came to the fore. "[D]uring the seventies, the deal maker became the principal driving force in the business," Dannen writes.

He continues: "A parallel event was the rise of the promotion man. The disco phenomenon lofted the promoter to new heights." Dannen's book goes on spotlight Neil Bogart's spectacularly decadent Casablanca Records, "the first label composed entirely of promotion people."

> Casablanca's unofficial motto, "Whatever It Takes," became the industry's rallying cry. The idea took hold that *selling* the product was just as important as—maybe more important than—the product itself. And it appeared to work for Casablanca and parent company PolyGram Records—but while Bogart's flamboyant label was conquering the charts with artists like cartoony metalmongers Kiss and disco royalty Donna Summer and the Village People, Casablanca was losing vast sums of money. Records may have been flying off retail shelves, but the expense of selling them—cash outlays for drugs, prostitutes, and promotional stunts negated any gains. "Whatever It Takes" was a recipe for profitless prosperity, and that is what the entire record business suffered in the end.

(The rise and fall of Bogart's profligate label is detailed in Larry Harris' 2009 memoir, *And Party Every Day: The Inside Story of Casablanca Records*.)

This promotion-driven business meant, too, that the *appearance* of popularity was at least as important as actual sales. Record companies shipped huge numbers of units to wholesale distributors regardless of whether there was actual demand for those records on the consumer end. The stratospheric sales spike of 1978, now obviously a statistical outlier, was interpreted in 1979 as the continuation of a promising trend—in fact, as the industry's new standard. For example, Dannen cites the case of RSO Records' soundtrack for the 1978 film *Sgt. Pepper's Lonely Hearts Club Band*, featuring some of the biggest stars of the day—Peter Frampton, the Bee Gees, Alice Cooper, Aerosmith, all interpreting beloved Beatles tunes—which shipped eight million units. The movie, however, was a resounding flop, five million unsold albums were returned to RSO, and countless others eventually found their way to the cutout bin. But since retailers had paid for the records up front, the huge initial shipment concealed subsequent soft sales, at least for a while. Most labels would accept returns in exchange for full credit toward another title—but as long as those two columns were kept separate, "shipping multiplatinum" stayed a viable marketing tool: it made underperforming records look like hits.

The major labels chronically over-shipped product during this period, even though they bore tremendous financial risk for their behavior; stores accepted the records, since they could just be sent back if they didn't sell. Dannen elaborates: "The record industry had never imposed limits on the number of records that stores could return. This meant, in effect, that retailers had no inventory risk. They could accept orders of any size, knowing they could return any unsold albums for full credit." But in 1979, as returns increased in the face of unexpected, industry-wide weak sales, labels started placing boundaries on these returns: limiting the time period during which returns would be accepted, or crediting only part of the retailer's initial investment. Record stores retaliated (and protected themselves) by ordering drastically fewer records than they had for the last several years. (Shoes would relive the same dynamic in the mid-nineties, when independent distribution suffered a similar—in their case, catastrophic—overreach-and-contraction period.)

"THE CRASH OF '79 WAS AT FIRST a retailing problem," Dannen writes. It rapidly accelerated into something else altogether.

In the 1986 book *Tarnished Gold: The Record Industry Revisited*, R. Serge Denisoff's sociological study of the music business in the 1970s and early 1980s, Denisoff pinpoints the moment of decline: "Beginning in the first fiscal quarter of 1979, sales plummeted. ... The objective fact was that the industry's growth was dropping a significant *eleven* percent per year."

Denisoff identifies 1979 as "a bust year." "For several decades, starting in 1955, the sales of the recorded product climbed steadily upward," he writes. "In 1979, 'The Great Disco Disaster,' as Robert Christgau termed it, reversed the trend." The industry had invested heavily in disco, and disco had crashed abruptly and spectacularly. Its fall left the industry reeling.

"The boom year, 1978, had produced 295 gold and platinum albums and 71 singles had fared as well," Denisoff chronicles. "By 1982, there was a forty-percent drop in these successful and prestigious albums. Only 24 singles went gold, the lowest yearly total since 1966." The traditionally recession-proof record industry was in a panic: "This period [was] fraught with contradictions, miscalculations, scapegoating, and corporate takeovers."

SOMETHING HAD TO BE BLAMED, and scapegoat candidates were abundant. Was it home cassette taping? Ken Buttice thought so; in a November 3, 1979 *Billboard* interview, he identified specifically the "Midnight LP" problem as a reason for soft sales: "[AOR stations airing full, uninterrupted albums at 12 a.m.] has been going on a while, but now radio stations are telling their listeners to gear up their tape machines. It's getting serious." Record sleeves featured a no-taping logo, and serious discussions about raising the cost of cassette recorders to dissuade piracy appeared in the music press.

Another possible culprit was videogame arcades, a relatively new phenomenon that had spread rapidly through the last half of the 1970s. (In 1974, one popular arcade chain, Aladdin's Castle, had twenty locations; by 1980, it boasted more than two hundred.) This explosion fundamentally changed the way adolescents spent their time and money—to the detriment of the music business, many believed.

The labels also blamed, to put it bluntly, the bands of the era. For half a decade, disco had been good to the industry financially, but when it crashed, the corporations that had backed it turned their eyes to the Next Big Thing—which in 1979 appeared to be power pop (sometimes known as "new wave").

However, with a few notable exceptions (such as the Mike Chapman-produced bands Blondie and the Knack), power pop failed to deliver the kinds of numbers the labels expected, indeed required, to meet the massive overhead they'd piled up during the disco era. The conventional wisdom of the industry then turned against the new bands, including Shoes. As Marty Schwartz says of the DIY foursome from Zion, Illinois, "They never connected at Top Forty radio. Everybody knew who they were, but it never turned into anything major. It was horribly disappointing to me, and the only time I would be proven wrong on something I personally believed in."

As it happened, Shoes actually made a respectable showing on radio, as evidenced by their quick "most added" designation nearly everywhere in America, but this did not translate into the Top Forty sales Elektra anticipated. In a November 10, 1979 *Billboard* article, "New Wave Wins Programming Okay," author Cary Darling notes that "new wave" was a new element on AOR radio. Darling writes:

> New wave rock, once solely associated with cult audiences in such media centers as New York, Los Angeles, San Francisco, and Boston, has become an integral part of the programming mix in radio markets outside those areas. ... A survey of 44 AOR stations, 11 in each region of the country, shows this new trend has entered into the mainstream of radio programming.

However, the article cautions, its incursion into radio didn't guarantee that corresponding records would sell. Darling interviews Tom Owens of KZWQ in Dallas, Texas, who says: "Sales don't tend to be outstanding on groups like the Beat, the [sic] Shoes, or the Pop, but radio reaction has been good." The reason for the discrepancy is not completely clear, though one likely culprit was a lack of distribution.

THE DIFFERENCE BETWEEN A MAJOR label and an independent is access to widespread distribution. When Shoes had released *Black Vinyl Shoes* through Jem, they had used Jem's network of many small regional distributors to get their record into stores. But a major label like Elektra did not have to cobble together a labyrinth of indie wholesalers for this purpose; they owned their own national distribution system—when it worked.

And in the case of *Present Tense*, there's some evidence that it didn't work particularly well. Though promotional copies of the album made it to radio stations—and onto their airwaves—promptly enough, *Present Tense* was often not available at retail outlets until several weeks later. Music fans could hear

Shoes' record on the radio and want to buy it, but couldn't do so if it wasn't for sale in their local record store.

Gary's younger brother Tim Klebe, a college student in downstate Carbondale, Illinois at the time, is one person who vividly recalls this gap between radio airplay and retail availability that fall:

> I would have skipped a few meals to purchase *Present Tense*, but the stores in town didn't have it yet. However, the radio station in town was playing it quite a bit, so I started calling the station and requesting they play the songs even more.

The point of radio play, of course, is to spur sales. But stores can't sell a product they don't have.

Theoretically, the promotion machine (the engine behind radio play) was only part of a complex mechanism of production and publicity that ensured a record would be available, get press exposure, and be heard on the radio at roughly the same time: promotion drove an existing product. But in Shoes' case, the system wasn't working quite the way it was designed to, because they were being shepherded by someone for whom radio promotion was the only element of the process that mattered—and so the promotion of *Present Tense* was way out ahead of everything else, including the availability of the record, and the press.

THAT SHEPHERD WAS KEN BUTTICE, the consummate promo guy. And even though Buttice had discovered Shoes, courted them, signed them, and guided them as if he were their A&R rep—"We really didn't work with anyone except Kenny," Gary affirms, "until much later"—he was still Elektra's vice-president of promotion. Technically, almost none of the A&R functions he performed fell under his label job description.

At Elektra, Buttice's radio-promotion skill conferred upon him an aura of success, and he surrounded himself with yes men—his own promo staff and loyalists in other departments, such as A&R's Carol Thompson. He carried himself like a winner, often getting what he wanted by sheer force of personality.

And Buttice wanted that transfer to A&R. A November 3, 1979 item in *Billboard*'s "Inside Track" column noted: "Scuttlebutt has it that Kenny Buttice, Elektra/Asylum's vice-president of promotion, may be shifted to a&r [sic]." The rumor's supporting evidence was laid out in the next sentence: "Buttice signed Shoes, which has a hot chart LP."

For their part, the band didn't quite understand the move Buttice was trying to make within Elektra; they just knew that he was always glad to see them and they genuinely liked him. "We loved hanging out with Kenny; Kenny was the king!" says John. They often sat in Buttice's office while he "held court"—calling various underlings into his office to discuss business matters in front of the band. They got an up-close look at his management style, which was colorful and bombastic: a good-natured bull in his own private china shop. As John puts it, "It was like hanging out with Tony Soprano."

Marty Schwartz, who worked closely with Buttice, describes him as "a street guy from Detroit, with really very little music sensibility. He was a good guy, but I never thought he had the acumen to be an A&R guy." Schwartz continues:

> [Buttice] just wasn't the right guy for the job, and his mentor, [then-president of Elektra] Steve Wax, was allowing him to run wild. Anybody at Elektra at that time in L.A. was running pretty wild. The boss just said, "Go make a hit record," and people did whatever they felt like.

And as long as there was that hit record at the other end, no one examined the process too closely.

It had become increasingly clear that Buttice had his eye on the label president's job, and just as clearly was using A&R as a stepping stone to get there; his rise at Elektra conformed to the general trend of the industry. Buttice was the new style of record executive: deal maker, salesman. And he wasn't waiting to transfer departments to do A&R's job for them.

But that meant that the more mundane aspects of selling records—the various threads of manufacturing and production and distribution—were less familiar to Buttice, and less control of these processes rested in his hands. If he wanted to rush the official release of *Present Tense,* the Elektra machine would do its best to make that happen—they'd fabricated a street date of August 29, though the test pressing of the record was still being tweaked on September 7, more than a week later—the company would get a few copies pressed up. But the creation of actual record albums for actual retail distribution was tied to laws of time, space, and distance that even Buttice could not bend. A certain number of units could be hustled out within a week or two—enough to stock radio stations nationwide—but not the hundreds of thousands needed for hit sales.

Shoes, never having been involved with an organization like Elektra, were largely ignorant of these logistics. The people they worked with, from Buttice to Carol Thompson to Bryn Bridenthal and her publicity department, treated them well; for their part, the band members were pleasant and unassuming, devoid of rock-star airs. "We liked the people at Elektra," John says. "And I think a lot of them liked us."

Billboard spotlighted Shoes' peculiar trajectory, seeing in it a new wave in the industry: in an October 26, 1979 article, "Shoes Typifying A&R, Promo Link," author Paul Grein states:

> The need for close communication between a&r [sic] and promotion departments is taken to its ultimate extreme in the case of Shoes, a four-man group from Zion, Ill, which was signed to Elektra/Asylum by its vice president of promotion, Kenny Buttice. … It is Buttice's first signing; all the other acts signed to Elektra since a&r [sic] director George Daly left the label earlier this year have been pacted by chairman Joe Smith or recently-departed president Steve Wax.

As long as they were at Elektra, Shoes were Kenny's band—and what Kenny said was gospel.

GENERALLY SPEAKING, BUTTICE'S predictions of Shoes' superstardom were good for the band, but he did encourage them to break some links with their past, not always wisely. For example, Shoes spent much of this period embroiled in a lawsuit with Jem, which was still distributing *Black Vinyl Shoes*.

Despite the fact that there was a direct link between Jem's licensing of *Black Vinyl Shoes* and the Elektra signing, Elektra was uncomfortable with the fact that Jem still had over three years left of legal rights to exploit *BVS*. The label did not want Jem benefitting from Elektra's promotion and publicity, selling the earlier album on the strength of the new one. Bomp! would employ the same strategy, re-releasing the "Tomorrow Night"/"Okay" single that fall. But in Jem's case, Elektra pushed Shoes to try and recover the rights to *Black Vinyl Shoes*. "Let's keep the catalogue together," they remember being told. In attorney Tom Leavens' words, "It was a strategy to clear the landscape for *Present Tense*." Elektra, Leavens stresses, "did not want something competing in the marketplace, causing confusion, boot-strapping on Elektra's promotion of *Present Tense*."

To be clear, there *were* genuine legal issues with Jem: the Sire imprint of *Black Vinyl Shoes* the band had inadvertently encountered during their London sojourn appeared to have been licensed by Jem without consulting (or paying) them: clearly a problem, with lawsuit potential.

Also, when Elektra's publicity department gathered material on the band for press kits, they talked to independent record-store owners and learned that *Black Vinyl Shoes* had actually sold well. Gary says label publicists spoke, for example, to "the head honcho at Bleecker Bob's"—ironically, the same Greenwich Village shop where Marty Schwartz had first heard Shoes over the store loudspeakers—who told Elektra that he had sold hundreds of copies. "And that was just one store," Gary points out. Indie rock legend-in-the-making Peter Jesperson, then the manager at Oar Folkjokeopus in Minneapolis, confirms that *Black Vinyl* moved off shelves with alacrity, both before and after the Jem release. "I remember opening boxes and boxes of them to restock," Jesperson says.

But Shoes realized that, as fast as things had been moving, they had never seen any kind of sales report from Jem at all, and thus had no idea how many copies of *Black Vinyl Shoes* had been sold, let alone whether they were due any royalties. When this was brought to Shoes' attention, according to Gary, they were stunned, and asked their manager and lawyers what to do. After seeking (and failing to secure) injunctive relief—mostly, just to force Jem to stop selling *Black Vinyl Shoes*—they went to court.

Shoes sued Jem—not for the unauthorized licensing (which they couldn't prove), nor for the failure to provide sales figures and royalties, which would have required a band-funded audit—but for the much more amorphous charge of "failure to advance" their careers. Marty Scott of Jem fought the lawsuit, calling it "a bizarre turn of events," since, demonstrably, the Jem release of *Black Vinyl Shoes* had advanced their careers significantly. "There were colorful claims," attorney Tom Leavens admits. "It was not a strong suit."

"We were naïve," says Gary. "We wouldn't have pursued the lawsuit if we were savvier. We didn't understand that we were being manipulated by Elektra." Still, once they had started the ball rolling legally, Shoes were stuck with the lawsuit.

Both parties settled out of court in 1980, with the resultant agreement nullifying the three remaining years of Jem's license, returning *Black Vinyl Shoes*' rights to the band. But Jem was still allowed to sell its remaining stock of the albums—piggybacking on Elektra's promotion of *Present Tense*, as Elektra had feared, thus avoiding an audit—and dodging royalty payments. In other words, each side got something, but neither was wholly satisfied.

IN EARLY OCTOBER, THE TWO front-runners for *Present Tense*'s first single were chosen to take center stage in a relatively new promotional medium for American bands—the music video—and that month, Shoes flew to Los Angeles to film. The videos were directed by Denis de Vallance, who had also directed hit videos for Queen: "Bicycle Race," "Fat Bottomed Girls," and "Crazy Little Thing Called Love." Jeff thought that de Vallance's production company had "had 'something' to do with the Beatles' 'Penny Lane' and 'Strawberry Fields' videos," helmed by Swedish television director Peter Goldmann, and they were the only music clips with any historical importance, any clout, as far as Shoes were concerned. Jeff continues, "We never heard exactly *how* they had been involved, but that was good enough for us, and they got the nod."

At this point, there was no MTV, and even the few American television programs and outlets that showed music videos (USA Network's *Video Concert Hall*, for example, or Philadephia's local PRISM network) were irregularly aired, often on obscure channels. Shoes were told that the videos they were making would be used primarily for the European market, since the band wasn't expected to tour Europe right away; video was a far more common method of promotion on the other side of the Atlantic.

The band members had seen video programs in England, and they knew they didn't want to do the somewhat cheesy "story" videos that were all the rage there, but de Vallance's proposal—essentially, a lip-synched live performance, shot on a stage set—seemed to preserve their dignity and display at least a little bit of cool.

Now that Shoes were in the process of marketing both their major-label debut and themselves, they began to get some pressure from Elektra to develop a "look."

The change in fashion had arrived: disco was out, new wave was in. Blondie's 1978 album *Parallel Lines* had made black and white de rigeur and reintroduced the skinny ties and monochromatic suits from the early sixties. The Knack had embraced the style and upped the ante—playing on their already obvious Beatles parallels, making new wave as much a fashion statement as a musical style.

Shoes' titular A&R representative, Carol Thompson, had some specific ideas about the image they ought to cultivate: she pictured them in the palette and the fashions of the coming decade. "Elektra wanted us in red, white, and black, in skinny jeans," John says. But Shoes balked at being costumed like matching paper dolls. As Dan Bourgoise says, "They didn't see themselves as part of any movement. They dressed as they dressed. What was happening in California at that time [e.g., the Knack] was far more calculated." Shoes dug in their heels. "We didn't want a makeover," John flatly recalls. "We wanted our 'Shoe'-ness."

Bourgoise was initially confident that Elektra wasn't attempting to tart up the band's look to appeal to teenage girls—"Elektra liked to think of themselves as hipper than that"—though the guys were certainly handsome enough, and many of Shoes' publicity pics played up their good looks. But Bourgoise now admits:

> There might have been some thought of [marketing Shoes as teen idols]. I don't think *we* entertained it, but there *was* an undercurrent of, 'Aren't the girls going to like them!' Still, once Elektra met Shoes, they'd realize that they weren't hammy enough to work as teen idols. It would have been disastrous. It would have compromised what they were doing.

But though Shoes weren't aspiring to hook Shaun Cassidy and Leif Garrett's pubescent fan base, the teen market was certainly becoming interested in them. For example, there was a full-page Shoes article (mostly photo) in *16* magazine's music publication *Rockline!*, and John remembers a few other similar features. And in the summer of 1979, Dave Bell Associates, a Los Angeles-based television production company, proposed following Shoes for a month in order to make them the subject of an after-school special. In addition, Shoes were offered the chance to appear on that decades-old-and-still-running mainstay of teen America's pop-music culture, *American Bandstand*. However, says Gary, "We turned that down. *Bandstand* really was seen as kind of corny and not cool." John concurs: "We wanted to prove we had a bit of an edge."

But defining that edge, in 1979, was a tricky business. They weren't punk, and they resisted being recast as power pop. Shoes wanted rock credibility.

Back in the early seventies, when John and Gary had fantasized about the moment they became rock stars—in their cartoon caricatures—they had literally pictured themselves as David Bowie and Alice Cooper: larger-than-life glam rockers with huge boots, enormous belt buckles, and spiked hair. But when the time came, they defaulted to being … themselves. Bourgoise wasn't the kind of manager who would push Shoes toward any particular image—that's a major reason why they liked him—and they had already dismissed the skinny-jeans-and-skinny-ties fashion advice of their well-meaning rep at Elektra. "We're pretty low-key and not very flashy," says John.

Left at last to their own devices, when Shoes showed up for the video shoot at a Los Angeles soundstage on October 9, they brought their own clothes from home: collared shirts, everyday pants, tees. "There were people there to do hair and makeup and stuff," John recalls. "But there wasn't really any wardrobe person as such."

Gary says that when he pulled one rumpled shirt out of his suitcase, an assistant grabbed it and set off to find a laundry. When the shirt came back, "it was not only ironed, I think they starched it," Gary cringes. "There was this military crease down the sleeve." John is more horrified now by the out-of-style bellbottoms revealed in long camera shots of the band—although, as he explains, "We were still wearing them in the Midwest."

Shoes' jeans width aside, the videos don't date too badly: clad primarily in simple, solid colors, Shoes avoided the fashionable trappings (such as red satin pants) that had been so enthusiastically adopted by prominent pop artists of the day, among them Rod Stewart.

And Shoes could easily have gone that way: disco may have been sinking, but its flotsam was strewn all around. For example, Jeff remembers that the next soundstage over was occupied by mirrored-ball mascots the Village People, then filming their movie *Can't Stop the Music*. "We encouraged Skip to run over to their set and ask if he could borrow the Indian chief's headdress so he could wear it in our video, but Skip wasn't going for it," Jeff teases in his memoir.

Elektra had sent noted rock photographer Neal Preston, whose credits included the Who, Led Zeppelin, Queen, and Fleetwood Mac, to take still shots of the video session. But the shoot turned out to be not much fun for the band. Shoes had never been filmed performing before, and they were jittery. While there were plenty of people around—the video crew and some publicity staffers from Elektra—the band was mostly on its own, walking onto the set with no preparation. "We were all pretty uptight and not sure what to expect," John says. "There was no one there to break the tense atmosphere. In retrospect, the end result looks more natural than it felt to film it."

Jeff says the video shoot was "preceded by perhaps the worst on-film interview of our careers," conducted by an inexperienced member of Elektra's publicity department. The band was visibly uncomfortable, picking their fingernails, slouching, staring at the floor. But "the interviewer was as nervous as we were," Gary recalls, and Jeff says, "That made us uptight about doing it." Jeff remembers him asking "lame, humdrum questions like, 'How did you get the name Shoes?'" Gary surmises that "he didn't know anything about us. There were no questions designed to evoke a thought-provoking answer; they were all superficial."

Recording directly to videotape, Shoes lip-synched their way through four songs under the unfamiliar, brutally hot lights in a marathon twenty-hour shoot, doing each song four or five times. "Too Late" and "Tomorrow Night" were obvious choices; everyone understood they had hit potential. The dark horses were John's raveup "Cruel You" and Jeff's bench-pressing love song "In My Arms Again," both of which were chosen at the shoot itself, and neither of which would end up being released as singles. John says that it was someone from Elektra who suggested "Cruel You" —adding that he would have preferred his much more honeyed offering, "Your Very Eyes," "in order to show a different side of our music."

By the time they got to "Tomorrow Night," the last song taped, Shoes were both physically tired and tired of the process, particularly because a smoke machine had been brought in to soften the videotape's sharp resolution. Says Jeff, "The end result is hot, sweaty, and smoky, just like we felt. We joked that it looked like 'Shoes playing in Hell.'"

MEANWHILE, SHOES EXPECTED TO support the record more traditionally, too—to go on tour after *Present Tense* was released—but Elektra did not push them to go on the road. "The label thought success would come from promo, not touring," says Gary. But despite their relatively modest live experience, Shoes saw the road as part of the game, and they were rehearsed and ready to go.

There was a problem, however, with finding the time. Much of the fall was spent travelling with Marty Schwartz doing publicity, mostly on the East and West Coasts. (Gary and John both remember that they were wearing lobster bibs at Boston restaurant Legal Sea Foods in October, when they heard that "Too Late" was climbing the charts.)

Shoes put in a multitude of public appearances in a multitude of locales. They all remember the Chicago party for parent company WEA (Warner Elektra Atlantic) that they attended in September, which celebrated the success of the Blues Brothers' self-titled debut album; John Belushi and Dan Aykroyd arrived in full black-suited-and-sunglassed regalia, Jeff recalls, and Belushi did his signature cartwheel through the room. Dessert was flaming Cherries Jubilee, brought in by waiters dancing to Fleetwood Mac's tribal new single, "Tusk."

And it was big news that Shoes were in the house; Jeff remembers first being "seated with the company brass like Kenny, and everybody bowing down to him." But the obeisance wasn't directed solely at Buttice. Gary adds, "People were turning around to stare at us when we came in, and when they introduced us, the room just *roared*."

There were other publicity jaunts and public appearances on the books that season too, from in-store appearances to music-biz Halloween parties, so Shoes' fall schedule was already pretty packed, even without live concert dates.

Another potential obstacle to touring was finding the right showcase. They discussed a slot opening for the Cars, who were then supporting their newly-released album *Candy-O* on their first arena tour. But Shoes were leery of pursuing that option: as with the *Present Tense* producer search, they took pains not to be too closely associated with Elektra's other favorite sons. "And we were maybe a little arrogant," Gary admits. "We didn't want to latch on to the Cars' coattails; we wanted to distinguish ourselves." Also, with the Cars touring behind their second multi-platinum record in as many years, the crowds they were drawing were enormous, and therefore sort of intimidating. Gary, with his chronic stage fright, was particularly concerned that this was no way to christen Shoes' new live identity.

Instead, the band opted for a tour of small Midwestern clubs—and even with a newly-acquired booking agent, that took months to schedule. But as Dan Bourgoise puts it, "The feeling was, you have to start somewhere." Playing clubs, they reasoned, would allow Shoes to sharpen their performing chops before the stakes got too high: they thought of it as a preparatory jaunt for the huge tours undoubtedly to come "when the record really took off," in John's words.

Buttice supported this decision. By sticking to clubs, Shoes would be playing primarily for the local radio-promo guys, Buttice's favorite cohort: a rock crowd, not a pop audience. Bourgoise continues:

> In some ways it would have been better if they'd played support on a big tour. But there was this whole idea of getting them out to small clubs and bars where the local radio guys hang out. Elektra's concern was what was good for the radio guys; not what was good for the band.

Kicking off just after Thanksgiving, Shoes' first tour was mercifully over before Christmas—they all still agree it was an almost unmitigated disaster.

BEFORE THEY'D STARTED OUT, Shoes' first step was to beef up their existing sound system, which they'd acquired much as they had their early guitars: via the local classified-ad paper *Trading Times*, or from people they knew who were upgrading their own equipment. It was thrown together, but it had worked for the few shows Shoes had done up till now. For this tour, though, they clearly needed something finer, so Shoes bought some new pieces and rewired others, built some new boxes and traveling cases. They rented another storefront in Zion to pull off this intensive revamping, just a few doors down from the dress shop. Dan Bourgoise hired two roadies in L.A. and sent them to Zion; they showed up in shirtsleeves, so Jeff and Skip loaned them winter coats for the duration.

Shoes' new equipment consisted of four custom floor monitors, Jeff says, enumerating the details of each one: "Two JBL K120 woofers, a 2440 HF driver on a 'potato masher' horn with a diffraction lens, and two JBL 2405 'slots.' Each three-way cabinet was bi-amped but the slots were crossed passively with a 3105 crossover." Jeff himself wasn't crazy about these monitors—"JBL tend to be very bright and harsh sounding, to my ears; they get loud, and they can cut your head off with that upper-midrange peak." (And in fact, the monitors blew up entirely during Shoes' first show, at the Edgewater nightclub in Twin Lakes, Wisconsin.)

They also attempted to streamline the setup protocol for their house speaker stacks, which broadcast the audience mix. The idea was to idiot-proof the process, so the band members wouldn't have to spend much time on it while touring. To that end, Jeff and Gary and the young road crew took the whole system to pieces and rebuilt it. Jeff describes:

> The main P.A. consisted of two "double scoop" cabinets with two eighteen-inch woofers, four modified 4550 cabinets with fifteen-inch drivers, four JBL 2440 high-frequency drivers on the ninety-degree radial horn, and eight JBL 2405 slots on top. We already owned most of the main P.A. stuff, but the crew modified the 4550 cabinets, and custom-wired the drive rack and cabinet jacks, so there was only one way to plug everything in; it couldn't be wired incorrectly. That way the woofer signal didn't accidently feed into the high-frequency drivers, which would blow out the drivers.

As it would turn out, their foolproof system wasn't indefinitely so: all the high-frequency drivers would indeed blow out in Indianapolis, one of the last shows of the tour.

SHOES HAD NEVER DONE A FAR-FLUNG road jaunt before; with the exception of the Dwight sets and Jay's Longhorn in the summer of 1978, every gig they'd played was close enough geographically for them to sleep in their own beds after they'd loaded out. But the grandiose vision of Ken Buttice—that Shoes were destined to be the biggest band in the world—had affected this aspect of their career, too. Though they planned to start small,

Shoes expected that, when *Present Tense* hit for real, they would tour for a long time—everywhere. With that eventuality looming, they had to assemble a crack travelling road crew.

Before, the band members had entrusted their old Zion buddies to take care of things offstage: Joe Higgins, one of the *Lime* gang, ran sound for some of the shows, and Garry Holverson—the friend of Jeff's who had co-signed that first loan for the TEAC 3340-S, as well as facilitating the *Zonker* hoax—ran the rest. In terms of bookings, transportation, and housing, well, they'd always handled all that themselves.

But these casual roles weren't going to work for an open-ended tour: a December, 1979 *Rolling Stone* article—"The [sic] Shoes Step Out in Style," by Chris Morris—mentions that "a tour of Australia, Japan, Europe and the U.S. is planned for early 1980." With that presumed scenario in mind, they hired professionals out of L.A. to run the tour. But the disconnect between Shoes' expectations and the reality of the professional rock world caused friction between Shoes and their road team from the very beginning.

Dan Bourgoise was in charge of assembling the crew in L.A. As noted, he had been Del Shannon's road manager, so Shoes trusted his expertise. Since Dan thought he was preparing Shoes for a national—make that international—tour, he was seeking a road manager with considerable experience. Bourgoise put the word out and waited to see who was available.

Bruce Sachs, who had managed the mustachioed crooner-turned-variety-show-star Tony Orlando, heard that Shoes were looking around for a tour manager, and contacted Bourgoise. "I had known Danny from way back, and I really wanted to work with these guys," Sachs recalls. "Everyone said they were great, and I wanted to get in on the ground floor."

Sachs, a compact, bearded man, says he turned down an offer from Styx in order to road-manage Shoes' tour. In addition to Orlando, Sachs had worked with Frank Zappa and the Kinks, handling mostly bookings along with logistics like housing, not the nuts-and-bolts of setting up equipment and transportation. On a larger tour, with a larger crew, Sachs' specialization would have been an advantage, but in the DIY, everybody-pitches-in world of Shoes, he seemed rarefied and out of touch.

For example, Sachs encouraged Shoes to wear "nice slacks" onstage, presumably to take advantage of their squeaky-clean image. "He wasn't rock & roll," says Jeff. "He had a more Vegas-type of background, and he didn't get it. We were into Talking Heads, the Ramones, Cheap Trick, and the whole wave of new music coming out; he was talking about what Tony Orlando would do."

The road manager's dubious sartorial counsel wasn't the only issue. The one thing Shoes really needed from Sachs was help dealing with the road crew. The tour was plagued from the start by technical problems, and as they mounted, so did Shoes' frustration with Sachs. "He washed his hands of the whole roadie and sound situation." says John. "That's what we needed him for, and he didn't do it."

And the road crew, more than anything else, was the bane of the tour.

Bourgoise and Sachs had found Shoes a small crew from A-1 Audio Lighting Rentals in L.A.: a light guy and a sound guy, Scott and Pete. They were just kids, John recalls—"maybe in their early twenties, no older"—with no real touring experience under their belts, and their inexperience caused major problems, costing Shoes weeks of subpar performances and thousands in broken equipment. Evidently, according to John, "The company just passed anyone off on us—we were green, so we got a green crew."

The youngsters habitually forgot routine tasks, such as turning on preamps and putting mics in front of guitar amplifiers. The band thought they could rectify some of the problems the two rookies presented by bringing aboard a third, more experienced roadie they knew, Dave, who had the additional draw of being a Midwestern local. Dave was a newlywed, and his wife came on tour, too. The band also tapped their old friend Garry Holverson to roadie: he was going through a tough time personally, and they thought the distraction would do him good.

But as the incompetence of the California roadies became obvious, Shoes looked to Sachs to deal with Pete and Scott, and he just didn't.

For Sachs' part, he insists that he was doing exactly what he had done on previous tours—bigger tours, with bigger bands—and that may well be true.

"He was very professional," Gary acknowledges. "He just wasn't a good fit for us." The scale of Shoes' tour was so much smaller than Sachs was used to that his specialization and uber-slick professionalism were not only out of place, they were an impediment.

And, they all recall, Sachs was deferential in the extreme to Dan Bourgoise when Bourgoise joined the tour in December. "Mostly, he kissed Dan's ass," Skip says bluntly. (Toward the end of the tour, Bourgoise lost patience with this behavior, John recalls. "He said, 'Don't worry about *my* coffee, *my* paper. What about the band? Are you taking care of *them*?'") Moreover, after Bourgoise joined the tour, he perused the books and spotted some unexplained expenditures. When Dan confronted the road manager, according to Jeff, Sachs insisted that he had provided vitamins for Shoes—to the tune of two hundred dollars a week—vitamins the band categorically denied receiving.

Adding to the stress of Shoes' inaugural road show was the presence of two journalists sent from *Time* magazine to follow them. The respected newsweekly's mid-December issue was going to feature the Who (then touring America) on the cover, with Shoes slated for a sidebar article on second-generation rock. The *Time* reporters—a man and a woman—came to a few rehearsals, talked to the band, took some pictures, and followed the tour's first few shows. "They were nice people," Gary remembers. "We sort of expected to be grilled, like Mike Wallace would do, but they didn't; they were really cool." Still, this wasn't an optimal time to have observers present, when everything was so disorganized. "It was pressure just knowing they were out there, witnessing the carnage," Jeff remembers. "It was like having a nightmare that you're in high school and your pants fall down at the senior prom. *Man*, did they fall down."

But the Shoes feature was never published: on December 3, the Who made unexpectedly horrific news when eleven concertgoers died and eight more were hospitalized after a crowd stampede before their show at Cincinnati's Riverfront Stadium. Shoes were understandably shelved for coverage of the tragedy, which brought to light an ongoing problem with unreserved "festival" seating at rock concerts.

THE TOUR HAD BEGUN ON NOVEMBER 30 in Twin Lakes, Wisconsin, with the monitors' self-destruction at the Edgewater. "As we stepped forward to do our first harmony, they just exploded," Jeff says. Dave was taping the show; listening to it at a party afterward, they cringed to hear how far off-key they'd been. "I know one thing," Skip later remarked in his journal. "If you can't hear yourself, you will sound like shit."

The next night, at the same club, the monitors worked for the first half of the show, then committed suicide again. Shoes officially hired Dave to run sound at that point, though they kept Pete on the payroll as a guitar tech. (Scott stayed on lights.) After that, it was off to Madison, Wisconsin; and then back to Illinois, at Haymakers in suburban Prospect Heights.

The last live date of the first week took place at a venue called the Rock Garden in Elmhurst, Illinois. Jeff turned 25 that day, and he celebrated by playing his new dark-blue Hamer emblazoned with the band name. In the house were two journalists who would become staunch friends and chroniclers of the band: Moira McCormick and Chuck Fieldman.

Alas, the night was a mess. Well in advance of the show, Shoes' road crew was supposed to have loaded their equipment out of the studio and into the club. But they'd shown up late, now having to rush—and in the bustle, one knocked over Jeff's Hiwatt amp stack, shattering several tubes inside. Plus, John noticed that his bass had been badly scratched up. The brothers turned to their respective roadies and gave them each a piece of their minds.

After those confrontations, Pete looked at Scott and said, "Let's get out of here," according to John, and the roadies simply split. Holverson was sent to fetch Sachs. "We made Bruce fire them; we weren't going to do it," says Gary. Sachs found the two in a bar just up the road from still-dry Zion and did the deed, then booked the now ex-roadies' flights back to L.A. that same evening.

THE BAND HAD ALREADY PLANNED A two-day break at that point, which was fortuitous: this allowed time for two new roadies to arrive. They liked Dave, but he wasn't really in a position to stay on tour indefinitely; he was obliged to get off the road in the interest of preserving new-marital harmony. But before he left, Dave set Shoes up with two friends of his, and this time, the band got lucky. "Beet and Steve saved us," Gary says simply.

Billy "Beet" Richardson and Steve Hurd both came to Shoes with long and impressive arena-rock résumés: Journey, REO Speedwagon, Alice Cooper, Boston, Nazareth, Golden Earring, the Doobie Brothers. The seasoned soundmen took the young band under their collective wing. Hurd remembers Shoes as seeming "like choirboys to us, naïve, polite, like they just walked out the church door." Richardson concurs, shaking his head at the supreme normalcy of their habits:

> We had come in off the road working with some heavy-duty people; people who, if you'd say 'good morning' to them, they'd tell you to go fuck off. And then these guys were there with their coffee and orange juice, and they were happy, and that's how it was.

These road-tested vets immediately sussed out the problems with the tour. Richardson explains:

> Shoes were getting messed over. Their crew was telling them, "You're gonna sound great, everything is going to work"—and we got there and nothing was right. They were playing on a Fisher-Price sound system; they were a vocal band, and had to hear themselves to do harmonies, but they couldn't even hear their vocals through the monitors. They weren't used to the environment of playing in a bar, through these speakers that didn't get any louder than your AM radio. They couldn't make it work, and they got frustrated.

Nevertheless, taken with the band's unpretentious personal style and absence of rock-star posturing, Richardson and Hurd took pity on Shoes, deciding to mentor them. On December 11, Skip reported in his journal that the band sat down with Beet, Steve, and Dave, and discussed the sound issues frankly; the roadies proposed workable solutions to the band's problems. "The days of taking things for granted are over," Skip wrote. Shoes obviously needed to monitor the sound situation more closely than they had been, and with these new advisors, they were ready to move ahead.

Beet and Steve mentored the band in other ways, too. Gary recalls one memorable nugget of Steve's wisdom: when he expressed hope at one point that they might meet some girls on the road, Hurd encouraged Gary to think more like a roadie: "*We* ain't lookin' for *nice* girls." Both he and Richardson tell of pounding on hotel-room doors in the middle of the night, trying to get the sleeping band members to wake up and carouse; Steve sighs, "They didn't really *get* the fun part of being on the road." Beet agrees: "We were used to the parties and goings-on and the things that happen on the road, and these guys were like some gospel band. They were four of the nicest guys—they were even *too* polite!—but we all clicked." Hurd and Richardson only travelled with Shoes for a few shows of that tour, but both the band and the technicians came away ready to work together again.

Around the same time, that first week of December, Ken Buttice decided to retire "Too Late" as a single in order to launch the second contender, leadoff track "Tomorrow Night." "Too Late" had been rising steadily through November, but not fast enough to please Elektra, and some AOR stations were already playing "Tomorrow Night." Says Gary, "I think that's the first time I realized we weren't going to be huge immediately, that fame wasn't going to happen as quickly and easily as Kenny said." And as Shoes became more familiar with the business, they could see that some decisions were being made more rashly than they'd expected from professionals. "Elektra was trying to hit that fast home run," Dan Bourgoise says, "and they were panicking. 'Radio isn't playing that one! Get another one out there!'"

SHOES' SHOWS RESUMED ON FRIDAY, December 7, in Burbank, Illinois. The club, called Pip's, was small, but Elektra people came out and told the band they sounded good. The next night, Shoes played in Bloomington, Indiana to a pitiful crowd, but as Skip theorized in his journal, the Who were appearing in Chicago, so the light turnout wasn't really a surprise (though Bloomington isn't exactly a Chicago suburb, being a good four hours south of the Windy City).

Between these two shows, Shoes were a bit taken aback to discover that their road manager wasn't all that knowledgeable about the actual road. Bruce Sachs had radically overestimated the travel time between Burbank and

Bloomington, insisting that the drive would take all night—a daunting prospect after the Pip's show, when all were exhausted. Holverson, who was supposed to drive the Winnebago, simply begged off and crashed in the back instead. The band members all looked expectantly at Sachs, who according to Skip's journal "reluctantly took over." Skip, too nervous to sleep, rode shotgun for a while, until he felt Sachs drifting off the highway shoulder. Rousing their drowsing-at-the-wheel road manager, Skip took over and finished the drive himself, arriving in Bloomington after just a few hours: as it turned out, the distance was less than 250 miles. The whole incident stoked Shoes' already considerable dissatisfaction with Sachs.

After Bloomington, it was on to Indianapolis—where Jeff describes the following night's concert, as "definitely the lowest point of the tour." Mortifyingly, Elektra brass and Dan Bourgoise were in the house. "I guess everything that could go wrong went wrong," Skip wrote the next day. "It was hotter than a bitch onstage. The monitors were feeding back. Guitars were out of tune. We played bad and sounded bad." Jeff describes the following night's concert:

> In addition to our own problems on stage, the P.A. blew out all of the high-frequency drivers. The cabling from the crossover to the power amps had jiggled out during transit, and upon turning the amps on, there was a loud ground buzz through the top end; the tweeters didn't survive. Had we played perfectly (which we missed by a mile), we still would have sounded muffled, like we were performing in the next room.

Shoes were so humiliated and angry that they didn't even greet their invited guests afterwards, and Dan summarily fired Dave, the sound man, after the debacle. The band proceeded to cancel as many subsequent live dates as they could—particularly those pending on the East Coast—but they were still obliged to finish out that week with a final show in Detroit on December 13. Skip's journal noted that "we're all a bundle of nerves tonight."

It didn't help that Shoes' apparently meteoric ascent from small-town home-studio rats to major-label recording and touring artists had created some bad feelings among their fellow journeymen rockers. As John said in an interview with Moira McCormick at the time:

[Chicago-area musicians] were going in [to see us play] with chips on their shoulders. ... They *wanted* us to be bad. So it was *great* when things were blowing up and we were tripping and falling on our faces. ... It was just one more reason to say, 'Why do Shoes have a recording contract and *we* don't? They obviously can't play a show; they're a studio band'—well damn it, what's *wrong* with being a studio band?

They had two more Midwest dates scheduled in mid-December, but by that point Shoes had had enough of touring. "Let's cut our losses here," John remembers thinking. "We were hemorrhaging money at that point," confirms Jeff. They announced to Elektra that they were ending the tour.

Unexpectedly, though, that pair of final shows on their ill-starred tour went markedly better—not just musically, but technically. Skip wrote, "It's almost too bad our tour is going to end, because I really believe the road crew is trying to get it together."

Still, fate wasn't quite done with Shoes yet. The last dates were plagued by bad weather—and even as they attempted to beat their retreat back to Zion, it was the Winnebago engine's turn to blow. Jeff estimates that Shoes' maiden tour ended up costing the band about $50,000 altogether.

THE MOST SIGNIFICANT LONG-TERM effect of the 1979 road stint was that it solidified the band's avoidance of playing live, of doing the kind of night-to-night slogging other bands did. "I remember saying I'd never get on a stage again," recounts Jeff, so deeply, deeply demoralized were Shoes by the events of December 1979.

Bourgoise now plays down the tour's problems, insisting, "It *wasn't* disastrous." But he also acknowledges that its modest scale may have caused more problems than it solved. The weeknight shows at pint-sized clubs, the sparse crowds: this was not what it was supposed to feel like to have a major-label deal, to be on the charts. Shoes were frustrated at the disjunction between their perceived success and their stunted reality. Bourgoise continues:

> Playing small, divey venues, not always full, makes it *feel* like a disaster. Had they gone out on [an arena] tour, supporting a better-known act, it would have felt more like Shoes were riding that wave of success. Yes, they would have been opening, but it would have been a bigger situation, and I think that they could have risen to it. ... In retrospect, they would have done much better *not* touring, maintaining their mystique and letting the record speak for itself.

Elektra didn't care that Shoes were abandoning the road. Gary says that their label preferred to see them play to their strengths, to return to the studio almost immediately: "They were all in favor of us stopping the tour. They wanted us to get back to work, to get the next record out." And the time frame was compressed. Skip's journal noted on December 13 that they thought they'd be in Los Angeles within weeks: "I guess we will finish out this month and maybe go to L.A. to do some pre-recording and do the album early so that it will be released in the early summer."

THERE WAS ANOTHER LAYER OF GRAVE disappointment added to the failed '79 tour: the performance of both *Present Tense* and "Too Late" on the charts. After an initial spike in November, both album and single declined swiftly while Shoes were on the road.

In early November, *Billboard* had reported that Shoes "had a hot chart LP." *Present Tense* had entered the Billboard Top LPs & Tape chart on October 13 at #145, but by the end of that month had risen to the upper half of that chart (#85). It continued to climb through November—while Shoes made promo appearances and refurbished their sound system—peaking at #50 on November 24. But as soon as they hit the road, it dropped precipitously back below 100, and had disappeared altogether by the end of the year.

The first single faced a similar fate. "Too Late" had been released in mid-October, and on October 20, *Billboard* had designated "Too Late" as a recommended "First Time Around" single: "Elektra's big fall push is on this group, which has a warm Beatlesque sound, highlighting tight, close harmonies, tasty guitar work, and an instantly accessible melody." Within two weeks of release, "Too Late" began to climb the charts—though

Billboard's Hot 100 erroneously listed the artist as "Mike Stone" in some issues—ανδ "Mike Stone and Shoes" in others. (Peculiarly, "Too Late" was only correctly credited in its debut week, November 3.) All through November it placed in *Billboard*'s chart, peaking at #75 on December 1, just as Shoes hit the road. But once December arrived, it too fell off the charts.

John hastens to assure, however, that Shoes' tour did not cause the decline, merely that both happened concurrently: "Our handful of shows in Cupcake, Illinois did not make *Present Tense* drop down the charts," he says:

> Elektra couldn't get the single to move—or it wasn't rocketing up the charts fast enough—so they released "Tomorrow Night," which ended up killing both "Too Late" and *Present Tense.*

But there's no question, according to John, that their sinking numbers had an impact on admittedly-shaky band morale. "We were already having enough problems on the road," he says, "and the sluggish chart action didn't improve our mood any."

Even though "in the long run, I guess it really helped us all toughen up," Gary says now of Shoes' fledgling road jaunt, when the tour ended at the close of 1979, they were just relieved it was over.

MEANWHILE, SHOES WATCHED THE bobbling continue at Elektra, helpless to right it. The single continued to be an issue: "Tomorrow Night" was given even less of a chance to make its mark than "Too Late" had been: in a matter of weeks, Elektra raced out a twelve-inch radio-only promo copy of "I Don't Wanna Hear It." All three singles had the same B-side, "Now and Then." (Jeff recalls being told that Elektra was using the song over and over because they didn't want to "waste" any potential hits on a B-side; John gave himself the mordant designation "King of the B's.")

But as with both its predecessors, there wasn't a fast-enough radio response to "I Don't Wanna Hear It," so *it* was pulled in turn for the Hail-Mary release of single number four, "I Don't Miss You" (this time with "In My Arms Again" on the flipside), just after the first of the year.

That made four singles issued in less than three months. Each 45 received less of Elektra's support than the last, and garnered less airplay. "It was a desperation move on the label's part," Dan Bourgoise says. "It was Elektra flailing around out there." By early 1980, Elektra had decided *Present Tense* was a "stiff"—a record that would not recoup its cost of production and promotion—and they gave up marketing it altogether.

SHOES' ELEKTRA DEAL CONFORMED to standard record-company practice in that the cost of everything—from the band's advance to the ale in the English limousine to the Jaffa Cakes to the blown speakers to the blown Winnebago engine—was being *covered* by Elektra, but not, in the end, actually *paid for* by them. Payment for all these expenses was intended to come out of Shoes' cut of album sales, which were respectable but not overwhelming: *Present Tense* sold about 125,000 copies in its initial run.

In the music biz at large, the number of label-provided goods and services classed as "recoupable expenses" had grown through the 1970s. By 1979, record companies seemed to function less as purveyors of music than as extremely specialized lending institutions—banks, essentially—which were also in the business of selling their clients specific services, the terms and costs of which they themselves determined. Labels provided the money and explained what it needed to be spent on, and then kept the books on the artists' income that was supposed to pay them back.

If sales of a given record went even reasonably well, the record company took no risk; no royalties would be paid to the band until the label had recouped all the artist's expenses. If sales didn't go well, artist owed label the balance of its expenses as long as they remained signed. It was this lopsided system that led the British prog-pop act XTC, for example, to spend seven years on strike in the 1990s, when they realized that despite several hit singles over the course of their career, their label, Virgin Records, was *never* going to pay them royalties.

In *Hit Men*, Frederic Dannen explains the central problem with record-company agreements:

> The key to understanding why the contracts are so bad is the word "recoupable." In a standard agreement, most of the costs of making a record are to be repaid out of artist's royalties rather than gross receipts. ... The way contracts are structured, the record company can make a profit off an album while the artist's royalty account is in the red. In fact, this is a frequent occurrence.

Discussing the XTC case in a 1997 interview with the *London Telegraph*'s David Gritten, music attorney Don Engel rhetorically queried: "Do you ever hear of an actor who has to give up his first million dollars [of] pay from a movie to get [the film] made? ... Yet all [musical] artists pay recording costs from their advances. It's counterproductive and unfair."

And of course, every band believes that they're going to be superstars, particularly once they're signed to a major label. Part of the label's job is to sell them on themselves, as Ken Buttice did for Shoes, convincing them to spend all the money their label makes available—which the band then owes back, as long they are signed—on recording, production, promotion, publicity: all the costs associated with making and selling records.

Shoes "were pressed to spend money on production and touring and videos," Gary says. "If we weren't spending, the Elektra staff asked us why not." Buttice may not have been successful in selling Shoes to the general public, but he sold the *idea* of Shoes to the four band members, convincing them to rack up a huge column of recoupable expenditures in a relatively short period of time.

But even with respectable earnings, more than enough to cover all the expenses a band is accumulating, labels can always keep what are euphemistically known as "reserves"—funds to offset possible *future* expenses a band might accrue. "They can hold back an extraordinary amount for that purpose," Gary says. "Theoretically, record companies have to release the money eventually," but the only way bands can prove that they've sold enough records to pay their debt to the label is to request and (more importantly) fund an outside audit of the company's books, and "most bands can't afford that." Under those circumstances, a recording artist just has to take the label's word regarding the state of their continuing debt.

The definition of a stiff depends on a number of factors. But compelling a band to feel personally (and thus financially) responsible for creating a stiff—to keep them from seeking money that might be owed to them—has obvious benefits for a record company.

In a 1981 interview with Don McLeese in the *Illinois Entertainer*, Jeff hints at Shoes' sense of culpability for the perceived failure of *Present Tense*. He cites the huge leap in units sold from their home-brewed masterpiece to their polished big-league debut—"Going from *Black Vinyl Shoes* to *Present Tense* saleswise—what more could you ask?"—but clearly feels that Shoes were to blame for not achieving the multiplatinum numbers they'd been told to expect. Jeff continues, "From a level of what Elektra had been filling us full of, what this record was going to do—well then, of course you go, 'It didn't do what they said,' so you try to figure out what you did wrong." The mere fact of recording and releasing a major-label album had been tremendous, of course, but Shoes had been led to expect so much more. And though Gary considers 1979, in many respects, "the greatest year of our lives," there is no question that by the end of that whirlwind period, Shoes were convinced that they had failed, even as Elektra continued to release singles, and *Present Tense* continued to be added to radio station playlists (as it was in Miami on Dec 9, fully three months after its release). The final year of the seventies closed with what Jeff calls "the most depressing Christmas of my life."

DECEMBER ALSO, FINALLY, BROUGHT the reviews. Though even then Shoes were known as critics' darlings—"If good reviews were money, we would have been set a long time ago," John observes wryly—it was only the seriously wonky music writers who'd heard *Black Vinyl Shoes*.

With *Present Tense*, the band got wider exposure, and it was overwhelmingly positive. Ken Tucker of the *Los Angeles Herald-Examiner* called the record "a little pop epic;" Ken Emerson in *The New York Times* declared it "an unabashedly melodic mash note." Stalwart Shoes booster Bill Paige designated the record "a pop rock masterpiece" in the *Illinois Entertainer*. The *Village* Voice's Robert Christgau gave *Present Tense* an A-, dubbing it "a formalist's delight." Max Bell in the U.K. rock weekly *New Musical Express* one-upped Christgau's evaluation, asserting that "Shoes are one group in a million who defy form," going on to declare that the band "call[s] their own shots. *Present Tense* is a record which defies expectations."

But some of the popular-music press saw Shoes primarily as representatives of power pop, that upstart genre the band members themselves didn't really know existed. "At the time, we were unaware of belonging to any power-pop movement," reminds Gary. "The only movement we felt part of was our own." He jokes that "when I first heard the phrase 'power pop', my first thought was, 'Man, I gotta check out some of this stuff.' I didn't make the connection until years later that they were talking about *us*."

Rolling Stone's respectable two-page feature on the band ran in December 1979, in the same issue as the magazine's review of *Present Tense*. But Shoes were lumped into an omnibus power-pop roundup that reviewed new discs from the Motels, the Beat (Paul Collins' American pop band, not the British neo-ska combo known Stateside as the English Beat), the Members, the Sports, the Pop, the Sinceros, and 20/20.

Writer Tom Carson praises Shoes' "Sixties-revisionist side of power pop at its most lushly romantic," but goes on to gripe that *Present Tense* "is almost too pretty and fragile, with some of the same wimp-music undertones that limited and dated so many of the Sixties radio bands."

The review was designed to focus on power pop as a genre, and though Shoes fared better than some of the other bands evaluated, it's clear that Carson simply disliked the genre—sneeringly characterizing it as "a definite step backward—an artistic retreat—from the daring of punk." The multi-band structure of the review itself was belittling, "back-handed," as Gary puts it. John agrees, adding, "I'd rather have a review of our own and have it be a bad one, than be lumped in like that."

As Dan Bourgoise explains, "The record business tends to identify trends and marginalize them. The Knack had a great record, but never really followed it up. They were left with skinny ties and matching jackets, this sort of Beatle-copy thing. Shoes got grouped into the same trend and dismissed by the press: 'We know what they're about: that power-pop stuff.'" No matter how carefully they tried to separate themselves from the trend, the

Rolling Stone review clearly demonstrated that for some critics, Shoes were just one more ingredient in the power-pop soup.

In any case, Shoes' coverage in *Rolling Stone* and numerous other publications did not appear until December, and at that point Elektra was already abandoning *Present Tense*, dashing any possibility of achieving the gold record Shoes had so fervently hoped for. Instead, the band sardonically presented Bourgoise with a gift: they took a copy of *Present Tense*, gouged it, warped it with a blowtorch, spray-painted it gold and mounted it. Bourgoise kept this "dead record" plaque hanging on his office wall for years, Jeff says: a memento of the frustrated saga of *Present Tense*.

John Alexander Dowie (left, in the garb of Elijah II) was a faith healer who founded Zion in 1900 as a religious refuge for his thousands of followers, as shown in the photo above. His dream was to make Zion City "heaven on earth."

Zion's religious and political leaders were partial to putting up instructional signs at the city limits.

NO ONE EXCEPT A **LOW DOWN SCOUNDREL**, A PERSON LOWER THAN THE **DIRTIEST DOG**, YES, LOWER DOWN THAN A **SKUNK**, WOULD CHEW OR SMOKE TOBACCO IN ZION CITY.

The center of Dowie's ministry was a chain of "Healing Houses" for the sick: part hospitals, part religious retreats. The 3-story Elijah House (right) was built by 500 workers over two months and, at the time, was the largest wooden structure in Illinois. All of it except the dome was razed in 1979.

Kid Shoes

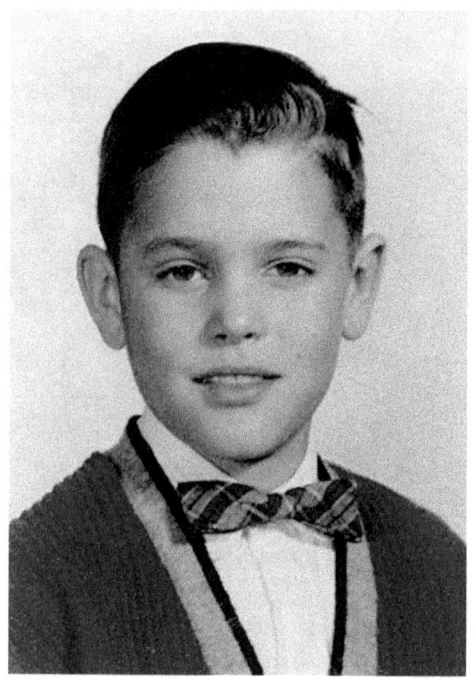

Gary, Spring Bluff School.

Jeff and John at 4 and 5 years old.

Left: John and Jeff meet the Beatles at a pumpkin farm in Pleasant Prairie, Wisconsin, October 1964.

Below: Jeff, with big brother John, proudly holds his prized possession: a new transistor radio.

1. Gary attacks!
2. Murphy boys & mom.
3. Gary gets dirty.
4. Gary's 12th birthday.
5. Jeff gets John in a ticklish situation.
6. John, sophomore year.
7. Gary, sophomore year.
8. Jeff, 8th grade.
9. Gary (age 12) towers over his 7-year old brother Tim, 1965.

John sent Gary this hand-drawn *Rolling Stone* cover before they had even recorded anything. Their letters at that time were peppered with doodles of oversized stardom.

Early Days

Jeff and John, Christmas Day, 1973.

Gary in the basement studio, 1974.

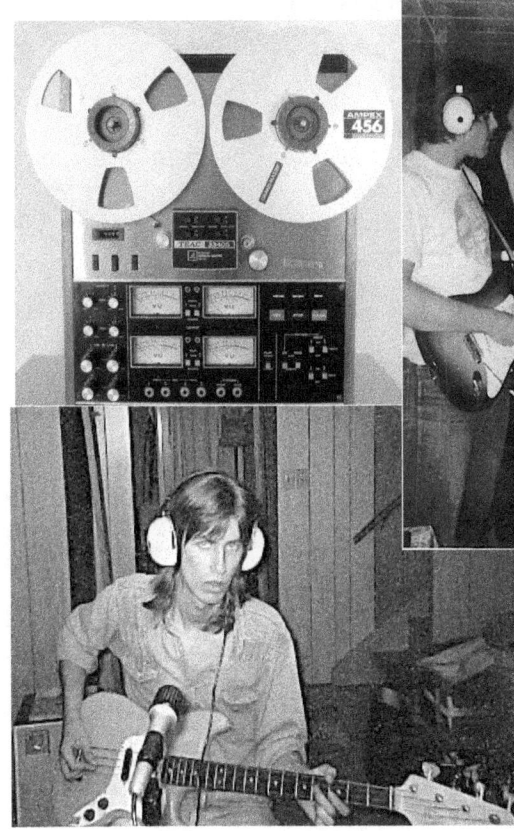

Middle left: The TEAC 3340S four-track recorder that fostered the birth of Shoes.

Left: John sits with his first Fender bass. The previous owner's band name was stenciled across the case: Rock Goat.

Above: Gary and Jeff plug in.

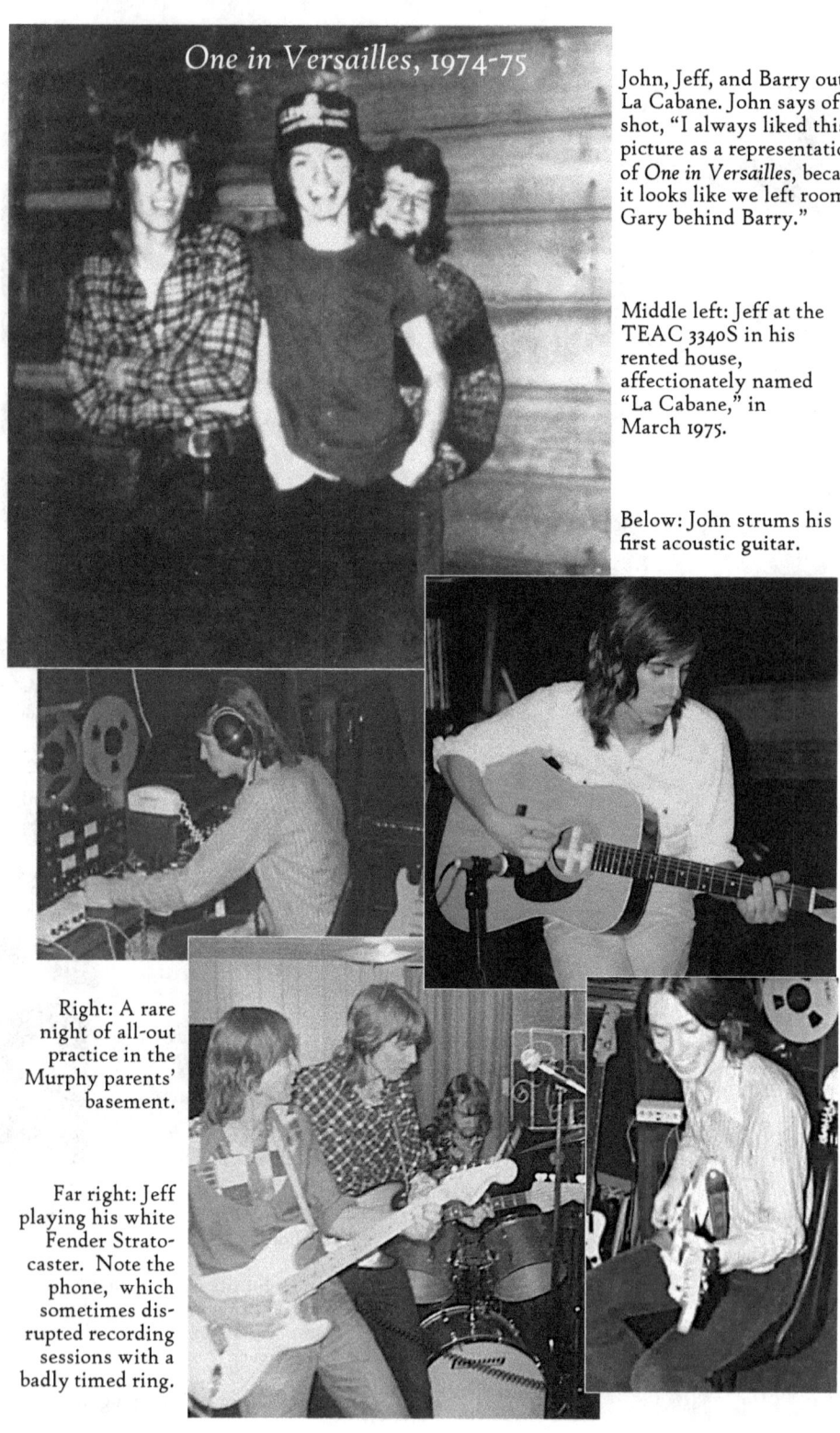

One in Versailles, 1974-75

John, Jeff, and Barry outside La Cabane. John says of this shot, "I always liked this picture as a representation of *One in Versailles*, because it looks like we left room for Gary behind Barry."

Middle left: Jeff at the TEAC 3340S in his rented house, affectionately named "La Cabane," in March 1975.

Below: John strums his first acoustic guitar.

Right: A rare night of all-out practice in the Murphy parents' basement.

Far right: Jeff playing his white Fender Stratocaster. Note the phone, which sometimes disrupted recording sessions with a badly timed ring.

Versailles, France

Gary's sole piece of correspondence from France before the postal strike, inserting his own face onto a comic French stereotype, baguettes and all.

Above left: Back in Zion, Jeff, John, and Barry strike a pose.

Above: Alone in his room, Spanish guitar in hand.

Left: Gary in Versailles, where he spent a year studying architecture while his bandmates continued recording. The palace wall is behind him.

Recording *Bazooka*, 1975

Casual Shoes

The reunited band hangs out, summer 1975.
The upside of having a name like Shoes is frequent free advertising.

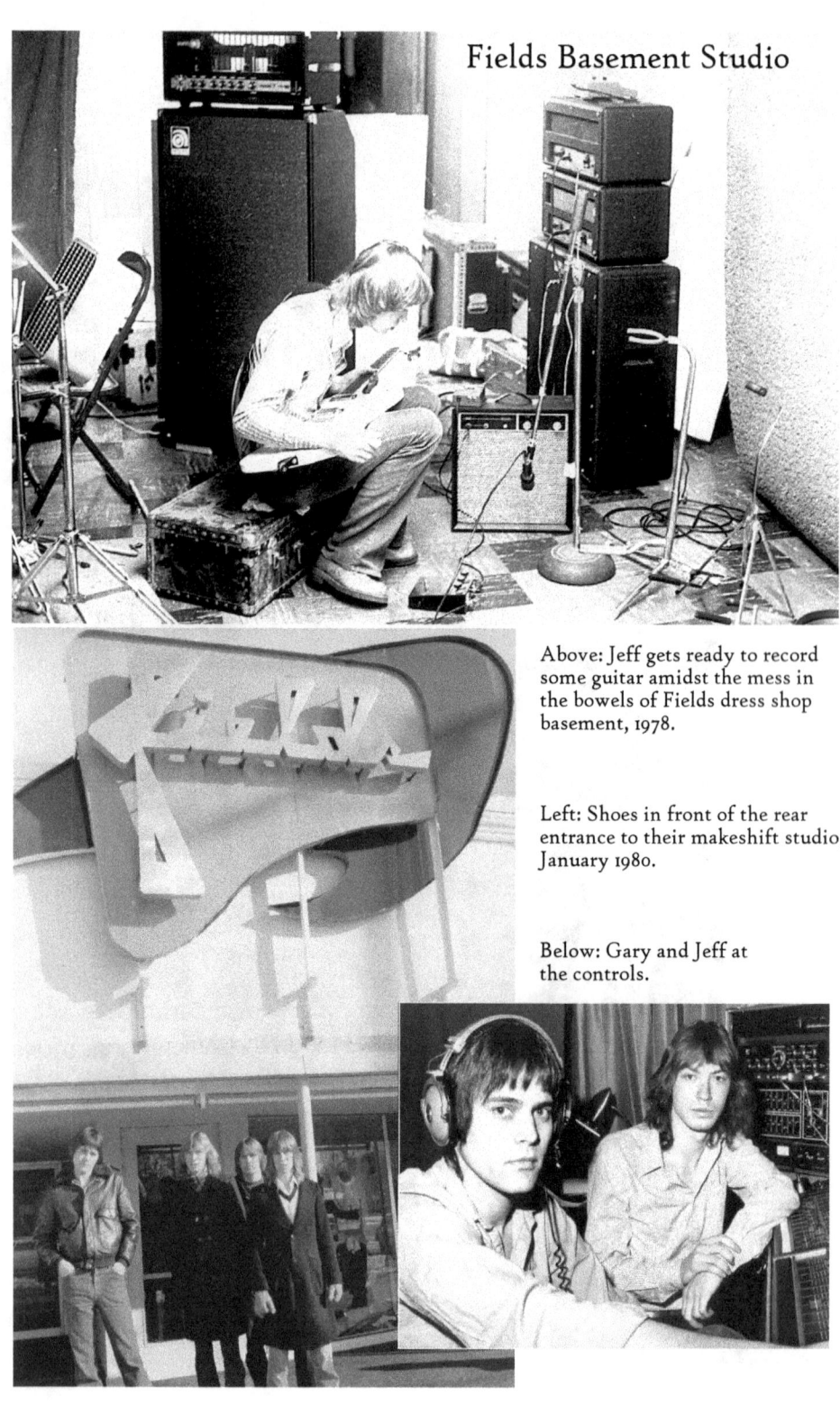

Fields Basement Studio

Above: Jeff gets ready to record some guitar amidst the mess in the bowels of Fields dress shop basement, 1978.

Left: Shoes in front of the rear entrance to their makeshift studio, January 1980.

Below: Gary and Jeff at the controls.

Top: Bomp! Records was an early supporter of Shoes.

Left: Gary records with his Gibson Explorer just before it was stolen from their rented space.

Right: John's Thunderbird bass was spared, but the thieves snatched his Fender Precision.

Bottom: You know you're officially a band when your name is on the PA cabinets.

Opposite page, clockwise from top:
1. Downtown Zion, 1978.
2. John's handmade poster for a local gig.
3. Photo from Shoes fan club application card.
4. Flyer promoting Shoes on the radio.
5. Shoes at My Brother's Pub, Pleasant Prairie, 1976.
6. A few miles away, vacationers ignore the nuclear power plant on Lake Michigan, a Zion landmark.
7. Power pop issue of *Bomp!* magazine.
8. Sleeve for the Bomp!-financed single, 1978.

This page: What a difference a couple of years can make. From sharing space with a weight-watchers club in the basement of a small-town dress shop in 1977 (above) to trying to keep straight faces at a photo shoot in a famed photographer's studio in Los Angeles (below), autumn 1979.

The Manor, Oxfordshire, England
Present Tense, 1979

Above: The main house of The Manor, the all-inclusive studio complex owned by tycoon Richard Branson.

Left: Gary runs through a song. Many guitar and bass overdubs were done in the control room.

Below: Mike Stone at the board under the watchful eyes of Gary and Jeff.

Above: Shirtless because of the heat, Skip lays down a rhythm track in the main house.

Right: Gary contemplates the next guitar part in his Big Star t-shirt.

Below: Jeff with his trusty Gibson RD.

Below right: John prepares to overdub with his Hamer 8-string bass.

Clockwise from top left: Gary and Skip try their hand at snooker. Gary nose best. Jeff on the streets of London town. Two of the three mascot Irish Wolfhounds monitor the progress of Skip's tan. John poolside at the Manor. A pensive Mike Stone.

Clockwise from top: Jeff readies his ax. Gary and manager Dan kickin' back in a London park. Even the loo was used for its ambience. A separate building was designated as the studio. John vocalizes.

Present Tense Promotion, 1979

Though music videos were still uncommon in the United States in 1979--and there was nowhere they could be broadcast regularly--Elektra encouraged Shoes to make videos for four songs off *Present Tense*. "Too Late" was in the process of being released as a single, and "Tomorrow Night" was considered the next front-runner, so they were obvious choices. The songs for the other two videos, "In My Arms Again" and "Cruel You," were selected at the last minute. Shoes taped all four videos in one marathon twenty-hour session.

1. Randee St. Nicholas photo shoot.
2. On the streets of NYC, autumn '79.
3. From *Rock Scene* magazine, Shoes appear at a Hamer guitar giveaway with manufacturer Jol Dantzig. (rockscenester.com)
4. Outtake from *Rolling Stone* photo shoot.
5. Shoes with manager Dan Bourgoise on the Bug office rooftop.

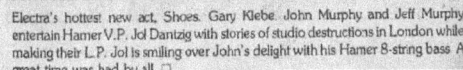

6. Greg Shaw, Bomp! Records.
7. Kenny Buttice & Carol Thompson, Elektra Records.
8. Ira Robbins, *Trouser Press*.

United Western Recorders, Hollywood
Tongue Twister, 1980

Top: Skip, Gary, Hernan Rojas, Richard Dashut (in Shoes t-shirt), John, and Jeff at UWR.
Middle: Gary helps out by tuning a drumhead. Jeff sets levels for his guitar.
Bottom: Hernan engineers a bass overdub by John. Richard ran sessions with an iron hand.

Top: Richard and Hernan concentrate on the business at hand.

Middle left: Gary tries to keep a level head through it all.

Middle right: Skip ready to do some serious damage to his drums.

Fireworks aftermath.

Drummers...always clowning.

Jeff enjoys an adult beverage.

Chicago Recording Company
Boomerang, 1982

1. Shoes take a call at CRC in the winter of '82.
2. Jeff solders.
3. Skip tunes up.
4. Producer Hank Neuberger.
5. Gary warms up his Hamer.

Top: Shoes in the woods, Winthrop Harbor, Illinois.

Center: John, Gary, and Skip sit for an interview in Jeff's apartment.

Left: Photo shoot for *Creem* magazine.

Eighties

1. The band standing tall in the control room of their 16-track facility, Short Order Recorder, Winthrop Harbor, 1984.
2. Gary moonlights as producer for Butch Vig's first band, Spooner.
3. John and Jeff do their best to impress at a home party.
4. John chills while defrosting.
5. Shoes among the mics.

Above: Horsin' around in the studio.

Middle: After relocating to Zion in 1986, SOR upgraded to 24 tracks in 1988.

Left: Publicity shot to promote the release of *Stolen Wishes*.

Platform Shoes

Opposite page:
1. Sharin' a mic in December, 1979.
2. Gary bears down, 1982.
3. First gig, Brat Stop, Kenosha, WI, 1976.
4. John, Rock Around the Dock, Chicago, 1978.
5. Jeff takes a solo, Milwaukee Summerfest, 1990.
6. Gary, Troubadour, Los Angeles, 1999.

This page:
1. Jeff rocks the skinny tie, 1979.
2. John gives his T-bird a workout, Milwaukee Summerfest, 1990.
3. John and Jeff at IPO, Abbey Pub, Chicago, 2003.
4. Gary stands firm, Milwaukee Summerfest, 1990.
5. Zion Leisure Center concert, May 1981.

1. With *Propeller* finished, the boys take a break, spring 1994.
2. *Stolen Wishes* tour with the whole crew, summer 1990.
3. Psyched for the *Propeller* release party.
4. Publicity photo, '94.
5. Huddling with acoustics, early 90's.

Twenty-First Century

1. Rockin' Millennium Park, Chicago, 2007.
2. Shoes hit Tokyo, 2009.
3. John befriends a lovable local.
4. Temple of Shoes.
5. Promoted as the Greasy Rockers' Party.
6. In tourist mode.

Ignition, 2012

1. Gary in his home studio.
2. John builds a bassline.
3. Johnny listens intently.
4. Jeff gets lost in reverie.
5. Gary mulls it over.

1. Jeff takes a turn at engineering.
2. John plucks a bit.
3. Monkeying with mic placement in the drum booth.
4. Check out that amp rack!
5. Gary ponders a playback, overseen by his cat, Psycho.

Shoes 2013

Top, Shoes perform at The Ginger Man at the SXSW Music Festival in Austin, TX, March 2013.

Left, John, long-time publicist Cary Baker, Gary, and Jeff outside Molotov before their first SXSW performance.

The cherished photos on these pages were taken by many different people over the years and selected from the personal collections of John, Jeff, and Gary. Unfortunately, in most instances, we are unable to identify the photographer of a particular photo taken many years ago. Those that we have been able to identify include Randee St. Nicholas, Neal Preston, Mark Siegler, Steven Gardner, Mike Zelenko, John Boydston, Harrison Jones, Sara Townsend, Tim Klebe, Chuck Fieldman, Durinda Quintin, Lorinda Murphy, Jeff Murphy, John Murphy and Gary Klebe.

We wish to thank them, and any others that we may have missed, for their contributions to the photo collection on these pages. Also, a special thanks to the Zion Historical Society for the use of the images depicting early life in Zion.

CHAPTER 7

TWIST AND BEND IT (1980-81)

AS THE NEW DECADE DAWNED, Shoes retreated to Zion and the studio. Buttice had given them a pep talk—"We'll get 'em on the next one!"—and they began the new record and the new year determined to do so.

But there were differences this time. Due to the confluence of *Present Tense*'s rush release, its muddled promotional life, and the lag time before its reviews appeared, Shoes were already working on the demos that would become their sophomore Elektra album, *Tongue Twister*, as the press for *Present Tense* began coming in. John points out that the creation of both *Black Vinyl Shoes* and *Present Tense* had largely been "pure, unaffected by critical opinion," but that "as soon as we started getting feedback [on *Present Tense*], we got self-conscious." Shoes were, for the first time, trying to figure out how to craft songs that would please the arbiters of taste, not just themselves. They had a handful of tunes already in progress—John's winsome "Karen" and propulsive "Hate to Run" had been demoed for *Present Tense*, as had a restructured version of Gary's ripping rocker "Jet Set"—and had re-demoed those almost immediately after getting home from the tour.

Now, still reeling from the whirlwind of 1979, but determined to get back to work, Shoes tried to think as Elektra and Buttice thought, that the secret to capturing the brass ring was high-charting singles. So the three writers hunkered down in their own apartments, each with an identical TEAC four-track, to write some hits.

JOHN, WHO HAD NEVER STRUCTURED his songs traditionally, was convinced that he had the most adjustments to make in order to consciously pen a chart-topper. In fact, he'd long preferred "sort of unusual, more subtle" songs that challenged conventional structures, like those in the folk-rock canon. He often buried titles in the verses (as in *Black Vinyl Shoes*' "Someone Finer") rather than making them the linchpins of choruses; indeed, he resisted the verse-chorus-verse structure in general:

> I had a tendency to not be obvious, to write songs like the ones I gravitated toward by other people. If a song just needs a chorus and a verse, why write more than that? I didn't even leave a space for solos for the longest time. But I could see the standard song structures on *Present Tense* were getting the attention.

Those were the tracks ("Too Late" and "Tomorrow Night") that had made it to the airwaves, the ones Elektra seemed more willing to push. Now, John thought, he'd better write something that would make it on radio as well. For his bandmates' part, they weren't pushing him at all. Jeff said then (as he has all along) that he considered John "a genuine artist"—praising the outside-the-box compositions John himself was beginning to shun. Gary concurred, and additionally lauds John's particular gift for composing ballads—which typically aren't considered highly marketable as singles. "John's stuff was somewhat more fragile, not as commercially-minded as what Elektra was looking for," Gary says. Being acutely aware that none of his songs from *Present Tense* had been selected as singles, John says, "You can't help keeping score in your mind. You worry about being left out; paranoia creeps in." He was determined, then, to figure out how to keep up with his bandmates—who, John thought, already had it all figured out. "Gary in particular was shaping his songs to be singles," John asserts.

On the surface, that observation would seem to hold water, as Gary had written or co-written three of the four singles on *Present Tense*. But he takes issue with John's assessment, insisting, "I wasn't *trying* to write singles." That said, Gary does believe certain song elements and configurations— which might happen to be radio-friendly—just feel "right" to him. But when his sense of "right" becomes his prevailing compositional standard, he assiduously keeps these self-imposed constraints from becoming formulaic. "Routine," Gary pronounces, "is the assassin of innovation."

As for Jeff's creative process, John had always believed it was uncluttered by doubt, almost instinctive. "Jeff was so outwardly confident and sure," says his brother. "He made it look far too easy." And while Jeff allows that this may have been what he was projecting, it's not necessarily what he was feeling:

> I was really only confident in my own taste. If I liked a song I was writing, I pursued it with a lot of focus. The reality was that I always felt behind the eight-ball, trying to keep up with John and Gary's writing, which I viewed as more sophisticated and mature than my own.

In this period of composing *Tongue Twister*, Jeff was particularly focused, rolling out song after song: the lush, gently Latin-spiced melodicism of "Only in My Sleep;" his fingers-crossed take on nightclub trolling, "Hopin' She's the One;" and the dreamy, reminiscent "Found a Girl." The last of these songs was included in the 2011 independent film *Inventory*, and Jeff discussed its genesis with the filmmaker on *Inventory*'s blog:

> In doing the numerous interviews and Q & A sessions to support *Present Tense*, I met a female journalist who invited me over for dinner. She lived over an hour away, so she wrote directions for me on a piece of paper. I approached the situation with cynical skepticism stemming from my previous break-up and had no expectations. ... The relationship eventually traced the meteoric arc

that is typical for people in their mid-twenties, but I wrote this semi-biographical song as a result of that first, optimistic encounter.

"Found a Girl" was praised for its almost photographic realism: longtime Shoes booster Cary Baker, writing in *Night Rock News*, called it, "a Badfinger-esque ballad [evoking] images of bedsheets strewn chaotically about any bedroom as the cold morning light pines in. The detail here is stunning."

Each with his own simple recording setup in his own apartment, Shoes' songwriters worked on new material worthy of bringing back to the still-operational dress-shop basement. Jeff admits they were "feeling more pressure, artistically and financially," though they remained basically confident about their writing. They were driven, too, by a force that had long been a benign, unspoken motivation, but which now seemed to take on a slightly less congenial cast: competition among themselves. John says that process began with the recording of *Present Tense*, which "started to isolate us from each other. The defenses started to go up. We each wanted to do things more on our own: 'I don't want any help; I'm going to make this hit by myself.'" The competitive vibe felt stronger than it had before, though not, at that point, harmful.

And as Shoes' composers started presenting works-in-progress to each other, they regained some of their confidence from the new songs. The Murphy brothers and Klebe were eager to share them with their record company, too, and specifically with Buttice, who was in the middle of transitioning to his longed-for prestige position of VP of A&R. Shoes were a trophy on his shelf: though *Present Tense* hadn't been a blockbuster, its reviews were strong, and Shoes were upbeat that they would, as Buttice had reassured them, "get 'em on the next one"—especially now that the expectations were clearer. As determined as Buttice was to break them, Shoes were equally determined to merit his resolve. "We wanted to give Kenny what he needed to make a hit," John says.

IT WAS JUST BEFORE VALENTINE'S Day when John initially started having difficulty seeing out of his right eye; he described it as a dark shadow rolling down from that corner of his field of vision. It didn't hurt, he remembers, and his response was more confusion than fear: "What the hell is this?" John didn't immediately see a doctor, as he hadn't had health insurance since leaving his city-planning job a year earlier. Hoping the condition would resolve itself, he let a couple of days pass—but the sight didn't return. When John finally sought medical help, he learned that his right retina had detached, and the left was likely to go at any time. Emergency surgery was in order.

Retinal detachment has a variety of possible causes; John recalls his doctors initially asking him if he'd gotten hit, since boxers often suffer from this condition. But they then determined that John's retinal issues likely stemmed from his premature birth. John's disorder, called retinopathy of prematurity (ROP), ran rampant in the 1940s and early 1950s, when pure-oxygen incubators were a common treatment for born-too-soon infants; excess oxygen is believed to have contributed to the blindness of Stevie Wonder, who was born prematurely in 1950. A 1951 study—infamous because researchers allowed the control group of infants to go blind—confirmed the link between the incubators and ROP, but clinical practice had not caught up by November 1953, when John was born. And so in February 1980, he found himself prepping for the surgery that would, hopefully, save his suddenly endangered sight.

This preparation included three days flat on his back to reduce ocular pressure, along with the removal of all the hair around his eyes—both eyelashes and eyebrows. "I looked like someone had taken an eraser and rubbed out my features," as he describes. The doctors reattached John's right retina, and successfully performed preventive surgery on his left.

Shoes' bassist's surgery was mentioned across the music press. Skip remarked in his journal, "One thing that was nice about John's injury: different radio stations picked up on it and said something over the air. 'Send cards,' etc. The newspapers did the same thing." Jeff notes that the Detroit area's Bozo the Clown sent a framed photo with his get-well wishes. Music-biz trade magazine *Cashbox* published an article, "The Strange Case of Mr. Murphy," that included Jeff's home phone number for concerned fans. "But we were almost constantly in the studio, so I wasn't home to get many phone calls," Jeff says now.

John was only hospitalized for a few days, but with two patched eyes and no one else at home, he moved temporarily into Gary's apartment to recover. John says that Gary offered his place partly because John needed a lot of care; Jeff was squeamish about applying the drops and ointments his brother's eyes required. "But John and I were so intertwined with each other's business," Gary remarks, "that it was really no big deal for me." He cut back his time in the studio for a couple of weeks, as well, to tend to his recovering friend.

During this period, John was understandably panicked. "Here I am lying on my back and thinking, 'How the fuck can this be happening now? I've got a recording contract, and a record to make. This is the most important time of my life, and now I'm gonna go blind?' I was freaking out." John's stress level only intensified because he needed new material, but he wasn't even supposed to sit up; there was no way John could write songs.

Gary and Jeff continued to work on their own tunes in his absence, Jeff layering "Strawberry Fields Forever"-style guitars on his aforementioned ballad, "Found a Girl;" Gary chipping away at his danceably hooky, heavier "Burned Out Love." John was only out of the studio for about two weeks, but was wowed (and more than a bit perturbed) by what they'd done without him. "I felt so out of it," John explains. "Don't think I didn't dwell on that."

He was antsy to return to work, and was back in the studio as soon as his eye patches were off. But it's no surprise that—aside from his already-existing "Karen" and "Hate to Run" (both written before the *Tongue Twister* demo sessions), and one other track, "When It Hits" (completed before his surgery)—John's new compositions on the twelve-track *Tongue Twister* are limited to the three group-penned songs: "Your Imagination," "The Things You Do," and "Girls of Today." (He did write and demo one song post-surgically—"In Her Shadow"—but that one wouldn't be recorded until the sessions for Shoes' 1982 album, *Boomerang*.)

ON EACH OF *TONGUE TWISTER*'S three group compositions, the percentage of composing by each of Shoes' troika of songwriters wasn't mathematically equal—indeed, as John points out, "It's not always thirty-three, thirty-three, thirty-three. But we decided that any collaboration would be credited to all three of us, even if the proportion of each one's contribution wasn't completely even." For example, Gary had brought the foundational instrumental structure of "The Things You Do" to John—and John wrote the lyrics and vocal melody over the top of it. Then Jeff added "the spooky guitar fill" that personifies the song. Three sets of fingerprints, three writers.

Other co-credited songs evolved accidentally. For example, Jeff brought what would become album opener "Your Imagination" to the table as a song called "Bad Habit." Going out of town for a few days, Jeff left John to put together the bass line without him, with Gary as engineer. John created the definitive, muscular riff that kicks off the song, and Gary suggested that he alter it slightly the second time through: that bass riff became the song's most distinguishing characteristic.

And although unbidden by Jeff, John and Gary started changing the words around too. John heard the piece as a relationship song—"A Heart to Play With," he called it—and ran with that theme lyrically. Jeff's bandmates were nervous about his response; after all, they'd done a lot to his baby without his knowledge. But Jeff says that when he heard the changes John and Gary had wrought, "I was knocked out, and the song was now officially a three-way collaboration," reprising John's solo towards the end "to further accent that cool bass part."

Shoes rarely shared lyrical duties as completely as they did on "Your Imagination"—partly because the lyric-writing process remained arduous for them individually; adding other perspectives only increased the pressure. John remarks on the tension surrounding the collaborative process:

> It helps bring out the best of everybody, but it's also somewhat more competitive; there's more critiquing, more chance of getting your feelings hurt. When someone brings in his own song, something he wants to sing about, okay, that's what he wants to say; it's fine. But if your name's on it, too, you're more critical. We would butt heads, usually over wording. We had some problems on songs where we'd worked it out musically, but not lyrically.

Lyrics from various incarnations of "Your Imagination" made it into the album version, and so some lines reference one version, some another. For instance, the phrase "Hold the fever down/Work the white heat," are original to "Your Imagination"'s ancestor "Bad Habit," but only the second half of the following phrase made it from the original: "You've got a heart to play with/it's such a drag to waste it." So the final lyrics are a true pastiche.

As "Your Imagination"'s lyrics kept changing, so did its title. They all liked the song, and kept a notebook of scribbled contenders for what to call it. Jeff found "A Heart to Play With" a little "too wimpy"—at that point, the working title was "Time to Make It" (as "Your Imagination" is, in fact, designated on *Double Exposure*, Black Vinyl Records' 2007 dual release of the *Present Tense* and *Tongue Twister* demos.) The final title is Gary's, but that wasn't settled until the last possible second, in the studio in L.A.

"Girls of Today," third of the three triple-credited songs, was written completely differently from the other two, and differently from *Present Tense*'s tuneful triptych "Three Times," to which it bears a surface resemblance. "Girls of Today" was genuinely penned as a group, all together in the studio. "It wasn't pieces that came in separately; we sort of jammed it out," Gary recalls. "We didn't usually do that, but it worked for that song. At some point, someone took it home to fine-tune lyrics, probably John, but it was really a group effort." As Shoes wrote and recorded *Tongue Twister*, they believed that "Girls of Today" would be the first single off the record—"I think there was a lot of unconscious lobbying for it," John says—but things wouldn't work out quite that way.

SHOES ARRANGED TO MEET KEN Buttice as he was passing through Chicago that spring on a triumphal tour to celebrate his finally-attained position as vice-president of Elektra A&R. The band can't remember now whether or not they had sent their demos to Buttice beforehand; certainly Buttice hadn't responded to them, if they had. But they took advantage of Buttice's travel to set up a face-to-face meeting at his high-rise hotel, Astor Tower, in Chicago's swanky Gold Coast neighborhood.

Despite his new status as VP of A&R, Buttice still partied like a radio-promotion guy. Marty Schwartz says that even after Buttice officially moved to A&R, "he never let go of promo; promo never let go of him." When Shoes arrived at Buttice's Astor Tower suite, a promo party was in full swing in an adjoining room. "There were a lot of people around," Gary recalls. "Coming and going. Okay, mostly women. Okay, they were hookers." A steady stream of industry folk poured through the whole night, too: promo guys, local deejays, Buttice's underlings. "Kenny was holding court," John says.

The nature of parties common in this era was described by super-manager Irving Azoff in a 1989 *Hits* magazine interview written by David Adelson. Asked to describe his favorite hotel-trashing incident, Azoff cites one involving Ken Buttice, along with famed guitarist (and notorious party animal) Joe Walsh plus assorted Elektra brass:

> [Walsh] once pushed a piano out of Joe Smith's top-floor suite at … the Astor Towers [sic] in Chicago. They pushed a grand piano through a plate glass window. It was Steve Wax, Kenny Buttice, Burt Stein and others. People like Lou Maglia and others were standing there watching. That sucker flew 22 floors and landed on the manager of the hotel's Cadillac. What was amazing was seeing them knock out all these plate glass windows to get that piano out. And it was all because they wouldn't let Walsh in the restaurant without a tie.

The band could tell from the detritus around them that night that they'd stumbled into a days-long debauch. This wasn't really Shoes' scene, and they waited patiently for Buttice to get free. In the meantime, Gary remembers hearing people laughing about "some wild night they'd had the night before."

Finally, Buttice sat down with the members of Shoes. As always, they watched him do his thing for a while. John tells of one Elektra rep from Chicago whom Buttice corralled and dressed down in front of them. "My boys tell me they're not hearing their songs on the radio," John recalls him saying. Shoes were surprised at Buttice's line of attack; by this time, they'd left *Present Tense* behind and wanted to know what Buttice thought of their *new* material. But he evidently intended for Shoes to see him ostentatiously fighting for them. John says Buttice threatened the rep with, "You've got two weeks to get them some airplay, or you're fired." In retrospect, this performance seemed to Shoes to have been a piece of theater—designed to disarm the band for the bad news that was coming.

Buttice was agitated, distracted. He spent much of the Astor Tower meeting digging under couch cushions, according to John; they didn't know what he was looking for, but assumed it was drugs. (Dan Bourgoise says that this was not unusual at an industry party: "Drugs were rampant, especially with promotion guys.") But Shoes weren't at Buttice's suite to party; they were there to work. Much depended on Buttice's reaction to the demos, and they were anxious about it. Gary remembers a strong feeling of nervous anticipation as they waited for their chance to give their mentor what they had.

Eventually, Shoes got a chance to play their demos. The band members are no longer entirely sure how many songs were presented, or which ones; the demos were basically finished, so he could have heard almost any of them.

But no one forgot Buttice's reaction. He was more serious and subdued than they had ever seen him:

"If I were you guys, I'd be scared."

Shoes were stunned. They understood Buttice to mean that the songs weren't good enough, that their careers were in danger. "It was completely unexpected," Gary says. "We had never heard anything from him but praise—and we were really proud of these songs. We were shaken by his response." John sees Buttice's curt dismissal as possible evidence that, despite his silence, he *had* vetted the songs with his people at Elektra. "He wouldn't have said we should be scared if Marty Schwartz or someone hadn't told him there was an issue," John theorizes.

Buttice went on to explain to them that they should be shooting more for the kind of songs written by his new find, Robbie Dupree. He played them Dupree's flyweight soul-pop tune "Steal Away," which would hit the top ten later that year. "It sounded exactly like the Doobie Brothers' 'What a Fool Believes,'" John says. "We didn't hear anything new or interesting there." They looked at each other uncomfortably. "That's not really what we do,"

Gary explained warily. But it was clear "Steal Away" was what Buttice wanted.

Shoes' relationship with Ken Buttice was always complex. He wasn't much older than they were—maybe thirty, to their mid- to late-twenties—but he'd accrued so much power and money that they were in awe of him. At the same time, they genuinely liked Buttice—the friendly, wisecracking aspect of their relationship would last as long as both parties were connected with Elektra. And the band thought Buttice was trying to wow them, too. "He loved thinking he'd just reached up his sleeve and pulled out this diamond in the rough [i.e., Shoes]," John muses. "He wanted to prove to us that he could make things happen." The concern Buttice expressed in this meeting, then, might have stemmed from his own feeling that he hadn't been able to deliver for them the success he'd promised on *Present Tense*—that it was *he* who had failed *them*, not the other way around—and he that feared he couldn't sell these songs either.

Other factors may have influenced Buttice's perception as well. The Astor Tower bash was at best a distracting environment, and though he should have heard the songs in advance, they couldn't tell with any certainty that he had. And now here the band was, in the middle of a party, pressing him for a reaction.

Though Buttice was now officially the head of Elektra A&R, he'd had little experience making his own musical-value judgments. He knew how to sell a salable product, but not necessarily what *made* a product salable, and that's what he was being asked to determine. He had not been in a position to okay demos for *Present Tense*; Marty Schwartz had brought him *Black Vinyl Shoes* and Maxanne Sartori had confirmed its quality. Now that he was obliged to listen to new material and evaluate its potential without his creative lieutenants, it was plausible that Buttice was shooting from the hip —unless he had already shared the songs with Schwartz and Sartori and was merely passing along their opinions. It just wasn't clear.

BUT WHEN SHOES LEFT ASTOR Tower that night, it didn't really occur to them that Buttice's negative response to their songs might be anyone's problem but their own; they shouldered all the blame themselves. "That was a long, quiet ride home," John remembers.

The next day Shoes' official A&R rep, Carol Thompson, phoned the band to apologize for Buttice's behavior—not his response to the demos, but for exposing them to the seedier side of the record business.

Though Thompson was on the staff of Elektra A&R, she'd started as an accountant, mostly managing recording budgets; Shoes were her first shot at being a creative rep. Thompson was also Buttice's faithful retainer, helping him adjust to his new department—"She knew the ropes of A&R and he didn't," Bourgoise observes—and she took increasing responsibility for guiding Shoes during their Elektra tenure. Over time, as she grew more comfortable in her new position, Thompson attempted to expand her influence beyond changing their look and protecting their innocence; Shoes found that her suggestions became more frequent, more intrusive.

Most of Thompson's contact with Shoes was through Dan Bourgoise. "We spent a lot of time together," he says of Thompson. The band teased Dan that Carol was flirting with him, and that for Shoes' sake, he should flirt back. "We had a lot of dinners," Bourgoise shrugs. "But I was always doing business."

Shoes were frankly amused that Thompson had felt the need to apologize to them for Buttice's Astor Tower carousing. It wasn't like they didn't know there were drugs around; as the seventies gave way to the eighties, recreational chemicals had permeated all corners of the music business. But even so, Gary says, "They weren't really offered to us." He remembers people constantly slipping off together, doing underhanded handoffs in elevators, that kind of thing. However, maybe because they were from a small town, maybe because they had a reputation as nice guys, Shoes were largely seen as being outside that sphere of influence, as too pure to corrupt.

Shoes didn't really mind being outside that part of the music business; only Skip had ever been much of a partier anyway. And as John notes, "We weren't judgmental." Still, band members say that apparent drug use by Elektra staff did at times affect the way they did business with Shoes. "You'd wonder: is it the coke talking, or the drink, or did you just want to get going to the strip club?" says John of Shoes' decreasingly frequent, and increasingly hurried, interactions with Buttice.

Kept off-balance by Buttice, amused by Thompson, Shoes returned to tweaking their almost-finished demos. No matter what Buttice thought, these were the songs they had, and these were the songs they were going to use on the new album.

By the end of March all the demos were done, and John had eyebrows again. It was time to get recording.

SHOES STARTED LOOKING AGAIN at record producers, and on March 24, Chris Kimsey—at that point engineering the Rolling Stones' album *Emotional Rescue*—flew to Chicago. Thompson picked him up to drive him north to Zion; Skip's journal entry reports, however, that when she left the airport, she accidentally headed south and ended up in Indiana before reversing course to Zion. But Kimsey was not yet finished with *Emotional Rescue*, and he couldn't free up his schedule quickly enough to take the reins on Shoes' new project. Geoff Workman, fresh off helming the Cars, was discussed as well, but according to Skip's journal, "Workman was waiting to hear from Foreigner."

Skip's next entry, on April 24, expressed the band's frustration: "We are really getting upset because we should have been in the studio months ago. I hope things don't turn out like last year."

But producer negotiations dragged on into the next month, with the band chafing at the delay. Finally, in mid-May, Elektra told Shoes to just come to Los Angeles. John says, "We left for L.A. because we were getting antsy; we thought we'd have better luck locking in a producer if we were out there to push in person." Once Shoes arrived on the West Coast, they remained until *Tongue Twister* was finished in September.

The last few months had convinced Shoes that Elektra's stance on them was "out of sight, out of mind," and they were equally convinced that they'd do a better job keeping on top of Elektra if they were based in L.A. When Shoes went west to pin down a producer and make their new record, then, there were serious conversations among them about whether this move should be permanent.

Shoes remembered too well wishing they had their own equipment while recording in England, so when they packed up this time, they took no chances: everything but the performance P.A. went on the truck. Shoes hired two roadies, Bill Barnett and Bill Russell, to drive the equipment to California. The road crew routed themselves through the South, collecting a huge cache of fireworks along the way.

Shoes were primed for a good, long California stay, though no one was sure how long it would last. "It was a calculated gamble," says Gary, "that we'd be there for a while." "We'd rented a storage barn to rehearse," John affirms. "We knew we weren't coming right back home, in any case."

SKIP, WHO CONFIDED IN HIS JOURNAL that "you can always tell how smooth things are going to be by the first day," reported that Shoes' arrival in L.A. on May 19, 1980 was decidedly inauspicious—flying into smog so thick, he wrote, that they couldn't see the wings of the plane. And Elektra had sent an absurdly puny car for them, a subcompact Chevrolet Chevron. "Here are five people [the six-foot-plus band members and the Elektra employee sent to fetch them] with 12 pieces of baggage getting into a compact," Skip chronicled. "I didn't think we would make it, but we did."

The band stopped briefly in Hollywood to see Dan Bourgoise at Bug Music, before continuing on to the Oakwood Garden condominiums, a luxuriously appointed complex often used by the entertainment industry for long-term residencies. Located just a few miles from United Western Studios on Sunset Boulevard in Hollywood, it had pools and tennis courts, a Jacuzzi and a billiard room. But most of Shoes' apartments were not ready; only Jeff's was fully set up for his stay. The others' lacked such basic necessities as bedding and toilet paper, and it took several days to get their living circumstances straightened out. There were professional problems, too—when Shoes first tried to rehearse, they found their assigned studio locked. (For his part, Skip wasn't all that disappointed; he was more eager to reassert his tennis skills against "Jeffy Connors.")

On May 21, when Shoes had been out west only a couple of days, they caught a performance by popular local band Great Buildings (whose guitarists/vocalists Danny Wilde and Phil Solem would later form nineties popsters the Rembrandts, of TV sitcom *Friends*' theme-song fame) at the famed Sunset Strip nightclub Whisky A Go Go.

It was backstage at the Whisky that Shoes met Richard Dashut, the already widely-renowned producer of such blockbuster Fleetwood Mac albums as *Rumours* and *Tusk*.

Dashut was a Tinseltown native and had been an aspiring sound engineer in 1972, working as a janitor at Hollywood's Crystal Sound recording studios— "I wasn't even allowed in the control room except to vacuum and empty the ashtrays," he remembers—when he met producer Keith Olsen. Olsen hired him away to work at Sound City Studios, where Olsen was head engineer. Dashut's first job at Sound City was, once again, maintenance—and while painting the control room on his second day, Dashut met then-unknown Lindsey Buckingham and Stevie Nicks, who were recording a demo. The three became housemates and fast friends almost immediately.

Soon after, Olsen took Dashut under his professional wing. Dashut went on to serve as second engineer on the Olsen-produced *Buckingham Nicks* (the pair's sole release) in 1973. When the American soft-rock duo were invited to join the British former blues band Fleetwood Mac two years later, it wasn't long before Dashut came along, too, first as a live sound engineer for their 1975 tour, and then a year later in the studio to produce gargantuan hit album *Rumours*. He was drawn into the over-the-top world of Fleetwood Mac: the parties, the drugs, the drama; he owed his loyalty to them before anyone else.

When Shoes met Dashut, he'd just finished two intensive years working on *Rumours*' follow-up, *Tusk*: over twelve months on the recording, and nearly a year on the road with the Mac's subsequent, chaotic tour. According to drummer Mick Fleetwood, in his memoir *Fleetwood: My Life and Adventures in Fleetwood Mac*, both he and Dashut developed a crippling fear of flying on that tour, driven by a rash of DC-10 disasters, including the one that had almost killed Shoes the year before. Dashut begged off the tour in March 1980, but before he left, Fleetwood writes, "We gave Richard a huge farewell party that turned into a bacchanal." At one point in the festivities, Dashut "had to grovel before Fleetwood Mac. When his degradation was complete, we made him swear eternal fealty to the band."

In his conversation with Shoes at the Whisky, Dashut mentioned that he had been back in L.A. for a couple of months. In fact, he had just bought a house in Malibu, was looking to stay in town for a while—and was at loose ends professionally. Dashut had said in a *Billboard* interview in late 1979 that he had "no plans to produce" any material: "That's something I may or may not do this year. For some reason, I don't have this burning desire to do something totally on my own … [but] if you ask me a month from now, I'll probably be biting my nails to get back in the studio."

The members of Shoes immediately sprang to the alert. "We had a short-list of dream producers," says Gary, "and he was on it." In 1980, Fleetwood Mac was, quite simply, the biggest band in the world. And here was Fleetwood Mac's producer, right in front of them and actually between projects.

Fleetwood Mac had been name-checked by Shoes in their 1977 *Chicago Reader* interview with Don McLeese, lauding the Anglo-American group's gleaming production style. "Fleetwood Mac was one of the few bands we liked that were on the radio," John says now. "We saw ourselves as doing the same kind of simple pop as they did. They had a guitar emphasis, but there was a pop sensibility in the guitars; they propelled the song." For Jeff, Fleetwood Mac had been one of his role-model bands when considering the importance of production: "I became acutely aware of the tone of the kick drum after first hearing the Keith Olsen-produced *Fleetwood Mac* LP. [Dashut engineered that 1975 mega-seller.] *Rumours* was a step up from that, in that the tone of each instrument was so distinctive."

And Shoes were taken with Dashut personally, enjoying the hit producer's affable, unpretentious manner. "He was like us, hanging out in jeans and a t-shirt," Gary says. "He seemed to have a similarly offbeat sense of humor as we do. And humor is very important in the studio; otherwise, things get pretty tense." John confirms Gary's initial impression: "We had met some producers who had an attitude, and we knew that's not what we wanted; Richard *could* have had one, based on his track record, but he didn't."

Though he didn't know their music, when Shoes casually asked Dashut that same night if he'd be interested in hearing their demos, he agreed to give them a listen. Just over a week later, Fleetwood Mac's multi-platinum producer was helming Shoes' new major-label album. In a 1981 interview with their local *Zion-Benton News*, John noted, "It was like fate decided we would work with him."

IN ADDITION TO COMMERCIAL success, Dashut brought many other useful attributes to the table once recording began. For one, he was accustomed to dealing with a perfectionist band with multiple songwriters, articulating several discrete artistic visions simultaneously, and he expected that process to take some time. In a 1979 *Billboard* interview, Dashut pointed out that "when you have five individuals in the group with different opinions, it takes time to get everybody's ideas." He saw the role of the production team—which on *Tusk* comprised himself and his co-producer Ken Callait—as a centering influence in the recording process, saying, "Ken and I take the energy of the band and focus it. ... We are the vortex." Indeed, Dashut was pretty much fresh from recording with a musician whose exactitude and urge to control made Shoes look like dilettantes: his friend and erstwhile housemate Lindsey Buckingham.

Fleetwood Mac were notorious for over-the-top studio conflicts, and Dashut knew how to deal with them. He was adept at wielding humor in tense situations, at convincing Shoes to take days off, at using studio time to decompress. The producer also knew, John said, "when to withdraw and leave us to shout it out," beating a strategic retreat with his Chilean engineer, Hernán Rojas. Dashut was like *Present Tense*'s Mike Stone, in that he was more of an engineer than a producer in practice. But unlike Stone, who had sought to keep the band members shoehorned into their prescribed roles—as performers rather than producers—Dashut took in stride Jeff and Gary's worrywart hovering over the recording process, even making the band co-producers. "Richard was way more collaborative with us," says Jeff, "probably because he worked so closely with Lindsey and had developed that position of cooperation. He supported just about anything we wanted to try."

Also, Richard Dashut took the demos very, very seriously, using them as the constant reference point the band had intended them to be—a clear indication that he respected Shoes' production of their own work.

Dashut, like Stone, had a preferred recording milieu: he wanted to work on Shoes' new album in Los Angeles. He owned a new house in Malibu, and having just returned from a year of globe-trotting, Dashut didn't want to travel.

But recording in L.A. was a far more fraught prospect for Shoes than it might have been for another band. "We were terrified about Elektra coming in and controlling the show," Gary says frankly. For *Present Tense*, Shoes had sought as much distance and isolation as possible, crossing an ocean to get it; did they really want to work right in the belly of the beast? Nevertheless, as Dan Bourgoise puts it, "Richard Dashut liked the system in L.A., and Shoes liked him." So L.A. it was.

Dashut intervened, too, in order to assuage the hit-fixated Ken Buttice, assuring him that the material for *Tongue Twister* had real chart potential. Since Dashut had steered monster albums that had sold about thirty million units in the previous three years, Buttice accepted his evaluation.

THE CONGENIAL DASHUT WAS also keen to welcome Shoes to California, inviting them out to his Malibu home the first weekend in June. John remembers him coming out to greet them accompanied by two new, relatively unusual, toys: he was riding a moped and listening to a Sony Walkman, both still largely unknown consumer items in America. The producer told the band he'd been touring with Fleetwood Mac in Japan when he picked up his personal cassette player; the Walkman's headphones were, at that moment, filling his ears with Shoes' demos for what would become *Tongue Twister*.

They proceeded up to the house for a meeting. Also present was Hernán Rojas, whom Dashut had asked to engineer Shoes' new record.

Rojas had been a musician in Salvador Allende's Chile when General Augusto Pinochet seized power in a notorious U.S.-engineered coup in 1973. Rojas' job—playing guitar in the backing band for the Santiago stage production of *Jesus Christ Superstar*—ended when the production was shut down under Pinochet's dictatorial regime. Rojas escaped north to the States, and like Dashut before him, was hired as a general laborer at a good-sized studio, the Village Recorder in Hollywood. He fell into engineering partly because he was bilingual: a Brazilian band was working at Village Recorder, and he was called in to communicate with them, Spanish being close enough to Portuguese to facilitate understanding.

As a house engineer, Rojas had met Dashut during the mixing sessions for Fleetwood Mac's single "You Make Loving Fun" (their fourth and final hit from *Rumours*), and was swept into Mac world from then on. In May 1980, Dashut called Rojas and said, "There's this young band that wants to work with me. Are you interested?" Rojas assented; at that first meeting in Malibu, he recalls, everyone kicked around ideas about which songs should make the record before going outside to look at Dashut's property.

The producer invited Shoes to try out his moped, an offer John gamely accepted. The bassist received a quick tutorial—"'Right grip accelerates, the left one is for brakes'—piece of cake, got it," he recalls thinking. But it didn't work out quite that way, in John's retrospective play-by-play:

> I twist the right grip and I lurch forward … twist again, lurch again … my legs are both sticking out, trying to balance the thing, and I'm wobbling down the driveway, toward the sandy road. I keep twisting the right grip, forgetting my instructions: right grip accelerates, left grip brakes. … I see a car coming around the bend and I'm about at the end of the driveway. I'm panicking, I'm jerking forward, off-balance, legs outstretched, trying to brake à la Fred Flintstone.
>
> I hit the narrow sandy road and I'm trying to stay on the lip of it, because of the approaching car, but there's also a little drop-off into the brush, so I don't have many options for where to head. The next

> thing I know I'm airborne, sailing over the handlebars as the moped stubbornly stays put. The car drives past, the guys run over to me; I'm lying in the road. I sheepishly get up, unhurt; while dusting myself off I look over to see Richard gingerly pick up his moped. I say, "Richard, I'm so sorry; is it okay?" And he graciously says, "It's all right; don't worry about it," as he props the wounded road-beast upright.

Once they'd assured themselves that John wasn't really hurt, Skip scribbled in his journal, "We laughed our asses off."

During *Tongue Twister*'s recording, the producer's visiting father took his own spill from the moped but fared less well; Gary says that the elder Dashut was bedridden for several weeks.

As Mike Stone had done, Richard Dashut started with the drums. But whereas in England this had meant finding a live-sounding room at the Manor to achieve the best ambient effect, this wasn't the case in L.A. Rojas says that "we were looking for a really big drum sound, like Led Zeppelin." However, United Western's Studio B had been an old big-band studio (Sinatra and Elvis had recorded there too, according to Rojas), and the rooms were huge and echoey—which necessitated a good deal of experimentation.

As Gary notes:

> United Western's studios could accommodate whole orchestras—and we took advantage of the large space to capture that natural, ambient reverb for the drums. When we recorded it, it had a larger sound than *Present Tense*. But during Dashut's mixing, *Tongue Twister* got dryer. It *should* have been a more ambient record.

Dashut, says John, spent "days and days recording one stick hitting one drum. Thunk. Thunk. Thunk. But we thought, maybe this is how you're supposed to do it, you know?" According to Rojas, not all the drums were recorded that way: "Some were done as an ensemble. But we were definitely pursuing the obsession to create a perfect drum track."

Shoes repeatedly told themselves to "man up—this is what the big boys *really* do," no matter how fixated Dashut's technique seemed. Gary remembers them all being intrigued by the process at first, enjoying the discovery of different tones and colors in the drums, and fascinated by watching the master, Dashut, at work; but eventually they wearied of it. (In fact, the painstaking process had serious repercussions at the end, when *Tongue Twister* went over time and over budget.) John in particular came to the conclusion that such extreme meticulousness sucked the life and momentum out of the recording process: "You'd go in all pumped to record, and *that's* all you'd do." Rojas says that Shoes' style was a factor, too, observing, "These guys were into the post-punk, new-wave drum patterns that were more complicated. But to [keep those complex beats], your inner clock has to be Swiss; it has to be perfect." If one drum at a time was what it took to get the beat just right, so be it. Dashut confirms that this was his preferred method: "I was a real drum freak. It was really important for me [that the drums] have good timing, and a good feel. ... But the goal was to make the record *sound* live in the end."

And Skip, on whose behalf all this was taking place, wrote in his journal, "It sure as hell took long enough."

It wasn't that Dashut forced Shoes to vivisect the recording process just to be difficult; this was simply the ferociously detailed procedure he was used to. "Not a lot of groups then recorded live—that's just not how we did it," Dashut stresses. "When I recorded with Lindsey Buckingham, it was *all* overdubs." Gary adds:

> He seemed to have this idea, I guess from working with Fleetwood Mac, that this was *supposed* to be a painful process ... In dealing with them, Dashut was convinced that there was a direct relationship between the time you spent on something and its outcome. He'd seen a lot of meticulous long-term projects become successes.

But even Gary, the most methodical and perfectionist of the three, recognized that Dashut didn't do Shoes' production process any favors in the long run: "That practice of painstakingly precise production was a bad thing for us to get into—after that, nothing was ever quite good enough." Still, Gary recognizes their own complicity in the scrimshawed production method, too, saying, "Dashut wasn't dictatorial at all, but we were impressionable." Or, as John puts it, "Who was going to say no to Richard Dashut?"

Every instrument received the same careful treatment as the drums. One United Western visitor recalls staying for several hours, listening to Gary (whose guitar was plugged directly into the recording console) hit the same three chords (a snippet of "Yes or No") over and over and over. Control meant separation, perfection. "The style of recording at that time was to isolate and keep the sound from being contaminated by other sounds," John explains. He remembers combing through completed bass parts in isolation, "to check for unnecessary squeaks or odd buzzing, variations in pacing, et cetera. It got a little OCD."

Shoes probably could have challenged Dashut's method, pronouncing a particular take good enough and moving ahead—certainly Dashut himself was easygoing enough not to take offense—but they were in awe of his skill and résumé.

The band had other production differences with their producer as well. Dashut tended to lean away from distortion, especially on non-lead instruments, but Shoes liked to use it—and lots of it: "Those fuzzy, buzzy guitars were a big part of our sound," John stresses. Rojas describes hunkering down in the control room with John, trying to coax the eight-string Hamer bass into some cool, distorted sounds; the engineer says his experiments with John were necessarily somewhat secret for that reason. John recalls that his distinctive bass line on "Your Imagination," for example, had "some flanging in the demo version … you can hear that kind of almost loose, bouncy, rubber-band sound on *Double Exposure*." Dashut had removed the effect during recording, but John and Rojas put some adornment back on— not the dramatic flanging, but a more subtle fuzz— during mixing.

Dashut wasn't all that keen on distortion with electric guitars, either. "He certainly didn't like it when I used it," Gary remembers. "He didn't see any reason for rhythm guitars to have effects at all." One of Gary's most distortion-heavy songs—"Burned Out Love"—met with a lukewarm response from Shoes' producer. "At one point I said to him, 'Richard, you just don't *like* distortion,'" Gary recounts. "It was an observation, not an accusation." Dashut countered that Lindsey Buckingham employed a lot of distortion. "But not the way we did," Gary points out. "Lindsey used it only on lead guitar; we liked it on every guitar." They did manage to sneak in a fair amount of fuzz, eventually, without directly crossing Dashut, for whom they had the utmost respect.

Shoes were learning from Dashut as they had learned from Mike Stone, and one vital skill they took from those sessions was the art of looping: taping a part they were happy with (for example, a guitar hook or a drum fill), and inserting it throughout a song.

Initially, Shoes were leery of the technique, though Dashut assured him he had used it on big hits, including Fleetwood Mac's "Dreams." When John ventured, "Won't people notice that?" Dashut casually shot back, "Did you?" On *Tongue Twister*, when they used looping, it was solely with the drums. "But only on some songs," Gary says, "and only a little." John adds, "We were overdubbing parts that would have been impossible for one drummer to do." Later in their careers, drum looping would become a crucial tool for them in their own production, when the role of Shoes' timekeeper would be a revolving one.

OF COURSE, DURING THE *TONGUE TWISTER* sessions Shoes had a regular drummer, and though looping took even more responsibility away from Skip, he cheerfully accepted this reduction of his role, taking up residence by the condominium pool; Bourgoise nicknamed him "The Bronze Adonis."

John, meanwhile, was hiding from the sun. Not long after Shoes' arrival in L.A., he'd been visited by a girl from Zion, who left him with the virulently infectious eye condition conjunctivitis, commonly known as pinkeye. Despite the visual trauma that had befallen him in early spring, he delayed dealing with the problem as long as possible. On June 24, Skip mentioned in his journal that John was having eye trouble and blaming it on dry air and his contact lenses; by June 27, it was clear that he had a serious infection. On June 28, Skip wrote that Gary said John needed to go to the hospital; they learned there that he had also scratched the cornea of one eye.

John remembers that all his bandmates accompanied him to the doctor, where his left *and* right eyes ended up patched—one to heal the cornea, the other to keep both eyes still—for the second time in four months, and John received a stern warning from the doctor about the importance of shrouding his baby blues for a while. But when his fellow Shoes drove him back to the condominium, they inexplicably dropped him off in the parking lot outside his apartment, alone and blind. John called into the darkness, "Jeff? Gary? Skip?" But they were gone. And so, violating the orders his doctor had just given him, John pried up the gauze on his good eye and found his way back to his apartment, exploding furiously at his oblivious bandmates when they returned.

COMPARATIVELY SPEAKING, THE pace of the *Tongue Twister* sessions was more relaxed than that of *Present Tense*, though Shoes were still working much of the time. "I guess that's the laid-back L.A. studio vibe that people refer to," Jeff says sardonically. Dashut had an hour's commute to and from his home in Malibu, so Shoes usually arrived and started without him, working with engineer Hernán Rojas, second engineer David Ahlert, or by themselves.

The studio environment at United Western was much looser than it had been the previous summer at The Manor. More than the usual complement of inevitable pranks were pulled; some inside the studio, some outdoors—often involving the roadies' fireworks they'd purchased on the way to California. Says Jeff, "There were ongoing launches and mayhem." "We were nuts," Dashut chuckles. They recorded some of the ensuing hijinks to fill out the breaks between songs on *Tongue Twister*. (Some of these snippets ended up being appended to tracks on Shoes' rarities-and-outtakes CD, *As Is*.)

One incitement to trouble was a receptionist at United Western to whom they'd taken a fancy. ("We all thought she was hot," John admits, and Gary insists she liked them all right back.) The receptionist, like most service workers in L.A., was an aspiring celebrity: she had modeling headshots lying around, and also wanted to be a singer. She'd had a previous relationship with English producer Mike Chapman—late of the U.K.'s Chinnichap bubblegum hit factory and producer of none other than *Get the Knack*—who was then ensconced in another studio in United Western's complex, working on *soi-disante* punkette Suzi Quatro's *Rock Hard* album; Chapman, they remembered hearing, also aimed to make the receptionist-cum-wannabe-singer a star.

This wasn't anything more than studio gossip until Chapman, through the grapevine, warned Shoes, Dashut, Rojas, and the other members of their crew to stay away from the receptionist and her friends, whom he termed "my girls." Naturally, the gang took it as a challenge, determined not only to woo these young women, but simultaneously to make Chapman's life miserable.

Dashut tells of having an ongoing feud with Chapman that predated the summer of 1980: "I've always had a thing about people who take themselves a little too seriously. Chapman had produced those two records [Blondie's *Parallel Lines* in 1978 and *Get the Knack*, in 1979, both multi-platinum] and thought he was king of the world." Dashut was determined to take him down a peg, and Shoes inadvertently—but enthusiastically—became pawns in the skirmish between the two mega-producers. "It was stupid," John says now. "I never even met Mike Chapman."

One battlefront was the arcade game Asteroids. There was a machine right outside Chapman's studio, and when Shoes arrived, the high scores all belonged to Mike Chapman. "It was Chapman's initials MDC, MDC, MDC, all the way down," Gary relates. "We were determined to wipe those off, and we replaced them, one by one." They didn't use their personal initials, however; by August, the high scores all read SHU, SHU, SHU.

Another *casus belli* was the girls—increasingly, The Girl. It is she who screams about the state of her clothing on the studio-vérité outtakes the band was collecting. (Her clip appears at the opening of "Thing of the Past" on *As Is*.) Rojas remembers their making United Western's receptionist an offer: "We promised her everything—'Oh, sure! We'll produce your demo!'" They even had her in to sing, in an apparently professional set-up. "But we weren't actually recording it," he says.

Shoes and their crew conducted a sort of guerilla campaign designed to disrupt Chapman's sessions, as well. United Western, which dated from the 1950s, featured an intercom system that was controlled from a central office. Someone (no one admits who) broke into the office and hijacked the intercom to Chapman's studio. There was a hardcore magazine sitting around their control room—*Velvet*, a sort of lesser *Hustler*—and it came with a flexi-disc called *Velvet Talks*, which featured a woman's voice feigning sexual excitement. They created a loop of that track, Rojas says, and played the loop through the intercom, pumping it into Chapman's session. "We were told [by second engineer Ahlert, who often brought them studio gossip] that Michael Chapman was fairly amused by the prank," Jeff says, "but the smoke bomb caused a slight postponement of the sessions over there."

Of all the escapades of the summer, the smoke bomb caper was indeed among the most consequential. Rojas says that one of their roadies sneaked into Chapman's basement studio while Chapman and company were on break and planted said device, which had a long fuse; thus, it did not detonate until Chapman and his musicians were back on the job. Smoke filled the studio, ending sessions for the day, and costing thousands of dollars in lost time.

It wasn't just Chapman and his crew that got bombarded; Shoes subjected each other to similar fusillades. Jeff was trying to record the lead vocal for "Your Imagination" when someone—he's not sure who—released a flurry of bottle rockets into the main studio. "It was a large room," he says, "so the bottle rockets ricocheted around and exploded harmlessly"—annoying, but not dangerous.

Dashut fared less well; when a similar barrage was unleashed on him, he was in the bathroom. Jeff relates:

> While he was standing at the urinal, he was subjected to a dose of bottle rockets; Richard was a great-natured prankster himself and said he deserved the same treatment as everyone else. Unfortunately, the bathroom was much smaller [than the studio] and, due to the white-tiled walls, *much* louder. One of the rockets exploded close to Richard's ear as he helplessly stood, completing his task at hand. He said his hearing became distorted

in that ear and he felt pain, so he went to the doctor, who told him he had blood in his ear, had burst his eardrum, and shouldn't be exposed to loud music for three weeks. We continued to work in his absence, but as I recall, he couldn't stay away for that long and would drop by occasionally—and returned for good before the entire three-week period had passed.

The prank's fallout was embarrassing, but not all bad: during his absence, Dashut visited the Elektra offices to vouch for the band's progress and production skills. (It was Dashut's vote of confidence, Jeff thinks, that would convince Elektra to give Shoes a shot at producing themselves on their next album, *Boomerang*.)

"Looking back on it now, as an adult," Rojas muses, "I feel responsible for doing all that playing when we were supposed to make a great album. But it was a very competitive environment, and we were drawn in. ... So much energy was put into those pranks."

THE BAND'S HIGH SPIRITS DURING the *Tongue Twister* sessions were manifested in other ways, too. For one thing, they were determined, Bourgoise says, to "open up the production process a little bit." Having gotten past their earlier concerns about label meddling, the band now invited Elektra executives, including Ken Buttice, to hear playback sessions—something unthinkable even a year earlier. But Shoes had recently realized the value of being seen as team players, which the band demonstrated by making their Elektra colleagues feel welcome in the studio.

They invited other people in to hear what they were recording, too—girls they had met through work, like Elektra's publicity staff and the forbidden females of United Western. In July, members of Fleetwood Mac took a month off from their ongoing marathon tour, visited United Western, and weighed in on Shoes. John reports that Lindsey Buckingham, who'd come to see Dashut, "didn't want to make it a big deal that he was there"—but remarked approvingly of "Burned Out Love," "Sounds like a hit." And they heard from Rojas that Stevie Nicks, who was dating Hernán at the time, "stopped by during mixing and was singing along with 'Karen,' trying to harmonize with it," John says. The band members were understandably flattered by these votes of confidence.

Shoes' strategy to establish themselves as a "company band" was to make friends with the label people so the Elektra folk might be more inclined to work the records enthusiastically; the band went all in on Elektra extracurriculars. Shoes gamely participated in company picnics, bowling tournaments, and a baseball game in which the record label took on the artists and their management. And Shoes genuinely did like the staff at Elektra—and baseball.

1980 WAS A BASEBALL KIND OF summer. Shoes sponsored a girls' softball team back in Zion, coached by their old *Lime* buddy, Ed Erickson. And Dashut organized another baseball game in L.A., this one with the band and crew versus the staff at United Western, something he had often done with Fleetwood Mac. "I really like baseball," Dashut says simply. "It's a good way to break up the pressure of recording."

In his journal, Skip—who was not at the studio for pregame preparation and practice—made note of his bandmates' excitement as the contest approached: "They have been buying ball gloves and baseball bats. Set up a carpet so they could throw a ball in the studio. I can see this is going to be a big deal."

Gary, the former jock, was mildly amused as the comparatively non-athletic Dashut took the lead in organizing the Shoes team, running practices on Elektra time. "He was trying to take control, and he wasn't really a ballplayer," Gary says charitably. "Meanwhile, I'm thinking, 'Okay, I'll stand over here and pitch and blow your mitt off.'"

Falling short on players for their team, Dashut called in a ringer known as Lurch to fill the roster, a towering fellow who dwarfed even the members of Shoes. "I used to tell people he was a roadie for Fleetwood Mac," Dashut recalls, "but he wasn't. He was just a friend of a friend; I brought him in to win games." During the match, says Rojas, Lurch hit one ball all the way into the street.

Two more slots on the team were filled by Rojas and a friend of his from Chile named Gerardo. Neither had ever played baseball before, "but Gerardo was a great sport person," Rojas says. "They did real damn good," Skip commented in his journal. He describes the end of the game:

> We were all really psyched up, Richard especially. He is just like a little kid [about baseball]. After we won, battling back to get five runs in the last inning and holding them, I came running from left and met Richard on third. He jumped up in my arms and went around in a circle with everyone else on the team joining in. It was like winning the World Series. He was really proud of us. In fact, [the staff of United Western] kept a low profile the next day. They all want a rematch now. But they can't say it wasn't close.

Having narrowly edged out United Western in its 23-21 win, the band threw a cookout to celebrate.

BUT THE MAIN BUSINESS OF THE summer took place in the studio, and it was there that Shoes sequestered themselves, ten to twelve hours a day, six or seven days a week. (Jeff's studio notes calculate that the record took 630.25 hours to record, and another 143 to mix.) "It would have taken a grenade to get them off course," Dan Bourgoise remarks. Dashut gave them confidence; Shoes thought the material was strong and were pleased with the tracks in progress.

Band members were accustomed to the professional recording process now, and confident that they could operate within it—in contrast to their state of mind while recording *Present Tense*, according to Jeff. "On *Present Tense*, we were timid and cautious," he recounts, "always assuming that there was some great secret to professional recording that we didn't know about. By *Tongue Twister* we had learned that using our own gear and following our own instincts was the best way to get the record to sound the way we wanted it to." Still, Jeff acknowledges, "We did defer to some of Richard's techniques like isolating instruments and looping, which were new to us."

Shoes also took a streamlined approach to their signature lush, layered sound, reaching for something more modern and clean; more rock, less filigree. Even the vocals that had characterized their most popular songs from the last record were reassessed, and Shoes ended up setting aside much of Stone's influence on their harmonies. According to John, "We didn't want to use the massive block of Queen-like backing vocals that we used on 'Too Late' and 'Tomorrow Night.' We wanted to hear the individual voices more, so we would pull back the number of overdubs on a harmony part. We'd multitrack Jeff, for instance, doing the high part, then me or Gary doing the lower part, rather than all three of us singing all the parts."

Jeff makes note of another aspect of Shoes' vocal production on the *Tongue Twister* tracks: "The lead singer didn't do backing vocals on that song at all. We stripped it back to using just the other two singers." This decision was purely aesthetic, and not because of the problems they'd had reproducing studio-polished harmonies on the 1979 tour, they all agree. "We have known people who wouldn't do things in the studio they couldn't do live, but that was never a determining factor for us," Gary says. "The record was always more important; we'd do what we needed to do for that, and wing it live."

In addition to these structural changes in production, the vocals were processed differently by Dashut. Gary notes that there was minimal reverb and echo in the vocals. Instead, says Klebe, Dashut preferred the approach he used with Fleetwood Mac, resulting in "clean, dry" vocals—(i.e., produced without effects)—and they deferred to Dashut's acoustic sense. (In a recent conversation with Hernan Rojas, Gary reports, they both expressed a desire to remix *Tongue Twister* and restore it to its original state.)

But in the summer of 1980, under the guidance of Richard Dashut, Shoes sought and achieved the modern aural cleanliness, free of ambience and reverb. As John puts it, "We did want to sound current. Fleetwood Mac records were clean, with uncluttered arrangements; the Cars were clean, very polished, high-tech (but edgy, too). I now felt the heavily upholstered production on *Present Tense* sounded a little dated, somewhat old-school." As Jeff points out, "The major releases of the time were very slick, polished-sounding productions, and we wanted to compete on equal footing." Jeff notes that of course Fleetwood Mac was among these bands, and (by 1980) Queen, too, but also lesser-known acts like Australia's Tarney/Spencer Band.

And as always, the long, long shadow of the Cars and Roy Thomas Baker set the tone. Gary adds, "Modern, prominent drums were a big part of the Cars' sound. We definitely wanted that."

Part of Shoes' acquiescence to this gleaming new standard was their sense that they were just small-town guys from nowhere, and that they had to conform to make it. Shoes tried to control what they could control, then, in order to walk unchallenged through this still-developing world. Jeff elaborates:

> I think we often got more focused on the execution and precision of a vocal part rather than maintaining an overall loosey-goosey rock feel. We were always feeling like we wanted to make sure it sounded "pro"—that we weren't just some flunkies from Zion, Illinois. We always doubted our own musical skills, but were confident in our production skills.

And Shoes made a conscious attempt to play up their rock side. Reviews of *Present Tense* having focused on its fragility and retro sweetness, "we wanted *Tongue Twister* to be a little more in-your-face," John says. Simplified arrangements and fewer vocal harmonies adorned muscular songs like "She Satisfies," "When It Hits," "Burned Out Love," and "Hate to Run," to try and bury the "wimp rock" label for good.

WHEN SHOES FINISHED RECORDING at United Western Studios, they started mixing *Tongue Twister* at the Village Recorder—the site of their first nightmare sessions in L.A. less than eighteen months earlier. But he shift posed some problems for the mixing process. "It's always risky, leaving a place where you know how the tracks sound, and going somewhere else," Rojas explains.

Jeff recalls that as Shoes got to work, "the staff was still talking about some session they'd done where several pieces of gear had failed. We told them that *we* were the band from that session, and they freaked."

Initially, Dashut took the mixing-process reins himself, but the pace of the summer was starting to catch up with all of them, producer included. "By that time, we were burned out," says Gary. "We probably should have had a fresh set of ears mix it." Dashut's avoidance of ambient sound, as well as vocal and guitar effects, meant that, as Gary admits, "Some of the life was mixed out of it."

But almost as soon as mixing began, Dashut's only months-old "eternal fealty" chit was already being called in. Though Fleetwood Mac had been supposed to take five weeks off to rest from their whopping *Tusk* tour, Mick Fleetwood decided that they had so much quality material recorded on the road that they should do a live album. Some parts would have to be overdubbed, and there were certain songs they wanted to tape again, live— and they of course wanted Dashut at the controls. He left to record Fleetwood Mac.

Hernán Rojas estimates that he ended up doing about eighty percent of the mixing and mastering. And without Dashut, Shoes were free to add back a little of their signature sound. The mixdown studio at Village Recorder had a recording room on the side, and Rojas says they used it frequently during mixing: "We did a lot of percussion in there—some cowbells, shakers, tambourines—whatever the song needed. Plus a couple of harmonies." In addition, they restored some processed guitars Dashut had deep-sixed. Jeff's studio notes confirm that during the mixing process, which started in early August, Gary added the grit and distortion back in to some of his Dashut-scrubbed guitar parts, and John replaced a little bit of the bass effect on "Your Imagination." Jeff himself re-recorded more vocal overdubs for "Found a Girl."

The mixing days were long, but Shoes were already over time, over budget, and under pressure. "But we were still preserving that obsession with clean sounds," Rojas remembers, adding that purifying the tracks—going through the instruments one by one, erasing stray hisses, pops, and clicks—in those pre-digital days was an onerous process: "You had to clean track by track, one at a time, muting and unmuting when things weren't playing." Even with this meticulousness, mixing only took a little over two weeks

At long last, *Tongue Twister* ended up with the sound Shoes were looking for. It was unquestionably harder and more pristine than *Present Tense*, they felt, and better showcased their songwriting and guitar skills, proving that a synth-less guitar band could sound contemporary. The oft-commented-upon designation on the inner sleeve—"No Keyboards"—certainly echoed Queen's signature no-synthesizer disclaimers, and set them apart from the trend of eighties synth-pop. Nevertheless, John insists, "That was never meant to be a manifesto. We were just pointing out that it was kind of cool that Jeff and Gary could get all those exotic sounds using only their guitars —we were not saying we'd *never* use keyboards."

Shoes completed mixing and mastering *Tongue Twister* just over one chaotic year after finishing its predecessor. Having been through this process once before, the band members braced themselves for another whirlwind round of publicity and promotion, expecting that this fall would be as jam-packed as the previous one. "We were happy to have a lot to do, and couldn't wait for more things to start happening," Jeff confirms. John, too, insists that Shoes weren't looking for a break in the action: "I think we were just so ready to get to the next level, the kind of success that Kenny first talked about." And they wanted to be back on store shelves, confident that *Tongue Twister* would get them there.

But it didn't happen that fall. Elektra would not release *Tongue Twister* for another full season.

No one in the band is really sure why. They were told at the time that Elektra's autumn promotion budgets had already been allocated by the time *Tongue Twister* was finished. Elektra's postponement till the first of the ensuing year (traditionally a lean time for new releases) meant, they were assured, that the label would be able to concentrate more fully on selling Shoes. That, at least, is the positive spin Shoes gave their fan club members in an October missive, enthusing, "Elektra's promotion department loved the album when they heard it and begged us to wait until after the Christmas rush so they could give it the 'big push.'"

Elektra did have four of the top ten records in the fall of 1980: the Cars' *Panorama*, though not as potent as either their 1978 self-titled debut or its follow-up *Candy-O*, was still charting high, as were the *Urban Cowboy* movie soundtrack and Jackson Browne's *Hold Out*. But the bulk of Elektra's efforts had no doubt been lavished on the monster record of the summer and fall: Queen's *The Game*. The album had scored a number-one single—"Crazy Little Thing Called Love"—even before its full release in late June 1980. And by the end of the summer, another new Queen single was climbing the charts, bassist John Deacon's stripped-down "Another One Bites the Dust" (whose funked-up bass hook was clearly nicked from Chic's innovative disco smash "Good Times").

There was no doubt, too, that Elektra's fall release schedule was already heavily populated. The label had high expectations for Queen's soundtrack from the film *Flash Gordon*, for example, expecting it to perform as well as *The Game* (though it did not). Also in the wings was a live Eagles disc, whose success would end up being fueled even more by the heavyweight band's onstage breakup that July. In the wake of *Urban Cowboy*'s success (and that of its crossover rock & bluegrass hit, the Charlie Daniels Band's "The Devil Went Down to Georgia"), Elektra threw a significant amount of money toward country music, including albums by down-home veterans Mel Tillis, Roy Acuff, and Eddie Rabbitt. And in the face of the music industry's economic slowdown, the label was re-releasing old, proven material: fall 1980 saw a rash of greatest-hits albums from established Elektra hitmakers including the Doors, Warren Zevon, and Linda Ronstadt.

As far as radio-friendly contemporary pop was concerned, Elektra had the field covered with the Korgis (their single "Everybody's Got to Learn Sometime" peaked at number eighteen on the American charts that fall), Blue Steel, and the Kings (though a December 20, 1980 concert review in *Billboard* ID'd their Siamese-twinned anthem "This Beat Goes On/Switchin' to Glide" as only "a semi-hit"). Shoes were fighting for space in a very crowded field.

The band was assuaged, more or less, by Elektra's argument that *Tongue Twister* would have been lost amid this flurry of new fall releases, though they found the delay frustrating. Still, Shoes didn't take it personally; Gary says, "I never got the feeling that Elektra thought it was a weak record and didn't want to go up against strong competition. And even if we could have forced them to release *Tongue Twister* when it was finished, that doesn't mean they would have supported it." Shoes tried to see it Elektra's way: that a few months more not only wouldn't harm them, it would help them in the long run.

THERE WAS NOTHING MORE TO DO in California, but the band members delayed their return to Zion while their label's decision to hold *Tongue Twister* was finalized. It wasn't just that Shoes wanted the record on the street; they were hoping a quick release would tip the balance of the decision they'd been considering for over four months—whether or not to move their center of operations from Zion to Los Angeles.

Gary and John generally thought it was a good idea; Jeff generally did not. Skip was equivocal about the situation: his journal notes that his then-current sweetheart "is really going to like being a California girl," but underlines his concern that without a huge hit record, Shoes wouldn't have anything to live on.

On September 12, Skip wrote:

> I just finished talking to Jeff. ... He was telling me that Gary is determined to move out here. At this point I find that hard to do because we don't have any money. He said John wanted to start looking for apartments. If he finds one, I don't know what he will use to pay for it. ... Gary figures he will die if he has to go back to Zion and live.

"We liked being there," Gary says simply. "It wasn't just the weather and the proximity to the label; it was living in a city and all that entails. Neville [Johnson, Dan Bourgoise's lawyer friend] took us out all the time to these great clubs. We liked the people. We were happy there."

On a professional level, the main argument for moving west was to increase the band's visibility to Elektra, and allow Shoes to become part of the more sweeping coastal music scene. However, as Dan Bourgoise cautioned, "A lot of bands that were out there were already being penalized"—or at least not helped—by their presence in L.A.

By the time Shoes were having this conversation, in the late summer of 1980, the Knack, the flagship band of the power-pop movement who'd ruled L.A.'s club scene the summer before, had released their underwhelming follow-up record. New-wave icons the Cars, too, had slipped a little in 1980.

Blondie, the only other new-wave band with a serious chart presence, spent much of 1980 trying to bounce back from the comparatively disappointing performance of their late-'79 album *Eat to the Beat*, though they hit it big thanks to their participation in the popular film soundtrack *American Gigolo*: Blondie's "Call Me" ended up as the top-selling single of 1980. But they were leaving new wave behind; by the end of 1980, Blondie's genre-bending "Rapture" had introduced a plethora of white rock fans to the exotic urban stylings of hip-hop.

A number of bands with whom Shoes felt comradeship didn't seem to be doing all that well in L.A. either. Groups like 20/20, the Beat, the Plimsouls, and Great Buildings may have made records, but those releases hadn't even cracked the charts. For these bands, having Los Angeles as home base was no magic bullet.

Pulling up their stakes would be a big risk and a significant financial commitment for Shoes, with no obvious, immediate benefit. It would mean taking day gigs—not even the kind of steady, career-oriented employment they'd walked away from eighteen months before, but the service-industry jobs most all aspiring Angeleno artists preferred (so that they could quit in a heartbeat when their big break inevitably came).

Shoes, too, had the typical small-towners' horrified reaction to the cost of living in a big city. Skip spoke with stunned disbelief about the rent on their condominiums, a staggering $550 a month. Jeff admits this was a roadblock for him as well:

> The fact that it seemed Hollywood was full of wannabes who ended up as waiters, store clerks, or gas-station attendants—instead of becoming the stars they aspired to be—scared me. Things were

expensive out there, compared to Zion, and we didn't know how much money we were actually going to make.

Zion was considerably more manageable financially (indeed, barring a hit record, it was all they could afford). John says that if Shoes *had* made the move, "I planned to keep my apartment back there just for visits. That's how cheap it was." But there were other reasons to stay in Zion, too; their families were there, and some of them had girlfriends. Even more than that, as Gary puts it, "We had our laboratory there." Recreating Shoes' studio space in L.A. would have been prohibitively expensive.

Dan Bourgoise became the deciding vote, and he encouraged them to go home. While Bourgoise acknowledged, "I know they enjoyed living in L.A.; it's a lot different from Zion," he felt Shoes "were far better away from the L.A. scene," instead maintaining their music-biz profile as "the mysterious men from Zion." Plus, Gary recalls Dan being anxious to protect them from "the phoniness of the West Coast industry." This wasn't a big concern when the band was out there recording—"They were encased in their own cocoon" during that process, Dan says—but things might have been different had Shoes lived there permanently, duking it out in clubs and struggling just to be able to make music at all.

And so Shoes accepted Bourgoise's advice and returned to Zion, leaving their fully gestated but unborn record on the shelf in Los Angeles.

NOW, THEY HAD FOUR EMPTY months to fill. Jeff and Gary kept busy, returning to their studio to produce other local bands. Jeff's was a power-pop quartet from Racine, Wisconsin called Take Me (whose drummer, Jeff Hunter, would play with Shoes on their 1990 tour).

As a group, Shoes produced a single for their old Spooner friends Butch Vig and Duke Erikson, called, "Where You Gonna Run?" backed with "You're the Lucky One." On his own, Gary worked with Vig and Erikson throughout the 1980s, producing Spooner's '82 debut *Every Corner Dance* and mixing '84's *The Wildest Dreams* with the band, as well mixing Spooner successor Fire Town's 1987 release, *In the Heart of Heart Country*.

Vig would go on to produce monster records by Nirvana (the paradigm-shifting, genre-defining *Nevermind*) and Smashing Pumpkins, as well as his own hit band, Garbage; Vig has repeatedly cited Shoes, and Gary in particular, as encouraging him to produce, and as helping him formulate his production methods. In a 2009 posting at the music-production website Gearslutz.com, Vig reminisces about these early years:

> I look back at my days with Spooner and Fire Town with fond memories, and now I realize how both bands were very influential on my becoming a producer. We had a DIY attitude (out of necessity really) and since we wanted to make records, I was the guy who sort of took charge and figured out how to do it. Gary Klebe (from Shoes, a great power-pop band from Zion, Ill.) co-produced the first album, *Every Corner Dance*, and he saw that I had an interest in recording, and told me one night, "Don't just be a drummer—you have an ear for recording; you should keep moving in that direction," and I took his advice to heart.

Vig gave Gary similar credit for his production technique in a 2004 interview for the book *Classic Rock Albums: Nirvana, Nevermind*, saying:

> In Spooner, the first producer we worked with was Gary Klebe from Shoes, who paid a lot of attention to detail. And [Klebe's methods] rubbed off on me. I understood what it takes—you take extra time and move the microphone around, or listen to it in the context of the guitars and the EQ, or whatever you're doing, and try and give the instruments more space or separation.

Shoes in general and Gary in particular, then, can justly lay claim to significant influence over one of the most prominent producers of the modern-rock era.

BUT IN FALL 1980, OTHER THAN production work, there wasn't a lot going on for Shoes. When they left L.A., says Skip, they'd felt good about *Tongue Twister*, but subsequent time away from the record created in them all a sense of rising panic about its quality. John recounts, "Those few months were agonizing, from my point of view anyway. I wanted to re-cut stuff, remix, substitute demos. ... I beat myself up over it—I had a severe case of demo-itis" (an artist's deep-seated fear that their original demo is better than the studio version).

To distract themselves, Shoes killed time. They joined a gym; they gave interviews in which they admitted feeling guilty for being idle. Still, "I don't sleep all day," John told a *Trouser Press* interviewer at the time. "But I can do laundry at eleven [a.m.] and play with the kids downstairs." They wrote; they rehearsed. But Shoes didn't get out and play live, since there was no record to plug. "We had too much free time," says John, "and we knew *nothing* was going to happen 'til that thing came out."

But while Shoes were waiting, the world was changing. Ronald Reagan was elected in November; the vision he brought to U.S. voters was fundamentally nostalgic for a nonexistent world in which the forces of conservatism, not those of rock & roll, won the culture wars of the sixties.

Then, an earth-shattering sea change occurred on December 8, when John Lennon was assassinated by a deranged fan on the street in front of his New York City home.

All the band members remember being deeply shaken by Lennon's loss—"Gods aren't supposed to die," Gary says simply—though skeptical that it had any effect on the radio and retail performance of *Tongue Twister*, released a scant six weeks later.

But as R. Serge Denisoff argues in *Tarnished Gold*, there were very specific market forces that shifted in the wake of Lennon's death:

> One consequence, observable in subsequent record sales, was a retrospective appreciation of 1960s music. The [Lennon] tribute broadcasts, some lasting a week, rekindled interest in the Beatles. Other 1960s stalwarts reemerged: *The Doors Greatest Hits* was a platinum record; the Who achieved a similar award for [their current album] *Face Dances*. AOR stations welcomed requests for oldies sounds. ... Some cynics suggested Lennon and Yoko Ono's *Double Fantasy* [released just weeks before] benefited from the mindless murder; it would sell three million units.

Clearly, the country was in a backward-looking state of shock, not just because John Lennon was dead, but because of the manner of his death. It was an act of irrational aggression toward a beloved icon. *Rolling Stone* reflected that the assassination "was the negation of a spirit and life force that embodied just about all of what was great and important about rock music, about life." And rock fans mourned by engulfing themselves in the Beatles' back catalogue.

The repercussions lasted well into 1981. As Denisoff writes,

> [The year] had begun on a fading memory of Lennon's departure and a music scene without any sense of purpose or direction. A few outspoken music journalists were already expanding Don McLean's [iconic lyric] "the day the music died" [from 1971 smash hit "American Pie"] to link Lennon's fate to Buddy Holly's [since both suffered tragic, early deaths]. There existed a handful of fairly obvious parallels: Holly's air crash marked the end of a mythologized music era, and Lennon's murder appeared to symbolize a similar termination.

The impact was economic as well: though 1980 had represented a slight recovery for the music industry, 1981 and 1982 would see it resume its slide into the red. Elektra was no exception to the renewed downward trend, something that would soon become apparent to Shoes.

Band interviews from this time, which mostly hit the street as *Tongue Twister* was being released in early 1981, show Shoes in a reflective mood. The trust they'd once had in the system, in the label, and even—despite their personal loyalty—in Buttice himself, was clearly shaken. As happy as they were about the forthcoming record, Shoes understood that there were aspects to the game that might not have been immediately apparent to them. Gary, for example, shared his perspective on dealing with the industry in a 1980 *Trouser Press* interview:

> We never really appreciated what it takes to make it. It's an understanding of not just your material, your art, but everything around it—the people that make it happen, especially. Of course

you're always concerned about developing as an artist, but if you ignore the [business] end of it, you're pretty much helpless.

It was a hard-won lesson, and as Shoes prepared for *Tongue Twister*'s release, they reassured themselves about the choices they'd made, and kept on trying to make the machinery of Elektra work for them. As John commented at that point, "We've proved to ourselves that nine times out of ten our instincts are right. Whenever we regret things, it's usually because we gave in."

And so Shoes walked a narrow path between self-assertion and playing the game, quietly doing things their own way—while still trying everything they could to get Elektra to give *Tongue Twister* a strong send-off, without the guesswork and poor planning that had marred the release of *Present Tense*.

It's hard to overemphasize the level to which *Tongue Twister* was intended as a corrective to *Present Tense*. Shoes understood that their first big-league record had been mishandled, and this was their chance to make it right; it was another opportunity for Elektra to do its job, too. If four months' lead time would allow for better distribution, timelier press and reviews, a clearer marketing strategy, and a decisive single, then Shoes were all for it.

But instead of preparing the groundwork for its release, Elektra seemed to forget about *Tongue Twister* altogether. When it finally came out, in January 1981, *Tongue Twister* hit stores without a designated single, without a promotional strategy, and without even the level of funding that had been available for *Present Tense*. The results were all too predictable.

Chapter 8

Under the Gun (1981-82)

Tongue Twister was launched in January 1981 with Elektra's favorite refrain, "Let's see what radio does." And John vividly recalls lying in bed one morning soon after, waking up to popular local deejay Steve Dahl's a.m. drive show on "The Loop"—and hearing the familiar guitar chords of Gary's blazing rocker, "She Satisfies": "'This is *it*,' I remember thinking, 'It's happening. This is the beginning of it.'" "It," of course, was the smash single they'd all waited for, the success Ken Buttice had kept assuring Shoes was right around the corner. They fully expected *Tongue Twister* to "push us to the next level," says Gary.

Dahl, though still a young disc jockey, had been something of a Chicago legend ever since The Loop's July 12, 1979 promotional stunt "Disco Demolition Night" at baseball stadium Comiskey Park. During the event, Dahl, dressed in army fatigues, appeared before an overflow crowd between the games of a White Sox double-header. Lugging a box of disco records rigged with explosives, Dahl proceeded to blow a hole in the outfield turf, but that was only the beginning of the chaos that ensued. Scores of fans surged onto the field, others flung like Frisbees their own disco records (which they'd brought to gain discounted tickets), and a full-scale riot was on.

Chicago forfeited the second game to the Detroit Tigers with the field unusable due to the crowd of lingering disco haters; dozens would be arrested. Dahl would be fired seven months later—but his celebrity status was assured.

Dahl was more a talk-oriented deejay than a music-driven one, and his anarchic style has been cited as a major influence on notorious shock-jock Howard Stern's development. But Dahl's show maintained a musical component, he was an unabashed rock fan, and he was playing Shoes.

THE BAND CERTAINLY DID NOT expect "She Satisfies" to be the first single. They all thought that honor would fall to the group-penned "Girls of Today," a sunny round of a song that bore a reasonable resemblance to the tracks that had gotten the most attention off *Present Tense*. "We thought it was a good representation of our sound." Gary says. "And since all three songwriters were credited, it seemed like a logical choice." Before Shoes had left California, Skip noted in his journal, they had proposed that song as a single to Ken Buttice. "He has the final say-so," Skip wrote on September 2. "He likes 'Girls of Today' also."

But "She Satisfies" had made it to radio, and that was the song pressed as a single, with another three-way collaboration ("The Things You Do") as the B-side. A picture sleeve was printed, with the stylized cover of *Tongue Twister* (a rainbow-hued sigma on a black background, done by Larry Vigon, who had designed the cover of Fleetwood Mac's *Tusk* and was recommended by Richard Dashut) on one side, and Randee St. Nicholas' separate portraits of each band member on the back.

The single was pressed and ready to drop when a small item appeared in *Friday Morning Quarterback*, the must-read music-industry tip sheet edited by radio veteran Kal Rudman. Rudman had heard *Tongue Twister* and focused on one particular song—the nostalgic ballad from the dark horse, John. Labeling "Karen" a "sure-fire hit" that was certain to be "hugely successful," the tiny *FMQB* piece threw everything into a state of panicked second-guessing. Shoes needed a hit, certainly, and who were they to contradict a recognized hit-spotter?

Dan Bourgoise recalls the band being "so unsure of what to do. But the piece got them all excited. Maybe *this* would get Elektra all fired up, because their interest had begun waning when the band didn't instantly hit with *Present Tense*." Buttice was still in their corner, a powerful champion, though Shoes had been skittish about him since the Astor Tower meeting. Richard Dashut and the past summer had healed some of the breach, but they knew things wouldn't really be the same until they provided Buttice with the hits he expected.

All copies of "She Satisfies"/"The Things You Do" were summarily destroyed, though for some reason, the picture sleeves survived.

After a brief delay, Shoes were told that "She Satisfies" and "Karen" would be issued as a double A-side single, and postcards announcing the release were pressed up and sent out to the press and their fan club.

The actual record, however, was never produced for distribution.

The concept of this particular double A-side was flawed in its inception, and demonstrates one of the major problems Shoes faced as they shot the rapids of the record business: Elektra just didn't know what Shoes were or how to market them.

Back in 1977, when Ira Robbins had identified in Shoes "the kind of multifariousness necessary to prevent singleness of direction," they thought that was a good thing. Robbins had opined then that Shoes' variety of voices ensured "they won't have any trouble coming up with a string of singles that will sound similar but different enough to stay creative."

But this very multifariousness was becoming a problem. Shoes didn't have an obvious frontman, and they didn't have an obvious musical niche. They'd never been comfortable under the power-pop umbrella, which had shredded by now anyway: Elektra simply didn't know what to do with them—indeed, even what kind of band they wanted Shoes to be.

Dan Bourgoise saw this lack of understanding as Elektra's blind spot. Since Shoes had a small but devoted following and generally good critical reception, even if mass sales eluded them, Bourgoise argues that the label could have played up Shoes' idiosyncratic appeal, had they chosen to do so.

> Elektra had no perception of how you deal with a cult band like that: that there may have been less conventional ways of marketing than they had done before. Elektra insisted, "This is how it's done! We're the record company! We know this stuff!" But things needed to be done differently with a band like Shoes.

If Shoes' role was to be critics' darlings, the open secret of the cognoscenti, then Elektra should have capitalized on that angle. Instead, the label kept trying to force the band into a pre-existing radio format.

The double-A side was a shortsighted shot, according to Bourgoise, at marketing Shoes as both rock and pop; all things to all stations. He continues:

> The shift from "She Satisfies" to "Karen" was Elektra's frantic attempt to remake the band to fit in some familiar category: "Are they AOR? Are they MOR [middle-of-the-road]? Whatever!"

But as Gary notes, these were "two diametrically opposed songs," style-wise—any station whose format would accommodate one of them would never accommodate the other, no matter which track was perceived as the "real" single. Not only that, each song was also radically different from the upbeat, midtempo *Present Tense* singles for which Shoes were known: one a soft ballad, the other an uncompromising rocker.

Shoes themselves had reveled in that contrast, deliberately sequencing "She Satisfies" right after "Karen" on *Tongue Twister*. John recalls a playback party at United Western where a rough cut of the album, with tracks in their final order, was played for the band's all-female guests. One young woman, lulled into a romantic haze by the end of "Karen," actually screamed out loud as the first stab of guitar on "She Satisfies" split the air.

"She Satisfies," was, at that point, one of the hardest-rocking songs the band had ever done. Gary insists that this was not a self-conscious attempt to shake the pesky "wimp rock" tag (though he jokingly offered, in one contemporary interview, to punch out a reviewer who had hung that label on the band). "Any changes," says Gary, "were based on self-criticism, not as a response to outside critics." And yet there's no question that the track represented a solid step away from the gauzy romanticism of *Present Tense*: more driving, more directly sexual.

Gary recalls that Jeff was the first Shoe to identify the song's potential; "I know he was listening to it in his car." Jeff says he liked "She Satisfies" because it "captures a great guitar rawness" that they'd sought to replicate in the studio. "Of course, our definition of raw is probably not what others would call raw," Jeff admits. But the dynamic tune's selection as a single came as a surprise to Gary, too.

"Karen," on the other hand, embodies Shoes in high love-struck mode, and is one of John's most wistful and enduring songs. Like much of his early writing (it was composed between *Black Vinyl Shoes* and *Present Tense*) it concerns the same girl he'd dated for several years in his early twenties—Sara Haack, whose first name scans similarly to the song title. It's a prime example of John's deeply-held belief that the more personal a song is to the writer, the more it will resonate with the listener:

> There really was a "Karen," and we were together a long time. But good things sometimes come from dire experiences, from that place where your nerve endings are exposed. It's all about using little scraps of real stuff, knowing how little it takes to get the idea across, but still mining that vein of hurt or confusion. Everything in the song is true. And—this is one of the few times I've ever done this—I even played it for her.

Shoes fans routinely cite the song as one of their favorites, although, being a ballad, it was never a staple of their live act.

"'Karen' is a great song," Gary affirms. "But when Elektra suddenly pulled the single that was all pressed and ready to release—without consulting the band—we just said, 'Here they go again.'" He continues:

260 *Boys Don't Lie*

> It's harder to break a ballad than a straight rock track. Still, lots of rock groups have their biggest hits with ballads: think about the Rolling Stones' "Angie" or Kiss's "Beth." So it's not *what* Elektra picked, but *how*. But they were excited by the *FMQB* thing, and if Elektra was excited, we were excited. Sure, it was a rash decision, but we were accustomed to rash decisions at that point—and if there had been a real, unified effort on Elektra's part, it might have worked.

Egos were set aside: the most important thing was the success of the band, not whose pen had authored it. If John, none of whose songs had been chosen as *Present Tense* singles, felt vindicated, he never said that. All that mattered was for *someone's* song to connect, big-time. One hit, and the whole system would reboot, all those doors of opportunity at Elektra would reopen.

John says he did receive a preliminary, white-label test-pressing of a single with "Karen" on both sides, but as noted above, the "Karen"/"She Satisfies" double-A side they had advertised was never manufactured for sale. Jeff thinks it might have been pressed for promo release to radio stations, but none of them recall hearing "Karen" on the radio. To exacerbate the confusion, promotion worked fine: the double-A side chosen as a "recommended" single in *Billboard* on March 28, 1981 (even though the single itself didn't exist).

It was the same scenario that derailed *Present Tense*, compressed and in fast forward: a late single, abruptly pulled in favor of another song. Gary observes, "I think *Tongue Twister* was even more botched in that respect than *Present Tense* had been."

DESPITE ALL THIS BOBBLING, *Tongue Twister* as an album fared pretty well in certain markets, particularly on college radio, where Gary says *College Music Journal* rated it number one in all four regions of the country for several weeks that spring. This despite the fact that Elektra had recently shut down its college music department; college radio was simply not recognized by the industry as a viable marketing tool. "We didn't take that stuff seriously,"

Marty Schwartz admits. "We didn't think about breaking bands through college radio. Modern rock wasn't even a recognized musical category in 1981." R.E.M. would become one of the first bands to parlay success in the college arena to the mass market, but in 1981, they were just releasing their first independent single.

When Schwartz left Elektra in 1982, he notes, it was to develop a modern-rock format commercially, starting at AOR giant KROQ in Los Angeles. "Given my frustration at trying to break Shoes in very archaic radio formats [like AOR and MOR]," he says, "the experience inspired me to start another format more relevant to a younger and much hipper audience." Schwartz helped KROQ transition from an AOR outlet with new-wave accents to one of the first real "modern rock" stations.

But in 1981, Elektra was only interested in mainstream airplay on mainstream radio. Dan Bourgoise recalls, "Elektra had the perspective that they had to break Shoes through singles." By any calculation, that would be a tricky thing to do, especially without any actual singles.

There may have been other issues facing Elektra at this point, too: the Crash of '79 leveled out in 1980 (a year R. Serge Denisoff calls "economically flat"), but by 1981, sales figures were slipping again for everyone. In other words, there may not have been sufficient funds to press another single.

Certainly, there was less money spent on promotion of Shoes' second Elektra album. Instead of the luxurious trips that had accompanied *Present Tense*'s release, the label informed Shoes that they could afford to fly only two of them to New York to do *Tongue Twister* press; John and Gary went in February. "There wasn't a lot of excitement [on Elektra's part] about the second record," Marty Schwartz recalls, though he emphasizes that this was because of the label's failed investment in *Present Tense*, not because Elektra considered *Tongue Twister* an inferior album: "We had put a lot into the first record and it didn't work." Consequently, *Tongue Twister*, as Skip says flatly, "just dropped off the face of the earth."

THE REVIEWS OF *TONGUE TWISTER* were generally strong, however, identifying in Shoes a purity of vision and spirit that stood in stark contrast to many of their contemporaries. Robert Hull, for example, whose *Creem* article pronounced the band "technically proficient and spiritually clean," concluded, "Shoes are the Cars and Boston with heart and soul still intact." *Rolling Stone*'s David Fricke identified Shoes' sound as "an exhilarating fusion of clean-cut British pop classicism and semipunk roughhousing in the grand Midwest manner of the Raspberries and Blue Ash." James Hunter of the *Village Voice* assessed the record as "uniformly first-rate." And Tom Carson, whose backhanded review of *Present Tense* in *Rolling Stone* a scant year earlier had so rankled the band, referred apologetically to that piece, and pronounced Shoes "heroically guileless" this time around:

> The [sic] Shoes' resigned accepting that life can't ever be what they want it to be makes them not so much losers as simply outsiders and naturally parallels their sense of themselves as alien to the musical mainstream as well; their deepest gratification comes not from the story they're telling, but from the amount of invention, care, and skill they bring to telling it.

In addition, Carson, who had hung the ignominious "wimp rock" placard on the band in that earlier review, now said that "She Satisfies" "puts any suggestions of wimp-out to rest by claiming the gutsiest guitar riff and the most charged vocal on the album."

There were some negative reviews, too, generally pegging Shoes (in spite of "She Satisfies") as too sweet: "*Tongue Twister* will have trouble lasting even half a hundred listens," one reviewer wrote, "but the [sic] Shoes are so cute and quaint, so irresistibly harmless and trite they provide plenty of perfect teenage fun." Another dismissed the album as "elevator music for the designer-jeans set."

Many writers simply misunderstood *Tongue Twister*. One argued that "When It Hits" was clearly about Ronald Reagan—despite the fact that the record was written and recorded well before the presidential election of 1980. Another cited a Greil Marcus assertion—"The secret message behind the election of November 4th [1980] was that some people belong in this country, and some people don't"—to argue that "if indeed there is a return to normalcy in America, then Shoes is as good a band as any to mark such a cultural transition." This author was obviously mistaking Shoes for poster boys of the Reagan Revolution.

These critics seemed bent on countering the critical contention that Shoes' obsession with personal relationships painted them into a thematic corner, arguing (incorrectly) that the lyrics were metaphors for sociopolitical issues. But their misinterpretations were generally framed as complimentary, so the band members didn't bother correcting them. Instead, they contented themselves with dismissing in interviews the very concept of politics in music. "The lyrics have messages, but they're not real big issues like political things. We're just trying to reach out to everyone," John explained to C.A. Wehrley in a magazine called *Thinker*. Gary was more abruptly dismissive in a *New York Rocker* interview: "I liked the punk stuff, but I don't give a shit about the lyrics. I mean, I don't care about anarchy in the U.K."

THROUGH FEBRUARY, MARCH, APRIL, and May of 1981, Shoes did more shows than they'd ever done in their lives, crossing and recrossing the region, and going as far afield as Minneapolis and even over the border to Toronto. Beet Richardson and Steve Hurd were the crew. Some shows were done with Take Me, the local Wisconsin band Jeff had produced in the fall of 1980; (and whose drummer, Jeff Hunter, would later tour with Shoes).

On March 10, Skip reports in his journal that they'd already played the Edgewater in Twin Lakes, Wisconsin (the site of their first disastrous gig in 1979), premier showcase club Tuts in Chicago, and venues in Rockford and Champaign. The shows were going fine, from the band's perspective, though they had all caught colds. By that weekend, Shoes were in Detroit, Skip reports, at a punk club that was "located in a real sleazy part of town. … [It's] supposed to be a hip place, but none of the press will go there because it is so crummy." On St. Patrick's Day, they played Haymakers in Prospect Heights, Illinois: the show went so well they were asked back. Then it was north to Minneapolis to Duffy's, a strip club by day and rock club by night. "That got us charged up," Skip remarks.

But things were still pretty tight financially: the band was barely covering the expenses of touring, and stiffing themselves to do so. Between songs, a fan at the Duffy's show handed Gary a note that contained a simple plea: "Please don't let John lose any more weight."

Then it was south to Madison, Wisconsin to do a show with Vig and Erikson's Spooner; Points East in Milwaukee; Edgewater again; then Haymakers, and Tuts. (Skip's journal makes note of the fact that their opener at Haymakers was a band called JYNX: hardly an encouraging portent.) They played a private jazz club in Kalamazoo, Michigan, and Harpos, a former movie theater in Detroit. Skip told his journal that Shoes were getting zero promo support from Elektra: "We get to a town and no one knows who we are. In fact, more people know about *Black Vinyl* than *Tongue Twister.*" Toronto followed; the hours before the show were tense since their equipment truck was hung up in customs. Then it was back to the States—Tom's in Bloomington, Illinois; Rocket North in Twin Lakes, Wisconsin; somewhere in St. Louis; and then Haymakers, twice more.

Reviews were tepid. A writer in Minneapolis called them "not especially dynamic guys;" another, from Toronto, went further: "As craftsmen of simple, uncluttered, teen-oriented singles, the band's hand is strong enough that someone conceivably could have excused Shoes' almost embarrassingly shy presentation, obvious lack of stage experience, and barely modest musicianship." Both reviewers noted, however, that Shoes' stalwarts seemed to like the shows just fine: the problem was that the fans were greatly outnumbered by largely indifferent attendees. (Skip notes that at this point, the band asked Elektra just to send them their own promo materials: at least they could put them up in the clubs themselves when they loaded in.)

SHOES SHRUGGED OFF THE REVIEWS and focused on their goal: the main show on May 23, when they sold out the biggest venue in their hometown, the Zion Leisure Center. "We always called it the Ice Arena because we thought it sounded cooler," John confesses. "We just didn't want our fans to think we were performing for shuffleboard players. And there *was* a rink."

No one's quite sure how the concert was booked in the first place; certainly it wasn't through Elektra, who never pushed Shoes to play live, and just as certainly it wasn't through their usual booking agents, who dealt solely with bars and clubs. Gary thinks an old schoolmate of theirs may have been working for the Zion Park District and proposed the show. Both John and Gary had had their first jobs working for the Park District: huge public areas and wholesome recreational facilities were a major part of Dowie's original vision of Zion, and those parks needed staffing and maintenance. John had rented out boats on a lagoon one summer; Gary did grounds maintenance.

No matter how the "Ice Arena" gig came to be, Shoes' May '81 Zion concert was much better attended than the shows leading up to it. Estimates range from several hundred to a thousand in the audience, and the crowd was far more enthusiastic than they'd been seeing.

John remembers driving up to the Leisure Center—located on Dowie Memorial Drive in the very center of the Union Jack map—and seeing the circular road lined with cars. "We later found out that there was some sort of event going on at the church, too," John notes. "They weren't *all* there for us." But it was by far the biggest crowd they'd ever played to, maybe even bigger than ChicagoFest's.

Shoes' opening act was another local band named Hot Mama Silver (featuring Herb Eimerman, who would later work with Jeff on his side project, Nerk Twins); their onstage introduction was provided by Ian Case, a deejay from Waukegan. (Gary recalls that one night around this time they stopped in at Case's station after they'd been out drinking, and he let them in for an impromptu interview. "I said 'fuck' on live radio," Gary says brightly.)

That night, the Leisure Center held a different audience from those Shoes usually encountered: larger, younger, *female*. "Usually, when we'd hear the crowd at a club or whatever, it was this low rumble of male drunks," says John. "But this time, there were all these young girls there, screaming. It was much higher pitched, and a *lot* louder." The band's parents were in attendance as well.

Shoes entered through the crowd—seeing as there was only a temporary stage—and the audience parted around them as they strode to the front, every inch the hometown heroes. John says, "Every so often, I'll still meet people here in Zion who say that was their first concert. That's pretty cool."

Shoes and their crew had brought over their trusty eight-track recorder from the dress-shop basement—just a few blocks away—in order to capture their live act. But as Jeff relates, "Unfortunately, though the crew immediately hit 'Record'—they didn't get around to setting levels until forty-five minutes in." So while the whole show was captured for posterity, only the last six songs were balanced instrumentally and vocally—and they just barely got those, according to Jeff: "The tape ran out during the final applause." The band eventually made up cassettes of the show, called *Shoes on Ice*, and offered the souvenir release for sale to their fan club members.

There were about five hundred people in Shoes' fan club, which was born from those first postcards that Greg Shaw had suggested in 1977. Members received irregular updates on recording and touring, merchandise offers, and greetings at Christmas and on Valentine's Day. The band members had been running the fan club themselves, but just after the release of *Tongue Twister*, that task was delegated to band buddy Chuck Fieldman, the aforementioned local journalist.

Despite the fact that Shoes' fan club was decidedly a side operation—and not even remotely a money-making venture—Elektra was angered that Shoes had released the cassette, even to such a limited population. They'd sold "maybe fifty, but I'm not sure," John says, but recalls too, that Elektra threatened to sue them if they did not cease distribution. In deference to their label Shoes pulled the cassette offer and put *Shoes on Ice* on ice. It would not reappear for over a year.

As the summer of 1981 wore on, Shoes became increasingly frustrated at the label's lack of initiative, at the non-start Elektra had given *Tongue Twister*, at the complete lack of money. With no single and no marketing, of course sales were lackluster, and as a result, the band members' personal finances were dwindling.

Not that this was an unusual state of affairs. Elektra had never paid Shoes, aside from their initial advance, production funds when they were making a record, and the occasional per diem. As an unrecouped band—one whose sales had not covered their costs to date—there was also no meaningful accounting of potential royalties, however. In a 1985 interview, Jeff noted that Shoes never made even $10,000 a year during the major-label phase of their career. The only money that came in was from playing shows, but since Shoes thought wide-ranging tours would be prohibitively expensive, they generally only performed in their own circumscribed region. Skip protested Elektra's stinginess by growing back his moustache; they took pictures of themselves looking grim and sent them to Buttice.

It was during this strained summer that Shoes were scheduled to headline a club in Milwaukee. Not long before the gig, the booking agent called them: would they mind sharing the stage? They'd still get top-billing, but they'd have to split the money—a respectable one thousand dollars—evenly with the other band. In their tough financial straits, and adhering to the principle that they should be paid what they'd contracted for, Shoes nixed the opener, an Irish band with just one record out. But that album (*Boy*, on Sire Records) had made a considerable splash—the band was U2.

That summer, Dan Bourgoise went to visit Mel Posner, then president of Elektra, to lobby for more funds. Dan explained that Shoes were broke, that in order to start another record, they needed preproduction money. Dan recalls Posner replying, "If they need money, tell them to get jobs." (Skip did, in fact, taking on irregular shifts as a bartender and installing window treatments for a friend's business.)

The other Shoes, however, were flabbergasted. "I didn't think Elektra wanted us to do that," Gary says. "But we were big boys, we'd signed the contract, we'd taken the chance that things might not work out. Still, what a slap in the face." It was a far cry from Buttice's promises a scant two years earlier that they'd never have to worry about money again.

Posner's cavalier attitude may have stemmed from the fact that, having completed two unrecouped Shoes records, Elektra had an escape hatch: they were not contractually obligated to pick up Shoes' option to make another record. Yet the band still had a friendly relationship with Buttice, and he was still vice-president for A&R. Shoes were thus protected somewhat by being "Kenny's boys." But in an economic crunch, that shield could only extend so far. As Jeff recounts:

> I have to say, it never really dawned on us that Elektra might actually drop us after *Tongue Twister*. We assumed Kenny still had enough strength in the company that it wouldn't happen; we were naïve that way. Besides, Kenny and the promo guys kept saying, "Don't worry, we'll get 'em on the next one!" So we assumed there would always *be* a next one.

When the preproduction money for the album that would become their third Elektra release, *Boomerang*, was eventually approved, Posner emphasized that the funding had not been automatic; even Buttice told them that there had been conversations about whether or not to extend the option on the band. Gary says they played it off lightly with Buttice—"Ah, c'mon, Kenny. You know you love us!"—but also understood that in this, at least, Buttice was dead serious.

IT SEEMED LIKE AN IMPOSSIBLE position: Shoes had gotten a stay of execution—their option *was* extended. It was clear, however, that Elektra was going to spend as little as possible on them, gauging success primarily by their presence on mainstream commercial radio. But in the world of early-eighties FM, playlists were narrowing radically, and for Shoes, that was a blueprint for disaster.

Prior to the Telecommunications Act of 1996, fairly strict regulations had governed how many media outlets in a given market one owner could hold, but even different owners were increasingly chasing the same format and audience: Top Forty aimed at white suburban males between the ages of 16 and 34.

Hunting this audience became a science in the 1980s, as FM radio playlists increasingly became the creations of "radio doctors"—consultants hired to turn underperforming stations around by focusing and limiting their playlists to specific genres, essentially replacing the program directors that labels like

Elektra had spent so much time and money wooing. People listened to radio, the governing assumption went, not to discover new music, but to hear songs with which they were already familiar, and ones that sounded just like them. Mike Joseph, creator of the "Hot Hits" format, embodied its driving principle when he asserted that "you can't be original with music. You can be original with everything else: sound, techniques, promotion, and news." But the musical playlists themselves should be familiar, with new songs added only if they met a preexisting formula.

In the early eighties, the dominant radio doctors were Burkhart/Abrams. Tailoring their playlists exclusively to the same white-suburban-male-16-to-34 demographic, consultants Kent Burkhart and Lee Abrams mixed old rock with new to create the "SuperStars" format. The idea appealed to desperate radio programmers in the economic crunch of the early 1980s: market research, callbacks, and other methods were used to determine what should be played—what type of music, statistically, would attract the most listeners, and thus the most advertisers. As Denisoff wrote in 1986's *Tarnished Gold*, "In light of [radio's] structural problems of the late 1970s and early 1980s, it is not surprising that radio doctors, regardless of cost, have become the 'in' thing."

But the search for scientifically guaranteed audiences, many felt, meant quashing the innovation that had long been the heart of FM radio's appeal. Asked about the role of Burkhart/Abrams in the history of FM, Paul Rebmann, a 25-year radio veteran, asks, "You mean the guys that killed FM radio?" If the consultants' goal was to program "SuperStars," by definition this meant non-superstars—that is, most new or unproven groups—didn't make the cut.

Consequently, the doctors missed innovative new artists: Denisoff recounts that, "Abrams himself once admitted to being 'almost a year late' on [future superstars] Duran Duran, Stray Cats, and ... Billy Idol." Others were even more direct, like Mike Harrison, widely credited with coining the term AOR in the 1970s, who dismissed the role of the "experts'" supposed scientific methods:

> These consultants have made both an art and big business of the old game of selling gut-level decisions to management via research. As a

result ... many of today's younger programmers actually believe that research is a magic substitute for ... individual human experience, intuition, and, most important, taste.

Consultants shrugged off the charges laid at their door: Kent Burkhart practically welcomed his critics' protests of radio homogenization, saying, "Well, McDonald's sells a lot of hamburgers, so I'll accept them." From the radio docs' perspective, there were no problems with marketing the same product, the same playlist, coast-to-coast, just like fast food.

But the ossification of commercial FM radio opened doors for other media; college radio, for example, came into its eclectic own during the radio docs' era. As indie chronicler Michael Azerrad writes in his 2001 book, *Our Band Could Be Your Life*, "Tightly controlled FM formats, mostly programmed by a small group of consulting firms, kept new music off the radio. College radio jumped into the breach, providing a valuable conduit [between bands and potential audiences]."

And then came MTV.

A FEW MUSIC INDUSTRY FIGURES understood the causal relationship between changes in FM radio and the rise of the pioneering music-video television network. In *Inside MTV*, his 1988 sequel to *Tarnished Gold*, R. Serge Denisoff quotes one who did:

> FM radio, once the savior of the industry in the 1960s, was stagnating. Les Garland, then at [Atlantic] Records, recalled, "How many times can you hear 'Layla' or 'Stairway to Heaven'? In my travels, that's what I found on every station. I thought, 'Gee, there ought to be something that radio is going to wake up and do.' MTV seemed like just what was needed."

But, Denisoff hastens to add, "[Garland] was in a distinct minority at the time."

MTV, then, was designed as a new arena for music promotion, offering an alternative to AOR and the work of the radio doctors.

And certainly early MTV was chock-full of the kind of music that just didn't get played on the radio. British novelty act the Buggles' "Video Killed the Radio Star" was the station's famous kick-off, and quirky bands like Haircut 100, Altered Images, Flock of Seagulls, Total Coelo, and the Vapors were staples on the channel.

It's important to note, however, that MTV *would* have played corporate rock if it *could* have: the early, innovative playlists of MTV were largely accidents of supply. The original intent of MTV, according to Denisoff, was to create a visual version of AOR radio. Like standard AOR, its target audience was young white men. But the sort of bands who populated AOR radio didn't usually possess videos ready to go: Bruce Springsteen didn't have clips, Clare Grogan did. As Denisoff notes:

> [MTV founder Robert] Pittman had to take what he could get in the way of "promo" videos. Candidly, [MTV programming executive John] Sykes admits, "We were missing a lot of artists at the beginning because video hadn't really done anything until MTV launched."

Artists who did fit the general AOR model and had fully-produced commercial videos were in short supply. But on August 1, 1981, when MTV made its debut from a restaurant basement in Fort Lee, New Jersey—Manhattan wouldn't have MTV for several years—the game went to those with videos ready to air.

Shoes did.

They couldn't tell, right away, that MTV would have any impact at all. Zion didn't have cable, so they weren't even able to watch the fledgling channel. "So many names—of radio stations and publications and towns [that were playing Shoes]—were thrown at us," Gary recounts, "and we were used to hearing that we were doing well in a certain market or whatever, but those successes didn't mean anything to Elektra." MTV ought to have been different from those other minor successes: like Elektra, it was, after all, a member of the Warner/AMEX conglomerate. But that relationship created a kind of sibling rivalry, and ended up doing more harm than good.

Warner executives had been privy to the whole development process for MTV in 1980-81. But that doesn't mean they liked the idea of "music television." Denisoff characterizes early resistance to MTV within the Warner family as coming from the music wing, rather than the TV division or even American Express, their financial partner. Still reeling from the Crash of '79 and its aftermath, labels saw the new channel as a drain on scarce resources rather than a potential marketing venue. Denisoff notes that for the labels, "an unspoken truth was the bottom-line reality that the industry was spinning its wheels as sales continued to drop and company employees received pink slips, even in the executive suites." Videos seemed an unnecessary expenditure in a belt-tightening time, and certainly not in keeping with the way promo had traditionally worked.

Record-company promotion people, Denisoff points out in *Inside MTV*, were particularly suspicious of the new medium, which directly challenged their business model. They simply were not ready for the transition, and resisted it as long as they could. "Most record labels, unless they had already produced a video-clip library [as some had, for European markets], took a wait-and-see approach. ... Promotion people were tied to radio despite the cries of AOR conservatism," Denisoff says. He quotes Warner Records' director of video and television, Jo Bergman, an early and comparatively enthusiastic supporter of videos, about the resistance they faced:

> "Record companies are still unconvinced about a visual medium, period. ... There's no way to prove that TV or video actually sells records, or what great a part it plays in the sales of records." Later Bergman would add, "It wasn't so much that *I* was skeptical ... I've been doing videos for so many years, I wouldn't continue to do it if I didn't think it made sense. But in terms of the sales and promotion people at *that* time ...."

So while Warner's labels had a leg up on the competition in terms of knowing about MTV's development, they were in general no more prepared to take advantage of it, largely because their promotion departments weren't interested.

Shoes' videos had been made primarily to be shown on European television, during those heady days after the recording of *Present Tense*, in lieu of international touring. European stations had many more outlets for visual music; video clips had been a standard marketing tool there for years. Consequently, European labels had much bigger video libraries than their American counterparts, something that skewed the content of early MTV in an attention-grabbing and unconventional direction. Denisoff recounts:

> "Most of what we [programmed] was from new-wave British groups," recalls Ronald L. "Buzz" Brindle, formerly [director of music programming] of MTV, "who were already very conscious of video's power. They had already cultivated a 'look' and a style, one that still dominates. ... Back then the British videos just looked better—they were instantly recognizable against the American ones." A sizeable number of these modern Brit-rock auteurs were bands virtually unknown across the Atlantic Ocean. This would prove to be a blessing in disguise, though, as [MTV's] desperation [for clips] would later become innovation.

MTV, then, leaned toward modern rock by default: there simply wasn't anything else to put in rotation.

Though MTV executives took great pains to conceal the underwhelming number of videos available for airplay in those early days, Denisoff puts the modest tally somewhere between 100 and 125. Thus it's no real surprise that all four Shoes videos—for "Too Late," "Tomorrow Night," "Cruel You," and "In My Arms Again"—were aired on MTV's first day, and remained in heavy rotation for months thereafter. Shoes were big fish, even though the proverbial pond was admittedly kind of small.

Shoes were a perfect MTV band. Their music was innovative but not overly quirky, tuneful but not saccharine. They fit Pittman's AOR ideal, but they also fit with the new-wave and modern-rock acts MTV backed into playing. They were photogenically handsome and clean-cut. And MTV provided them additional support in subtle ways: veejays wore Shoes t-shirts onscreen; Shoes posters appeared on the walls of the faux-casual crash-pad that was the MTV set. Here, at least, Shoes were stars. And "MTV was *begging* us for new Shoes videos," Gary recounts.

Throughout 1981 and 1982, the role of video was hotly debated in the music industry. In November 1981, *Billboard* hosted a Video Entertainment/Music Conference; their third, but the first since MTV had launched in America. There, the ambiguous position of music videos was discussed: were they a promotional tool, like radio play or a commercial? Were they an art form in themselves, like a TV show? Len Epand of PolyGram argued, "We're not making advertisements for records. We're making video art." Jeff Ayeroff of A&M countered that promotional videos had been successful in Europe: "Why is it promotion in Europe and art in America?"

At issue, of course, was money. Should labels be expected to provide free programming to a medium seemingly unrelated to their business? Or should MTV pay labels for the clips they used, just as any station would pay a production company for a show?

The money question rested on whether or not MTV exposure sold records. Though few at the time seemed to realize the impact MTV would come to have, its effect seems (with the benefit of hindsight) predictable.

MTV brought an unprecedented level of pop-culture hipness, not to major cities where kids might be expected to encounter trendier music and styles anyway, but to third- and fourth-level markets: those places that lacked significant broadcast television channels and thus depended heavily on cable for content. Small-towners suddenly had access to the kind of cool underground music once only available to their urban cousins, and they went to their own local record stores looking for the music they now heard—and saw—on television.

These minor markets had been completely overlooked by record companies. Heavyweights in the industry similarly dismissed the effect of MTV in those secondary (and tertiary and quaternary) cities. But precisely because the playing fields were so small, MTV's effect was dramatic and calculable.

On October 10, a scant two months after MTV's launch, *Billboard* ran an article by Jim McCullough entitled, "MTV Cable Spurs Disk Sales of Artists Aired." McCullough presented evidence from record-store managers in some of these smaller markets chronicling the direct effect of MTV on sales. Shoes were mentioned specifically as one of the bands benefitting from the new medium. McCullough's article clearly lays out the causality:

> Steve Mitchell, manager, Sound Warehouse in Tulsa, indicates, "We've seen a strong impact. Sales of certain LPs have picked up in direct relation to what's being shown on MTV. Directly, it's influenced the Buggles, the [sic] Shoes, and the Tubes. ... There was a time when you depended on radio to break acts like that. No more. This has to be the way newer artists get exposure."

McCullough's piece recounts a similar tale from a Syracuse, New York record-store manager who simply states, "I have the [sic] Shoes on reorder because of MTV."

Shoes themselves were largely oblivious of the new medium. Zion didn't have it, and like the rest of the industry, the band members weren't sure what it meant yet. If they thought about MTV at all, it was to cringe at the amateurishness of their videos. But aside from Shoes' own self-consciousness, they had no tools to contextualize *Billboard*'s news about MTV's retail impact. Gary says:

> We never knew how many records we sold, anyway—Elektra never told us—so we wouldn't know if there had been a spike in sales. It's possible that somebody mentioned MTV to us, but I don't think we understood the significance of it. I don't think it registered more than, say, the college radio thing.

Dan Bourgoise, however, understood MTV's significance immediately. "It was like a bolt straight from heaven!" he says now. "This was our second chance!" Bourgoise's enthusiasm was catching: he convinced Shoes that the television exposure—and the record sales it sparked, which they learned about only when they read it in *Billboard*—would give them leverage to bargain with Elektra.

Shoes and Bourgoise went, as usual, to Ken Buttice, and requested funding to shoot a video for one of the songs off *Tongue Twister*—possibly "Your Imagination," John thinks. The album had been out for nearly a year, but, they reasoned, *Present Tense* was older than that, and if *Present Tense* had gotten a boost in sales from video exposure, it was reasonable to expect that the more recent record might, too.

Buttice—with the skepticism of a promo guy and the insider's knowledge of MTV's weak financial position—turned them down cold. Jeff remembers Buttice's words: "We know all about that MTV. It's a flash in the pan. We own it! If it sold records, I would know." They pointed out that *Billboard* had cited new sales of *Present Tense* post-MTV, but Buttice dismissed the article as meaningless. Bourgoise recalls Buttice's rejection: "It's a stiff! And the last record, that's a stiff, too! Why would we make videos for a stiff?" Disappointed, Dan Bourgoise asked if Buttice would mind if he took his request all the way to label chief Joe Smith. "Go ahead," Buttice replied to Bourgoise, as Jeff recalls. "But he's going to give you the same answer I did."

This time, Bourgoise went alone, armed only with the copy of *Billboard* stating unequivocally that, where MTV was available, the music channel was having an impact on record sales. As Buttice had predicted, Smith was unconvinced. But, according to Bourgoise, it was this meeting that persuaded Smith to extend the band's option and allow them to start recording another album, a sort of consolation prize for turning down video funding.

There is no question that Elektra missed the boat with Shoes and MTV, or that Shoes lost a valuable opportunity because of the label's lack of vision. Jeff calls it "perhaps the biggest marketing mistake of our career," which implies that it was *their* mistake; but as signed artists, they had to work through their label, and if the label didn't want to fund videos, it wouldn't. Yet as events eventually transpired, money was not the real issue.

AS DENISOFF OBSERVES IN *INSIDE MTV*, Elektra had plenty of company in their skepticism of the music channel's potential; indeed, it was conventional wisdom in the record business. MTV's reach was limited, and confined to markets that didn't matter much in the power centers of New York and L.A. Denisoff cites Jo Bergman: "It's one thing to have field reports, and selling Buggles records in Phoenix, now, that's nice, but it's not the kind of thing that [makes] decisions ... in sales and promotion." She identifies MTV's "real" launch as being January 1983, when it finally premiered in Manhattan:

"It's one thing to have reports coming in from the field, it's another to go home at night and put it on in your bedroom." But even once the music channel's clout had been proven and its reach expanded, labels still quibbled over who ought to be paying for video production.

For their part, the band members are skeptical that Dan's plea for video funding resulted in Shoes' option getting picked up: the Murphys and Klebe think that the decision had far more to do with Elektra's fear that, though they had not been able to turn Shoes into a blockbuster success, another label might do better with them, making Elektra look bad. Such a rationale may seem petty, but in the increasingly chaotic world that Elektra Records' Los Angeles office was becoming, it's as plausible as any other possibility. Keeping Shoes on Elektra's swollen roster didn't hurt the label—as critical darlings, the band accrued favorable press, and they enjoyed a loyal fan base even if they weren't selling many records—and it concealed, to some extent, the disorder at Elektra, even from the band members themselves.

SHOES WERE UNAWARE THAT, BY late 1981, the L.A. Elektra office was in a tailspin; no one appeared to be in charge except Ken Buttice. "This was a crippled company," Gary now reflects, "losing their A&R department to a promo man." As Marty Schwartz puts it, "They'd brought me out to L.A. [in 1980], and then signed some real crap music. Some of the worst music I've ever heard was signed out of that L.A. office between '80 and '82." The Elektra roster is littered with also-rans like the utterly forgettable Beds, the girl who sang "Aquarius" in the 1979 film *Hair*, and inconsequential solo albums by lesser members of Queen, Jefferson Starship, and the Eagles. Most sunk out of sight without a trace.

Back in Zion, Shoes were starting to get worried. They would lose contact with the label for weeks at a time, and hardly ever spoke to Buttice. "Kenny was disconnected from us after *Tongue Twister*," Gary recalls. "He was preoccupied, and that made us nervous."

Still, Shoes stayed busy, playing shows, roughing out demos, and making decisions for their next record, but their impression was that things in California were in disarray. No one seemed to be able to green-light anything. There were discussions about releasing the six live songs from the Zion Ice Arena as a twelve-inch EP; Gary and Jeff took their tapes to Hedden West to master them professionally for Elektra, but the idea appeared to fade into the ether. During one rare conversation with Buttice, he proposed to Jeff another six-track twelve-inch EP, but as Skip told his journal, only Jeff had songs ready to go. Not that it mattered: as with the suggested Ice Arena EP, the idea for this one just vanished. As Gary observes, "I don't think anyone had the reins. No one was making decisions." Marty Schwartz confirms, "People did whatever they felt like."

As was the case across the record industry, layoffs had started at Elektra: staffers Shoes had worked with just disappeared. Buttice had been their savior, their champion, and their friend, but he was running the L.A. office into the ground. By the fall of 1982, Buttice and everyone who worked under him would be fired.

In October '81, Elektra announced the formation of a new label, Elektra/Musician, to be administered out of New York. Veteran Columbia Records executive Bruce Lundvall, tapped to run the new imprint, said in a contemporary *Billboard* article, "We have a very strong commitment to artists who want to live here [in New York] and have their business done on the East Coast. With a two-headquarters kind of company, artists on the East Coast, [in] Europe, or the South who were a little concerned about dealing with the West Coast now have an opportunity to get answers at the source." Buttice, still senior VP for A&R in Los Angeles, was given a brief nod as a consultant, but it's not hard to see that the action was shifting east, and away from Ken Buttice.

STILL, AS LONG AS THEY HAD FUNDS for recording their next project, which they did once Elektra picked up their option, Shoes were there to make music, and by the end of 1981, they had enough songs to move forward on the record that would become *Boomerang*. They were proud of the songs, all of them feeling that they were developing as songwriters and performers.

They shipped these demos to Buttice, and he was particularly taken with Jeff's luminous ballad, "The Summer Rain." They also sent Gary's chipper ode to television, "The Tube," appending the famous Rocky-and-Bullwinkle cartoon routine—"Hey, Rocky! Watch me pull a rabbit out of my hat!" "Again?" "Nuttin' up my sleeve … Presto!"—to the beginning of the track, but that one received no response.

Buttice did fly out to Chicago in November with Carol Thompson to see Shoes live at the WLS RockFest on Thanksgiving weekend. Sandwiched between the Go-Go's and fellow Chicago-area band Survivor, Shoes held their own in front of the cavernous International Amphitheater's crowd. Chuck Fieldman, who was backstage, recalls that Buttice was denied access to the restricted backstage area, but that he spotted Fieldman and got his attention. "Will you tell these assholes who I am?" Fieldman remembers Buttice shouting, gesturing toward the security staff. Later, Buttice and Thompson drove up to Zion to hear the new demos. "They liked some and not others, but as usual, [the demos] are in rough form," Skip reported.

At this point, Shoes had come to understand that the new visual medium was going to be important, despite Elektra's reluctance to fund promotional clips. As Skip recalls, representatives of MTV queried the band several times: "Where's the next video? What's going on with you guys?" So when Shoes were approached about making a new clip by David Braga—a videographer at a small local TV station in Madison, Wisconsin and a mutual friend of Butch Vig and Duke Erikson—they leaped at the chance.

As the band saw it, after months of waiting for the label to act, Elektra had clearly turned its back on Shoes videos: it was time to do something on their own. They had always had a DIY ethic, the clock was ticking, and they had to act. Dan Bourgoise says:

> Now exposure is all about Facebook, Twitter, YouTube, MySpace, blogs. Everything is much more immediate. Back in 1981, Shoes *needed* that immediacy, because they were trying to reach a young audience. That lack of instantaneous exposure is one critical factor in why Shoes don't have the recognition today that they deserve. If we could have worked on Shoe time, not Elektra time, they'd have been better off.

With videographer Braga, Shoes decided to choose from the demos for the new album, which sported the working title *Animation*. The song they selected was John's lively rocker "In Her Shadow," which had been demoed for *Tongue Twister*, and then re-demoed that summer. John's not entirely sure, in retrospect, why that one was selected; ordinarily they'd lean toward newer material. But Shoes had been trying out a lot of the unrecorded songs live, and John does recall that their corps of followers seemed to like "In Her Shadow."

The single-day shoot was done "completely on the fly," Gary says. As with Shoes' previous clips, it was a performance video on a soundstage. "In Her Shadow" was a new song, the band members looked okay, and Braga did a capable job editing together the footage. Shoes had done it all without taxing Elektra's almost-nonexistent resources, and they released it to MTV.

But once again, as was the case with *Shoes on Ice*, the label was not pleased with this end-run around their system. "We got some static from Elektra," Gary confirms. "I think they threatened to sue us," adds John. The label demanded that the unauthorized video be pulled from MTV immediately; in fact, Shoes are not sure it was ever shown. But Elektra's response indicates that financing was not the real issue for the label in regards to making additional Shoes' videos: it was apparent that Elektra was anxious to claim creative control. If they said no videos, they meant *no videos*. That was news to Shoes, but they got the message, loud and clear.

And as had happened with *Shoes on Ice*, Shoes did not challenge the label's right to call the shots—in this case, on the MTV question. They just quietly pulled the clip and prepared to record the next album.

But unbeknownst to Shoes—quite possibly, unbeknownst to Buttice himself—Elektra's economic failures of the last several years had put the VP of A&R in a perilous position. Shoes could tell something was wrong back in L.A.—phone calls weren't being returned, and sometimes they couldn't rouse anyone at all at the office—but the band members just weren't sure what the problem was. So they kept their heads down, worked on their demos, and hoped for the best. After their experience with the first two Elektra records, Shoes may not have thought Buttice was making the best decisions on their behalf, but his was the star they were hitched to, for better or worse.

SHOES' PREPARATIONS FOR THE RECORD they called *Animation* were noticeably different from those that had marked their two previous studio outings. For one thing, John says, producers were not paraded before them, smorgasbord-style, because it had been decided fairly early on that Shoes would produce themselves.

There's some debate now among the band members about how that decision was made. Jeff tends to see it as a vote of confidence from Elektra: at the time, he said that Shoes "convinced Elektra brass to let [the band produce] ourselves," and called it "a natural progression for us." And certainly, they were anxious to make their names as producers—that had been part of the original Elektra deal, after all, and both Jeff and Gary had produced outside bands when Shoes weren't recording.

But this glass-half-full interpretation ignores the very real fact that, for Shoes' third Elektra album, the label's resources were constrained across the board. Producing themselves was simply cheaper. As Dan describes, it was "tough to swallow, going from when Elektra couldn't give them enough to Elektra giving them nothing." Elektra had extended the band's option, and set out a budget for another album. As their original contract stipulated, production funds increased from *Tongue Twister*. But it was clear that their label would have no patience if the band went over budget this time.

As their own producers, the members of Shoes chose a high-end, albeit local, studio: Chicago Recording Company. John confirms that they felt the sea change: "'First we're in England, then we're in Hollywood, now we're in Chicago. We're gonna end up back in our own backyard.' And we did, eventually."

To man the studio controls, Shoes turned to CRC's chief engineer, Hank Neuberger. They had met Neuberger several years earlier; in fact, he had put out feelers about producing the band as far back as *Present Tense*. Neuberger didn't have much in the way of straight rock credentials, though his engineering résumé was sterling, including stints with revered folksinger-songwriters Steve Goodman and John Prine, and the seminal R&B-funk band Ohio Players. And his days at CRC were spent producing commercial jingles. But Neuberger was a fan of Shoes' records—this was the first time they'd collaborated with a pro who knew and liked their music going in—and "he understood, better than anyone we ever worked with, what we were going for," Gary says. "We did argue about some stuff, but in hindsight, I tend to think he was more right than I was." Neuberger himself doesn't remember the sessions as contentious at all: "They were really nice guys, and we got along well."

As working musicians, Shoes were already, by necessity, pretty much night owls. But these album sessions turned them into full-on graveyard-shifters, recording all through the night when the studio was empty (and rates were lower). They occupied CRC's basement ("the catacombs," as John called it), going into the studio about nine-thirty or ten o'clock every night, and working until seven-thirty or eight in the morning: "Then we'd sleep all day, get up about five p.m., and do it all over again." Still, John recalls, the whole setup had its advantages:

> If you're going to do something like that, it makes sense to do it in the dead of winter. Because when we were in England, we really wanted to get out and see tourist things and go places. That was true in Hollywood, too: there were fun things to do that weren't recording. Not in Chicago in the winter. This time, there were no distractions.

Shoes generally worked about six days a week. The schedule was fixed by Neuberger, who was operating the studio during the day in addition to presiding over Shoes' sessions at night. "We ran him ragged," they all agree. Neuberger notes that he didn't always work these double shifts; sometimes he handed the sessions off to his engineers, and sometimes he took days off. Once in a while, Neuberger grabbed a catnap on the couch in his office while waiting until he was needed. But at least part of the time, he was working essentially twenty-four-hour days, and weekends off were absolutely necessary.

Neuberger's need for a break was exacerbated by the fact that these were not easy sessions for the band. "I knew they were under stress," the chief engineer recalls; he bore the brunt of the pressure as each Shoe, in turn, drove the recording process to his own exacting specifications. In retrospect, the members of Shoes are uncomfortably aware of how difficult they made it. "It was tense and it was hard on Hank," John says. "He was doing therapy sessions for three guys. As soon as one guy is done with his song, now here's the next guy with his." In a band with a single creative center, recording requires coddling a single auteur psyche, so that the strain of recording waxes and wanes. But with Shoes, particularly on this record, each song's author was fervent about his own material, so the strain of recording never let up.

The tension was particularly pronounced between Jeff and Gary, the most production-oriented band members. Early in the recording process, Skip jokes in his journal that the two are "jockeying for pole position" at the board. When they retired to their apartments in the morning, each complained to his roommate about the other. "Jeff is saying that Gary is hogging the board," Skip wrote. "John says Gary's saying the same thing about Jeff." Skip and John, outside this production rivalry, did their best to keep the peace. Skip makes note in his journal of a moment early in the recording process when Neuberger looked at John and him and "asked us if we were in the same band [as Jeff and Gary]."

In addition, while they were still supportive of each other's writing, the members of Shoes weren't necessarily *equally* supportive. John grouses that "I always felt at the eleventh hour like those guys would have something in their back pocket" that they would pull out for their *own* songs—a riff or effect or fill—they had withheld from his: "It was like, 'Okay, *now* we're gonna get out the cool stuff!' and I'd say, 'Well, wait a minute! My song could use something else! You didn't do that for me!'" John hastens to add that he doesn't think anyone was intentionally sabotaging anything, but that the low simmer of competition that had always existed was creeping closer to the boiling point.

John recalls one particular altercation over his desire to go back and re-record his vocal for the rollicking "What Love Means," something the schedule didn't allow and his bandmates sneeringly dismissed: "'Oh, I want to re-record this, I want to re-record that,'" he recalls them mocking him. Others might not have felt the stresses among them, yet for the generally courteous Shoes, treating their friends and family with such disdain was a major breach. "We were like rats in a cage," says Gary. They were trying hard to keep it together, but increasing demands—internal and external—were beginning to take their toll.

Even Skip was getting in on the dust-ups, something he'd long steered clear of. During the sessions, when he roomed with Jeff, they repeatedly discussed Skip's desire to sing backing vocals. Jeff explained (Skip notes in his journal) that if he wanted to sing, he'd have had to be present when vocals were being demoed, something that had long bored him. "Another reason I should try to stay down at the studio is so that I can get in on some background vocals. Jeff told me I had to be there and take my chances," he wrote on April 6. "Of course I'll have to make sure my voice is better than adequate ... Little do they know of my hidden talents." Skip asked again to sing, on April 14, and was left unsatisfied:

> So I was there and Jeff was doing one of his songs and they marched right by me and did the background vocals. So they didn't ask [me to sing] and another [issue] is that they sing so fucking high I can't reach it. ... Well anyhow, I was pissed when I left the studio.

Leaving was the problem, as he learned later, when Jeff told him that they generally recorded the high parts of the backing vocals first, followed by the lower harmonies. Skip was simply never there for the stuff in his range. Once he understood that, he was determined to wait it out, and as he wrote triumphantly on April 29, "I got in on the vocals last night."

Neuberger clearly felt the strain of overseeing these sessions—one contemporary *Billboard* account calls him the "engineer and referee." Sometimes, he would simply hide out, handing the session over to one of his second engineers—Tom Hanson, Mike Szarsynski, or Paul Klingberg—and sleep on a couch in his office.

At other times, Neuberger would plead quietly to Elektra to credit him as producer or at least co-producer, arguing that he was doing more than an engineer's job in smoothing these particular choppy waters. For example, after the instance in which John was ridiculed by Jeff and Gary for wanting to re-record his vocal for "What Love Means," the bassist was withdrawn for several days—reliably showing up at the studio, but uncharacteristically quiet and restrained. Neuberger sought him out and asked what the problem was, and when John confessed that he really wanted another crack at the song, Hank made it happen, John says.

Neuberger's negotiations with Elektra were partially successful: he would be listed as "Associate Producer" on the eventual *Boomerang* sleeve.

Though Shoes felt like they were fighting for their professional lives, recording their third big-league album wasn't all nonstop *agita*. They rented a pair of apartments in the same downtown building, within walking distance of CRC, with John and Gary in one, Jeff and Skip in the other. They were in a hip city neighborhood, and Neuberger's schedule meant they got to go out some nights. MTV News came to Chicago to do a feature on the band. They were close enough to Zion to return every couple of weeks, listening to the rough mixes through their own studio speakers, and Gary's folks even came to CRC for a look-see one weekend, the first parental visit to any Shoes recording sanctum.

Women came to visit, too. At this point, they all had regular girlfriends, and were working close enough to home that their ladies could stop down for a few days. (Skip remarks that this required some negotiation in the shared-apartment situation, since one guy generally got the bedroom, and the other the couch.) Jeff was having a temporary reunion with the girl who'd broken his heart when he got home from England; John with the young woman he'd been dating in California. Gary had met someone through the band, and Skip had been dating the same girl since before *Tongue Twister*. One weekend, when all four women were supposed to visit at the same time, Skip reported that only Jeff's date made it. "Three lone wolves out on the town," he wrote wryly. "What a laugh! Three young studs went out alone and came home alone. I think I'll call home."

On March 8, Skip's girlfriend, Jill, made it to Chicago for her birthday, and had to wait for them at CRC. He relates what occurred when Shoes had finished their work for the evening:

> We got goofing around in the studio. John and Gary on the piano, Jill on snare drum, me on vocal, Jeff on whatever. We taped it but I haven't heard it back yet. ... I told Jill she would be famous now.

So Shoes pressed on, focusing on their work, trying to have fun, all the while aware that their tenure at Elektra was in danger.

"They did see the writing on the wall," Dan Bourgoise says. They knew that the stakes were high and that they were swimming upstream now."

IRONICALLY, ALL THIS TENSION AND worry came at a time when Shoes had never felt stronger about their craft. Nineteen eighty-one had been, by financial necessity, a heavy concert year for them, and they were confident their performances and songwriting were more finely honed than ever.

But at the same time, they were writing in isolation. "I wonder if it wasn't a reaction to the reaction to *Tongue Twister*," John muses. "Those group compositions, which we really liked, were totally overlooked." As far as he recalls, no one even suggested writing together this time.

Instead, every song on the record is credited to a single composer. Jeff explains:

> The co-writer thing changed as we became more self-confident and learned more. I always liked the collaborations because of the feeling of being part of a team, but I'm as guilty as the next guy of creating songs that were almost solo projects.

The songwriting process was a little more complicated for *Boomerang*, because when Shoes' songs had been composed back home, Jeff and Gary were still living in the same apartment building in Winthrop Harbor. Each wrote primarily in his own apartment, and each worried about being overheard by his bandmate. Jeff continues:

> We still wanted to surprise each other with a new song. Everyone likes to have that "ta-da!" factor where we surprise each other, and it became harder to do unless the songs were more and more

complete-sounding. It was a little tough to make a fully developed demo while living in the same building. You couldn't get too loud when you worked at home.

But one man's hoped-for surprise is another man's suspected secret, and it's not too hard to see that the writing of *Boomerang* was fraught with more of the looking-over-the-shoulder suspicions that had begun to creep into their songwriting process during *Tongue Twister*. That mutual mistrust was the direct result of Elektra's demand for a hit single, along with each person's determination to be the one who provided it this time around.

As Gary puts it, "We were gone if we didn't have a hit. It would have been different with a boutique company like Sire or IRS, but not Elektra." And by 1982, Shoes had become increasing skeptical that Elektra would give *any* of their songs a shot.

They acknowledge that these stresses came out in their songwriting, too, most notably in Jeff's "Under the Gun," which, he says, "was definitely a response to the record-company pressure." Gary concurs, noting that his deceptively sunny-sounding "Double Talk," while only obliquely referential to their relations with Elektra, certainly expresses the sense of wariness that pervaded their experiences at that point. "Watch your step, I'm on to you./All your double talk, all your lies, don't push your luck with me." "We went from being trusting to being untrusting, and that's a big change in a person," he reflects. "We realized that we always had been on our own, that anything Elektra did for us was in their own interest. These weren't fans trying to help; it was a corporation."

Many of the songs on *Boomerang* weren't painted exclusively from Shoes' usual boy-girl palette. For example, while Jeff's aggressive rocker "Mayday" could be taken as referring to a relationship, it is in fact the apocalyptic cry against the Reagan Revolution that critics had been so anxious to find on *Tongue Twister*. "Mayday, it's too late to stop it," Jeff wrote. "Mayday, the time has come/Mayday … the ending for me and you."

Gary's aforementioned "The Tube," another off-topic offering, "started as just a title":

> That was my generation; we were raised by TV. TV's been there my whole life, from the time I was four years old and rolling around on the floor watching the Three Stooges. It's not intended to be a very serious song, though I guess people saw it as ironic or whatever. It's more lighthearted.

John notes that the channel-changing sample included in the song is also considerably more low-tech than it seems: "Nowadays every sound bite would be chosen. We left it completely to chance. I don't remember spending all that much time on it; we just pointed a mic at the TV and changed channels until we found something that sounded cool."

John's "Tested Charms" was another non-relationship song, a sympathetic portrait of an aging beauty desperate to recapture her lost allure. Says John:

> One of the strengths of our group is that we're not afraid to be vulnerable. I think it's fine to show that range, if that's what the song needs.

But John recognized that if the goal was to deliver singles, he'd essentially handicapped himself by including the contemplative ballad among his contributions to the record. "Tested Charms" was unusual musically, too: it was built around a little rhythm track created by a Casio mini-synthesizer—something Shoes took heat for, given the unintentionally proclamatory "No Keyboards" note on their last record ("Keyboards? The Casio was a *calculator*," John scoffs).

And it didn't exactly *fit* the mood of the record. In fact, John says, Shoes put "Tested Charms" at the end of *Boomerang* because there simply wasn't anyplace else for it that wouldn't disturb the album's momentum.

Shoes' official A&R rep, Carol Thompson, told John his song made her cry. But, he adds wryly, she also asked, "Could you speed up the middle?"

THOMPSON, WHO HAD BY THIS time been promoted to general manager of A&R was, like Buttice, not really a music person. Her expertise was in budgets and accounting. Though she had been Shoes' A&R rep in name ever since their signing, Thompson had never actively involved herself in the recording process before. But in the power vacuum that afflicted Elektra's L.A. office in 1982, she took to A&R with a vengeance. Perhaps it was an attempt to defend her position in the face of company cutbacks—a need to be seen doing *something*—or perhaps she genuinely thought that Shoes urgently required her guidance. In any case, Thompson became a much more regular fixture in their lives, proffering advice on lyrics, band presentation (she thought Jeff should be a more obvious front man, which he dismissed immediately), and production. Dan Bourgoise saw Thompson's "trying to flex her A&R muscles" as "excruciating. But they were scared, and she could do that."

All three band songwriters recall Thompson's critique of the intentionally abrasive-sounding vocal track for "Mayday." Since it was a cry for help in the face of America's rightward turn, the song was *supposed* to sound strained; the unusual (for Shoes) raspiness was even more pointed given the fact that it was Jeff, often designated as the most mellifluous vocalist of the group, who was doing it.

Thompson didn't like it. Hearing a rough mix, she encouraged Jeff to re-record the vocal, to make it smoother and more in keeping with Shoes' usual style; she asked them to remix the song, too. Happy with "Mayday" as it was, the band didn't change a thing from the mix they'd sent earlier in the year. But when they played it again for Buttice, Thompson, and other label brass in L.A. that May, she apparently couldn't hear that there'd been no change, and assumed they had re-recorded "Mayday" as she'd requested. Thompson reportedly leaned over, touched Jeff on the arm, and murmured confidentially, "Now aren't you glad you took my advice?"

This meeting, during what would end up being Shoes' last trip to California during their Elektra tenure, took place in a crowded conference room at label headquarters, with Buttice still holding court over his crew. Shoes, Buttice, Thompson, and Marty Schwartz (along with as many staff members as they could cram in) sat and listened to what the band thought was the final version of *Boomerang*, blaring through huge speakers wheeled in for the occasion. Though Shoes received a standing ovation—possibly genuine, possibly obligatory—everyone was apparently getting into the advice business: Marty Schwartz leaned over to Buttice and whispered, "Side two should be side one."

With previous albums, Shoes had generally been pretty sanguine about Elektra suggestions, despite their contractual guarantee of creative control. Anything that got the label pumped up and in the mood to help them was fine by them—"Whatever, we didn't think *that* would be the single, but okay," John offers as example. "We didn't want to dampen Elektra's enthusiasm." But in the case of resequencing an entire album, Shoes demanded a negotiation.

Even switching the sides created issues. They'd already given much thought to the placement of "Tested Charms"; the new sequence would put it in the middle of the record, where they had decided it didn't belong. Jeff balked a little, too, as his "Under the Gun" lost its lead-off position to John's "In Her Shadow." The decision was made, then, to switch the first three tracks from each side to the other side, and rearrange the rest of the tracks slightly to prevent the same vocalist from having two songs in a row, something the band prided itself on avoiding. Once all that was settled, the mastering process for Shoes' third Elektra album followed immediately.

But there were other issues to deal with as well. Just before the Los Angeles trip, John had received a copy of *Billboard* that boasted a full-page ad indicating that someone, somewhere, had screwed up badly. Elektra had long been aware that Shoes' working title for the record was *Animation*. The title and the visual ideas it suggested engaged the band's creativity. Proposed images had been discussed between Shoes and Elektra, and a graphic artist was paid to create a series of band pictures (featuring color-blocking on selected articles of their clothing) that simulated real animation, by rearranging the figures—now Jeff was in front, now John, etc.—all of which would appear on the back of the LP cover. "We want to include a flip-book in the album," Skip noted in his journal.

But what no one had bothered to tell Shoes was that at the same time, another member of the WEA family—one with more pull—had released a record with the same title. Yes vocalist Jon Anderson issued his solo project, *Animation*, on Warner subsidiary Atlantic, just as Shoes' *Animation* was being completed. Once informed, they came to California for mastering hoping against hope that they'd be allowed to keep their title, but Elektra declined. "These people could fuck up a one-car funeral," Skip commented bitterly.

Chagrined, Shoes went through the mastering process at Precision Audio with their now-nameless record. Over the course of that trip, an ominous feeling grew. In Skip's journal, he is clear that both Buttice and Thompson are in trouble at Elektra; he never mentions that Shoes might be, too, though his bandmates had already figured that out.

They were busy on that trip; two days were spent with Randee St. Nicholas doing a photo shoot they expected to use for the inner sleeve of *Boomerang*—maybe for the flip-book, according to Skip. (But in fact, not only did Elektra refuse the flip-book idea: they refused to do an inner sleeve altogether: Shoes made the lyrics available through their fan club.) St. Nicholas took dozens of shots of the band in full male-model pout. After a day and a half, they were getting edgy, so they took cans of shaving cream and started spraying each other, sculpting their hair into weird shapes and generally fooling around. "Mine was supposed to be a Mohawk," Skip noted, "but I think it looked more like a fish fin." Without cleaning up, they returned to their hotel; Skip laughed that the doorman was hesitant about admitting them to the building.

When Carol Thompson called to invite Shoes out to dinner at tony Beverly Hills restaurant The Palm one night toward the end of their trip, they accepted, despite the fact that they had just eaten. "We figured that this might be the last time Elektra was willing to feed us," Gary says. At dinner, they all recall, Thompson was openly patronizing toward the band and Dan Bourgoise, presumptively trying to order food for them all. "She collared the waiter," John recalls, "saying, 'New York strips all around,?' but he came to each of us individually, and we all ordered these four-pound lobsters." Thompson ended up borrowing money from Dan Bourgoise to cover the bill.

Over the meal, Thompson floated various alternative album titles to them, all forms of the one they couldn't use—*Animated? Animate?*—and when John blurted out *Boomerang*—a title they had actually briefly considered early on for the record, they jumped at it. "Plus I think we were just relieved we could all agree on something without going through the Name-the-Album process again," John says. Serendipitously, both *Animation* and *Boomerang* had nine letters, which meant that the cover's redesign would be minimal; and the layout, with the band's name and the album title set at right angles to each other, even looked a little like a boomerang.

Shoes headed home after delivering the record—resequenced and renamed—at the beginning of June. "When we left L.A., we knew something wasn't right," Gary reflects. They heard conflicting rumors about *Boomerang*'s fate: first "Bound to Be a Reason" and "In Her Shadow" were supposed to be paired as a single, then "Mayday." A twelve-inch of "Mayday" was pressed and may have gone to some radio stations: Skip's journal cited a report that the "Mayday" single had been released on July 26. The album's street date was pushed back from July; it officially came out on August 6, 1982.

BUT WHEN THE RECORD WAS RELEASED, Skip barely noticed it: his father had become seriously ill quite suddenly in mid-July. Mr. Meyer's sickness was swift, merciless; it attacked seemingly every system in his body at once. An only child, Skip was close to his parents, so he put everything on hold to be with his mother at the medical center in Madison, Wisconsin.

On July 29, Skip wrote:

> My dad went into the hospital two weeks ago. At first, it was his pancreas. ... then they found a tumor on his kidney. My mom and her son freaked out. Now we are in Madison where they diagnosed him with having an ulcer in his duodenum so they have been treating him for that. Today, he went in for a biopsy on the tumor. We are waiting for the results. I wish they would find out because this hospital living is driving me crazy.

Gary—who knew all too well about dealing with parental illness while a record was looming—went to Madison as well, staying with his friend Butch Vig and accompanying Skip to the hospital.

The other three Shoes all had a curious relationship with their drummer. He had long been one of them, subject to the same circumstances and travel and money problems, but he was outside of them, too. Skip didn't write songs or play the guitar, though he often promised himself in his journal that he would. (He notes now that he did write a few songs, but never showed them to his bandmates.) Skip also hadn't been allowed to sing, a proscription he'd taken quite personally, as noted above. By *Boomerang*, the separation between the three songwriters and the drummer was structural.

But his bandmates liked him personally and had become accustomed to his manner, which remained, even in these stressful times, self-deprecatingly (if a little bitterly) humorous. Being around Skip was a relief, a way to decompress —to be inside the band, but outside the intensity of the recording process. "If you wanted to vent, you could always go hang out with Skip," Gary says, "since you knew there'd be a fight with anyone else."

When his father got sick, it was the worst possible time professionally. Jeff and John stayed in Zion to handle press for the new record; Gary and Skip camped out in Madison.

And on August 10, less than a month after he'd taken ill (and four days after the release of *Boomerang*), Skip's father died.

Skip reported the news flatly in his journal, but did not write again for over two months. His bandmates tried to be supportive, though he didn't reveal much of his grief. "It was scary how fast he seemed to bounce back," Gary comments.

AND THE BAD NEWS KEPT coming: *Boomerang* had barely hit the streets when they found out that Ken Buttice had been fired.

Buttice had long been a decidedly mixed blessing for Shoes. A consummate salesman, he'd sold them on a vision of themselves so grandiose that they were now a quarter of a million dollars in the hole with their label, maybe even more than that. But the charming former promo man had given them a confidence in themselves they'd had never had. Shoes knew that others at Elektra were much more skeptical, watching the bottom line a lot more closely than didthe label's cheerfully heedless VP of A&R, but they had always assumed that Buttice, by sheer force of ambitious will, would protect them as his first real investment. And now he was gone.

Firings were not generally publicized, but in an August 28, 1982 "Inside Track" posting in *Billboard*—one fraught with tales of roster-slashing at CBS, Atlantic, Columbia/Epic—Buttice is referred to in the past tense: "Elektra is said to have dropped 12 acts Wednesday ([August] 18) from its roster. The groups were signed when former a&r [sic] chief Kenny Buttice oversaw the department."

The band members looked at each other, back in Zion, and their response to the news was simple: "We're fucked."

Chapter 9

When Push Comes to Shove (1982-87)

With Buttice gone and Elektra in desperate financial straits, *Boomerang* got even less of a launch than *Tongue Twister*; this time, there was no travel to the coasts, and media outreach was primarily local. The press kit for *Boomerang* (penned by an anonymous Ira Robbins—"That kind of work kept a lot of us in pasta in those days," the veteran rock scribe says wryly), adheres to an upbeat tone, focusing on the benefits of self-production and the MTV effect:

> As a result of their unanticipated MTV windfall, Shoes plan to translate several tracks from *Boomerang* to video for cable viewing. Like everything they do, the group plan to exercise control over their video output and have discussed storyboarding and taping.

That was the official line, anyway. Of course there had been no real windfall—monetary or otherwise—from MTV, and Elektra refused to discuss music videos at all. Shoes *had* talked about videos among themselves, but as far as they recall, there was zero contact with anyone at the label except the publicity department. And even there, housecleaning was going on figuratively and literally—some of the girls they knew were being laid off, and one of them, on her way out the door, packed all Shoes' publicity materials in a box and mailed it off to Dan Bourgoise, who forwarded it to the band.

As bungled as the single selection (indeed, the entire release process) had been for *Present Tense* and *Tongue Twister*, Elektra evidently gave up entirely for *Boomerang*: there was no single release at all. A twelve-inch of "Mayday" was pressed for radio stations, but never made available for sale to the public.

Nevertheless, Shoes' whole future with Elektra hung on *Boomerang*.

Just a month after its release, Jeff told Moira McCormick in the September 18, 1982 issue of *Billboard* that "*Boomerang*, like previous Shoes LPs, has been slow in taking off." No surprise there; not only did it lack a customary lyric-printed inner sleeve, the standard low-budget promotional materials were also absent this time around:

> So far, says Murphy, they've even had to make do without benefit of *Boomerang* posters, cutouts, and the usual paraphernalia. But in the classic do-it-yourself Shoes spirit, their fan club is taking up the slack with buttons, notepads, and lyric sheets, available to members. "It costs us a fortune," Jeff sighs, "but the fans are worth it."

Elektra's only acknowledgment that *Boomerang* might deserve a push at all was the free bonus disc included with *Boomerang*'s first 10,000 copies: the belated *Shoes on Ice*—which the band had recorded and mixed themselves. For his part, Jeff believes that many of the *Shoes on Ice* discs were never used for their intended purpose, as a perk for *Boomerang* buyers; instead, he says they were generally kept behind the counters of record stores, distributed at the discretion of sales clerks—assuming they even remembered the bonus discs were there.

McCormick noted in the *Billboard* article that Jeff "realizes that this is not the most sanguine time in the record industry's history to be trying to make a splash." The recession of 1982, which bottomed out in November of that year, saw greater unemployment and more business failures than had been experienced in the United States since the 1930s. Things were bad out there, and the record business was not exempt.

Shoes at least had the cold comfort of knowing they weren't alone in their plight: in 1982, the "Crash of '79" was being reenacted.

ON SEPTEMBER 30, WITH *BOOMERANG* still in its hopeful new-release stage, *Rolling Stone* ran an article entitled, "Record Industry Nervous as Sales Drop Fifty Percent." "The U.S. record industry is in the worst shape of its history," authors Kurt Loder and Steve Pond flatly state. Their piece cites a number of reasons for the decline: no-longer-dependable superstars (Blondie's 1982 record, *The Hunter*, sold 500,000 copies, Loder and Pond point out, as compared to over a million of their 1981 release *Auto-American*; Fleetwood Mac had gone from twelve million units on *Rumours* to two million on *Tusk* to one million on *Mirage*, et cetera); lack of marketing and advertising on the part of record companies; and the rise of the Walkman coupled with the blank cassette. The record industry as a group only really recognized the last of these problems, zestfully demonizing home-tapers. (Ken Buttice had been a particularly avid advocate for adding a royalty onto the cost of cassette decks to offset presumed losses due to their use, a proposal that was never enacted.)

At the same time, labels were spending exorbitant amounts on contracts for acts they still assumed would produce huge hits. "For example," Loder and Pond wrote, "it was recently reported that Glenn Frey and Don Henley, the two former leaders of the Eagles, had been paid advances by Elektra/Asylum of $1.5 million and $2 million, respectively, for their debut solo albums. Frey's record has sold only 200,000 copies, and only 100,000 copies of Henley's LP were even shipped, leading to speculation that those deals alone might tip the balance in the label's already precarious financial situation."

Joe Smith, chairman of Elektra, is quoted acknowledging that, yes, "we do make ridiculous deals." However, Smith immediately points to *someone else*'s bad contract in order to illustrate his point, citing CBS's $5 million-per-album deal with Billy Joel. The *Rolling Stone* article continues, "Smith says the record business may be off as much as sixty percent this year, 'although that may be a little drastic. ... Queen's latest album [*The Game*] sold 3.5 million [units], and the new one [*Hot Space*] hasn't hit 1 million yet; but that doesn't mean the business is off sixty percent—it means that the new Queen record is not as good as the last one. It never would have sold 3.5 million, because it doesn't have the hits on it.'" Smith, who would be replaced by the end of the year, clearly illustrates the way the blame game was played: if a record did not sell, that was the fault of the artist, not any other forces.

Another industry executive commented anonymously, "Nothing is selling. It's grim out there and we're all getting hit in a heavy way. In 1979, business dropped, but lots of companies bounced back and made money the next year. This time around, people are saying that nothing like that is going to happen. They say this is going to be the new record industry." The industry itself compounded its financial woes with a shortsighted new returns policy: whereas previously the labels would ship units and collect payment after each record was sold, now they were placing a sixty-day limit on the amount of time retailers could hold onto a record without paying for it. Unless retailers paid for a shipment up front, then, the records themselves were straitjacketed into a two-month shelf-life, giving them a scant eight weeks total to catch on before being returned to the label.

The music-biz pie was getting ever smaller, and those who still got a crack at it were taking larger and larger pieces. For example, that November saw the release of the biggest-selling album of all time, Michael Jackson's *Thriller* (29 million units sold in the U.S. by 1984; at least 110 million globally by the end of 2011). But such blockbusters crowded out smaller acts, and Shoes were on the wrong side of that equation.

EVEN WITH THE BONUS DISC, *Boomerang* sales were disappointing. Shoes never got any actual figures from their label, but it was clear that the record was nowhere near the breakout they'd hoped for.

Reviews were still favorable, of course. Parke Puterbaugh in *Rolling Stone* found *Boomerang* to be "brimming with the virtues of youthfulness and tunefulness, and recall[ing] the spirit of bygone days when music worked like a kaleidoscope, giving artful, patterned expression to our fondest wishes and deepest fantasies." And longtime supporter Ira Robbins, in *Trouser Press*, praised the band for its "durability":

Anyone familiar with the previous *Tongue Twister* or *Present Tense* will find no surprises here. Shoes are so good at their chosen form that it would be unnatural for them to alter course. Neither fear of typecasting nor commercial frustration can deter them from what they've always done, which is breathy, guitar-dominated pop.

Back in Illinois, Shoes hit the road again in the circumscribed geographic range they had set for themselves in the spring of 1981. The band performed a healthy number of shows that fall and through the next spring, mostly in the same upper-Midwest club-and-college circuit they usually played. It brought some money in, though as Shoes had grimly learned in 1981, not really enough for four people to live on. The now-silent Elektra didn't offer any tour support whatsoever, and so, as before, the band members just kept their heads down and moved ahead.

Their road crew this time out was organized by a scrappy Chicagoan named Lee Popa. Popa had been running sound since high school. By the time he got to Shoes four years later, he had served as a house sound man at Club C.O.D., doing blues acts on weeknights, and traveled with local rock groups on the weekend; he estimates that he'd worked with more than two hundred bands during that time. Popa recalls, "I was living at my mom's and had all Shoes' records—when they called me, I was thrilled."

Popa began working with Shoes in 1981, first as a sound man, but by '82 he was unofficial road manager, finding friends to do sound and lights for them. Popa remembers his time with Shoes fondly:

> They were way more intelligent than most bands, more intellectual; I learned a lot from them. They were fine song craftsmen. What they do looks simple, sounds simple, but it's hard to recreate. You can't buy what they do, can't teach what they do. There's a relationship between the guitar lines, and among the guitar and bass lines, that's almost syncopated, like balls bouncing at different speeds. They weren't trained. It just came naturally to them. ... And really nice guys. They were funny, never mean. We'd joke around, but there were never any temper tantrums, never any weirdness.

The shows Popa ran weren't huge, he recalls, but Shoes played hard anyway: "The band would be cranking, [even] to half-empty clubs."

Popa, a musician himself, was sensitive to the requirements of Shoes' music, and tweaked their sound system to maximize the band's strong points, easing some of the audio issues that had plagued them:

> I tuned the P.A. like a soul P.A: I changed the speaker horns' frequency crossover so the vocals would come out of both the lower-frequency [midrange] horns, which were tuned up, and the high speakers.

What Popa did for them, Jeff says, was to ensure that "our voices were coming more from the mid-range 'coned' speakers and less from the high-range compression drivers (tweeters)." The effect of the change, Jeff continues, was to temper the sometimes "piercing and edgy" effect of Shoes' vocals issuing from the high-range speakers. "We tend to sing fairly high, with high harmonies, so Lee 'warmed' the sound up by sending more through the paper-coned speakers than through the bright tweeters."

Popa was dedicated. Prior to a November 6, 1982 show at the Thirsty Whale in River Grove, Illinois, he unexpectedly stopped by the club for set-up: unexpected--because he had gotten married earlier that day, he told the band, and was still tuxedoed as he helped with sound check. (Popa now insists that he was merely breaking in his tux in preparation for the wedding the *next* day, but confirms that his dressed-to-the-nines appearance was an impromptu visit.)

And Popa, who went on to enjoy a measure of success with his own skate-punk band, the Slammin' Watusis, says he learned from Shoes musically as well: "Working with them, I picked up a lot of power chords." These days, Popa is a guitar instructor—"and I'll catch myself teaching kids to play a G-chord the way they did, with a finger on the D, too," he laughs, explaining that Shoes customarily augmented the G with an extra note. "They did it with the A chord as well," he recalls. "The effect is to make the guitars sound a lot fuller—more like a harp, almost, especially when all the guitars were going at once, even the bass. I think they might have gotten it from George Harrison." Shoes themselves didn't think their style was all that unusual, but as Jeff points out, "Being self-taught, we do some wacky things because we never learned the proper way to do them."

Popa characterizes Shoes as being more serious craftsmen than feckless rock stars. "We didn't set hotels on fire," Popa says. "We just played some solid-ass sets." Reflecting on Shoes' legacy, Popa concludes, "They chose not to be a household name. They didn't want to play the shallow game of the music industry."

A DECENT CLUB SHOWING THANKSGIVING weekend at Haymakers got Shoes invited back for Christmas night. But on December 23, the band received devastating news: Elektra, poised to elevate a new president, was buying out the remainder of Shoes' contract. In some respects it was a fortunate break; four years of spending at rock-star levels without rock-star sales figures left the band deeply in the hole to Elektra, though even now they're not sure by quite how much. In his journal on January 18, 1983, Skip estimated that Shoes owed Elektra about half a million dollars. But because their initial contract had included an "in-for-one, in-for-two" provision, Elektra would either have to let them make another album, or pay to break the contract. The company chose the latter option, part of a mass wave of divestitures that cost the label millions.

Bob Krasnow, the incoming Elektra president, had identified the problem plaguing his label as being weak sales by underperforming artists; a 1989 *Los Angeles Times* profile states that, by his own account, Krasnow had gone "through the roster with a hacksaw." Number estimates vary—some sources say he winnowed Elektra's 150 artists to 20, some that 120 shrank to 46—but in any case, it was clearly a bloodbath.

The *Los Angeles Times* article, which pronounces the new president "Elektra's Comeback Kid," is sympathetic to Krasnow:

> Bob Krasnow remembers one week of January, 1983, as the worst of his professional life.
>
> The veteran record executive had just been named chairman of struggling Elektra Records and faced his first chore: closing the

label's Los Angeles office and firing more than 200 of the company's 300 employees.

"I had to give the word to people who had been at Elektra for 20 years—people in accounting and other (support areas) who weren't to blame for the mistakes that were made by others in signing acts. But they had to pay the penalty and it was a horrifying experience."

"By the end of 1982," says Jeff, "most of the people we knew had been fired." Marty Schwartz says simply, "It all came apart."

In order to accomplish this complete disassembly of Elektra's L.A. wing, the *Los Angeles Times* reported, "Krasnow spent over ten million dollars buying out artists' contracts and moving the company's headquarters back to New York City." The term "downsizing" would not become a standard corporate euphemism for several more years, but Krasnow practiced it zealously, "adhering to a 'small but beautiful' philosophy."

Getting axed by Elektra wasn't completely unexpected, but losing their record deal was still a serious blow to Shoes. Dan Bourgoise says that getting dropped is "like a breakup of a marriage, with all that same kind of emotion and self-hurt. For musicians as tied in [to the entire culture of recording] as Shoes, what they felt was helplessness." Bourgoise also experienced guilt over his own presumed role in Shoes' dismissal, certain that there was something he could or should have done: "I felt as bad as they did. I felt responsible. You think, 'Isn't there someone higher up that I can convince? Can I go beg somewhere?'"

Shoes themselves were confident, however, that they would be picked up by another label. After all, they had a name, a following, a track record on MTV, and a string of critical plaudits. That Christmas night, in a boisterous showing at Haymakers, they told the crowd that they'd been released, earning their now ex-label a full-throated thumbs down from their supporters. Nevertheless, John assured the fans, "We'll carry on." The audience—sizable for a holiday—cheered Shoes' bravado.

BUT IT WASN'T *JUST* BRAVADO; Shoes had reason to be self-assured. They were landing excellent showcase gigs, often supporting bands with substantial followings. On New Year's Eve, Shoes opened for Kiss in Illinois at Rockford Metro Center, a 10,000-seat venue in Cheap Trick's hometown. It was one of the earliest shows on the enduring glam metalmongers' *Creatures of the Night* tour. According to *Kiss and Sell: the Making of a Supergroup*, penned by C.K. Lendt (an employee of Kiss's then-management, Glickman/Marks), the tour was a serious disappointment for Kiss; Lendt writes that it featured "a much-reduced show and costumes that were sharply trimmed down from the dazzling Vegas look of the Super Kiss period." In contrast to Shoes, of course, Kiss were still glitzy and over-the-top; Eric Carr's drum kit, for example, was mounted in a gun turret. But the headliners were having a bad road jaunt, as Lendt reported:

> Turnouts were anemic. Shows were booked then unbooked. In Sioux Falls, South Dakota, a third-string promoter claimed insolvency on the night of the show and disappeared. ... In San Angelo, Texas, local migrant workers, not the usual union stagehands, put the show up to keep costs down. The promoter skipped the building and stiffed the workers before the night was over. Kiss got stuck with the bill.

The Rockford date wasn't sold out, either, though the crowd was heftier than Shoes were accustomed to.

Despite the fact that they shared a stage, Shoes met the headliners only briefly—Kiss arrived late, and their roadies broke a water main backing a truck into the venue, pushing start time back even further. Jeff recalls that womanizing bassist Gene Simmons seemed pretty taken with Skip's girlfriend (if his sticking his tongue in her ear was any indication). Shoes had heard through the grapevine years earlier that Simmons, an avowed fan of British Invasion-style pop, was an admirer of theirs; Chuck Fieldman remembers Simmons himself telling them so that night. And John notes their preshow send-off from singer Paul Stanley: as Shoes took the stage (and Skip ascended the gun turret where the drum set sat), Stanley stood in the wings and remarked, "Good luck," as they prepared to face the unfriendly horde.

Packed with Kiss Army soldiers, the audience greeted Shoes as might have been expected, with the metalheads—all geared up for a raucous New Year's Eve—screaming, "You suck!" But as Shoes' set went on—edited to focus on their more hard-rocking material—the crowd unexpectedly warmed to them, and the night ended up going pretty well. As Fieldman recalls, "After Shoes had finished playing, the guys eventually came out and sat in some unoccupied seats. A number of people who were there to see Kiss came over and asked for autographs."

But the real ramifications of Shoes' improbable connection with Kiss were still several years away.

SIGNING TO ANOTHER LABEL proved more elusive than the post-Elektra band had anticipated: in the midst of the recession, record companies were gun-shy. Dan Bourgoise stressed that relying on Shoes' name alone was not going to be enough to get them signed again, that they were going to need new songs, new demos. (Gary, for one, found this a little insulting; he thought that their existing catalog ought to have been enough of a résumé for anyone.) Shoes' reputation as reclusive studio geniuses who didn't sell records didn't do them any favors, either. But if Bourgoise needed demos, the band would have to find a way to make them, and so Shoes took their separation check from Elektra—a respectable $50,000—and set up a new studio in which to record them.

The basement of Field's, though it had served them well, wouldn't suffice for this next phase of Shoes' career. "The dress shop had time and noise restrictions," Jeff details. "We wanted to establish a more professional studio atmosphere where we could work undisturbed, anytime." Plus, after the storybook splendor of The Manor, and the capacious professional studios in L.A. and Chicago, a shared space with seven-foot ceilings and no windows was dispiritingly claustrophobic. "It really wasn't healthy down there," Gary adds, citing the musty raw cement and lack of ventilation. They began looking for another recording space, if not in Zion proper, then in the surrounding area.

It wasn't long before the band rented a vacant storefront—sandwiched between a beauty parlor and a typesetting shop—in Winthrop Harbor, the only Illinois town between Zion and the Wisconsin border. Situated just a few blocks from where Jeff and Gary still lived in the same apartment building, it was part of a three-store plaza on the main (practically the only) street through town.

Shoes were free to arrange the store's interior as they saw fit, so Gary, deploying his architecture training, drew up some plans for a real studio, dubbed Short Order Recorder after their original digs in Jeff's living room. They built a wall to separate the control room from the recording space, mounted some second-hand UREI monitors, yanked out carpet to make the room reverberate, and outfitted it with the best recording equipment they could afford, using some of the Elektra severance money to do it. Jeff says, "I don't think we spent more than three or four thousand dollars remodeling. It was basic, but functional." In June 1983, *Musician* magazine did a one-page write-up on the space, and Shoes posed for an ad for the 16-track Tascam mixing board, which, with a 16-track Panasonic Ramsa semi-pro console, and a one-inch tape machine, formed the nucleus of the new studio.

To save money, Shoes built everything themselves. John remarks that he and Jeff had never really done construction before, but that he found it to be kind of fun: "Gary and Skip *had* worked in construction, and they taught us how to do it. The first time I saw how a wall was built on the floor, I was fascinated." Creating the new studio was the band's job now, and they spent the better part of each day building. "We were a pretty good crew," Skip jotted approvingly in his journal.

Another fresh piece of equipment was a Roland Juno 60 synthesizer, which pushed Shoes to experiment with novel sounds, unexpected tangents. "We didn't place any limits on ourselves at all," Jeff says. "All the rules were thrown away." Gary agrees: "The gear drives the songwriting, to a certain extent, and if we had a new piece of equipment, we were certainly going to use it to write new kinds of songs."

From Shoes' perspective, then, the experiments that would eventually comprise their first post-Elektra album, *Silhouette*, grew naturally out of the gear they had acquired, though those who'd mistaken *Tongue Twister*'s "No Keyboards" disclaimer for a manifesto were sure to be shocked. "We had avoided synthesizers because we were a guitar band," John reflects. "But then we got this big Roland, even though we weren't keyboard players. And we said, 'Let's use this puppy.'"

Playing with the new toy got Shoes really moving again, which was worth the investment. Dan Bourgoise reflects, "They were trying not to let [losing the label deal] destroy them creatively, [because] it *can* be soul-destroying. If you come out of it with dignity and self-respect, that's a lot." The fact that after such a crushing disappointment, Shoes were back making music again mere weeks later—and not just making music, but growing and innovating and pushing their own envelope—is, in itself, a major accomplishment.

RECORDING THE NEW DEMOS BEGAN in March 1983, and throughout March and April, Shoes even toured again.

As before, they stuck to their own region, visiting a handful of familiar clubs like Tuts and Haymakers.

One notable change in this slew of dates, however, was that the shows leaned heavily toward colleges. Western Illinois University in Macomb, Northern Illinois University in DeKalb, and Southern Illinois University in Carbondale all saw Shoes that spring, as did two campuses of the University of Wisconsin (LaCrosse and Green Bay), and St. Norbert College, also in Green Bay. They were playing institutions of higher learning for a reason: post-Elektra, Shoes were returning to an independent music scene that had evolved in their four years at a major label, and colleges—college shows and college radio—were an increasingly important part of the equation.

And the independent music scene was burgeoning. By 1983, R.E.M.—signed to the upstart A&M imprint, I.R.S. Records—were getting glowing write-ups in national magazines. They would be widely considered as the first band "made" by college radio. By 1983, the Replacements' *Hootenanny* was expanding that influential Twin Cities post-punk combo's reach well beyond the Midwest. By 1983, fellow Minneapolitans Hüsker Dü had begun to temper their hardcore foundation with more melodicism; their *Metal Circus* EP also found a place on college radio.

Michael Azerrad, in his indie-rock chronicle *Our Band Could Be Your Life: Scenes from the American Indie Underground, 1981-1991*, identifies Hüsker Dü's evolution—toward punk with pop and acoustic elements—as the development of a new musical category: "college rock".

Azerrad argues that, regardless of the kind of music the college-rock bands played, the driving ethic was punk:

> Doing an end run around the Powers That Be will always have an inherent ideological spin. ... [T]he key principle of American indie rock wasn't a circumscribed musical style; it was the punk ethos of DIY, or do-it-yourself. The equation was simple: if punk was rebellious and DIY was rebellious, then doing it yourself was punk.

In 1983, Ira Robbins gathered together twenty independent tracks from across the nation and compiled an album: *Trouser Press Presents America Underground*. Shoes' "Like I Told You," an unreleased track made in the dress-shop basement in 1978, appeared halfway through side one. In his liner notes, Robbins wrote, "In the end, we wound up with a blend of well-known groups—who have released numerous major-label or prominent independent records—and near-forgotten obscures—who made one glorious home-brew 45 and were never heard from again." Shoes were the former, of course, and they were pleased to be included in such company.

At this point, a number of terms were employed to label this rising movement: Robbins favored "underground rock" in *Trouser Press* ("America Underground" was a column before it was an album); "alternative music" was more common in England; programmers of FM radio stations in some large cities like Los Angeles (KROQ) and Boston (WFNX), as well as some suburban areas (WLIR on Long Island) had claimed "modern rock"; and the catch-all moniker "college rock" was becoming more common, pointing to the prominent role college radio and college tours played in its development. R.E.M.'s success had depended heavily on college support; they were from the university town of Athens, Georgia and had made a splash on college radio before achieving mainstream renown.

Shoes had always done well with degree-seeking audiences; *Tongue Twister* in particular had gotten a lot of play on college airwaves. And now, in the spring of 1983, they played in front of the biggest crowd of their careers, opening for the Kinks at the University of Illinois Circle Campus (now the University of Illinois at Chicago) in front of 15,000 people. Chuck Fieldman, who had helped them secure the Kinks gig, says that Shoes were dazzled by sharing a stage with these bastions of the British Invasion, who were then experiencing a renaissance touring behind their album *State of Confusion* and its sparkling, surprise-hit single, "Come Dancing." John remembers playing one of his new songs—"Turnaround"—which they had been road-testing regularly, even though it was only half-written.

Still, Shoes had to admit they simply were not satisfied with this new niche: they wanted back into the major-label system, and would consider themselves failures unless that happened.

BACK IN WINTHROP HARBOR, Shoes redoubled their efforts to fight their way back to the majors. The first three songs they produced at the brand-new Short Order Recorder were John's "When Push Comes to Shove" (which he'd shelved "Turnaround" to work on: "I took some heat from the guys for that—they wanted me to hurry up and finish the song I had"); Gary's effervescent, percussive "A New Sensation;" and Jeff's bouncy confection "Oh, Angeline." They created a package for the resultant cassette and sent it off to Dan Bourgoise as soon as it was ready, sometime that spring. Bourgoise says he shopped it to every major and most of the minor labels in the country.

Nobody bit.

The record business was still reeling; after all, three of the last four years had been disastrous. Many label reps didn't even bother to acknowledge receipt of Shoes' demos, and as Bourgoise recalls, even those that did often said, "If Elektra can't do anything for you, we can't."

It's possible another manager could have sold the demos; certainly Bourgoise wasn't a salesman at his core. Shoes had hired Bourgoise to function primarily as their liaison with Elektra, a role they didn't need anyone to play anymore. But Dan was honest; if a label did nibble, they'd need a man on the ground in L.A., and they genuinely believed he was doing his best for them.

Still, Bourgoise didn't seem to be able to deliver a record contract, the one thing Shoes needed most. They had gone into their latest demos with a certain amount of momentum, optimistic that they had the talent and tools to attract a new label. But the demos, from Shoes' perspective, were going out into the void, and moving forward was getting harder.

Still, they did keep moving. Nobody liked those songs? Okay, they'd do some more. A second set of three demos, comprised of Jeff's sexy dance-floor number "Will You Spin for Me?," John's deceptively chipper-sounding "Bound to Fade," and Gary's guitar-propelled "Running Wild," took them into the summer.

AS 1983 WORE ON, SKIP, WHO had taken another bartending job, was getting harder and harder to locate when Shoes needed him to record. He had always spent less time in the studio than the others, content to play his parts but not hanging around afterward; to some extent, Skip's absence initially seemed to be just an extension of that behavior. He kept up his end in some ways—paying his share of the studio rent, for example—but sometimes when they called to ask him to come in and drum, he just wouldn't show. "He was pretty slippery," says John. Skip's family had a vacation home up north, and the drummer spent a lot of time there, incommunicado. Gary points out that Skip, who'd joined during the heady rush of recording *Black Vinyl Shoes*, had never really seen anything but the good parts about being in the band—the run-up to the Elektra signing and the flurry of activity that followed. This was the first really tough period he'd faced.

The other three, Gary says, had a different perspective. They were ready to do whatever they had to do to keep the band going: "We took care of Shoes; Shoes didn't take care of us."

Skip acknowledges that his interest *was* waning once Shoes lost their major-label deal. In fact, "I just checked out," he says. His detachment reactivated the three-against-one tensions, initiating a crisis within the band that wouldn't come to a head quite yet, but was imminent.

That was a tough season. "The broke-est I ever got was the summer of 1983," says John. "I was living on pretzels and Diet Coke."

And while Shoes were mostly happy with what they were recording, the work was being done under far-from-ideal circumstances. Jeff remembers, "It was a tough process and trying time for us." Gary was going through a breakup, "and that, along with the intense heat in that un-air-conditioned studio, made for some very somber recording sessions," says Jeff. John recollects that laying down the "big backing vocals" on his "Bound to Fade" was particularly rigorous: "We were sweating buckets doing them. Everyone was sweating; no one was talking."

From the West Coast, there was almost complete silence. Dan Bourgoise's job, as he saw it, was to protect Shoes from bad news, and what label news he did have for them consisted of rejections. As a result, contact between Shoes and their manager had gotten more and more sporadic. Bourgoise didn't ask for money; Bug Music was doing just fine, and Dan always made sure Shoes got their publishing checks, no matter how tiny—it was the only income they saw some months. But they fought back a growing panic in the face of his silence, fearing they'd made a mistake in staying with him. The band members started talking among themselves about severing their managerial relationship sometime in the fall, as they launched into demoing a third set of songs. Toward the tail end of 1983, Shoes let Bourgoise go.

"I didn't really see it as a firing," John says. "It was more like we relieved him of this frustrating duty. He was a tremendous cheerleader, and he'd believed one-hundred percent we could do it ourselves."

Gary in particular remembers the period surrounding this termination as a distressing one:

> That was the first time we saw a decision as a business move rather than following our gut feelings. ... We were backed into a corner and acted against our instincts. Here we were, scared, embarrassed, and at the point of having to find jobs in this small town where

> everybody knows you, knows your business. ... I never felt so bad in my life. I regret firing Dan more than anything I can think of.

He continues:

> What bothers me most is that Dan was the only truly good person we met in the music business, the only one with power who was really trustworthy and honest; a good man. Ironically, we gave that partnership up, we thought, to keep our careers going.

True to form, Bourgoise was sympathetic to why Shoes dismissed him; Bug Music has remained Shoes' publisher, and both parties still have a warm relationship.

But having lost their manager, Shoes now needed someone to sell the demos they were still producing. The band members reached out to some industry contacts they'd made in 1979, most notably Freddy DeMann. He'd been a friend of Ken Buttice's back then, but in 1983 was between superstars, going from managing Michael Jackson to handling a new act, Madonna. Feelers also went out to Al Bunetta—who the previous year had founded Red Pajama Records with his most prominent client, Chicago folk-rocker Steve Goodman—and Stan Plesser, the Kansas City concert impresario who had also managed country-rock outfit the Ozark Mountain Daredevils. But no one would take Shoes on as management clients, or even give them any encouragement.

AFTER A YEAR OF STRUGGLING ALONG on essentially nothing, apparently *for* nothing, Shoes were dejected as 1984 dawned. Reality was staring them in the face, and they could no longer postpone some hard decisions. If Shoes were going to go on as a band, they couldn't wait for a label to rescue them. Once again, they needed to go DIY, which meant they needed money.

The band members did have some options, even if they weren't ideal. They had each been employed before Elektra, after all; even though it had been almost five years since the Murphys and Klebe had worked regular jobs, presumably they were still employable. Additionally, they were partners in a significant group investment: Short Order Recorder had been built as Shoes' own workshop, but there was no reason they couldn't use it for outside clients, if they chose. As seasoned songwriters, performers, and engineers, they had the skills and drive to help young bands—bands they saw as being like themselves—get their sound down. Shoes could go on, if everyone put his neck in the yoke and pushed in the same direction.

John and Gary went back to non-band work in early 1984. John returned to graphics, landing a job at the typesetter next door to the studio, designing menus and résumés. The pay was terrible, but the work was easy, and frankly, at that point John was just glad to be employed in the art field. Gary, who still needed about four more years' experience to qualify for the Illinois architecture licensing exam, was fortunate enough to go back to the firm where he'd spent the first part of his post-college internship. But as Gary points out, "A mainstream job was symbolic: it meant we'd failed. The new jobs also drained us, so that we didn't have as much time or energy for the band."

Jeff, on the other hand, had returned to being Shoes' main engineer as they kept working away at the songs that would become *Silhouette*. Jeff offered his services to other bands as well, placing an ad in the *Illinois Entertainer*, the local monthly music paper, advertising studio space and production skills for hire. Jeff recalls:

> I started doing outside sessions and even freelancing at other studios. My first couple of projects involved local bands to whom I said, "For $800, I'll give you a single by the end of the weekend."

Jeff was also producing at suburban facility Remington Road Studios—the new name of Hedden West, where Shoes had recorded the "Tomorrow Night"/"Okay" single, and mixed *Shoes on Ice*.

Remington Road's head engineer was still Michael Freeman, whom they'd met their first time there. He steered a fair amount of the studio's engineering work to Jeff, who was starting to build a reputation for himself as a pop producer. A young Ric Menck, employed part-time at the studio, describes seeing Jeff roar up in an orange Saab Sonett convertible—every inch a celebrity, as far as the awed youngster was concerned. Before too long, Jeff was eking a living out of producing.

Freeman says he liked having Jeff work at Remington Road. As a self-taught engineer, Jeff understood sonic experimentation and trouble-shooting. Also, he was "easy to get along with," according to Freeman:

> Perhaps because he'd been a musician himself, the clients really liked using Jeff. He understood what it took to make a session comfortable, and get the best out of people.

Jeff would engineer and produce other artists for the next two decades.

OVER THE COURSE OF THE WINTER of 1984, Shoes completed recording and mixing what they had now decided was not just a set of demos, but an album: *Silhouette*. It took a little longer than they'd planned; not only did their outside jobs and projects interfere with recording time, but both John and Gary decided to change out some of their songs they'd written earlier for more current compositions.

Gary, cautious about straying too far from Shoes' established path, had started to become a little disenchanted with the synthesizer while *Silhouette* was still in progress. He traded his synth-heavy "A New Sensation," the first *Silhouette* song he'd written, for a cleaner, leaner guitar sound— dropping even the distortion he'd long favored—on the more traditionally Shoes-y "Get My Message," which they decided to use as the album opener.

Similarly, John sidelined his rhythmic, contemplative "Pieces of Glass" for the much more playful, sixties-style raveup "Twist and Bend It." In a 2011 interview for the aforementioned independent film *Inventory* (which included several Shoes tunes on the soundtrack), John discussed the song's inspiration:

> Lyrically, it's sort of stream-of-consciousness. ... The title came from the directions on how to use the wire ties from a box of plastic garbage bags ("Step 2: Twist and bend").

It was during this period that Jeff came in with "Will You Spin for Me?" notable for its unabashed dance beat. Of course Shoes were shooting for something commercial—that had always been the goal—and thematically, at least, the song was in the same general aspiring-pick-up vein as "Do You Wanna Get Lucky?" or "Hopin' She's the One." Nevertheless, John and Gary both recall glancing warily at each other as Jeff played it for them the first time. John says, "I think we were all on board with a change in direction, but we thought, 'Are we really going this far in?'" At the same time, John acknowledges this was one of the first times they had really seen his brother's gift for stylistic metamorphosis, now readily acknowledging, "Jeff can tackle any genre and make it work." For his part, Jeff says he was simply stretching a little, trying to see what noises the new studio gear would make. Ultimately he'd come to a realization:

> The synth became a mixed blessing. It was fun to tinker with, but I think it led us into areas where we weren't comfortable. "Will You Spin for Me?" was an example of that experiment.

But it was an undeniably irresistible dance track with a deeply infectious melody: when Shoes released *Silhouette* in France on the New Rose label, New Rose selected that song as the single.

As for John's "Twist and Bend It," the track was also notable partly because all of the drumming was done by its composer. "When we recorded it, Skip was MIA," Shoes' bassist relates, "so Jeff and I cooked up the drum track. We did it piecemeal; Jeff engineered and I whacked the skins." This wasn't actually too unusual at that juncture; by the time Klebe and the Murphys finished *Silhouette*, they had simply adjusted to not having Skip around.

Their drummer's absenteeism had continued throughout the *Silhouette* sessions, and by the time John, Jeff, and Gary had completed the record in spring, their patience had dried up. "We had enough morale problems without that going on," Gary says. When they finally called him in for a band meeting, "we hadn't seen Skip for weeks," John notes. "We needed his share of the rent, and we wanted to know what was going on."

In a tense, terse meeting at the studio, the three singer-songwriters laid out their position to Skip. John recollects that he started the talking, because everyone else was staring silently at the floor. Gary says that eventually he chimed in, laying down the law while John played the good cop. "We've decided you're not in the group," Gary recalls saying. "You're out. If you want back in, you have to show us you're serious about it."

John was more diplomatic: "We're not going to shut the door, but prove to us that you're really into this, or we're going to assume you don't want to be in the band anymore."

Skip heard the ultimatum rather than the open door. "He called us all individually at our homes," John recounts, "and said, 'Whatever happens, happens.'"

By that summer Shoes were operating as a trio.

SILHOUETTE'S RECORDING HAD CONCLUDED, but the new album needed two things in order to be released. One was graphics; that was John's department. The other was distribution, which, without a label, was going to be complicated.

The graphics issue was simply a matter of finding the time. John knew that he wanted the same high-contrast imaging he'd used for the "Tomorrow Night"/"Okay" single, plus a color-blocking similar to what he'd conceptualized for *Boomerang*. The photo was chosen from a Randee St. Nicholas shot taken in their Elektra days, cropped to remove Skip.

Doctoring the picture was easy enough for John. He was back at a graphic-design firm, so he had access to state-of-the-art equipment—though being employed full-time, finding the opportunity to do the actual work was tricky. The lettering was even trickier: John was looking for a very specific, somewhat careworn style, and doing it by hand was time-consuming. (He ended up, Jeff recalls, painstakingly dipping each letter stamper into salt or sand before hand-pressing it onto the paper.) As 1984's spring and summer wore on, Jeff and Gary grew increasingly testy about the fact that the graphics were still unfinished, John ruefully admits—though he maintains he spent no more time with graphics than his bandmates did on musical production. Jeff says he eventually queried his brother, "Remember the typeface the Beatles used on the back of *Sgt. Pepper's?*"—to which John replied, "No." "Exactly!" the younger Murphy exploded at him. But *Silhouette*'s graphics still weren't completed until almost the end of that summer.

Finding a label was another matter entirely. Jeff says that reactivating Black Vinyl Records and putting the album out themselves was not even considered: "We didn't have the money or will to release *Silhouette* ourselves. We wanted someone else to do that end of it." Bug Music used European labels as sub-publishers, and so through Bug, Shoes' lawyers set up relationships with three European labels—New Rose in France, Line in Germany, and Demon in England—even securing the band a small amount of advance money for each release. Since these were labels, and not just distributors, the European companies produced the discs themselves from Shoes' masters. "But aside from the advances," Jeff says, "we didn't see a lot from those releases." An attempt to find a new American record company proved fruitless, despite swirling rumors that this or that label might take the project on. Until Black Vinyl Records re-released it on CD in the early nineties, *Silhouette* was only available as an import in the United States.

AFTER THE FINAL MASTER OF *SILHOUETTE* was shipped off to the European labels with whom they'd contracted, Shoes started looking for other musical projects, to keep them moving while they waited to see if their new album would have any impact.

Someone—possibly Bug attorney Neville Johnson, possibly Bourgoise—hooked them up with a filmmaker in Los Angeles who was working on a movie called *The Dirt-Bike Kid*, starring Peter Billingsley (who'd played *A Christmas Story*'s iconic Ralphie two years earlier). The film tells the story of a young boy whose fondest wish is to own a dirt bike; when he finally gets one, it turns out to be magic.

Shoes heard rumors about the film—for example, Jeff remembers one about Teri Garr being considered for the mother's role—while they roughed out demos for the first explicitly instrumental music they'd ever created. Each of Shoes' singer-songwriters put together one song apiece that summer, with the others contributing; everything on what John calls "The Soundtrack That Wasn't" is triple-credited.

Similarly triple-credited is the song Shoes provided at the request of their European labels as the all-purpose B-side of the singles each had chosen to release from *Silhouette*. New Rose was issuing Jeff's "Will You Spin for Me?" and Line and Demon were releasing John's "When Push Comes to Shove." So Shoes went back into their studio that fall to record a hasty composition of John's called "Dormant Love." He'd worked it up with Jeff at the studio, using a fair amount of trickery to get around the fact that they were now drummer-less—as Jeff describes, "We created one artificially with drum loops and delays, then overdubbed cymbals and fills"—and then Gary came in and added some punchy guitar to the chorus. So they went ahead and credited "Dormant Love" to all three songwriters.

JOHN RECALLS WITH A LAUGH the fact that, despite the song's downbeat, characteristically Shoes-y view of the male-female relationship—"Precious hours, forgotten years/We stood there without a tear/And your eyes said 'Where will it end?'/ Every heart breaks if it won't bend"—he was actually pretty happy at the time. That summer, he and Jeff had met two sisters, and both were now heavily involved in their first serious relationships in a long time. John says his new girlfriend was not impressed that the first song he produced during their relationship was "Dormant Love."

Jeff and Lorinda met first, at the beach in Zion. She was sitting with her friends, and as soon as Jeff saw the fetching blonde, he was hooked. Lori took one look at Jeff, she told him later, and was so rattled that she jumped up and ran into the lake. Though only in her twenties, Lorinda had grown up fast: she'd married young and was the mother of two little boys. As was the case in a lot of small towns, early marriage was common in Zion; as bachelors who were then in their late twenties and early thirties, Shoes were something of an anomaly in their circle of friends.

It wasn't long before Jeff and Lori introduced John and Durinda at a dinner party. Like her sister, Durinda had also had a youthful marriage, but by the time they met the Murphy brothers, both young women were divorced. Jeff cautions, however, against reading too many biographical parallels into his songs from this period, like "I Knew You'd Be Mine" and "She's Not the Same"—though both songs appeared on *Stolen Wishes*, the first album made after they met. Lyrics may begin by referencing a real-life situation, he says, but other stories and ideas are grafted onto the words in the process, and rarely is a one-to-one correlation in play.

Gary, who so often felt as though he were the fifth wheel tagging along in the Murphy Brothers' band—a perspective aggravated by the number of press features that emphasized John and Jeff as the core of Shoes—found this chronic feeling exacerbated by these new relationships. He'd had girlfriends, sure, but nothing as steady as his bandmates now had. He often found himself at loose ends, ready to record but unable to schedule time with his colleagues, who were understandably distracted by their new loves. Gary's focus, he says, was still on Shoes, on getting back to a point where they could make their livings as musicians.

Nothing much seemed to be happening with *Silhouette*, which was available only as an import in the U.S. The band received a few copies from each European label, but neither Shoes nor the labels sent the record out for review—and *Silhouette* was not generally covered by the major national music magazines. As John says, "You put a record out in a foreign country, it's like putting it out on Mars."

But where it was reviewed, the notices were upbeat. The album got a positive write-up in *Creem*, for example, where Moira McCormick described *Silhouette* as "a characteristically well-crafted pastiche of '60's pop shadings, '80's techno flashes, and big-beat dance rhythms, spread thick with [Shoes'] trademark three-part harmonies." In the *Illinois Entertainer*, Guy C. Arnston's review was strong, if quirkily hockey-themed. "If John were a Chicago Blackhawk," he wrote, "he'd get two minutes for hooking on 'Bound to Fade,' plus five for his false ending." Lloyd Sachs in the glossy *Chicago* magazine worried that the album was "too self-referential," griping that "the band members have given up all consideration of playing for anyone but themselves" and then immediately declaring that "Shoes' devotion to the craft of making bright, idiosyncratic pop music ... [justifies] that self-involvement." All the American reviews encouraged fans to seek out the record in the import bin of their local record store.

Among the band members themselves, things were tense. "We'd had a huge ass-kicking; we were back in Zion," John explains. "We were just looking for a reason to go on." Gary claims that they barely spoke to each other in 1985; John says that's an exaggeration—they still hung out—but admits they rarely talked music. When conversation did drift toward the band, they often argued, because no one had any idea what to do next. "There were a lot of nights I'd get out of Gary's car and I'd just be so angry," John remembers. "Of course I didn't want to be feeling that, so I'd go see my girlfriend." Jeff, amorously distracted himself, was generally not even on hand for these arguments.

So in 1985, it didn't look like there was very much holding Shoes together. If they were going to survive, they had to keep moving forward.

The problem was, no one knew which direction "forward" was.

SHORT ORDER RECORDER WAS NOW GIVEN OVER almost entirely to other acts. Jeff was producing demos for several area bands, including a Waukegan quartet known as Roc Sinatra (based around some former members of Hot Mama Silver, who had opened for Shoes at the Zion Leisure Center), and a young suburban Chicagoan named Leroy Bocchieri; both would become long-term Short Order clients. Ric Menck and his partner Paul Chastain laid down some demos as a retro-pop duo called Choo Choo Train. Another regular customer was a brash Chicago guitar-pop trio fronted by an ambitious, occasionally obnoxious, singer and guitarist named Jim Ellison. This first Material Issue lineup was not the one that would go on to make a name for themselves in the coming years, but the long-term professional relationship between Jeff and Ellison began during these troubled times for Shoes.

Ellison was young—barely 21 and still a student—and unschooled. He couldn't tune his guitar, Jeff remembers, adding that his amp was "some broken-down piece of junk." However, says Jeff, Ellison was "a great fan of Shoes and—regardless of how 'un-popular' pop music may have been—he was an unabashed pop fan." Jeff says he and Jim Ellison produced four songs together in this first round of recording, and that he influenced Ellison's guitar sound in a very specific, practical way.

Jeff had been playing through British Hiwatt amplifiers—long the amp of choice for the Who, immortalized in their 1974 song "Long Live Rock"—for several years, attracted originally by their relative rarity in the Midwest ("You didn't see many local bands playing Hiwatts," he remarks) but ultimately won over by their tone and quality:

> I'd wanted to use an amp that was a bit less common; I stumbled on my first Hiwatt at a local music store and bought it used. Happily, I discovered a well-built amplifier with a unique tone that complemented Gary's Marshalls. ... The Marshall is an amp that creates a strong midrange-based distortion, while the Hiwatt seems to introduce a lower-order harmonic that makes it feel fat. Both amps have that warm tube sound—warmer than solid-state amps, due in part to the fact that tubes naturally compress when driven hard and add even-order harmonics when they distort—so it worked out great. The Hiwatts were originally constructed from surplus military-grade components, so they're built like tanks. They also have what is probably the most concise construction of any tube amp. A beautiful piece of engineering.

Jeff especially liked the sound of the powerful, characteristically clean Hiwatts when it was muddied up a little with distortion. "I had mine modified to create more overdrive," he says.

Now, Jeff brought these amplifiers to the attention of young Ellison:

> I introduced Jim to Hiwatt amps, which became a big part of Material Issue's sound. ... Jim had been coming in with these old junkers that were cool aesthetically, but sounded bad. I loved Hiwatts, and that's what was in the studio, so I encouraged him to play through them. Apparently he liked the sound too, because soon he had acquired a Hiwatt of his own, and then picked up a few

more. ... I encouraged bands to use our studio gear, because I knew I could get good sounds out of the equipment quickly.

In an unpublished April 1985 interview, Jeff and John are outwardly upbeat about Shoes. They express confidence about doing everything on their own, and though they'd like to sign to another label, of course, they also recognize that working alone suits them. As Jeff puts it:

We can record material without having to go through months of budget meetings and negotiating [about] what studio we're going to use, finding producers, all that stuff. We have the ability to be autonomous. It would be hard now to give up that freedom.

But the bruising they'd taken over *Silhouette* left Shoes fearing that Elektra had stigmatized them—as "a band that exists but doesn't sell records," John mused in the interview—and that they'd have to fight to overcome that image.

AROUND THIS TIME, SHOES WERE approached by a suburban-Chicago television producer named Lou Hinkhouse, who told them he was a fan of their music. Would Shoes be willing to make a video for his little local-cable music show, *The Pulse*? Shoes didn't see why not. They talked at some length about which song to do, settling on John's "When Push Comes to Shove," which had been a single in Germany and England. They kicked around some ideas for the video: "We knew what we liked," Jeff says, "and what we didn't." They were hoping, he details, for a clip that was "non-lip-synched, non-literal, but was more cinematic or plot-based, with the look of film." But they hadn't quite decided what such a video would look like when Hinkhouse simply called them one Saturday to announce that he was en route to Zion with his camera and a small crew.

Of course, Shoes weren't prepared to shoot a video. But they gamely went along with Hinkhouse, whom they liked, and his associate—an aspiring young screenwriter named Bill Kelly (who would later go on to script Hollywood films *Blast from the Past* and *Enchanted*). Hinkhouse simply filmed Shoes performing in the studio, goofing around, walking through Zion's streets, and down on its beach. The videographer returned several times that spring and summer with his camera and friends in tow. "Sometimes he'd only film for like twenty minutes, and then we'd just hang out," Gary relates. "But he had tons of footage by the end."

However, throughout the whole process, Gary's attitude—not just about the video shoot, but about the band and its future in general—was becoming ever more downcast:

> Lou wanted to go down to the beach and do interviews, and I just refused. I didn't see the point of it at all. We were losers, failures, I thought. What were we going to even talk about—the past? We weren't making music; we were barely speaking at that point.

Jeff participated in some interview footage, showing Hinkhouse around Short Order, but after that the videographer changed direction. Instead of conducting more band interviews, he brought an attractive young woman (a friend of his then-girlfriend's, named Bunny) to stand on Sheridan Road in Zion like a roving reporter, and ask passers-by, "What do you think about Shoes?" Several elderly men, some little kids, and a young couple all answered her seriously, assuming she was referring to footwear. "I insist on shoes at all times," one man says. "I like 'em!" a youngster chirps, while an elderly gent enthuses, "I think shoes is wonderful!"

Eventually, Hinkhouse edited all the disparate vignettes together to create two different music videos for "When Push Comes to Shove": one primarily comprised of the studio material, the other a compendium of the street footage. The Murphys and Klebe generally prefer the latter. "That video has a kind of home-movie quality I like," John explains. "Not the studio stuff so much, but the Zion parts, and the beach." Hinkhouse screened the clips on his program, *The Pulse*, but after that, the videos were never aired again.

THE STRESSES OF 1985 WERE NOT all internal. Another source of worry was an ongoing feud with a new business that had taken up residence in Short Order's strip mall—a pizza parlor. Most of its business was carry-out, so it needed quite a few transient parking spaces. The pizzeria's parking needs were diametrically opposed to the recording studio's, which needed fewer spaces, but longer-term. The pizza parlor's proprietors were unhappy about what they saw as Short Order's parking-lot-hogging.

One evening, while Jeff was watching *Monday Night Football* and talking to Lorinda on the phone, he was started by a nearby *kaboom*! and subsequent sirens. Glancing out his back window, Jeff was stunned to see his car ablaze—and the fire department already on the scene. "As they were taking an axe to the trunk to try and open it," he recounts, "I yelled out to them I had the keys, if they needed them." Though there's no doubt the fire was malicious, Jeff insists he wasn't the target: "There was a local Mafia guy who had a car like mine. I think the arsonist thought it was his." John and Gary, however, are skeptical of this theory; they suspect their neighbors were asserting their parking rights with a none-too-subtle threat. As the engineer, Jeff was the one most often at the studio, and thus his car the most obvious mark.

As the year progressed, intraband relations continued to be strained, particularly between Gary and the Murphy brothers. But ultimately, the threat of losing what they had built together became the impetus for refocusing on Shoes—and figuring out what they had to do to push onward.

Sometime in the fall of 1985, Short Order Recorder's strip mall was sold. Its new owner wanted to put a bar in the storefront adjoining the studio, separated from Shoes' space by a simple stud wall that would do little to block the sound of their drums and guitars. He had big plans, John says, for a booming clientele sparked by a new local marina, and having a rock band next door was not part of those plans. For the sake of his own business, the owner placed new restrictions on Shoes' lease, set to roll over at the beginning of 1986. They would no longer be able to make noise after six o'clock in the evening.

This was impossible. Gary and John were working full-time jobs; if they were going to do *any* recording, it would have to be after six p.m. Plus, their indispensable outside clients worked nine-to-fives in the Chicago area, which was some fifty miles away, so *their* sessions also had to take place in the evenings. "Sometimes," says Jeff, "we wouldn't even be able to start a session until eight or ten o'clock, even midnight."

Clearly, Shoes had got to get out of that place. But to do what? To build another studio? To start all over someplace else? With what money? And to what end?

John describes this as a time of weary desperation, of seriously examining themselves to see if they had it in them to do it all ... over ... again. They would come to recognize that the debate over rebuilding the studio business was really a debate over something much larger: it was about whether Shoes, as a band, existed anymore.

"That was a pretty big crossroads," John says now.

And surprising themselves, perhaps, as much as anyone else, Klebe and the Murphys decided to keep Short Order—and thus Shoes—alive. "The studio *was* the band," Gary says. "And we did not want to give it up." Jeff agrees: "We concluded that Shoes was still first and foremost in our priorities, and the studio was the means to that end."

REVITALIZED, SHOES BEGAN SCOUTING local properties for a new studio site. It wasn't long before they settled on an old concrete-block retail building on Sheridan Road, Zion's main drag. "When we were kids, it had been Butler Electric," John remarks. The space was freestanding—precluding any more difficult neighbors moving in and sharing a wall—and rock-solid. "There was a bomb shelter in the basement," Gary recalls; the subterranean vault was also occupied by a car-upholstery business owned by a friend of theirs, Roger Stried.

The building certainly "wasn't pretty," says John. "The first time we looked at the interior, there was an oily car engine in the middle of the floor. But we definitely knew the space was right." "You just needed to see past the surface things," Gary says. "We were really excited about the *dimensions* of the space; it was perfect." It was larger than their old place; if Shoes were really going to run a commercial studio, even part-time, more square footage was an absolute necessity. Where the Winthrop Harbor Short Order had been rather cramped and bare-bones, this new facility boasted high ceilings, loading docks, and a concrete floor, which would give them more or less complete control over how much reverberation the room produced.

They could build their state-of-the-art studio right there in Zion.

Thinking in terms of roomier digs meant virtually everything needed to be reconsidered. Studio design was changing in the mid-eighties, Gary says now. In studios with one main recording space, the traditional design placed the live area—with hard, reflective surfaces that bounced sound back (creating an infinitesimal delay in the echo)—in the front of that space, and the dead area—carpeted and baffled to control sound reflection—in the back. All of the outside studios Shoes had used in the past were set up along those lines, according to Gary.

By the mid-eighties, the thinking went, a bit more reflection was desirable in order to make every recorded sound seem more natural. Jeff and Gary were fascinated by how to control these delicate shadings. The new Short Order was thus designed for this more ambient sound, with the live section in the back of the space, and the dead section toward the front, adding a barely-there echo. In addition, they hung nearly floor-to-ceiling baffle panels from the exposed gridwork of beams atop the studio space; this allowed for almost any configuration of live or dead areas they could possibly desire.

Another important design element Shoes knew they wanted was a more capacious control room. "In old-fashioned studios," Gary notes, "the control rooms were small and the recording rooms large. Over time, this had reversed, and we always liked the newer, larger control rooms better." And for the band, this wasn't merely a preference; it was an absolute necessity. "Aside from drums, ninety-five percent of our work is done in the control room," Gary points out. Because Shoes produced themselves—with Jeff or Gary often working alone—the Shoe at the board needed enough room to play an instrument while still having access to the recording console. At the same time, they wanted a discrete recording area, for outside clients and drums, so they designed the space to accommodate both options.

Shoes taped out the proposed location of walls and potential speaker placement on their future studio's floor. They set up portable, floor-based baffles, moving these barriers around to mimic actual walls, while positioning and repositioning their monitors to get the best sound. "We set a chair where we figured the board would be, and aimed the monitors at an angle that focused about a foot behind where the engineer's head would be, roughly forming an equilateral triangle," Jeff explains. They were trying to avoid, he says, the kind of scenario they'd experienced so often, in which a track that sounds tight in one control room sounds trite in another. "We'd always been *very* frustrated after recording at other studios," he details, "because what we heard at home didn't sound like what we'd heard in those studios. But mixes coming out of Short Order Recorder—when we played them elsewhere—sounded pretty darn close to what we heard right when we mixed them."

Looming over their painstaking design process was the fact that time was of the essence. Shoes were paying two sets of studio rent, after all, and since Winthrop Harbor was still serving recording clients, they needed to leave it set up absolutely as long as possible. The band members knew their budget—already strained by transforming the electrical shop into Short Order II—couldn't stretch enough to cover new equipment right away, so the 16-track board at Winthrop Harbor (still only three years old, fortunately) would be utilized to get the new studio up and running.

Another economy measure was the use of mill-ends of Ozite—a thick hybrid of corduroy and carpet—to insulate the dead section of the room. Shoes got a deal on them from a large industrial site, and on the bitterly cold Sunday of Super Bowl XX in 1986, the Murphys and Klebe drove out to a warehouse west of Chicago and purchased huge discounted rolls of the salmon-colored stuff. (Having bought more than they could use, however, they sold the leftovers to Butch Vig, who was then outfitting his new venture: destined-for-fame Smart Studios in Madison, Wisconsin.) Gary had been experiencing back problems and had trouble lifting, John reports: by that evening, as the Chicago Bears were easily obliterating the New England Patriots 46-10, about all Gary could manage was to lie on the floor in Zion, connected by phone to his college friends at their Super Bowl party in Chicago, doing shots along with them after every Bears touchdown.

As before, Shoes constructed the studio entirely by themselves. Gary handled most of the carpentry, assisted by John; Jeff installed almost all the Ozite singlehandedly—a huge job in itself—and did the majority of the audio wiring.

Renovations took six months. John remembers that it was 'round about the Fourth of July when he looked around and decided that the new space looked more or less complete. "We're done here; I'm gonna go see my girlfriend," he announced. The move-in took place soon after. Gary recalls that it was pretty hot when they moved, and the members of Shoes all recount how Jim Ellison, whisper-thin, a smoker, and not particularly strong, showed up to help, carrying a four-foot hunk of track lighting he'd offered them to offset an outstanding bill for studio time.

To Shoes' credit, their regular recording clients didn't miss more than a day of work, because they broke down Short Order Winthrop Harbor and assembled Short Order Zion within the same day.

But Shoes didn't use it for themselves right away. Their move to the new, improved studio had eased some of the last few years' tensions, but they weren't quite ready to make music. Gary's fairly sure that he, at least, did not start working in the new Short Order for another six months, at the beginning of '87. At that point, he says, "I had to remind myself how to use all this equipment I hadn't touched in more than two years."

As a professional recording facility, however, Short Order took off immediately in its new location. "People would come in to make a demo," Jeff says. "But they'd leave with a professional-sounding single." Material Issue recorded demo sessions there that they went on to release in 1987 as an entire EP, the band's self-titled debut recording on their own independent label, Big Block Records.

BUT EVEN AS SHOES WERE BUILDING THEIR state-of the-art recording facility, a major paradigm shift was looming over the music industry, one already holding the seeds of the demise of analog studios like Short Order. As the twelve-inch vinyl platter increasingly gave way to the compact disc, music was becoming digitized, by necessity, for the new medium (though most projects were still recorded in analog format, and then transferred to digital after the fact).

At this stage, CDs were still largely the territory of classical music; orchestras had enthusiastically embraced the sharper, more pristine digital sound. (An October 6, 1984 *Billboard* article—"Dealers, Manufacturers Upbeat in CD Discussion"—noted that, though CDs only accounted for about five to six percent of all music sales, they represented about thirty percent of classical receipts.) Rock fans and major rock labels were slower to adopt digital music formats; manufacturing, shipping, radio, and retail were all still configured for twelve-inch LPs.

The cost of CD players and the discs themselves was another prohibitive factor, though they were not as expensive as many consumers believed. In the same October 6, 1984 issue of *Billboard*, the "On Target" column states that, while CD players were selling for as little as $250, most consumers still believed them to be in the $750 to $1,000 range. The costs of pre-recorded discs did remain high, hovering near $20 even as the technology to produce them dropped in cost. (Thirty states, led by New York and Florida, sued the industry for price-fixing in the early 2000s.) Some artists, like David Bowie, digitized their entire catalogs early on, but as had been the case with music videos, most labels took a wait-and-see approach.

IN 1987, THREE THINGS HAPPENED to create a perfect situation for Shoes— now in digital form—to reintroduce themselves to the world. Technologically, legally, and inspirationally, they felt ready to test the market.

In 1985 and 1987, Jeff attended the New Music Seminar in New York at the urging of Ira Robbins. This conference, which began in 1980 as a small gathering to help unsigned artists make their mark, had grown to a massive, must-attend schmooze-a-thon for the music industry: in '87, according to *Billboard*, there were 6,500 attendees. Jeff says that on his first NMS trip, "I kinda-sorta tried shopping some of the songs from *Silhouette*, but soon realized that not only am I not a good salesman; it was hardly the type of environment that I do well in. I don't feel comfortable pitching our music; I like finding ways to get the music out there and talk about what we do, but don't ask me to convince anyone how good we sound or how many copies we'll sell." Jeff felt out of place among the swarming crowds of young aspirants, even as he recognized friends and compatriots in the throng:

> There were thousands of people hawking their tapes (yes, we were all still in the days of cassette-tape demos). Ira [Robbins] told me that most of the tapes people gave out were often left behind in the panelists' ready rooms. I ran into Peter Holsapple [of North Carolina's jangle-popmeisters the dB's] and [pop musician/producer] Don Dixon there. ... I also met Jody Stephens from Big Star, and the studio tech from The Manor; he recognized me in the big panel room. There must have been five thousand people in that room.

In addition to the networking opportunities, the New Music Seminar was a good place to learn about the latest developments in digital technologies, according to Jeff: "I picked up literature regarding CD replication at the 1987 NMS, and that gave us the information we needed to release Shoes' catalog on CD."

Prior to this time, the software and hardware needed in order to digitally master and produce compact discs had not been widely available, hampering CD production and sales, and pushing up unit cost. But by the mid-eighties, these problems had mostly been solved, and production was increasing rapidly. Nevertheless, the digital music business continued to face a lukewarm response from the major labels, so it had turned to the indie labels as a market.

According to a July 26, 1986 article in *Billboard*—"CD Manufacturer Makes Pitch to Independent Labels"—LaserVideo, a CD-manufacturing company out of Anaheim, California, attended the NMS in 1986 to pitch their product specifically to an indie market. At that time, LaserVideo chairman James H. DeVries confirmed that CDs were still struggling to establish "credibility" with the majors, but "a strong base of committed consumers [was] more likely to derive from the independent market"—presumably because the indie market was comprised of serious music fans as prone to be interested in improved fidelity as classical-music listeners.

CDs were an exciting new technology, and Jeff says he remembers Ira Robbins encouraging him at the 1987 NMS to digitize Shoes' catalog, reasoning that the painstakingly detailed production they had already put into their *oeuvre* would be displayed to its best advantage in this format.

Jeff was already interested. On June 1 of that year, *Sgt. Pepper's Lonely Hearts Club Band* had been released on CD. And as Jeff says now, "That proved to us that the CD format was well-established."

NINETEEN EIGHTY-SEVEN also marked five years since Shoes' separation from Elektra, a threshold that meant the band was now free to release the music from their three major-label records themselves. Though Shoes didn't have "hits per se," as John says, they'd created quite a lot of songs they considered strong enough to re-release, and the idea of a best-of compilation started to develop. At NMS, Robbins mentioned a similar idea to Jeff. So it was that in the fall of 1987, Shoes decided to compile what would become *Shoes Best*, a collection of music spanning their career, and put it out on compact disc.

"It was an experiment," Gary says. "We wanted to see if we *could* digitize our music and release a CD—and we wanted to see if anybody gave a damn about our music anymore."

Klebe and the Murphys collected what they considered their best songs, which at that point existed on the analog masters they'd gotten from Elektra, as well as their own analog masters. They chose five songs each from their three Elektra records and *Silhouette*, plus one from *Black Vinyl Shoes*, and a new song, Jeff's gently propulsive "Love Is Like a Bullet." They only processed those twenty-two songs—not any extras for even alternate choices—since the digitization method was quite involved. Jeff recalls the complexity of this then-new procedure:

> You had to establish the sequence and time-lags between the songs, then EQ and level-match each song to the ones around it. After that, the songs had to be recorded onto the master tape non-stop, in an analog format called Sony U-matic, which had to be on three-

quarter-inch videotape, with a SMPTE [pronounced "simpty," short for the Society of Motion Picture and Television Engineers, the organization that defined and utilized the standard] time code and a "frame-accurate log sheet." This way, the pressing plant could insert each song's start and end times, along with index numbers for the CD (called the P and Q codes).

Once Shoes had a master tape of the twenty-two songs, the compilation could be encoded in digital form onto CD.

Shoes did not possess the encoding equipment, of course; few studios did. "There weren't many facilities in the area where we could do the digital mastering," says Jeff, "so we found a place outside Chicago called Classic Digital, which was just this guy in his house with the gear. He mostly did classical music, because that was most of what was on CD in those days. I don't think he had done much rock before us, if any. So our first transfers were recorded fairly quietly, to stay well below the digital overload threshold of the time. That's why, compared to later rock recordings, the volume level of our early digitized tracks is fairly low."

Gary says that it took several sessions to get through everything; it's no surprise that when Shoes went on to upgrade their equipment at Short Order in 1990, they made sure to install their own digital-processing capability.

SHOES BEST WAS MASTERED IN September. The band reactivated the now-ironically-named Black Vinyl Records and released it themselves, with liner notes by Ira Robbins. It was reviewed in several major music magazines—unusual for an independent release—and praise was copious.

Rolling Stone hailed *Shoes Best* as "a feast of shimmering neo-sixties power pop, distinguished by intricate layerings of whispery schoolboy singing and orchestral clusters of fuzz guitar." Reviewer Paul Grant, in *Option* magazine, actually thanked Jesus, because "this loving tribute to 22 pop masterpieces stands to remind us that the [sic] Shoes were pretty much the finest at blending lilting, melodic '60s pop with the best of late '70s/early '80s sophistication." *Stereo Review* called *Shoes Best* "reason to be cheerful." Almost all the reviews express pleased anticipation at the promise suggested by Jeff's "Love Is Like a Bullet," from the tail end of the *Silhouette* sessions; it was tantalizingly listed as coming from their forthcoming—already named, but not yet recorded—follow-up album, *Stolen Wishes*.

Shoes made a live radio appearance, that fall, on WXRT in Chicago, singing "Love Is Like a Bullet" on Johnny Mars' afternoon-drive show. Chuck Fieldman recalls hearing the performance and asking which instrument they used to get the curiously harmonica-like "ah-ha-ah-ha" background on the chorus. They told him it was simply John and Gary, alternating the "ah"s and "ha"s vocally.

And sales of Shoes' first CD were "encouraging," as John puts it: "At least we knew that if we *were* to do another new record, people still remembered who we were. They still cared." In fact, *Shoes Best* moved about 15,000 units almost immediately.

By the end of 1987, it was beginning to look more like another all-new Shoes project was in the works, too. One hopeful sign was that Gary was in the studio more often than he had been since he'd returned to a regular job; once he'd started visiting Short Order in January, Gary had rapidly realized that making music and working full-time were not going to coexist peacefully for him. In June, only a few months shy of qualifying for the arduous Illinois architecture licensure exam, Gary quit his job (though he was immediately hired by the same firm as a consultant: essentially the same job with more flexibility). It would take a little longer to get his license working part-time, but Gary knew it was the only way he could do Shoes, too.

And so as '87 waned, the men of Shoes all had reason to be cheerful—and none more so than Jeff. At the end of November that year, he married Lorinda, holding the reception at Short Order Recorder.

And then one day, out of the blue, Gene Simmons called. The bassist for Kiss was starting his own label, Simmons Records. He had seen a write-up on *Shoes Best* in *Billboard*. "I'd like to sign you to my label," he told an incredulous Jeff.

It was the beginning of a very strange interlude in the saga of Shoes.

Chapter 10

Never Had It Better (1987-91)

Ironically, after all that effort and worry about finding a label, reactivating their own Black Vinyl Records seemed to be Shoes' key to sparking outside interest.

The call from Gene Simmons was completely unexpected. Though the band members had met Kiss's fire-breathing bassist years earlier when they shared a stage with him, Kiss's lascivious, over-the-top glam-metal and Shoes' boy-next-door pop-rock would appear to be strange stylistic bedfellows. "But Gene was a huge fan of British Invasion-style pop, and he liked our work," Jeff explains.

In his 2002 autobiography, *KISS and Makeup*, Simmons represents his decision to found Simmons Records almost as a Charles Foster Kane-like whim: "It suddenly occurred to me that I would like to have a record label." Now, as a would-be music mogul, he was hunting talent. He had read about *Shoes Best* and wanted to talk to the band about possibly doing business together. Would they send him a copy?

They did, and for several weeks, several days a week, the members of Shoes talked on the phone with Simmons at all hours. Sometimes it was Jeff, sometimes Gary, sometimes John, sometimes two or three of them at a time.

"Gene called almost daily, in late 1987," Jeff remembers. "He was always phoning after gigs from his hotel room, and I talked to him a lot."

Simmons was on the road with Kiss, and gave them his code name so that they could reach him at his hotel. Gary thought these calls were made just to get acquainted—"He wanted to talk music, mostly." Klebe got the sense that Simmons "wanted to debate" them about certain aspects of songwriting and structure. As characteristically non-confrontational Midwesterners, each of the three would politely agree with Simmons' assertions even if they thought he was mistaken—but he'd challenge Klebe and the Murphys, pushing them to disagree. Both parties were getting to know each other in these conversations, and John thinks that Simmons was trying to get a sense of Shoes as artists: "The conversations were pretty much about our work." They all recall that Simmons had put a lot of thought into what made Beatles' songs effective—for example, he pointed out that early Fab Four tunes generally didn't mention specific girls' names, instead focusing on a non-specific "I" and "you"—and noted that, with a few exceptions, Shoes had already modeled their own writing on that principle.

Jeff says that these dialogs clearly indicated Simmons' intention of signing Shoes—they weren't discussing whether they *would* sign, but detailing the specifics of their work when they inevitably *did*. "We talked about musical styles as well as the production process," Jeff says, describing their new friend—part guru, part overseer—as being very specific about Shoes' duties as a Simmons Records act: "'You'll record the songs in your studio, give the tapes to me, and I'll release them on my label through RCA,'" Jeff recalls him saying. Simmons was equally clear about his sales objectives. "I'm only signing four bands," he told Jeff, "so each one has to go at least double platinum."

A new recording contract was what Shoes had long hoped for, and if there were in Simmons' pitch echoes of the big, empty promises of Ken Buttice, none of them voiced any concerns about it.

Simmons' goal as a label chief appeared to be refining an act with some preexisting public recognition; the other major band he was courting at the time was based around Gregg Giuffria, former keyboardist for L.A. glam-metal act Angel. His solo band, Giuffria, enjoyed a measure of success in

1984 with their Top Twenty single, "Call to the Heart." But when they signed with Simmons Records, Simmons took the reins and rebranded the group entirely, changing their name and exerting complete artistic control. In his autobiography, Simmons explains his method:

> I signed Gregg only on the condition that I would executive-produce his records—I would have full control over the name, the look, everything. I didn't want the name to be Giuffria. I wanted them to be House of Lords, which was a name I owned and had trademarked. I wanted to direct their image.

John and Gary recall that the Giuffria signing made more sense to them than Simmons' apparent enthusiasm to sign Shoes: Angel and Giuffria shared stylistic ground with Kiss, but Shoes' music had little in common with any of them. The Murphys and Klebe noted, however, distinct similarities between Giuffria's *career* and theirs, since Simmons "was more interested in artists who were already established," says John. Agrees Gary, "He didn't seem to *want* to discover someone brand-new."

But Simmons was a mega-successful recording artist, and he had sought Shoes out; they were certainly willing to listen to what he had to say about their work and how they could be marketed.

BY LATE JANUARY 1988, SHOES had received an invitation: would they be interested in coming to New York to talk contract terms for signing to Simmons Records?

Simmons flew the band out shortly thereafter, putting them up for a night in New York before their meeting the next morning at the midtown Manhattan office of Glickman/Marks Management, who handled Kiss's business affairs. But from the moment Shoes arrived, John says, he knew something was not quite right: Simmons had them cool their heels in his reception area for a good half-hour first.

When Simmons finally did deign to receive the band, they recall his first words as being rather ominous: "I may have been a bit premature in bringing you out here." It got worse: "But since you're already here you might as well come on in."

While Simmons did make a point of greeting each band member individually as they entered the office, it appeared that John's sense of foreboding had a basis in fact. Simmons and Howard S. Marks, whom he introduced as his business partner, had just been in the middle of a serious disagreement about signing Shoes. And there was no question who wielded the power in that room: Marks sat in the big chair, while Simmons stood deferentially behind him.

The meeting began slowly, according to Jeff, with Simmons and Marks "reminiscing and joking about the old days when Gene and [Kiss's lead singer] Paul Stanley recorded commercials for Hertz Rent-A-Car. "Imagine, Gene Simmons from Kiss working on commercials!" they remember Marks guffawing.

Beneath the veneer of congeniality, however, was the cold fact that Marks clearly didn't think Shoes were a sound investment for Simmons Records.

According to C.K. Lendt, the vice-president of Glickman/Marks Management who authored the 1997 book *Kiss and Sell: The Making of a Supergroup*, Simmons Records was a "letterhead company": it barely existed at all beyond its corporate stationery. (The same was true of Man of a Thousand Faces Management, Simmons' foray into artist representation, Lendt said in a recent interview) "They didn't have any offices, or any staff associated with them; they used the Glickman/Marks office as a base of operations."

During the meeting, Simmons was in the awkward situation of having invited a band to his office to talk turkey, but evidently not being able to do so without his manager's say-so. (Unbeknownst to Shoes, Marks' decisive role in this meeting was complicated by the fact that legal proceedings for the dismissal of Glickman/Marks had begun; Lendt reports that Kiss had been clearly planning on firing their management during a January 15, 1988 meeting in Cleveland; Shoes' appointment took place some two weeks later.) Simmons seemed, in Gary's view, determined to present a united front with Marks, even if that meant breaking his word to Shoes. Though Gary describes Simmons as "pretty obviously embarrassed and frustrated," he had evidently turned tail: instead of laying out the terms of their promised contract, Simmons made Marks's case for him, as if he were the other man's lawyer. "Howard just doesn't hear the songs," Simmons shrugged.

Simmons put *Shoes Best* on the stereo and clicked from track to track, commenting flippantly on the drums, the lyrics, the musical style in general. He said Gary's upbeat "Double Talk" sounded "like a marching band," for example. Some of his criticism morphed into a backhanded compliment, indicating he didn't want to dismiss them altogether: when Simmons told them, "You guys are white bread; you have no soul," he then hastened to add, "There's a place in the market for that." "I don't even think he had thought about what to say," Gary surmises. "It seemed like he was just shooting from the hip. It was pretty humiliating to be in that room."

The Kiss bassist picked apart their songs, their image, even their name, until Gary finally said to him, "Gene, what did you ever *like* about us?"

Simmons gave a heartfelt sigh. "*Everything.*"

THE PROBLEM, SPECIFICALLY, WAS that Marks did not "hear a hit." The five men debated, for a while, what a "hit" sounded like, and Jeff says that the subject of "Love Is Like a Bullet"—his new-direction song from *Shoes Best*—came up. According to Jeff, Marks didn't like it much:

> He said, "'Love Is Like a Bullet.' It's a bad title! It's a bad title and I'll tell you why. It's a bad title, because the only people that can identify with a song called 'Love Is Like a Bullet' … is people that's been shot!"
>
> When we reminded [Simmons and Marks] that the Police's massive hit "Message in A Bottle" appealed to more people than just those stranded on a desert island, their response was, "That's the Police. They got Sting!"

Rather amazingly, the meeting wasn't all bad. Simmons did like "The Summer Rain" and "Pieces of Glass." He told Shoes they were good-looking guys, and "ten times the songwriters I am." "But," he continued, "you have to be, because you write pop. I write rock & roll." These compliments were scant encouragement, however, and when the band was dismissed after less than an hour—sent home with the familiar imperative to "write some hits!"—they knew they'd been here before. And they knew that wasn't good.

Klebe and the Murphy brothers spent a long afternoon dejectedly trudging around Manhattan, before flying back to Chicago that night.

Though Simmons assured them they'd hear from him soon, it was more than two months before he called back.

WHEN SIMMONS DID CONTACT Shoes again it was early April. He was apologetic; Kiss had fired Glickman/Marks Management in March under a cloud of financial impropriety: in the case *Kiss Co. et al. vs. Glickman/Marks Management Corp, et al.*, the band sued their former handlers for $17 million. A 1997 *New York Times* feature quotes Simmons on the complaint: "There were tax shelters we were put into that backfired, and we let [Glickman/Marks] go because we thought they had failed in their fiduciary responsibility." The same article goes on to state, "Kiss contended that the two managers took commissions on sound and light bill reimbursements to which they were not entitled, costing the group $605,000. The managers said they were entitled to the payments."

But now that Glickman/Marks Management was out, Jeff says Simmons "just picked up from where he'd left off in New York, like we had continued talking the whole time. 'Jeff! It's Gene! I'm ready to cross the t's and dot the i's! Let's do this deal!'" This time, Simmons had a much more detailed arrangement in mind, closer to the Giuffria/House of Lords deal: now he was also seeking creative control over Shoes. Simmons wanted to manage the band, as well as manufacture and distribute their records. In fact, he intended to reinvent Shoes. "As far as Gene was concerned," John says "it was Day One now."

Simmons' management proposal came with a laundry list of requirements, of course—changes that he wanted to make to the band and their image—and though Shoes were skeptical about the validity of these ideas, they considered them gamely. He'd grabbed the brass ring himself, after all; plus, as John puts it, "After what we had been through up to that point, we were willing to entertain just about any reasonable suggestion."

IN THE CATEGORY OF "REASONABLE suggestions," Shoes remember Simmons wanting them to re-record some of their old songs. In some cases, they were songs that could legitimately be considered lost gems, like "Pieces of Glass," which had been recorded for—but not included on—*Silhouette*, and only appeared on *Shoes Best* in America. In other cases, Simmons wanted changes made to existing work. Jeff says that, though Simmons had complimented his song "The Summer Rain" during the New York meeting, he now objected to the chorus's lead-in—"It seemed so easy/It came so hard"—and wanted it cut. They test-edited a version for him without it; Jeff says of the abridged mix, "It sucked."

Simmons wanted Shoes to re-record their two most well-known songs, "Too Late" and "Tomorrow Night," as well. They don't recall him asking for stylistic changes, however; just a more-or-less straight reiteration. "It was about control," Gary says frankly. "Shoes owned the songs, but Elektra owned the licenses. If we re-recorded them, Gene would have had the licenses. He wanted everything free and clear."

But Shoes felt that Simmons' demand to re-record their existing catalog had artistic implications, too, which made them distinctly uncomfortable. "It was like he was telling us those other records didn't matter—that they had never existed," John says. "We didn't want to torch our past like that."

Simmons also envisioned Shoes doing covers of other artists' songs—John specifically remembers him suggesting "Turn Down Day" by the Cyrkle, the bubblegum-folk band (and Brian Epstein protégés) behind the bouncy 1966 hit "Red Rubber Ball." Shoes didn't reject that idea out of hand; "Turn Down Day" was a melodic tune well within their purview, one on which they could put their own stamp. Other bands, they reasoned, had covered vintage songs, and this one wasn't even as well-known as those: Van Halen had charted with a cover of Roy Orbison's "(Oh) Pretty Woman," and Shoes' longtime idols, Cheap Trick, had done fitting covers since their first album (which featured a version of the Move's "California Man")—their newly-released *Lap of Luxury* included a cover of Elvis Presley's "Don't Be Cruel."

Throughout their career, Shoes had in many respects modeled themselves on Cheap Trick, the commercial trajectory of whose *Lap of Luxury* is instructive about the state of conventional wisdom in the 1988 music industry—and offers some context for Simmons' directives to Shoes. The first hit off *Lap of Luxury* was the hugely successful yet critically-drubbed "The Flame." This formulaic power ballad—penned by an outside songwriter—may have hurt their artistic credibility, but Cheap Trick scored a number-one hit, something they'd never managed before. And in its wake, "Don't Be Cruel" would crack the top ten on Billboard's Hot 100 Singles chart later in the year. *Lap of Luxury* appeared to be Cheap Trick's long-awaited return to form after nearly a decade of movie soundtracks and so-so sales; maybe these were the compromises that had to be made to sell records.

Simmons didn't insist Shoes use a commercial hired gun (like "The Flame"'s composer Diane Warren) to write them a hit—their songwriting was what he liked about them, he insisted—and the covers he suggested were feasible, they thought. But his suggestions grew more invasive as the spring wore on: now Simmons wanted Shoes to entertain the idea of renaming themselves, and, Jeff recalls him recommending they consider "putting a chick in the band."

"Clearly," Jeff opines, "he was looking for ways to make us easier to market."

Gary thinks it's possible that Simmons' increasingly outlandish ideas were tests, and not meant to be taken seriously. "Gene had respect for us," says Gary, "but he had no interest in doing business with us if we were going to be the kind of band we *had* been. Were we willing to do what he wanted to get us there?" He wanted Shoes to put themselves in his hands, unquestioningly, but they naturally balked at ceding the kind of control Simmons insisted upon.

For several months, Shoes delicately balanced his demands with their own proclivities for self-determination. They were willing to accommodate what they considered reasonable requests, in their own way. As far as Shoes were concerned, John says, they still had negotiating room: "If it came down to an ultimatum, we would have crossed that bridge then."

MANY OF THEIR CONVERSATIONS WITH Simmons during this second round of discussions involved the nature of Shoes' lyrics, and what he thought should be done to play up their strong points as writers—in particular, accentuating the barely-hidden sexual content their songs had always carried. Simmons wanted Shoes to push the boundaries, to take their chosen theme of the male-female relationship to its logical conclusion: to be more directly sexual in their lyrics. "Don't just fuck her, make her come," Simmons told Shoes. Simmons insisted that if they were going to write love songs, they had to be sex songs. "Make the girls wet," exhorted the composer of "Tunnel of Love."

They did their dutiful best. "Want You Bad," "Can't Go Wrong," "I Knew You'd Be Mine," "Inside of You" ("I was gonna call it 'The Heart of You,'" John says, "but I figured Gene would like the double entendre better"), and "Feel the Way That I Do" were all crafted to follow Simmons' particular guidelines.

Simmons charged John and Gary each with writing a song called simply "I Want You." (Jeff recollects the proposed title as rather more direct than that: "I-Want-You-I-Want-to-Fuck-You.")

John put "I want you" directly into his song "Feel the Way That I Do"—"I want you, and I want you to feel the way that I do"—though he turned rock convention on its head by composing it about the *female* orgasm. Simmons wasn't happy with it. Gary stuck closer to the specific assignment: his song was called "Want You Bad," but even then, Gary recalls, Simmons complained that the word "bad" was unnecessary; the title was not what he had specified.

When he asked Gary to read him the lyrics to "Want You Bad," Gary says Simmons stopped him at the line, "Anything you desire/Anything you require," decreeing, "You can't use the word 'require' in a rock song! That's a college word!" (The college-educated rock star's animus toward higher education was not news to Shoes; according to Gary, Simmons often affected blue-collar bravado and "talked a lot about kicking college kids' asses.")

John remembers his bandmates' genuine surprise at Simmons' reaction to their completed homework: "We thought we were doing what he wanted." Even those that hewed most closely to his recommended formula, like Gary's alpha-male anthem "Can't Go Wrong," didn't quite pass muster. "I really thought I'd hit the nail on the head with that one," Gary muses, "but Gene didn't like it." As the process continued, the band and their Svengali wanna-be began getting irritated with each other. "He was exasperated and we were exasperated," says John.

But despite Simmons' obvious annoyance, "we *weren't* saying no to him," John points out. "Look at the songs on *Stolen Wishes*. They're mostly 'I' or 'You' songs, mostly structured around the words 'want' or 'need.' We were doing what the teacher wanted, though we were obviously interpreting the assignment." Jeff concurs: "'Love Does' was originally called 'London' in a nod to Dwight Twilley Band's 'England' [from their classic, influential debut *Sincerely*], but was reworked to make it a relationship song, at Gene's prodding."

SHOES SENT DEMO TAPES TO Simmons through the spring and into the summer—hoping, John says, to distract him from the idea of re-recording their old material. But with demo after demo, Simmons still claimed he "didn't hear it," says Gary. And he kept Shoes dangling with the promise of remuneration—that is, once they'd served up something he liked. "I'm not opening up the coffers until I hear the goods," Simmons told them. It was 1983 all over again: Shoes were writing demos in the increasingly vain hope of getting paid to make a record. Eventually, Simmons did agree verbally to a small advance in the outline of the proposed contract.

All this time, Shoes were being told by their then-lawyer, Russell Carter, that ongoing negotiations were tied to Shoes' double identities: as artists signed to Simmons Records, and as clients of Simmons' Man of a Thousand Faces Management. In a letter dated April 20, 1988, Simmons assures Shoes that these are two discrete deals, that as their manager he will take no cut from Simmons Records, and that he genuinely believes they can make money together. "I have better things to do with my time than to spend it with someone I don't think can 'make it,'" he wrote. Simmons also speaks of both sets of paperwork as though they are already in the mail: "[Y]our attorney will soon be receiving a contract between you and Man of a Thousand Faces," he wrote. As noted, the band members had seen the contract outline; Gary characterizes its terms as "generally okay." And Jeff remembers Simmons saying "that RCA had approved him signing us."

Neither contract ever arrived.

Shoes were never quite sure what happened in the end—it wasn't like there was a blowup or a formal closing of negotiations. Carter told them, "They're dragging their feet. I don't know why." "Simmons kept balking and asking for more songs," Jeff recalls. Gary remembers that as negotiations came closer to a final deal, the band members dug in their heels somewhat, being a bit more insistent about charting their own path (or at least hesitant about Simmons' more egregious suggestions), and Gary thinks maybe that's what tipped the balance. John muses, "Some people have told us that we should have done whatever Gene wanted," whether that was re-recording old songs or renaming the band or adding a female singer. "But we thought we still had some clout, some status; it wasn't crazy to think we could be successful again." That is to say, successful on their own terms.

As time went on and Shoes continued working, Jeff says, "Gene's calls got less and less frequent, until they stopped coming."

SIMMONS' WANING INTEREST MAY have had less to do with Shoes, however, than with the troubled business relationships of Kiss. According to C.K. Lendt in *Kiss and Sell*, by 1988 Kiss was bleeding money. A decade of so-so album sales and declining concert attendance numbers, paired with lifestyles marked by extravagant expenditures (and resistance to any attempts to rein in spending) had left the over-the-top headbangers nearly broke. By the time they fired Glickman/Marks, Lendt says, "the astonishing sums of money accumulated from 1975 to 1988 were gone." In other words, Simmons may not have *had* the capital to front Shoes at that point.

Shoes were disappointed, sure. But as much as the previous six months had resembled the frantic scuffle of making the *Silhouette* demos, Gary recalls that it also felt like 1978: if no one else came through for them, they would simply come through for themselves. "We knew we had options," he says. *Shoes Best* had demonstrated that they could successfully produce, distribute, and market an album on their own; they felt sure these songs would see the light of day somehow.

Simmons may have jump-started the process of creating what would become *Stolen Wishes*, John thinks—but Shoes were making the record in any case. He was, Jeff reflects, "basically a means to an end" as far as Shoes were concerned. He continues:

> We'd wanted a third party to help with the burden of manufacturing, marketing, and promotion, but we obviously had the mechanics in place to release it on our own on Black Vinyl Records—which we eventually did. Gene's interest in us provided some motivation to get things together more quickly, but we were going to record and release *Stolen Wishes* one way or the other, either with him or without him. After all, *he* had initially contacted *us*, *we* didn't contact *him*.

So as the work on the new record progressed and Simmons' calls petered out, Gary relates, "We just said fuck it, this is *our* record, we're going to do it *our* way."

BY FALL 1988 SHOES HAD GIVEN up on Simmons Records and—much as they had done four and a half years earlier with *Silhouette*—recognized that, despite the lack of a label deal, they had more than half a record written, as well as some serious recording momentum behind them.

And not just from *Stolen Wishes*: they had been contacted by Patrick Mathé, co-founder of New Rose Records (the French label that had released *Silhouette*), to contribute a song to a planned Buddy Holly tribute album, *Every Day Is a Holly Day*. Targeted for release in February 1989, coinciding with the thirtieth anniversary of Holly's death, the album included tracks from a number of independent musicians, including critical darling Elliott Murphy (no relation), and New Rose artists like the Slickee Boys and Imitation Life. Shoes were a fairly late addition to the project, but they were able to contribute "Words of Love," their favorite Holly song; as John exclaims on the *As Is* liner notes, "[W]e couldn't believe no one else had chosen to cover this one." Their interpretation owes a bigger debt to the Beatles' 1964 version than to Holly's 1956 original—it's more a lushly harmonized pop hymn than stripped-down rockabilly tune—and they spread the vocal duties out equally, playing round-robin with the verses—John, then Gary, then Jeff.

Back in Zion, as *Stolen Wishes* continued taking shape, Shoes felt rather unusually positive about this new project; John remembers Gary saying to him, fairly early on in the process, "This is going to be a *good* record." John continues:

> Gary didn't always say things like that. But we were working on the demo for [John's heartbreaker] "Torn in Two," and he liked that riff, and I guess he knew what songs he had in the pipeline, too. Of course, Jeff had "Love Is Like a Bullet" done—that was a pretty high bar that had already been set. All that helped to push us along.

With all three Shoes feeling confident about their writing, and excited about each other's, the recording process felt more vital than it had in a long, long time.

Stolen Wishes was the lengthiest album they had done since *Black Vinyl Shoes*—fifteen songs—and its writing and production consumed every spare moment. Of Shoes' self-produced albums—five, over the course of their career to that point—*Stolen Wishes* was by far the most sonically polished. "It's a lush record," Gary says, "kind of like *Present Tense* in that way." The layers and textures took time to assemble, though: altogether, the recording of *Stolen Wishes* lasted nearly two years. Shoes averaged about a song a month from July 1988 to September 1989. Nights, weekends, holidays—they were always in the studio. "We threw everything we had at that record," John says.

THIS WAS ALSO SHOES' FIRST album without an official drummer; Ric Menck was brought on board to play the sessions. But digital technology had rendered a drummer's job very different from what it once had been.

They began by adding Menck's live drums to the Simmons demos, but also had Menck play on electronic drum pads in order to create a digital impression of his stickwork: an impression that could be manipulated through the computer. Gary was particularly taken with this new technology:

> When Ric hit the pad, the strikes and intensity were recorded to MIDI [Musical Instrument Digital Interface, used for digitizing sound], then that triggered the sequencer [with pre-recorded drum sounds]. We had an old PC with a DOS program called Cakewalk; Ric's performance was recorded using that computer program, rather than tape. Every drumbeat was associated with a note in the sequencer—it was all numerical.

Once Menck's performance was stored in the computer, it could be altered in any number of ways: sped up, slowed down, even changed from a tom to a snare drum.

Jeff describes some of the programs and tools Shoes used to build the drum sounds on *Stolen Wishes*:

> Gary and I worked together quite a bit on the album; we almost had to because we were all learning how to use the technology together, like synching the sequencer to the tape machine—a technique that was in its infancy then.
>
> We spent hours and hours correcting the drum pulses in the computer, nudging a pulse a few clicks one way or the other, because the resolution would quantize, or shift, Ric's drum hits to the nearest resolution; so in some cases a hit would shift and be off by four to eight milliseconds, which is quite noticeable because the synchronization of the track would be off. We also had a sampler to contend with, which is the module that stored the actual drum sounds, and there was a learning curve for that, too.

The sampler, a Roland, could take these drum pulses and make them sound like any part of the drum kit Shoes wanted: a snare, a kick, a tom.

Of course, this level of manipulation, while making technical perfection possible, also took the human, creative element out of the drummer's hands and placed it into the engineer's.

Menck—a Shoes fan since their late-seventies, Rock Around the Dock days—had gotten to know them when his own band, Choo Choo Train, had recorded at Short Order. Menck had drummed with Shoes at a benefit show in 1986, telling Chuck Fieldman backstage, "Now I know how Ringo [who famously filled in for ailing Beatles drummer Pete Best] felt."

Menck was thrilled to be recording with Shoes, though he decidedly less enthusiastic about being removed from much of the process:

> My parts were recorded during several separate sessions, after which they overdubbed all the other instruments. Unfortunately, they were using these weird electric drum pads, which I absolutely hated the feel of. I remember they were very particular about my drum fills; they were used to the way Skip played, and his economy was part of Shoes' sound.

In retrospect, Menck's not sure the drum pads were the right choice. By eighties standards, they sounded real enough, he observes, but "I don't think these digitized drums they used have aged particularly well." And in fact, Jeff now admits he's of a similar mind on that score: "I think the demo version of 'Feel the Way That I Do,' which has Ric's real drum kit on it, has a much more organic groove than the finished, CD version."

But using the digital drum information, while it lacked the warmth of live drums, gave Shoes a lot of leeway to use the samples for a variety of purposes (much as they had once done with taped drum loops.) And in the absence of a human drummer much of the time, Shoes' perfectionism was given free rein.

The digital drums liberated them in another way as well. Since the percussion sounds were being built on the computer rather than on tape, they only took up one of the sixteen channels the studio featured, rather than the usual three or four. That meant more room to layer guitars and voices, resulting in the "lush" sound Gary refers to on *Stolen Wishes*.

SINCE SHORT ORDER RECORDER WAS very much a working studio by the fall of 1988, and Jeff was keeping regular studio hours; he was pushing himself hard to record his own material for Shoes as well as run client sessions. In fact, Short Order was busy enough that Shoes were beginning to have difficulty shoehorning their own recording in around their customers', as Jeff details:

> Things definitely had to be *scheduled* at that point. Weekdays and weekday evenings were the easiest to hold open for Shoes, while most clients wanted weekends and nights. So I priced the weekends and nights higher to try and attract more sessions during the weekdays.

Jeff recorded his own songs when there were no outside sessions; as his own engineer, he really didn't need anyone working with him. Gary had the same freedom—by this time, he was doing mostly freelance architectural work and had a lot of flexibility in his schedule. He arranged his sessions for complete privacy, usually working in the wee hours of the morning. John's full-time day job in graphics meant he had the most difficulty finding recording time; his available hours were the same as their clients', and John needed one of his bandmates—usually Gary—as engineer.

Jeff was keeping more-or-less regular business hours at Short Order, approximately ten a.m. to six p.m., as often as he could manage it. Throughout the *Stolen Wishes* recording process, he was not only managing and maintaining the studio, but also doing the bulk of the label work for Black Vinyl Records—which now had another release. In the fall of 1988, Shoes had packaged together their first two Elektra albums, *Present Tense* and *Tongue Twister*, for sale as a double album.

That meant wrestling with manufacturing and distribution, the kind of issues they had hoped a major label would handle. But as Shoes worked at these record-biz nuts and bolts, they became more proficient, building a network of independent regional distributors, learning the ropes and the customs of this unfamiliar field. These were skills that would continue to serve Shoes well.

It was a lot of painstaking labor, but as the months wore on, Shoes stayed focused on their primary goal: getting *Stolen Wishes* done. "I kept telling myself that nothing was going to happen for Shoes until it was finished," John says:

> There was one night, maybe in the spring of '89, when Gary and I were leaving the studio late. We felt really good—there were a lot of things in the pipeline, songs at different stages. But I did the math in my head and calculated that, at this rate, we'd still be working on it all through the summer.

Each song was demoed, then re-recorded, then passed around to the other guys to see what they would add—sometimes several times. That was the simple math: with limited hours and a lot of careful layering work on each song, recording took X times three, or six, or nine. Not until everyone had had a good-sized shot at embellishing every song would Shoes declare the record finished.

Another factor that affected the pace of recording was the installation of a bigger mixing board: Shoes traded out the semi-pro Ramsa console, which they'd acquired with the last of the Elektra buyout money, for a Neotek board in the summer of 1989. The concomitant transition from 16 to 24 tracks required some rewiring and reconfiguration of the control room, so the studio was out of commission for about a week.

It wasn't empty, however; Matthew Sweet was rehearsing to tour behind his new album, *Earth*, and Ric Menck (who drummed for Sweet on the tour) had recommended Short Order as a practice space. While Shoes tinkered with their new system, then, they got to listen to Sweet and his band work.

Over Memorial Day weekend, John and Gary recorded through an entire night to get the vocal track down for "Never Had It Better." "I didn't even have the lyrics done when we got there that night," John recalls. "I wrote and recorded them in one shot." As they left at dawn—"The sun was rising,"

John remembers, "the birds were singing, we were both exhausted"—Gary asked his bandmate, "What time are we getting back here today?" John replied incredulously, "Man, I don't know, I'll call you later." When he did, he told Gary he had plans: *"I'm* going to a picnic—I'm taking a day off." Gary rarely did so himself—John tells of driving by the studio one Christmas Eve and seeing Klebe's car parked there—and thus seemed not to have considered that some people didn't work on holidays. "But literally *one* day off in eighteen months didn't seem unreasonable," says John.

Even with the punishing schedule, perfecting *Stolen Wishes* was a protracted, thoroughly Shoes-ian process, because Shoes were, as always, determined that it was going to be as flawless a record as they could make it.

One regular habit, which they'd fallen into as far back as *Black Vinyl Shoes*, was that a given song's composer left open a number of bars for one of his bandmates to write his own guitar solo. These additional elements—little guitar or vocal fills—were the mature version of what Shoes had been doing since *Bazooka*. "We always wanted to be part of another guy's song," says Gary. "We always wanted to add something to make it just a little bit better, like putting the cherry on top." That, after all, was the point of having a band rather than being solo performers. But as each member brought in more and more fully-developed demos, it got harder to find a place for those garnishes. "People have said that our music is overproduced sometimes," John acknowledges. "But whose stuff are you going to trim back? The writer's? The guitarist's?"

On *Stolen Wishes*, the one exception to this general collaborative rule—the only song that's essentially a solo project from start to finish—is also the album's sole ballad, Jeff's "I Don't Know Why." Although, as usual, it could be interpreted as a relationship song, its exceptionally melancholy tone reveals its underlying inspiration: the suicide of a childhood friend: "I don't know why/You couldn't find a way/To let your feelings show/You should have tried to let somebody know," Jeff wrote.

As Shoes finished up the record in the fall of '89, they again considered the question of distribution. Should they try one more time to approach a label? Black Vinyl Records had done the job for *Shoes Best* and the *Present Tense/Tongue Twister* re-release (and as they worked on *Stolen Wishes*, they were preparing to reissue *Boomerang/Shoes on Ice*). But *Stolen Wishes* was new music, and might need to be handled differently. John and Gary were convinced that finding a label was absolutely necessary; Jeff was equally certain they could do it all themselves. Jeff recalls:

> I'd gotten on the phone and called wholesalers, and collected enough info to put together a network of maybe fifteen or twenty independent distributors across the country for *Shoes Best* in 1987 and the *Present Tense/Tongue Twister* release in 1988; that system was in place for us to use on *Stolen Wishes* and the 1990 *Boomerang* re-release.

It took a daunting amount of work to self-distribute, sure, but Shoes would have a lot more control than when wholesale was handled by WEA—and they would make an immediate profit on each CD, instead of just tossing them into the label machine and trusting that machine to pay out at some unknown point in the future. By the time Shoes had completed the record that fall, Jeff had talked his bandmates into distributing *Stolen Wishes* themselves.

They mastered the album and rendered it into digital form for CD at Chicago Recording Company, the studio where they'd cut *Boomerang*. Their old friend Hank Neuberger stuck his head in to say hello.

As Shoes finished up the musical portion of *Stolen Wishes*, the graphics started to take shape. John had found a book of old photographs in a used bookstore, and he really liked the faded, fuzzy-looking quality of the pictures. The band contracted a local photographer, Randi Shepherd, to shoot pictures in that style, and set their favorite shot—a wistful, smeared-looking photo of John, Jeff, and Gary—atop a piece of marbleized mauve paper. "It didn't reproduce quite right," John points out. "It looks more pink than purple. But the concept is basically what I wanted." Printing and pressing all those discs and inserts took several more weeks.

By the time the pieces were assembled, it was almost Christmas, and Shoes held a listening party for *Stolen Wishes* at Short Order the week before the holiday. They began sending out discs in January 1990—the first year of the last decade of the Twentieth Century.

THE INITIAL REVIEWS WERE ENCOURAGING. Longtime supporter Don McLeese was first out of the gate, declaring in the *Chicago Sun-Times* that *Stolen Wishes* was "strong enough to make anyone who ever loved Shoes fall in love again":

> As pop formalists, they celebrate the love song as though it were the musical equivalent of the sonnet or the haiku, delighting in its conventions as they replenish its possibilities.
>
> Though their songs almost invariably concern romance—yearning for it, recovering from it, drowning themselves in it—Shoes' major romance would seem to be with pop music itself.

Other early press was similarly supportive, often pointing to the band's long and storied history. The *Chicago Tribune*'s Greg Kot called the new album "a triumph of will," and *CMJ New Music Report* said Shoes were "just as great as ever. ... while time and trouble have taken away some of their naïve lilt, and sophisticated synthesizer textures update the sound, they're still as twee as ever and the songs still take your insides on that roller coaster ride that all great pop does."

As the buzz surrounding *Stolen Wishes* grew, reviewers from around the country phoned Zion to request copies. Even Gene Simmons' secretary solicited one on behalf of her boss. Jeff also fielded a phone request from writer David Wild at *Rolling Stone*.

THE *ROLLING STONE* REVIEW—hardly de rigeur for an indie release at that time—was a solid boost. "We were shocked that they would touch an independent," says Gary. "In another couple of years, sure. But at this point it was pretty unusual."

In the first six months of 1990, *Rolling Stone* reviewed over a hundred records; only eighteen of those were not on or distributed through major labels. Of those eighteen, only four had sufficiently limited distribution for the reviewer to include a mailing address for orders. *Stolen Wishes* was one of those four.

When a staffer called to tell the band that the review would be running in the March 22, 1990 issue, Jeff nervously inquired, "Can you tell me how it did?" "Four stars," the staffer answered. Jeff's jaw dropped. "They were pretty stingy with stars in those days," John recalls. "That really *meant* something." In fact, during that same six-month period, only one record earned five stars (Muddy Waters' posthumous collection *The Chess Box*), and three racked up four and a half (from Little Richard, Johnny Cash, and Sinéad O'Connor: the review of her monster album *I Do Not Want What I Haven't Got* led the section in the same issue that contained the *Stolen Wishes* writeup.) Shoes were one of twenty or so acts to hit four stars during that time, and one of only three independent artists to do so.

But the band wouldn't be able to read Wild's actual words until the magazine hit newsstands a month later. It was in this waiting phase that Gene Simmons—who had received his own requested copy of *Stolen Wishes*—rang Jeff back.

The point of the call was to tell Shoes that he didn't much like *Stolen Wishes*. "I don't get it," Jeff recalls Simmons sighing:

> He said it wasn't going to "excite fourteen-year-old girls." When I said we were shooting for a more alternative, college-type audience, he described them as "the geeks and nerds that wore glasses. The kind of kids I used to beat up in school." I told Gene that *Rolling Stone* was going to be running a four-star review. He said, "Reviews don't sell records." That was our last conversation with him.

This rather hostile intervention was out of character for Simmons. In their previous encounters, the members of Shoes all agree, he had been exacting, but basically businesslike and polite. Yet this exchange exhibited a level of animosity that took them by surprise. "I think we'd feel a lot differently about everything that happened if he hadn't made that last call," John reflects.

But when the *Rolling Stone* review was published, it exceeded Shoes' highest expectations. Wild pronounced *Stolen Wishes* "a great, unpretentious pop album that deserves to be heard by a mass audience" and "Shoes' "strongest effort yet":

> [T]he album sounds bright and fresh, more lively than any of their major-label releases. More important, Shoes are making the most passionate music of their career—"Feel the Way That I Do," "She's Not the Same," "Love is Like a Bullet" and many of the other twelve infectious songs on *Stolen Wishes* display a ballsy edge and irresistible force that has sometimes been missing on earlier efforts.

The review's effect was seismic. Wild had included Black Vinyl Records' address and phone number, allowing members of the public to order copies directly from the label, rather than through stores, "That about doubled the amount of money we got to keep," John remarks. "He really helped us with that."

And *Stolen Wishes* moved briskly through the distributors, too, who supplied record stores and other retailers. As orders heated up, one of Shoes' stable of wholesalers called them: "You've got a hit on your hands!"

OF COURSE, THIS TURN OF EVENTS also increased Shoes' workload exponentially. Gary had begun to take over some of the label business at the end of 1989, and once the word about *Stolen Wishes* was out, he and Jeff were swamped with orders. "We were going nuts filling them," Gary recalls. "Every day, tons of letters just poured in. And sending *Stolen Wishes* out to individuals wasn't like mailing multi-unit boxes to the distributors. We had to hand-pack each CD, with the receipt and Black Vinyl flyers. It was pretty time-consuming." And it was a constant race to keep the discs and cassettes in stock: the initial pressing of two thousand CDs and five hundred cassettes sold out, as did the second and the third; Gary thinks they had to reorder from the pressing plant at least five times, maybe more. But it was heartening, too, this hands-on access to a process that had been invisible to the band since the first pressing of *Black Vinyl Shoes*.

After years of not even knowing how many copies of an Elektra album were sold, now Shoes were intimately involved in each sale. Happily, they even needed extra manpower, hiring Chicago-based guitarist Jay Whitehouse to help out a few days a week.

As it was with so many people Shoes worked alongside, their association with Whitehouse had begun when he was a musician recording at Short Order. His band, the Indigos, had cut a demo with Jeff at the original Winthrop Harbor Short Order, as well as a full album at the Zion studio in 1988. By 1990, Whitehouse had a few years under his belt working with Bruce Iglauer at Alligator Records, the renowned independent blues label out of Chicago. Under Iglauer, Alligator's founder and president, Gary says, Whitehouse had learned a certain no-nonsense approach to the wholesaling business that Black Vinyl sorely needed: he knew how to handle independent distributors.

Whitehouse was a brand-new father; his infant son slept under a piano in Short Order when the studio was empty, and stayed strapped to his dad's chest in a Snugli the rest of the time. This often meant that the baby (now an adult) heard his dad doing the work of an enforcer, using sometimes vivid threats to get recalcitrant distributors to pay for discs they'd been shipped. Gary recalls overhearing Whitehouse pressing one wholesaler's employee for payment: "He said, 'By Friday, I want to see either our money or your boss's liver on a platter!'" Whitehouse admits that his son "heard more colorful language in his first year of life than the average child." But Black Vinyl Records needed Whitehouse's business savvy, and his skills helped to buoy them financially through this period.

THIS EASING OF MONEY PRESSURE allowed Shoes to plan for the future. That spring, they bought the studio building they'd been renting and refitted it with better equipment, including digital mastering capability. They reorganized their business relationships under a new corporate umbrella, Trinoceros. The Murphy brothers and Klebe also invested in Shoes as a band, promoting the new record in ways that simply would not have been possible without these resources.

First, they went on the road, travelling farther than they ever had before, playing shows on both coasts. Second, Shoes invested in a truly professional music video.

Touring was as much about being seen as about promoting the record. And it wasn't just fans who wanted to see Shoes play: the interest of the major labels was piqued as well, and the tantalizing vision of a potential record contract loomed yet again. A good showcase might seal the deal.

In the wake of the *Rolling Stone* review, labels started phoning the Black Vinyl office, slowly at first, but then the pace increased. "I talked to *everybody*," Gary says. "Probably a couple of dozen different labels called." Mostly, they seemed interested in floating trial balloons rather than making concrete offers, he thinks: "When an unsigned band gets four stars in *Rolling Stone*, you don't want to be the one label that didn't notice."

Shoes had seen this dynamic before--from the positive side in 1979, when several labels came courting but only Elektra put their money where their mouth was; and from the negative side in 1983, when no one company seemed willing to risk a penny unless other labels were willing to jump first. (Today, the band members often comment on the groupthink that still plagues the music industry; as Gary tartly observes, "A label's initial question is always, 'Who else is interested?'")

In the spring of 1990, lots of folks were. The buzz on Shoes was rising again, and it was an exhilarating time for them. One call came from movie director Michael Gottlieb in California; he had just been signed to write a sequel to his romantic comedy *Mannequin*, which had done respectable box office in 1987 and, more significantly for Shoes, launched the soundtrack song "Nothing's Gonna Stop Us Now" into a hit for weatherbeaten rock act Starship.

"Feel the Way That I Do" was offered a slot on the soundtrack for *Mannequin: On the Move*, and Shoes accepted the offer, knowing little about the original film's plot, and even less about that of its sequel. (The movie was widely panned and a box-office flop; only Jeff actually saw part of it, the portion with their song.)

IN THE WAKE OF *STOLEN WISHES*' RELEASE, Shoes knew they should get out and tour. As they were now on their own, the band members decided on a compact national run: five dates on the East Coast, two in the Midwest, and three in California. To be clear, while ten shows would be a small order for many bands, for Shoes it was a serious commitment of time and energy.

They also had to find a drummer. By the summer of 1990, Ric Menck was deeply involved in his new project with Paul Chastain, and thus unavailable; Velvet Crush were poised to cut their first album for the U.K.'s Creation Records. But while shopping at a local music store one day in Kenosha, Wisconsin, Shoes ran into an old friend, Jeff Hunter. It was a serendipitous meeting.

Hunter had been the drummer for the Chicago-area power-pop outfit Take Me, who'd had some success in the early eighties while working with Jeff, starting as far back as the dress shop. Take Me had a pop sensibility similar to Shoes' own—"The first time we saw them, they covered 'Too Late,'" Gary remarks—and had opened for Shoes as well as for prominent eighties new-wave acts like the Psychedelic Furs and Duran Duran. Take Me played support for the latter band in 1982, when its video-fueled album *Rio* was sweeping the charts; as Hunter puts it, "[Duran Duran] were winning Grammies while we were opening for them." An appearance with Shoes had drawn the attention of Elektra A&R, who offered Take Me a deal in the early eighties, but as Hunter explains, "We were already moving away from pop, going for a more [neo-psychedelic] Echo and the Bunnymen-type thing, and we turned them down. But then Elektra fell apart anyway." Shortly thereafter, so did Take Me, after a band member's illness caused an extended hiatus. When Shoes asked Hunter to play drums on the road with them, he consented.

But there was another problem: though *Stolen Wishes* used the synthesizer a lot more selectively than *Silhouette* had, there were still songs that couldn't be done live without someone other than Jeff, John, or Gary manning it.

Shoes turned to multi-instrumentalist and longtime Short Order client Leroy Bocchieri for help. He, too, agreed to come on the road, playing synthesizer, extra guitar, maracas, and the occasional tambourine.

Shoes were amped up to go on tour, especially to support a record that had gotten such a positive response. Even Gary: "Don't think that I didn't want to tour; I did. We were all excited about the possibility of reviving our careers." And the additional members were a decided bonus. "It was like going camping with the guys," John says, "except there was a show every night."

Though Shoes had customarily scheduled their live dates themselves, this time they went through a Los Angeles-based booking agency, Triad Artists. Brad Gelfond, an agent there, helped them assemble the tour. "He did a lot for us," says Gary, "though we were limited by our day jobs—John still had outside employment then—and the studio." Gelfond possessed a particularly important attribute: he had the ear of Hale Milgrim, then president of Capitol Records. In May and June, as Shoes prepared to go on the road, Milgrim wrote and called several times to assert Capitol's interest in the band. Gary was the point person for the Capitol talks.

The East Coast was first on Shoes' itinerary; their records had always done well there, and *Stolen Wishes* had garnered a flurry of positive reviews from regional press. They started in Boston on June 24 (after stopping on the way for what would be a rainy, rather miserable trip to Niagara Falls, which none of them had ever seen).

SHOES' NINETY-MINUTE-PLUS set in Boston featured selections that spanned their career—emphasizing the new record, as one might expect: of twenty-three songs, over a third were from *Stolen Wishes*. The Elektra catalog was respectably represented, and *Silhouette* showed up, too. (John's "Turnaround" was part of the main set, and his "When Push Comes to Shove" and Gary's "Get My Message" made the encores.) Even *Black Vinyl Shoes* popped up in the list, via Jeff's "Capital Gain."

The East Coast shows weren't particularly crowded—not surprising, given that most of these were midweek gigs—but the fans who did attend were pumped up. People who had waited years to see Shoes live came to Boston, New York, Philadelphia, Baltimore, Washington—five cities in six days. One admirer even crossed the Atlantic from England to follow that leg of the tour.

For some attendees, the mere fact that their reclusive idols were finally in the house was reason enough to be psyched. Whipping up the crowd for an encore in Philadelphia, the emcee screamed, "We've waited thirteen years for this!"

Drummer Jeff Hunter, for whom Shoes were hometown friends and colleagues rather than mysterious sequestered geniuses, had opened for some monster bands, but it had never occurred to him that Shoes might garner a similar response. He describes being a little awed by their fans' ardor:

> Shoes always drew this crowd, and it was everywhere we went. Shoes *fanatics* would show up, these people for whom Shoes was *it*. They were nice people, it wasn't like they were nuts or anything, but the band had a lot of fanatical fans who knew *everything* about them.

Over the course of two weeks, Shoes grew more comfortable with the attention, and with playing live again. John, who stood stage center, was the default front man, cracking jokes and fielding requests. An added jolt was provided by Leroy Bocchieri, bouncing and dancing from his perch behind Jeff in a way that had never been seen on a Shoes stage.

But by the standards of other bands in concert, according to Jeff Hunter, Shoes were still restrained. He attributes this quality of their live performance to two factors. First, Hunter thinks that their relatively late entry into the rock & roll game—they hadn't been musicians young enough to have made fools of themselves in cover bands, like so many of their peers—had an impact on their stage personae:

> Shoes were never just crazy young kids playing rock star in a cover band, like we were in Take Me. And when early Take Me played live, we didn't have to worry whether the songs we were covering were

good; they were proven to be that. But with Shoes' early shows, they *did* have to worry, because they were playing untested original material.

Second, the members of Shoes themselves were not outgoing; the shy demeanor they projected was no act, as Hunter puts it:

> I don't think their personalities adapted well to playing live. John has the gift of gab, but even he doesn't have that over-the-top gotta-be-the-center-of-attention thing that a lot of front men have. Shoes weren't really "performers" in that way.

Hunter believes that Shoes' relative discomfort onstage was a function of the way they'd developed, thinking through the process before they started. "They were more intellectual than a lot of other bands, maybe *because* they started later," he proposes. "They had their recording studio right from the beginning; they were just more sophisticated."

SHOES' TOUR CONTINUED IN THE Midwest on Independence Day, with an appearance at Milwaukee's perennially popular rock festival Summerfest.

On this brutally hot Fourth of July—it was over a hundred degrees—Shoes took the Summerfest rock stage right after their old friends Fire Town, the reincarnation of Spooner. Butch Vig, who John remembers looking as if someone had dumped a bucket of water on him, shook his sweat-drenched head as he came offstage. "Good luck," the drummer said to them. "It's horrible out there." Vig wasn't joking: though it was a great crowd—exuberant, scantily clad and steaming—Shoes were miserable. John remembers glancing over at a beet-red Jeff and worrying about him passing out; they were concerned not only about each other's state, but about their own. Gary says he concentrated his entire energy on staying upright.

Three days later, Shoes played a date at the Cubby Bear in Chicago, a sports bar across the street from Wrigley Field. It was sold out, and the crowd was fired up. Press estimates of the turnout cited 900 people in attendance (in what is officially designated an 800-capacity room). Critic Greg Kot, in his *Chicago Tribune* write-up, called the gig "something of an event, with a local

Who's Who of the music community and hundreds of fans pressed against the stage in the jam-packed club." Kot reported:

> "This is like Woodstock," said Shoes' bassist John Murphy, and he was exaggerating only a little.
>
> A Shoes concert is about as rare these days as the huge outdoor festival on Max Yasgur's farm 21 years ago.
>
> That almost perverse aversion to live performance is just one of several reasons why Shoes is merely one of the world's most respected pop bands, instead of the most popular.

Kot praised the band's showing, characterizing the harder edge on their sound revealed by live performance as "an epiphany."

But Shoes didn't have a label deal, and they still had bills to pay; epiphany or no, the band had to take a road break after two weeks out to catch up on Black Vinyl and Short Order business. "The problem with touring was that the cash flow stopped," Jeff explains, elaborating:

> We *never* paid ourselves when we played gigs. The money we made always went into the band coffers to cover bills, road crew, hotels, truck rental, new equipment, et cetera. So before we went out west for the rest of the tour, we did need to recharge the financial end in Zion for a bit.

The rest of July and early August 1990 were spent doing just that.

ONE WEEKEND DURING THIS PERIOD, Klebe and the Murphys went to Detroit to make a professional music video. As early MTV stars, they'd long wanted to give it another shot—"I didn't think we'd ever really been 'caught' on video," John says—and now, as their own bosses, they could simply decide to do it.

In this case, the video had come to them, rather than the other way around. Mark Malboeuf, a young videographer who had done some freelance audio-production work at Short Order, owned a little company in Chicago called Screentracks, Inc., a side business from his day job in advertising. Malboeuf had traveled the country filming TV spots for Ford, but once back home, he really wanted to develop his own production business—and Shoes seemed like a good bet for an inaugural project. Malboeuf asked them for permission to develop a video concept for "Feel the Way That I Do."

Along with his Chicago ad-biz friends Steve Hirsch and Dorn Martell, Malboeuf proposed an intricate video concept. He details:

> It would be a very light, fun, *Wonder Years* sort of thing, featuring performance footage intercut with handheld eight-millimeter video of kids playing—as if they were home movies from Shoes' youth. Since this footage was going to be vintage-looking stuff, we would distress it in post-production to make it look like it was old. We got very excited about it, as it was very much in line with the feel of the song, and would be a lot of fun to make.

Malboeuf, Martell, and Hirsch would be donating their services and only charging the band for materials. Advertising was their profession, but this video was about "creative freedom and the fun of working on a cool project," Malboeuf says. And Shoes liked the idea as proposed. But they were about to run up against a cold, hard reality about the independent versus corporate music-biz worlds; they were operating on a radically different financial plain. Malboeuf explains the problem:

> We were shocked that Shoes were shocked by the [five-figure] cost. Many of us routinely worked on thirty-second commercial spots that cost in the hundreds of thousands. So shooting multiple locations in multiple formats, creating and editing a four-minute music video for just the cost of the film, processing, studio time, equipment rentals, travel expenses, et cetera was a screaming deal. It was just more than they could afford. We thought about it, but there was no way to do this concept for less money.

Everyone was disappointed. Malboeuf and his team went back to the drawing board.

Mindful of the budget restrictions, he says, they headed in an emphatically different direction. "One of the things we had said in the planning stages was, 'We're not going to make a "girls in underwear" video,'" Malboeuf says of that done-to-death eighties MTV motif. But once the concept had to be restructured, Martell, the team's creative leader, evidently no longer felt constrained by that taboo, according to Malboeuf, because he "proceeded to draw up a sort of David-Lynch-style, girls-in-meat-bikinis video over one weekend."

Malboeuf and his crew knew Shoes had serious reservations about the revamped concept, but given the amount of time and work already put in by the creative team, everyone soldiered on. Had Shoes had a record label to intervene, even a manager, they might have been able to walk away at that point. But they hadn't, of course, and given the fact that Malboeuf's team had now sketched out two videos, essentially for free, Shoes' sense of obligation was significant. Resignedly, the band set off for Michigan to film for a weekend.

Once the members of Shoes arrived at Martell's studio—a warehouse in a Detroit industrial zone—it seemed that the director had no intention of using them in the video itself. So they spent all day Saturday standing around, flirting with models, and watching Martell shoot apparently unrelated images of girls in their underwear—one sporting an actual, alarming meat bikini—along with small dogs, and animal skulls in shadow.

By Sunday morning, they were weary of watching—"It was like we were visiting someone else's video set," says John, "and not like it was our video at all"—so they finally asked what was going on. Martell explained that he was making a concept video, using *Twin Peaks*-style imagery to parody the conventional rock-video objectification of women. Men were dogs, he explained to them patiently, and women were meat.

Shoes were skeptical, but as long as they were stuck in Detroit, they insisted on being included onscreen. "No one's seen us in ten years," John says he argued to the director. "We want to be *in* this thing." The crew filmed some footage of the band lip-synching, playing guitars, messing around. Asked to pose wearing pig heads, they did so, but felt kind of silly, and when it was all over and they went home, they had no idea what to expect of the finished product. "We knew that movies are shot out of sequence, and we hadn't seen everything they'd filmed, so we hoped it would be okay," says Gary. "We knew the video would depend a lot on the editing," says Jeff.

By mid-August, Shoes were ready to begin the California leg of their tour. They had never played the West Coast before, and they were jazzed.

Contact with Capitol had been sporadic but ongoing ever since spring, and Hale Milgrim really wanted to see Shoes live. Serendipitously, one of the band's longest-standing boosters, Cary Baker, was also working at Capitol, heading the publicity department. Baker told them that Milgrim's wife, Anne, was a huge Shoes fan, and it began to look like everything was sliding into position to get them the major-label deal they still believed was their best shot at stardom.

Shoes flew to California on a Monday. It was the middle of that night at their hotel when John suddenly awoke: "Uh-oh, I thought. I'm sick." Running to the toilet, he got violently ill, trying not to wake Gary, his roommate. John collapsed on the bed again and passed out, but before too long, he was running back to the bathroom; what he brought up this time was an alarming purple hue. Dazed and disoriented, John managed to return to bed; when he needed to purge again soon after, John used the room's trash can, because he felt Gary should see what was happening.

By morning, John was thoroughly wiped out, and understandably anxious. He recalls awaking with one very clear thought: "I'm gonna die." Still, he waited until Gary woke up to show him the trash can's contents.

"I hate to do this to you—but what does that look like?" John asked, already knowing the answer.

"Looks like blood," Gary said tersely. "We've got to get you to a doctor."

Shoes didn't have a doctor in Los Angeles, of course, so they called their publisher's office, where Dan Bourgoise's brother Fred gave them the name and address of his personal physician. Gary helped John into the rental car, and set out. Once there, while Gary distractedly flipped through magazines in the downstairs waiting room, John waited in the upstairs office. John didn't have an appointment, and Fred Bourgoise's doctor didn't have time to examine him, but he did listen to a description of John's frightening symptoms. "I'm not equipped to deal with this kind of thing; get this guy to an emergency room," he told Gary. They raced back to the car in a state of near-panic, and started looking for the nearest E.R.

They drove without knowing where they were going, but then Gary spied a hospital sign. "So we pulled in," he says. As bad luck would have it, this was a Kaiser-Permanente hospital, though the name meant nothing to these out-of-towners. Thus they weren't aware that Kaiser hospitals—which didn't exist in Illinois—weren't open to the general public; the chain was built during the Depression and World War II to serve only its own subscribers.

They parked and walked for what felt like miles, John remembers, and then waited and waited in the E.R.—only to be told that, because John's health insurance was not Kaiser, they couldn't see him. Though emergency rooms have been required by federal law since 1986 to take all patients regardless of their insurance status, that law only requires emergency rooms to save lives and stabilize patients before moving them elsewhere. From the outside, John looked ill, but not in imminent danger. His bleeding was internal and he was stoically determined to remain conscious, so it didn't *appear* that he needed emergency treatment. The Kaiser medical staff refused to look John over or even take his vitals, Gary remembers, sending them away abruptly (and almost certainly illegally).

Frustrated, Gary all but carried his bandmate back to the car. John was so weak from loss of blood that he was white and shaking. The Kaiser people had given them directions to another hospital just two miles away, however it was in a much sketchier neighborhood.

At this emergency room, at least, no one asked for John's health insurance; it appeared to serve primarily an indigent population. But the E.R. was crowded, and the wait was interminable. Gary began to be concerned about something else: if John was going to lose consciousness, which looked more and more likely with every passing minute, he wouldn't be able to answer questions or approve procedures. Gary knew a family member's consent would be necessary, so he called Jeff Murphy and Jeff Hunter back at the hotel, who came and joined them in the waiting room; John by this point was sliding in and out of consciousness on one of the vinyl couches as they waited, and waited, and waited.

All present agreed they had to do *something*, but as Jeff recounts, they were worried about upsetting the staff. "We'd had a hell of a time finding a hospital that would even *take* John, so we didn't want to rock the boat too much," he says. "But John was in bad shape." Finally, a frustrated Gary dressed down the inattentive desk nurse. "Do you see this guy? Do you understand how sick he is? Look at him!" Gary's intervention worked: she quickly found a doctor who, when he saw John, also chastised her for making this patient wait.

Not long after, John was moved from the emergency department to a regular patient room. There, the staff pumped his stomach and discovered the source of the blood: stomach lesions—possibly caused by a perforated ulcer (though there'd been no previous indication he had such a thing), possibly just a tear from that initial round of vomiting.

John had lost so much blood that he feared he'd need a transfusion. Though federal law had mandated that all donated blood in the United States be screened for the HIV virus since 1985, he and his bandmates had a residual concern that a transfusion placed John at risk for AIDS. However, he narrowly escaped having to undergo the procedure.

Still, the lesion needed to be cauterized, and John stabilized: he was going to have to stay in the hospital, at least overnight.

That presented a problem to the touring band, since they had a show that night, at a club called Trancas in Malibu. And so for the first time since the snake-bit tour of December 1979, Shoes canceled a gig.

Over the course of the next day, Jeff and Gary became aware that John's doctors were watching him more closely than his now-improving condition seemed to warrant. When they began asking the patient detailed questions about his health and habits—"Do you have a girlfriend? Boyfriend?"—his bandmates paused to assess his appearance as an outsider might. "John's got this hair standing up straight and he's so thin, and he was pretty pale at that time," Jeff Hunter describes. Plus, John was a musician.

Heroin was making one of its periodic comebacks in 1990, especially on the West Coast—and especially in the music community there. At the same time, AIDS was still a life-threatening, untreatable condition, a de facto death sentence—not until protease inhibitors were introduced in the mid-nineties would survival rates improve. And AIDS was associated with lifestyle factors, such as sexual activity and intravenous drug use, in which musicians might reasonably be assumed to indulge. Further, the blood of patients who were deemed infection risks was considered a biohazard, being the carrier of HIV, the mysterious AIDS pathogen.

A gaunt, pale musician from out of town therefore appeared to be a likely AIDS candidate, and that is, indeed, what his doctors feared. John readily agreed to be tested, though he knew he didn't have any major risk factors. The test was, of course, negative.

As soon as his condition stabilized, John started pressing for release. Not only did Shoes have another show coming up the next day, but the bassist had had to lie there while his bandmates did media interviews—mostly radio—and went sightseeing. (Gary jokes that he and both Jeffs needed to take the Universal Studios tour to recover from the trauma of John's health crisis.) By the time his doctor started teasing his nurse—"We've got to get him out of here! He's got a *show* to do!"—John was more or less recovered and ready to go. They let him out on Thursday, with just enough time to walk up and down Melrose Avenue—the popular Hollywood tourist and shopping destination—before heading off to the gig. "But even that tired me out," John remembers.

The show at Bogart's in Long Beach paired Shoes with their recording clients, Material Issue, with the younger band opening for their longtime friends. The crowd, Gary recalls, was "great," animated and welcoming. Located in Los Angeles' outlying oceanside residential area, Long Beach was more suburban hang than downtown hip, and Shoes were happy to be there—and John managed to stay on his feet through the whole show.

Shoes' set—by now well-rehearsed—went smoothly, though perhaps not surprisingly, they were more subdued than their opening act, still being worried about John. "I had one eye on him all night," Gary says. And predictably, Shoes' bassist was exhausted and pale by the end of it.

One Californian who—like so many on that long-awaited tour—was seeing Shoes for the first time was a psychology professor from Irvine, David Bash.

Bash had known about Shoes since 1978. As a student at Manhattan's New York University, he had seen *Black Vinyl Shoes* in the bins at Zig Zag Records in Brooklyn, but hadn't heard it until WNEW-FM started playing "Do You Wanna Get Lucky?" "I didn't know what it was, but it was a really great sound, like a low-fi Lindsey Buckingham," Bash remembers thinking. "When they back-announced, I found out it was Shoes." He went back to Brooklyn to buy the record.

Prior to *Present Tense*'s release, Bash saw Elektra's ad in *Billboard* and headed straight for over-the top chain store Crazy Eddie's ("Our prices are *insane*!" their ads hollered) the day the record came out. "Every song just blew my mind," says Bash. "There started the love affair. It was supreme music; they've always been in my top few favorite bands."

When Shoes played California, then, Bash made sure to be there, and to meet his idols: "It meant a lot to me. I was a fanboy."

Bash was struck, too, by Material Issue. It was years later, after leader Jim Ellison's shocking 1996 suicide, that Bash would adopt the name of the title track of Material Issue's first album for his traveling music festival: *International Pop Overthrow*. Shoes' appearance at Bogart's in Long Beach was the first time Bash heard the band (and quite possibly, he thinks, that song.)

FOR SHOES, BOGART'S WAS A WARM-UP for the one night that really mattered: the Saturday show at Club Lingerie in Hollywood.

This was it, the point of the trip. Shoes had been talking to several labels, on and off, but it seemed that their best signing chance was with Capitol, whom they were trying to convince either to reissue *Stolen Wishes* with wider distribution—now that it had garnered such strong reviews and sales—or to sign them for another record. The Lingerie gig was thus a crucial showcase for them, and Capitol brass would be in attendance.

Shoes were co-headlining with Canadian alt-pop favorites The Pursuit of Happiness, then supporting their second Todd Rundgren-produced album for Chrysalis Records, *One-Sided Story*. The previous year, TPoH's first major-label release, *Love Junk*, had made a respectable showing on both the Canadian and the independent charts, and its single—a re-release of their anthemic 1986 hit, "I'm an Adult Now"—charted once again. With a new record out, TPoH were widely seen as still-rising stars.

It was a well-matched double bill; as TPoH lead singer Moe Berg notes, "I was a big fan of Shoes." In one comic misunderstanding, however, Gary mistook TPoH singer Susan Murumets, chatting with John, for a groupie—and asked her to leave the dressing room while Shoes got ready to perform.

Like most bands, Shoes always needed a moment or two alone before taking the stage in order to tune guitars, warm up voices, connect with each other. The dressing-room-as-VIP-lounge, a scenario Gary says was especially common in California, represented something of a problem for them—*especially* Gary, for whom taking the stage was hard enough. "Of course I want to hang out with people, but *after*," he says.

But sharing a bill meant sharing a dressing room, and the uncomfortable moment with Murumets was one unintended consequence of that situation. "Gary was polite, and Susan was gracious and left while we got ready," John recalls. Jeff adds, "TPoH were cool about it, and we hung out with Moe and the band afterwards."

In the house that night were label president Hale Milgrim and his Shoes-fan wife Anne, as well as Cary Baker. But Tim Devine, Capitol's head of A&R—the one who would ultimately decide Shoes' fate—was not.

In his *Los Angeles Reader* review of the show, Chris Morris—who had written the 1979 *Rolling Stone* feature, "The Shoes Step Out in Style"— recounted the band's long history, as did nearly every other writer who covered *Stolen*

Wishes and its tour. But Morris, in this 1990 review, also emphasized their current *oeuvre*:

> Shoes are musicians working in the nineties, not pop archeologists handing in new translations of some rock 'n' roll Dead Sea scrolls. … Shoes, by virtue of its craftsmanship, dedication, virtuosity, and sheer *zeal*, remains with us, and it's to the band's immense credit that it never for a second sounds like it's shadow dancing in the rubble of music ephemera. (Morris does observe that "some of Shoes' accomplishments may have been purchased at the price of virtual monkdom," pointing to their reputation for staying in Zion and not touring.)

The writer also noted John's recent illness, implying that it was the result of nerves—"an ingrown terror of live performance"—and described John as "pale and hollow-cheeked, planted onstage between the saturnine Klebe and the appallingly youthful Jeff Murphy." According to Morris, "the adulatory audience reacted at first with near-disbelief, then pure glee."

While taking issue with some of the set's pacing and song selection, Morris was pretty adulatory himself, declaring Shoes "a group to be cherished":

> It works in a stylistic region—classical sixties-derived pop—that is rigorous in its formal demands and traditionally resistant to artistic resuscitation, and it never fails to make music that is hearty and vibrant. In that, Shoes remains a unique and prized American band.

The unique and prized band members agree that the Club Lingerie show was quite satisfactory. But it had been very hot onstage, and the pace of the trip was beginning to catch up with John, who was still wobbly. He started feeling faint onstage, and toward the end of the show, leaned over to Gary to tell him that he wasn't going to be able to do "Hate to Run," which had been Shoes' final-encore, customary closer for a decade. Luckily, the double bill meant that there wouldn't be any encores, and John stumbled offstage, searching for a chair.

He recalls:

> There were people everywhere—those were the first shows we'd ever done in California—and everyone wanted to say hi and congratulate us and stuff. People knew I'd been sick, too, so a lot of people wanted to ask about that. But I just wanted to sit down.

A day or so later, Shoes flew home, exhausted and triumphant.

BACK IN ZION, THERE WAS PLENTY to do. Jay Whitehouse had kept Black Vinyl Records running in their absence, but clients for the studio were pouring in, and Shoes still had to finish up the work they were doing with Dorn Martell for the "Feel the Way That I Do" video.

The editing sessions took place in Chicago in September, and when the band was shown the finished product, they were markedly unhappy with the result. The final cut interspersed three unrelated narrative lines with Shoes' footage: in one, a dominatrix with a whip attempts to prod a small dog through a hoop; in another, a lingerie-clad model wields an electric knife and a weed whacker; and in the last, two menacing Secret Service agents shield what appears to be an impound lot full of dancing girls from the camera's probing eye. In addition, stray impressionistic shots of dinosaur skulls, melting dolls, and still more models—some clad in steak and sausage—were interspersed, purportedly a further parody of the "men-as-predatory-dogs, women-as-forbidden-meat" theme.

Martell's intent may have been to critique rock-video clichés, but instead he appeared to be dutifully in thrall to them. As Jeff says:

> The video started out as a parody of how bands use women in videos just to sell the music. But the way it ended up, it just looked like we were buying into exactly what we had set out to satirize.

Shoes didn't give in to Martell's misleading *mise-en-scène* without a fight, but at that point they were already so far into it financially that starting again wasn't an option. "We did make them recut it once," Jeff says, "to get more footage of us in there." But aside from that minor tweak, Shoes figured they were stuck with the video as it was.

Dismayed by "Feel the Way That I Do," they didn't release the clip to MTV or VH-1, according to Jeff: "Since we weren't real happy with it, we focused more on indie cable outlets and alternative-type video shows. I have no idea if it ever received any airplay."

BESIDES, THERE WERE MANY OTHER pressing items on Shoes' agenda. Fall 1990 saw the re-release of *Boomerang/Shoes on Ice*, packaged together, just as Elektra had proposed eight years earlier. There were negotiations with European labels for the overseas release of *Stolen Wishes*, which took some time—New Rose in France even issued it on vinyl, a format that had almost disappeared (for consumers, anyway) in the United States by then. The *Mannequin 2* soundtrack deal was progressing, and there were also rumors (unfounded, it would turn out) that Shoes would be asked to contribute to another film soundtrack, the Tom Cruise-Paul Newman action vehicle *Days of Thunder*.

But all this business—the deals that made it through and the deals that didn't—was a distraction from what the band really wanted to do, which was simply to make music full-time.

Shoes patiently waited for the major labels to offer them something concrete while they saw other acts—with shorter track records—plucked from the indie labels all around them: Chicago's Smashing Pumpkins went from small-time Caroline Records to big-time Virgin Records with their Butch Vig-produced debut, *Gish*; industry legend (and Asylum Records founder) David Geffen was courting indie icons Sonic Youth for his own WEA imprint, Geffen Records; a furious bidding war was waged over Superchunk, a prominent indie band spawned from the fertile scene in Chapel Hill, North Carolina who—like Shoes—operated their own label (Merge Records) and whose radio-unfriendly song "Slack Motherfucker" had been a huge underground phenomenon in 1990. (Superchunk actually ended up forswearing the majors and signing with another indie, New York-based Matador.) When Nirvana was tapped by Geffen in January '91, Vig—who had produced the scorching Seattle neo-punk trio's demos and was favored to helm their first major-label record, too—called the studio requesting advice, knowing Jeff had been through a similar scenario with Material Issue. (Gary put Vig in contact with their lawyer.)

And when the labels finally did call Shoes back, late that summer, Shoes were stunned to learn that their recent modest success with *Stolen Wishes* was actually working against them: some record companies feared that its 30,000 units sold had tapped out the album's potential market. "How many more people are out there who still want to buy this record?" Gary remembers being asked. Even Capitol—which had looked like such a sure thing—was hesitant, and it was Hale Milgrim himself on the phone with the bad news, informing Gary that his head of A&R, Tim Devine, saw Shoes as "retro."

Cary Baker confirms that Capitol's zeitgeist in that early-nineties era was all about shedding older talent—from venerable, previously chart-topping singer-songwriter Carole King to former teen idol Donny Osmond—and acquiring younger ones, including stylistically disparate alt-rock acts Blind Melon and the Beastie Boys. "Capitol was reaching for modernity," Baker says. (One notable exception to this rule, according to Baker: rootsy chanteuse Bonnie Raitt—a good two decades into her professional career—had a huge year in 1990, winning three Grammys (Best Rock Performance, Female; Best Pop Vocal, Female; and Album of the Year) for '89's *Nick of Time*.)

Shoes may have still fit loosely under the "alternative" umbrella, but in their mid-thirties at this point, they were more of an age with the acts being pensioned off than the acts being signed.

The band now found itself in a generational dilemma: older than the kids at the core of the alt-rock scene, hipper than their own contemporaries, they were in the all-too-familiar position of not conforming to major-label categories.

It was an old story, and one in which Shoes had formerly played the ingénue.

SOMETIME IN THE MID-NINETIES, they met pop legend Joey Molland of the Beatles-protégé band (and power-pop progenitors) Badfinger. After a string of hits in the early seventies, Badfinger had imploded due to bad management and infighting, leading to the 1975 suicide of founding member Pete Ham.

But in 1979, Molland, together with his old bandmate Tom Evans and some American musicians, had rallied and released Badfinger reunion album *Airwaves*. It did respectably, in fact selling a little better than the early-seventies LPs considered Badfinger's hits, and the single "Love Is Gonna Come at Last" had charted on *Billboard*'s Hot 100 that year. But their rebirth was cut short by the same Crash of '79 that had plagued Shoes; Molland and Evans descended into competitive infighting and split up, and by 1982 Evans, too, had ended his own life.

When Shoes encountered Molland more than fifteen years later, he was clearly still stewing over the lost opportunities of 1979. Backstage at one of the innumerable music venues of northern Illinois, it appeared Molland had been drinking, and when Shoes introduced themselves, he promptly blamed them—maybe the whole power-pop movement, but maybe *just* them—for the fact that Badfinger's second shot hadn't quite cleared the fences. "Yeah, we could have had a comeback if it wasn't for you lot," Gary remembers Molland saying bitterly. "We were doing fine, and then you guys just *bumped* us out of the way."

"He kept saying that," Gary recounts. "'You just *bumped* us out of the way.'"

But by that point in the mid-nineties, Shoes had found themselves on the Badfinger side of the equation, and knew all too well how very galling it was.

Chapter 11

Rugged Terrain (1991-96)

NOT GETTING SIGNED AGAIN WAS a bitter pill, but Shoes were more cheerful about swallowing it than might have been expected. After all, they had an indie hit, and they'd learned something very important: being independent could, under the right circumstances, be preferable to being on a major label. They had complete creative control—final say over release dates, titles, scheduling, and other crucial components that had frustrated them in the past—and financially, there was no comparison to the crumbs for which Elektra forced them to beg.

The process had taken a whole lot of man-hours, sure, but *Stolen Wishes* had, to put it succinctly, *worked*. The marketing and distribution and press had functioned harmoniously, achieving concrete, quantifiable results. Ideally, Shoes still wanted an outside entity to handle things like distribution, publicity, and promotion, to allow them to focus on their music—"to be Shoes full-time," as Jeff says—but in the short term, at least, what they *had* done seemed like a decent blueprint for what they *could* do. "There was hope," Gary says. "We could see a whole different way of doing this, a parallel system." Shoes had the production and administrative facilities—and the skills—to make their indie career viable.

None of the major labels had really given the band a firm "no," of course. They had all deferred for now—neither picking up *Stolen Wishes* for distribution, nor offering a contract for a new record—cordially and noncommittally. Some labels asked Shoes to let them know when they had new material, but that was all.

Gary, who still manned Black Vinyl Records' phones, had always been the one most committed to the idea that Shoes needed big-league support. When labels told him to "let us know when we can hear something new," Gary took that to heart, determined to give them something as long as they were still interested. "I wanted to strike while the iron was hot," he says. When the band was still working *Stolen Wishes*, in fact, Gary was already back in the studio cutting his first track for the next record, a pounding rocker called "Animal Attraction."

Jeff, on the other hand, had a lot of other things to think about. In a November 1990 *Billboard* article, "Short Order Recorder Is Cooking—Thanks to Shoes' Sure Fit of Biz & Band," he speaks of his high hopes for the studio, observing that if even one artist were to strike it big, the profile of the studio would rise significantly. "Look what happened to Mitch's [Easter] Drive-In Studio in North Carolina after R.E.M. [broke through]," Jeff points out. Clearly, Jeff saw Short Order in the same class; he was focused on making things happen as an independent studio.

At this moment, the brightest feather in Short Order's cap was Material Issue. Their major-label debut *International Pop Overthrow* had been recorded as demos at Short Order between 1988 and 1990, and was set to come out as an album on Mercury Records early in 1991 with almost no changes; the demos *were* the album. "We made a few vocal corrections and re-mixed a few songs, but it was probably ninety-eight percent as-is," Jeff recalls. The fledgling trio hadn't done much yet, but front man Jim Ellison was supremely confident, the label had high hopes, and Material Issue looked poised to go far.

And it wasn't just Material Issue. Other Chicago-based pop bands were finding their way to Zion, drawn by Shoes' reputation, by positive reports from friends, or just by meeting one of the band members. It was Material Issue's bassist Ted Ansani, for example, who introduced Mike Galassini and his band, 92 Degrees, to Short Order Recorder. Ansani and Galassini had been classmates at a Jesuit boys' high school in Chicago and remained friends; Galassini reports being awed when Ansani told him he was recording at Short Order with the reclusive Shoes:

> Of course we all knew who they were. Everyone knew their story. They were do-it-yourself legends for any kid with a band in the Midwest. The idea of recording there was almost symbolic for my band. There was just this aura around Shoes, and around the studio; Zion was *our* Zion.

Galassini recalls that the first time he drove north to meet them, Jim Ellison was his ride. Ellison blew past the Zion exit on I-94 without slowing down, Galassini laughs. Then, slamming on his brakes in the middle of the highway, Ellison proceeded to back down the shoulder of the road for a good half-mile to reach the exit.

Other clients came along accidentally. For example, John was supposed to judge a local battle of the bands in Kenosha, Wisconsin when he met the Swingset Police, from nearby Lake Geneva. Member Mike Braam says that, when he and his bandmates (who were also his brothers) heard that there was a Shoe judge, they were excited; they thought their kind of pop would appeal to John, giving their band an edge. "We were on him like white on rice," Braam chuckles. But the battle of the bands never happened that day:

> Some idiot in a four-wheeler drove over the snake [the multi-thread cable connecting the mixing board to the microphones onstage] and broke it. They didn't even try to hold the contest. We just talked to John all day, and invited him out to our own little studio and practice space.

And when Swingset Police were ready to record, they too sought out Short Order and Zion.

Shoes were well on their way to making their studio genuinely profitable—even though it was in a small exurb far from a major population center.

Understandably, Jeff's attention was mostly concentrated on Short Order business. In the wake of *Stolen Wishes*, there were renovation projects at the studio—new offices in the basement, a new roof, and new air conditioning—plus the structural changes that the upgrade from sixteen to twenty-four tracks had made both necessary and possible.

"We weren't really writing at the time," Jeff says, "just concentrating on keeping *Stolen Wishes* going. We still hoped that someone would scoop it up for distribution on a more massive level, but in the meantime, we kept expanding our indie distributors as that landscape kept constantly changing." In truth, the patchwork independent distribution system—upon which so much of *Stolen Wishes*' success had depended—was actually a weaker link than Shoes realized. But as long as *some* of their distributors were paying *some* of their bills, Black Vinyl Records could go on, even if a few collapsed.

But they never expected the whole house of cards to come tumbling down at once.

UNLIKE HIS BANDMATES DURING the post-*Stolen Wishes* period, John went straight back to his full-time job, as a graphic artist, in the fall of 1990. He didn't have much choice economically: *Stolen Wishes* had earned Shoes more than they'd ever seen from Elektra, but it was an ingrained habit by now to sink most of their income back into the operation. And unfortunately, in most cases those investments had been profitless (the tour), fruitless (the video), or endless (the building).

Shoes had lost money on the road promoting *Stolen Wishes*, despite the encouraging press; California, especially, was a gamble that hadn't worked, financially speaking. The band had spent thousands producing "Feel the Way That I Do," a clip they ultimately preferred no one saw. And while buying their studio building was a nominally sensible investment, it locked them into sizeable, ongoing monthly expenditures like mortgage and utilities payments. In addition, Shoes' decision to take Short Order seriously as a commercial studio space necessitated regular equipment upgrades. "The studio was like a hungry beast," Gary says grimly. "We had to feed it all the time."

John was the only one whose livelihood kept him away from Short Order. Jeff could get paid by clients when there were sessions (which there usually were at this point, largely based on his growing renown as an engineer/producer), and Gary had finally accrued enough hours as an architect to take his licensing exam. He passed it in 1990, and the license qualified him for freelance work—something he squeezed in around the unpaid hours spent running Black Vinyl Records. But this granted Gary a flexibility that John, the full-time graphic artist, didn't have.

Plus, John (more than the others, it seemed) was feeling consumed by the relentless pace of the past three years. *Stolen Wishes* had eaten up 1988, 1989, and 1990, from the Simmons talks to the recording to the promotion and tour. "I remember saying toward the end of *Stolen Wishes*," John says, "that I'm never doing another record like this again. It was so intense, blowing everything else out of our lives except making that record—and then we immediately did a full year of promotion." And all this, he reminds, while he was working a regular forty-hour-a-week day gig. "It was hard to sit in my little crappy job," John reflects, "saying that I helped make a four-star album, but nothing had really changed."

For a brief time after *Stolen Wishes*, the members of Shoes had allowed themselves to withdraw funds from their band account, but it was never enough to live on. And when John asked that fall if he could draw a regular paycheck in exchange for more administrative hours, there just wasn't enough money. Sales of *Stolen Wishes* were slowing down; they could no longer afford their one regular (albeit part-time) employee, Jay Whitehouse. Now Shoes' only supplemental help was Jeff's old friend, producer and engineer Michael Freeman. "After Remington Road closed," says Jeff, "Michael freelanced, so I used to hire him to do overflow sessions at Short Order." Jeff would also bring aboard various second engineers (the guys who set the mics and did the studio grunt work), paying them hourly. Adding to Shoes' already overextended payroll wasn't an option.

John admits that heading over to the studio after work was getting harder to do at this point. "We were like Paul Newman in *Cool Hand Luke*," he describes, referencing the late film actor's Sisyphean doggedness in an iconic fight scene:

> We kept getting knocked down, and getting back up punching, but we didn't even know what we were punching at. In reality, we were just punching at nothing. We'd had all this acclaim, all this critical success, and it didn't make a damn bit of difference. It was hard to get moving again after that, because I, at least, was having trouble seeing the point of it all.

And indeed, when the whirlwind of *Stolen Wishes* settled down, it seemed that Shoes were right back where they'd started.

So the Murphys and Klebe went on as though *Stolen Wishes* had never happened. Gary pushed ahead with his songwriting, and eventually so did Jeff. And though John began to feel the familiar pressure to keep up his end, he wouldn't write anything usable for the next two years.

MATERIAL ISSUE'S ALBUM *International Pop Overthrow* was released in February 1991 to critical plaudits and respectable sales, moving about 200,000 units. The shimmering track "Renee Remains the Same" had been getting airplay in Chicago even before the band got signed; the first official single, "Diane," got decent airplay too, and the second, "Valerie Loves Me," made it to number three on *Billboard's* Modern Rock Tracks chart. But *IPO* wasn't a monster record; it was not going to do for producer Jeff Murphy what Nirvana's *Nevermind* and Smashing Pumpkins' *Gish* had done for Butch Vig. Still, Jeff wasn't in a bad position professionally: when Material Issue began recording again that fall, they would to go back to Zion and Jeff and Short Order, which was certainly a vote of confidence.

In "Bands on the Run," a March 1991 feature in glossy suburban publication *North Shore* magazine about Chicago-area unsigned bands trying to make a living, Jeff represents the senior-statesman end of the continuum. The article's lead photo shows the three band members sitting in front of Short Order's board, bolstering the piece's positing of Shoes as the one band with the stability and experience to foster others along.

Reporter Cindy Pearlman observes that "Shoes has been one of Chicago's most successful music acts," before briefly sketching the band's career. Pearlman writes:

> Since opening their recording studio in 1984, Murphy has been in the position to help other bands, like Material Issue, whose new album he produced. He has worked with the Bad Examples and a solo act called Leroy. "Of course, you are much more plugged into the business in New York or Los Angeles," [Jeff] says, "but you are also forced to plug into the hype and the glitz. We are a Midwestern band. There is definitely a work ethic here."

Jeff gives a realistic and sober evaluation of the Chicago scene, remarking on the generally disempowered regional label reps and the relentless demands of club owners, but saving his real critique for what he sees as indifferent radio and tepid crowds: "We've learned that Chicago just does not support its local bands like New York does. In that club scene, you get a following. In Chicago it's, 'Oh, those guys again.'"

MIDWAY THROUGH 1991, JEFF had a brainstorm. Several years earlier, before his marriage to Lori, he had sneaked her two sons into the studio to record a Christmas song for their mother, under the cheeky-cuddly moniker The Puddles. "Christmas List" had become a family favorite, never failing to bring a tear to his wife's eye, and Jeff wanted to release it more broadly. As autumn set in that year, inspiration hit: Shoes were part of a respectable alternative-pop community, so why not ask their colleagues to contribute songs to an alternative-pop Christmas album? Other multi-artist rock & roll holiday albums, like 1987's mainstream-star-studded *A Very Special Christmas*, had done well, suggesting that there was a market for such a project.

Yuletunes brought together a who's who of the alt-pop scene at the dawn of the nineties—Matthew Sweet, Material Issue, Don Dixon & Marti Jones, Kelley Ryan, Spooner, Bill Lloyd, the Critics, 92 Degrees, the Spongetones— artists and producers who had determined the shape of much of independent music in the mid- to late eighties. Sweet was riding the crest of his breakthrough album. *Girlfriend.* Dixon had produced R.E.M. and a laundry list of other noteworthy acts, from the North Carolina scene and elsewhere, along with his own work—and was showing no signs of slowing down. Spooner's Butch Vig was poised to become *the* name in alternative-rock production once Nirvana's *Nevermind* hit the streets that September. Even the lesser-known contributors on *Yuletunes* included such luminaries-to-be as Big People's Bill Kelly, the old friend of Shoes who had been Lou Hinkhouse's assistant in 1985 and would later go to Hollywood.

Unlike the traditionally-based *A Very Special Christmas*, the vast majority of *Yuletunes* was comprised of original material. (Only Dixon and Jones' soulful "Every Day Will Be Like a Holiday" was a cover, originally penned by Stax Records' William Bell in 1967.) Some of *Yuletunes*' contributors had Christmas songs already in the can Longtime critics' favorite Bill Lloyd had written and recorded the romantic jangle-pop carol "Underneath the Christmas Tree," for example, when he was approached by Jamie Hoover of the Spongetones to contribute a song to *Yuletunes*; it seemed like a perfect outlet. Pop songstress Kelley Ryan—an old friend of the band through her husband, former Shoes manager Dan Bourgoise—had a fetching ballad she'd written with collaborator Steve Toland—"It's Not Christmas"—ready to record; her contribution would cement her relationship, not only with Toland (with whom she worked for the next decade in L.A. power-pop act astroPuppees), but also with Don Dixon and Marti Jones, who remain to this day her regular collaborators. Ryan reminisces:

> I had met Shoes before ... but this was such a great personal step musically, because their acceptance of me as a songwriter, as well as a friend, really kicked me into gear and started me on a serious path of recording.

Nearly half the *Yuletunes* tracks were cut at Short Order with Jeff behind the board. And it went fast, he says: "*Yuletunes* was conceived in August of 1991 and put together in September"—a remarkably efficient production.

At the outset, *Yuletunes* was Jeff's idea, though his bandmates and business partners soon saw the project's potential and joined in. "We were looking to expand Black Vinyl Records," Gary reminds. "We were all for it." Jeff and Gary put out feelers to a lot of potential contributors, and the fall was a blur, with Jeff racing to record new tracks, Gary rushing to get the contracts and legal permissions in place, and John hastily conceiving and executing the disc's festive graphics—as well as penning Shoes' own song.

In fact, Shoes themselves were a little concerned that John's cheerful slice of holiday encouragement, "This Christmas," was not going to make the deadline—unlike some of the other acts, Shoes didn't have a holiday song already finished—but as usual, John slid it in under the wire. Still, the disc's late start meant that the 1991 holiday sales season was nearly over before *Yuletunes*' release. The mastering date was December 5, scarcely time to get it into stores by Christmas.

The launch party was held at a new Chicago nightspot in the Fulton Market warehouse district, called the China Club. Emceed by actor Mark DeCarlo (a friend of Leroy Bocchieri), it was a festive night. As many bands as could make it came and played their *Yuletunes* songs for the holiday crowd. Shoes, Material Issue, Spooner, 92 Degrees, Herb Eimerman, Leroy, and astropuppees were all there. Kelley Ryan, astropuppees' frontwoman, recalls that, though she "had knocked around L.A. as a 'solo-girl-with-her-guitar' for a few years," the *Yuletunes* release party was "the first time I ever played with other people on stage." They shared equipment to keep the show moving, and Eimerman sat in with Shoes, playing bass on "This Christmas."

The album reviews were uniformly positive. *Rolling Stone*'s David Fricke called it "traditional in its own charming way," and went on to note that the disc was comprised of Shoes and "fifteen other jangle 'n' pop purists, mostly worthy up-and-comers, cooking up tasty, original holiday-themed treats in time-honored Beatlesque fashion." Another writer called *Yuletunes* "a precious beauty" while (curiously) likening it to a firearm "so loaded [with killer tunes] as to require a five-day waiting period between ordering and possession." Yet another enthused:

> These songs, free of pretension and affectation, are the charming stuff of a pop purist's Christmas dreams: jangling guitars, contagious melodies, and buoyant harmonies abound at every turn. … Traditional in spirit if not in execution, *Yuletunes* is a highly recommended addition to rock 'n' roll's Christmas catalogue.

Though it got a late start that first year, *Yuletunes* continues to be a seasonal favorite, and from time to time delighted Shoes fans will still catch it playing over retail loudspeakers while holiday shopping.

As soon as *Yuletunes* was essentially in shape, Jeff was back in the studio, handling production duties on the second Material Issue album, *Destination Universe*—the first time in Jeff's producing career that he had major-label distribution going in. *International Pop Overthrow* had sold well, and Material Issue was seen by their label, Mercury, as a band on the way up. They were under pressure, then, to produce a killer record. And that pressure was aggravated by Material Issue's intense and mercurial front man.

Much has been written about Jim Ellison's complex, driven personality, especially in the wake of his 1996 suicide. He was at once charismatic and alienating, confident and needy. Like Shoes, he was caught between two sometimes contradictory desires, one for astronomical success, the other for complete artistic control. As Material Issue bassist Ted Ansani said in a 2008 interview with Ed Shull, posted on the website *Filthy Lucre*:

> It sometimes seemed that [Jim] would take the band three steps ahead, but then he was taking us two steps backward, because he was fighting battles he shouldn't have been fighting. He wanted so much control. He didn't always work so well with everybody, and because of that we would be burning bridges that we were standing on.

This trait was especially apparent in the studio. Jeff, who had worked with Ellison since the first Material Issue demos in 1985, was accustomed to his confrontational manner and urge to control *everything* that happened in the studio. The producer had developed techniques for coping with Ellison— "I used to give Jim the day off when other band members were working," Jeff offers as an example. But if Ellison had been challenging in a demo atmosphere, that was minor irritation compared to the *Destination Universe* sessions. Jeff remembers "walking over to Burger King during breaks and literally shaking. ... Jim could be so sarcastic and intense."

One problem was that Ellison, for all his writing and singing talent, wasn't exactly a virtuoso on the guitar; in one contemporary review of a live show, the *Tribune*'s Greg Kot describes Ellison as "grinding out one simplistic car wreck of a solo after another." It was a problem in the studio, too. Jeff talks of routinely staying post-session to record guitar parts that "Jim wouldn't or couldn't play," adding that Ellison called him "the phantom guitarist." And as he'd done on Material Issue's debut, Jeff wound up contributing stray keyboard and rhythm-guitar parts as well—uncredited, of course.

Bassist Ansani also dubbed some guitar parts. "Ninety-nine percent of all the guitars were done by Jim," Ansani says, "but when he'd come in after Jeff or I had recorded something, he'd say, 'What's *that* weird part?'" Yet the larger issue was Ellison's rock-star attitude, which he'd been carrying around since college, but which had been intensified by *International Pop Overthrow*'s success. He had a tendency, Jeff recalls, to try and bluff his way through obvious errors, exacerbating his inexpert playing by his arrogant refusal to admit he'd made a mistake. In a 2004 interview with the online magazine *Perfect Sound Forever*, Jeff described one such incident:

> [Jim] was not at all technology-based and would not even tune his guitar; I did it for him. He once broke a string during recording while doing a lead, and the guitar went flying out of tune. When I stopped the tape and told him to re-string his guitar, he argued that he 'meant' to do that. But that was just Jim.

Midway through recording *Destination Universe*, Ellison, driving recklessly, got in a car accident that made him miss several days of work. "But it didn't delay the record," says Jeff, "because I was able to do overdubs with Ted and Mike; mostly backing vocals with Ted, and additional percussion and guitar and keyboard fills that I played." Still, Jeff thought Ellison was being wildly irresponsible, and berated him for jeopardizing his success by taking dumb chances in a car. Ellison shot back, "Rock stars are supposed to be reckless!"

But producing Jim Ellison, as infuriating as it could be, was worth it, says Jeff: he valued working with someone whose pop sensibilities were very much in line with his own. Many critics at the time recognized the continuity between the bands; indeed, in Material Issue's early press, it was considered a given. One critic, in *Spin* magazine, hailed "the simpatico production of Jeff

Murphy" on *International Pop Overthrow*. And a *Los Angeles Times* interviewer didn't even bother to lead into his abrupt question to Ellison: "How 'bout those Shoes?" (Ellison immediately--and a bit backhandedly--praised his studio hosts: "Those guys are legends in the Midwest. They make great records, but they're not a big road touring band.")

THERE WAS A FAIR AMOUNT OF discord among the band members themselves, mostly having to do with Ellison's insistence on staying with Jeff as producer. While Mercury Records had released *International Pop Overthrow* as an album, it was, as previously stated, really just a collection of demo tracks recorded irregularly over eighteen-plus months and produced by Jeff one at a time. For *Destination Universe*, drummer Mike Zelenko told interviewer Darren Robbins in 2008:

> We went in knowing we wanted to use a big-name producer. Our manager and A&R guy wanted us to work with Jerry Harrison [of renowned post-punk art rockers Talking Heads]. Ted and I were behind that decision, but ultimately it came down to Jim and ... he was against the idea. ... [Ellison] wanted to have the band co-produce the record with Jeff Murphy, which allowed him to record the album in Zion—away from the record company, who would have preferred we record in New York or L.A. to keep tabs on us.

Ellison was enthusiastic about two major advantages Jeff and Short Order could provide. First, Material Issue's front guy wanted co-producer credit for the band itself—official recognition on the record jacket that Material Issue's creative input encompassed more than writing and playing. Second, just as Shoes had done a decade earlier with *Present Tense*, Ellison sought privacy for the recording process. "Basically, Jim didn't want to be bothered [by Mercury]," says Zelenko. Short Order could be Ellison's Manor, a place where the record company would not interfere—or so he'd thought.

But Mercury interfered anyway, becoming downright pushy during mixing, according to Zelenko: "They [wanted] to see us have a big hit record this time out, and were making a lot of suggestions."

Recording for *Destination Universe* was completed early in 1992, and mixing was well underway when Jeff ran up against a time constraint. Ten songs were done, four left to go, when a vacation to Mexico he'd planned months earlier reared its pre-booked head:

> I told the label and Material Issue I was taking a break for ten days and we'd finish when I got back. But John [who had returned earlier from the same group vacation] called me when he got home, telling me everyone was freaking out about my absence and that I needed to call the label and the band as soon as I got home.

Mercury was furious that Jeff had left Zion in the middle of mixing. While he was in Mexico, the label had second engineer Ron van Staley make a duplicate of the masters for "What Girls Want," the swaggering pop track being eyed as the album's first single, which Jeff had already mixed.

Jeff says he'd long been aware the label didn't think he was enough of a name to helm Material Issue's new record: Mercury had been pressuring the trio to have Jeff call on his friendship with Butch Vig, and persuade the smoking-hot producer "to mix a song or two so they could put his name on the album. I'd refused to use my friend in that way," says Jeff, "and had told them if they wanted to have Butch do it, they should contact him themselves."

With Jeff out of the country, Mercury gave two other engineers a shot at mixing "What Girls Want." One was Chicago-based *enfant terrible* and underground punk legend Steve Albini (Pixies, Breeders, Jesus Lizard), whom the members of Material Issue brought to Short Order for the session; the other was future Grammy winner Andy Wallace, who had mixed Nirvana's *Nevermind* for Vig.

According to Mike Zelenko, Albini got first crack at the track: since "the record company hated 'What Girls Want,'" Albini's punk sensibilities, Mercury reasoned, would bring out Material Issue's aggressive side.

When Albini came to Zion, Gary showed the producer around Short Order's control room and helped him get set up for mixing. Gary says he did overhear some of Albini's subsequent mixing session, "but I kind of thought they were working on an alternate version, a special mix—not looking to replace the one Jeff had already done."

John also listened in on Albini and Ellison in the control room, as an anxious-for-approval Ellison demanded, "Do you like it?" followed by Albini's dismissive response: "It's not my kind of music, Jim." Bassist Ansani remembers Albini being bemused that he had been brought in at all. He "threw his hands up," Ansani recounts, "and said, 'I don't know what you guys want me to do. It sounds like it sounds—use Jeff's mix.'"

But Mercury had insisted on a version with Albini's imprimatur, and so the band pressed him to make an immediate mix. When he did, they were not happy with the punk auteur's handiwork. "His mix buried the vocals, made the drums sound muddy, and just put guitars on top of everything," Zelenko says. Albini's version—called the "Head Wound Mix"—appeared on a 1992 Polydor import CD single from Britain.

The second outside mixing engineer Mercury tried was the aforementioned Andy Wallace, whose credits at that point (in addition to Nirvana) included hardcore acts Slayer and Sepultura. "His mix sounded so great that we wanted him to remix the whole record, but for whatever reason, that didn't happen," says Zelenko. Jeff liked Wallace and his work, though he notes that "no one consulted me about employing him." In any case, Jeff's and Wallace's styles were so similar, interestingly, that the final version of "What Girls Want" is actually a combination of the two mixes. Jeff observes:

> Even Andy's location of the individual instruments in the stereo field were the same as mine—tambourine on the left, guitar fill on the right. ... Once I matched the levels, I edited both versions together for the final mix. But I didn't even get to hear Andy's mix until I was in New York at the mastering lab, so I had to make a snap decision and do the edits and level-matching there.

Material Issue's *Destination Universe* was released in March 1992, but failed to achieve much commercial altitude.

In a 2008 *Popdose* interview with Darren Robbins, Ted Ansani said that Material Issue had used their major-label funding to make a high-gloss record: "Since we had an actual budget, we figured we were going to polish stuff up, add more layers, throw in [extra] percussion, and do some things that we weren't normally accustomed to doing."

But in the next breath, he wondered if that was a mistake, if that polished production style worked against them in a musical world just being conquered on a mass scale by the jagged guitars, sludgy bass and drums, and slurred, angst-ridden vocals of grunge, the punk-metal fusion that Nirvana's *Nevermind* had unleashed on the mainstream six months earlier.

Just like Shoes, Material Issue didn't quite fit into the clearly-demarcated categories of the music scene at that point. Ansani continues:

> I honestly felt that [Mercury Records] was frustrated over what to do with us. We weren't grunge; we weren't from Seattle [grunge's epicenter]. Green Day and Weezer, bands we ultimately would have much more in common with, hadn't happened yet.

Material Issue moved on from Jeff Murphy and Short Order when they cut their third record, working in Los Angeles with Mike Chapman—the veteran pop producer whose feud with Richard Dashut had so impacted the tenor of Shoes' daily life in summer 1980, while they were recording *Tongue Twister*.

Chapman, says Zelenko, had a very different production style from Jeff: "He taught us to let loose, capture some raw performances, whereas we'd been more precise when working with Murphy." Ansani agrees, remarking that Chapman was prone to starting sessions with shots of Stoli, and would routinely overdrive the amplifiers. "Chapman was blowing fuses in the amps fifteen or twenty times a day," Ansani relates, adding, "Jeff would never let things get that out of control."

Jeff is philosophical about the professional split with Material Issue, and its effect on his relationship with Ellison: they were alienated for several years following *Destination Universe*. But, Jeff says, they reconnected shortly before Ellison's death, remarking, "I read an interview with Jim where he said he considered me his older brother, in a way." Shoes maintained good relations with the other members of Material Issue, too, even asking Zelenko to drum for them during the sessions for their 1994 album, *Propeller*.

Jeff never really got another major-label production shot like *Destination Universe*, but the lure of big-time producing was not powerful enough to pull him out of Zion: "Butch Vig's situation exploded into mega success for him, which was great. But for me, the prospect of it scared me as being almost uncontrollable, and I didn't want to spend extended periods of time away from Lori or our studio." Moving to New York or Los Angeles, Jeff says, while it would have been more financially rewarding, "was never a real consideration."

From Jeff's perspective, "Short Order Recorder's primary purpose was not to attract outside clients, but to serve the recording needs of Shoes. Everything else was supplemental." And while Short Order Recorder has never had the same platinum-generating cachet as Vig's Smart Studios, Jeff doesn't regret it, because keeping things on a manageable scale worked for Shoes. "Financially, [a multiplatinum reputation] would have been nice," he allows, "but we always wanted success on our own terms."

As for Material Issue, the big studio and big producer turned out not to be the magic bullet they'd hoped: their Mike Chapman-produced album, 1994's *Freak City Soundtrack*, sold less than *Destination Universe*, and soon after, Material Issue and Mercury Records parted ways.

It's hard to pin down exactly why an artist does or doesn't hit. In Material Issue's case, hindsight suggests that the band, under pressure from their record company not just to replicate but to exceed the sales of *International Pop Overthrow*, was tinkering with the formula that had worked for them. But at that time, Material Issue was following the same blueprint of major-label, one-size-fits-all production and marketing—"Do this, and this, and then this, and you'll have a hit record"—that Shoes had seen fail so dramatically themselves. As Ira Robbins pointed out in his *Rolling Stone* review of *Destination Universe*, pop artists are "heretical enough to envision the potential for real popularity in power pop (generally a fine notion that is the exclusive refuge of idealists and altruists)." In many ways, the fate of Material Issue mirrored that of Shoes—and by extension, the fate of many fine pop bands who never quite managed to grasp the platinum ring.

But just as previous iterations had been swamped by psychedelia in the mid-sixties, disco in the mid-seventies, and synth-pop in the early eighties, this wave of pop was steamrolled in turn—by the juggernaut of grunge.

That Nirvana-led monster truck was just revving up in 1992, and Shoes unconsciously adjusted.

PROPELLER IS UNQUESTIONABLY THE hardest-rocking Shoes album. Aware of the trend toward simpler song structures and stripped-down production, the band members describe the stylistic transition from *Stolen Wishes* to *Propeller* as an echo of that from *Present Tense* to *Tongue Twister*. "A return to basics from what some critics had felt was lavish overproduction," Gary explains.

One significant change was the reappearance of real drums; Shoes were backing off from the highly synthesized and manipulated drum sounds they'd used for more than a decade. "I really liked the more organic feel of this disc," says Jeff. "It felt like we were back to a more natural recording process—using real drums, and less sequencing and synths."

This description makes it sound, however, as if live drummers were an integral part of *Propeller*'s recording process as it occurred, which was not the case; all drum tracks were added *after* instrumental and vocal tracks had been committed to tape (with click tracks cuing the beat). The two drummers who appear on *Propeller*, Mike Zelenko and Ric Menck, were assigned their particular tracks through luck of the draw. As individual songs neared completion for Shoes, according to Jeff, they'd call both men to see which had time to come to Zion and lay down his track. "Whatever song was ready," he says, "got the drummer that was available at the time."

Neither Menck nor Zelenko saw himself as part of *Propeller*'s creative process. "I was a drummer for hire; I did what I was asked," Zelenko says. Menck agrees: "I just blew through town quickly, adding drums to tracks that were already complete, or nearly complete."

For Jeff's part, he found himself backing away from the glossy studio perfection Shoes had always striven for. But instead of pushing for the raw-power aesthetic that was all the rage in the wake of Nirvana, Smashing Pumpkins, Pearl Jam, and other bands of the grunge movement, Jeff says that he "personally really opted for a sloppier feel to songs like 'Treading Water' and 'Slipping Through Your Fingers,' rather than doing multiple takes to get the 'perfect' track." John generally concurs: "I think we were definitely being a little less precious about performances, vocally or instrumentally, so we didn't baby all the tracks like we normally might have." Though Shoes weren't consciously seeking the punk-influenced aura of grunge, its authenticity of spirit was appealing to them. And Gary points to Shoes' largely timeless sound to dispute this characterization of *Propeller* as less polished in response to grunge—but agrees that *Propeller* is more elemental, more reproducible in a live setting, and more of what he characterizes as "a *band* sound."

The irony of all this is that, in making *Propeller*, Shoes functioned less as a band than they had on any of their previous records. The moderate success of *Stolen Wishes* had done to them what even the silent thud of *Silhouette* had not: it had isolated them from each other.

Jeff and Gary each worked completely alone, and when John came in at night, it was almost always just with Gary as an engineer. Jeff was usually gone for the day before he arrived. "We worked," John says, "in onesies and twosies."

Each one did more instrumentation, exercised more control on his own songs, than he ever had before. The album-credit details alone demonstrate that even established Shoes customs like leaving room for John's bass line were left behind: Jeff played bass on his own "Treading Water," Gary on his "The Last of You" and "Bittersweet." They did retain the tradition of writing each other's guitar solos most of the time, though this too was starting to evolve; Gary contributes his own solos on his songs "Animal Attraction" and "Never Ending," and Jeff does the same on "Slipping Through Your Fingers."

FROM OUTWARD APPEARANCES, it seems as if *Propeller* should have been an easy record to make—Shoes had a building, a studio, a label—but its production was fraught with tensions, mostly raised by the higher expectations its predecessor had prompted. *Stolen Wishes'* success had allowed them to set up a structure to preserve Shoes, but keeping those investments viable was now a treadmill they had to trudge daily. The aggregate income from the two main sources—label and studio—was barely enough to run the building most of the time. The necessity, now, for success measured in financial as much as artistic terms was pushing the three toward open conflict.

The problems that vexed *Propeller* had little to do with time, particularly not for Jeff and Gary. Jeff was at Short Order more than forty hours a week, between writing his own songs and producing other bands in the upstairs facility. Gary was in the building more than full-time, too, running Black Vinyl Records out of the basement as well as recording his own material and engineering John's. Gary would lay down tracks whenever he could, mostly working late at night, when the building was empty of clients and BVR business was tied up for the day. And John, though he had kept his outside job, was certainly in no worse a position—financially and in terms of available time—than he had been for *Black Vinyl Shoes* or *Stolen Wishes*.

But the comparative freedom of his bandmates to work on music was a constant affront to John. Yet if he was going to cut back on his outside job, he needed to be paid by Black Vinyl Records—and administrative work wasn't in the shoestring budget. Only Jeff got paid, and only for studio time (though not nearly what he was worth, in John's view) but this did exacerbate tensions among them, particularly between Jeff and Gary, who was eking out a living on irregular freelance architecture jobs.

Things were stressed, then, between all three Shoes, so they avoided open conflict by avoiding their bandmates.

It was toughest for Jeff and Gary to steer clear of each other, since they worked in the same physical place. When both were in the building at the same time, they sequestered themselves on separate floors. And it was just easier for John not to show up at all. From his perspective, there was so little time to write anyway; getting angry about internal politics wasn't going to help him get his songs done.

Jeff, whenever he could manage it, not only shunned late-night "musician's hours" but tried to get home for the evening meal; he lived a scant two blocks from Short Order, and so even if he had an after-six session, Jeff could usually swing dinner with the family. But this meant, from John and Gary's perspective, that Jeff was ready to take off right about when they were ready to start recording. This was especially true for John, who would just be getting out of his job at suppertime.

These intra-band tensions reveal themselves in various ways on the record. Listening to *Propeller* in hindsight, it's not hard to get the same sense of grim foreboding Beatles' fans had watching their revealing 1970 documentary film *Let It Be*: this is the work of a band whose individual components are all going in opposing directions. Though each member of Shoes disputes this characterization, it's difficult to ignore the implications of a plethora of *Propeller* song titles, including "Don't Do This to Me," "Silence is Deadly," "A Thing of the Past," "Tore a Hole," "Slipping Through Your Fingers," and "Never Ending," (the title of this last one does not necessarily indicate trouble, but the lyrics—"Don't make a promise to me/I only believe what I see/Don't even open your mouth/You don't ever mean what you say anyway"—indicate an undeniable problem.) "Rugged Terrain" and "In Harm's Way" also came from these sessions, and were released later; if anything, they strengthen this interpretation. All of the titles *could* be taken to refer to relationships—after all, these were Shoes songs—but the weight of them together suggests something more ominous. When the just-hanging-on-themed "Treading Water" passes for upbeat, something is very wrong.

The difference, of course, is that *Propeller* was *not* Shoes' *Let It Be*; it did, however, turn out to be their last foray into the studio together for many years. And speaking about these sessions to any of the band members is likely to bring up bruised feelings nearly two decades old. But each was operating according to what he thought were his own self-interests, whether that was seeking monkish seclusion or observing strictly-enforced family time or just carving out room to stay sane. "Everyone was right, and everyone was wrong," Gary sums up. "We had never been further apart than we were on that record."

Musically, too, *Propeller* is more somber than any of Shoes' previous outings. There are two reasons for this: one, John had borrowed a Fender Jazz bass and, he says, "played it throughout the album, so there was a deeper bottom than my more midrangey-sounding Gibson Thunderbird, which we usually used." Jeff agrees that instrument unquestionably influenced the mood of *Propeller*. "It's a more bass-heavy record than *Stolen Wishes*, so it sounds darker."

Two, the shunning of studio perfection allowed Shoes' performances to be rawer than ever before. John mentions that he didn't even want his ballad "In My Mind" to seem "too pretty." Jeff comments that he was using a lot more feedback across the board: "'Silence Is Deadly' opens and closes with an acoustic guitar feeding back through an amp. I wanted a constant drone, like a sitar-type sound." And he admits:

> I was going a bit overboard with my guitar feedback on "Tore A Hole" (which I recorded in the control room by feeding my Strat through my Hiwatt amp through the Auratone studio monitors, and placing one of the monitors a few inches in front of my guitar). John and Gary even asked me to scale it back a bit—you should have heard it *before* I did that.

Between grittier guitars and coarser singing—Jeff says the backing vocals for both "Silence Is Deadly" and "Tore A Hole" owe a debt not to grunge, but to the Beatles' corrosive, inadvertently Charles-Manson-inspiring "Helter Skelter"—*Propeller* ended up with a noticeably more primal tone. However, Jeff acknowledges, "In hindsight, I wish it had been mastered a bit brighter, and the vocals could have been a bit louder in some of the mixes."

In terms of sheer craft, though, *Propeller* is an achievement of which Shoes are all justifiably proud. John points out that the three songwriters trespassed a bit on each other stylistically—he, for instance, with the frankly raw, Gary-esque rocker, "Tore a Hole;" Gary with his contemplative, John-like reverie, "The Last of You." The resulting confusion among some listeners over whose song was whose delighted John. "I liked tweaking people's expectations," he says now.

This was the first time since *Boomerang*, Jeff points out, that they'd had twenty-four analog tracks to work with from beginning to end. It allowed Shoes to experiment, each on his own, with expanded instrumentation (including strings) and alternate interpretations of songs (there are two radically different versions of John's "Thing of the Past," explained below)—and then play with the results. (However, as Gary notes, the return to live drumming tied up a lot more tracks than had the digital drums of *Stolen Wishes*: ten or twelve channels, as opposed to one.)

When John had asked Jeff to come up with a solo for his plaintive "Don't Do This to Me," his brother's initial pass featured "a lower-register, slidey guitar," which, John says, he found "a little too laid-back." Jeff took another crack at the solo in "a higher register, without the slide." The eureka moment came during the mixing process, John says, after "we unintentionally combined both of Jeff's takes on two different tracks and then left them both in."

They were all pleased with the fresh, out-of-the-ordinary result, however accidental; the solo's two melody lines use the same notes, but they *feel* completely different: one upbeat, one subdued. As Jeff describes, "The guitars kind of swirl in and around each other."

One serendipitous side effect of Shoes' comparative isolation from each other during recording, then, was recapturing the now-elusive art of surprising each other.

Two other guitar solos on *Propeller* were nerve-wracking not for themselves, but because of the worries that each Shoe now had about the others' reactions, searching for criticism where none existed. These were Jeff's solo for Gary's "The Last of You," and Gary's for Jeff's "Treading Water."

For Gary's song, Jeff says he had written something with "a Chris Isaak, rockabilly-smolder feel to the part." He was pretty happy with it, but of course it still had to be presented to Gary. As Gary was right in the studio building's basement, doing so was easy:

Gary was down in the office and I asked him to come up and give it a listen. He suggested a very slight change in the solo section, but it was done in almost no time, and I really liked the feel of that song.

Jeff recalls being a little nervous about the ease of the operation, especially the quick adjustment: the way Jeff saw it, Gary could be skeptical of anything that seemed done too fast, whereas he himself liked the immediacy of first inspirations. But Gary said he was "thrilled" with the new part, declaring it "perfect."

Gary had a comparable fear about Jeff's response to his more deliberate working style. Jeff says he had basically completed "Treading Water," nurturing the psychedelic track and admittedly "hogging more of the instrumentation than usual," including the bass line. But as they had planned, he handed it off to Gary for the guitar solo.

A full two weeks passed before Gary came back with his contribution, a characteristically uncluttered passage that both fits in with and offers a counterpoint to the intricate instrumental wash of "Treading Water." Jeff recalls loving his bandmate's work, calling it "one of Gary's best solos *ever.*" But at the time he delivered it, Gary remembers Jeff's response as subdued. "I don't think he wanted to show too much enthusiasm, because it had taken me a while," Gary thinks. "But I'd wanted it to be right ... I walked away thinking that Jeff thought it was acceptable, but not necessarily great."

Even when things were going well, then, the members of Shoes tended not to express it out loud. "We're terrible about that with each other," John admits. "Sometimes the compliment comes *years* later."

Shoes continued to explore new territory on *Propeller*. One innovation was the first session musician Shoes had ever hired, cellist Peter Szczepanek, who was brought in to adorn John's pensive ballad "In My Mind." John had written the part on a synthesizer, but Jeff suggested that they find a real string player, in keeping with the more organic feeling of *Propeller*. John agreed, and Jeff made some inquiries.

Initially, they tried a bass violinist they'd located through a client, but the tone of that instrument was too deep. "What you need is a cello," advised the string player, whereupon they found cellist Szczepanek, a seasoned musician who performed with several Chicago-area classical ensembles. Szczepanek came to Zion one evening, quickly learning his part off a computerized score created from a MIDI file.

The resulting track is warm and textured—sophisticated—a counterpoint to the largely rough-and-tumble *Propeller*. Jeff observes that the more mature, almost elegant vibe of tracks like "The Last of You" and "In My Mind" "really gave the disc a refined, classy feel."

Another first for *Propeller* was Shoes' pushing their harmonies in some different, intriguing directions—the only instance of their all working together during the sessions. For example, John's "A Thing of the Past" abstains from Shoes' standard block harmonies in favor of a syncopated, rhythmic harmony line.

"A Thing of the Past" was noteworthy in another way, because it boasted two completely different incarnations—the banjo-based version that appears on *Propeller*, and a guitar-based interpretation found among the odds and ends on *As Is*. "We wouldn't usually do that," remarks Gary, who provided both versions. "When we worked on each other's songs, we'd mostly just add a fill or a solo. This time, I did a whole alternate take."

Gary had been skeptical of the banjo idea ever since John proposed using one on the track; John had even borrowed the instrument specifically for that purpose. As he recalls:

> I had wanted a banjo feel in "A Thing of the Past," and said that to Gary. When I went to the studio that Saturday, Gary was trying to pick it *Deliverance*-style, and he doubted it would work. I told him that I just wanted something simple in there. A "banjo-ness," I said. I fooled around a little with it and came up with the beginning bit, but asked Gary to play it because I figured he'd be more accurate than me. ... It took a while to get it down, and Gary questioned his performance. But I was satisfied with it It was nothing fancy—just a bit of banjo-ness.

Banjo wasn't, of course, a typical instrument for Shoes, though they'd used it all the way back during *One in Versailles*. (It makes a brief, beginner-level appearance on John's novelty tune of the same name.) As far as John was concerned, the inclusion of the banjo part put "A Thing of the Past" to bed.

Gary wasn't satisfied. It was just before final mixing of "A Thing of the Past" that Gary went in—as was his custom, late at night, alone—to do a fill with a distorted guitar. Almost by accident, he says, a whole new version of the song took shape. "It sounded good to me, a different direction to go with the song," he says.

The next day, Gary sprang the alternate version on John as a surprise, and the change was radical. The song went from being an acoustic-guitar-and-banjo frolic—with the music standing in stark contrast to the elegiac words—to a darker, deeper rumination on loss, the music's overall tone now of a piece with its lyrics.

There wasn't much time to determine which version to use, according to John: "We had to make a fast decision because we had to mix the next day." John resisted using Gary's retooled version on the finished record, explaining, "It's the same rhythm tracks, same pace, but it sounded slower to me for some reason." Gary is convinced that he didn't lobby for either one, but John expects that Gary's feelings were probably a little hurt that his work had seemingly been wasted.

In the end, though *Propeller* was challenging, at times arduous, to make, it's an album Shoes are proud of, perhaps in part *because* it was a challenge overcome. The record was finished in late 1993, with the packaging and pressing readied for release in early spring 1994 (just a few months before the suicide of Nirvana's Kurt Cobain).

SINCE BEFORE *STOLEN WISHES*, Shoes had been working steadily at building Black Vinyl Records as a business. As Jeff steered the development of Short Order Recorder on the main floor of their building, so Gary oversaw the expansion of Black Vinyl Records in the basement.

The evolution of Black Vinyl's mail-order wing, which had existed in a modest form prior to *Stolen Wishes*, illustrates the shift. In fall 1990, a Black Vinyl Records flyer advertised all eight of Shoes' available products: four albums (*Boomerang/Shoes on Ice, Present Tense/Tongue Twister, Shoes Best*, and *Stolen Wishes*) and four items of merchandise (a button, a photo, and two t-shirts). The parallel flyer from spring '94, on the other hand, features twenty-two records, ten from Black Vinyl itself and twelve others on various imprints from like-minded acts—many of whom were Short Order clients releasing their own music on their own labels.

Still, the first non-Shoes record released by Black Vinyl was not a Short Order recording; it was made by the Spongetones in their North Carolina studio and delivered to Zion as a completed album.

The Spongetones weren't a new band when vocalist-guitarist Jamie Hoover called Black Vinyl Records in spring 1991. Hoover, bassist Steve Stoeckel, guitarist Pat Walters, and drummer Rob Thorne had been playing together nearly as long as Shoes, forming in '78 as a Beatles tribute band and quickly evolving into writing original songs. A 1982 album, *Beat Music*, and a 1984 EP, *Torn Apart* (both recorded for the South Carolina-based Ripete label), had featured such luminaries from the southeastern pop scene as R.E.M., Mitch Easter, and Don Dixon, and had earned accolades in the national music press, including *Rolling Stone*. *Where-Ever Land*, released in 1987 on their band label Triapore, was something of a departure from the Spongetones' customary evolved-Merseybeat sound, but by the time Hoover was looking around for help manufacturing and distributing his band's 1991 album, *Oh, Yeah!*, they had largely returned to their British Invasion roots.

Hoover, figuring that Shoes and the Spongetones shared a lot of the same fans, phoned Black Vinyl's office out of the blue and asked Gary whether Shoes had ever considered signing any fellow indie bands to their label. "We've been talking about it," Gary acknowledged. Hoover asked if he could send along the rough mixes of *Oh, Yeah!*, then nearing completion, and Gary agreed to give them a listen. When the tapes arrived, Gary was more than impressed:

> I couldn't believe what I was hearing. These weren't demos—this was a finished record, an incredible record. It struck me we needed

to put this out. And it seemed like there wasn't a lot to lose; they had already garnered some press.

This wasn't a standard record deal, but a manufacturing and distribution agreement; after all, the album was finished. Black Vinyl would handle the pressing, packaging, and distribution of the Spongetones' *Oh, Yeah!* for five years—not unlike the deal Shoes themselves had struck with Marty Scott at Jem back in 1978. The Spongetones' contract with Shoes' label is dated July 12, 1991.

"They were so nice, so businesslike," Hoover effuses. "Genuinely honest, and a bright spot in our otherwise rough career."

There was never any question of how many copies of *Oh, Yeah!* were being sold, or what the Spongetones' cut would be: Hoover says that his band received regular sales reports from Black Vinyl. In a 1996 interview with *Goldmine* magazine, Hoover observed appreciatively, "Black Vinyl's done an excellent job for us. ... Our own Triapore label was much less organized and professional. I mean, wow, these guys have their own fax machine!"

At the same time that the Spongetones' deal was being inked, work was moving ahead on *Yuletunes* (with the Spongetones' "Christmasland" included), and *Silhouette* was being issued for the first time in the United States. These various threads all represented possible paths to making Shoes' business end work. "Our own industry was on the rise," Gary says, "and it looked rather optimistic at the time."

Running an independent label and recording studio wasn't what Shoes had set out to do originally, but this was 1991; major labels were looking to the indies for ideas, inspiration, acts. And there was a niche for Black Vinyl: artists like the Spongetones, the clients who flooded Short Order Recorder, and some of the other alt-pop acts on *Yuletunes* (such as Bill Lloyd) appealed to an underserved market, and the idea that Shoes could keep themselves afloat by helping other DIY bands had real appeal. "The talent was right in front of us," Gary says.

Black Vinyl could use Shoes' cobbled-together network of independent regional wholesalers to help their friends on the alt-pop scene, along with

Shoes themselves, by ensuring that these distributors saw Black Vinyl as a regular source of new music. As Jeff noted in a 1996 *Goldmine* profile of Black Vinyl Records, "It became obvious that to get paid on a regular basis by our distributors, we would need a more constant product flow from the label. A bigger stable of titles helps us to be taken more seriously on a retail level, too."

The subsequent rapid expansion of Black Vinyl Records, then, was part community service, part business decision, and part survival mechanism.

The following year, Black Vinyl Records began selling albums made by other independent imprints. These were still primarily the work of Short Order Recorder clients, and sometimes just friends of the band. There was a distinction between Black Vinyl's titles—primarily Shoes and Spongetones recordings—and the other releases. "With Shoes itself we were a distributor and a record store; for other acts, we were just a record store," Gary details. In other words, they'd use their independent distribution network to get Black Vinyl albums in stores, but discs on other imprints were sold strictly by mail order. "And with every release," says Gary, "we thought we'd be closer to becoming a significant independent label like Matador or Sub Pop."

As always, Black Vinyl's overarching goal was the promotion of Shoes; building a network, they believed, would be good for the band in the long run. Ironically, it never really worked out that way: Black Vinyl Records' strongest, most reliable product was always Shoes' music. Nothing else provided as secure a source of income.

SHOES HAD ALWAYS BEEN relatively early adopters of new technologies, and Black Vinyl Records continued down this path by developing an Internet presence early on. Much of the credit for this innovation goes to Steven Gardner, an Internet service provider on Long Island, New York and a lifelong Shoes fan, who contacted Jeff sometime in the late 1980s.

Then, most people still did not have online access in their homes; computers were freestanding data-collection devices and little more. As the Internet developed, one of the first platforms for marketing and communication was the electronic bulletin board system (BBS), where businesses could connect with their customers, if not in person, then at least in cyberspace.

But Gary took over the business end of Black Vinyl just as the BBS was ceding way to the World Wide Web, as bandwidth expanded and it began to be possible to embed graphics and sound in websites—and reasonably expect that at least some people could see them (albeit at dial-up speeds). Steven Gardner offered Shoes server space and advice, as Gary painstakingly taught himself HTML and began developing a site for Black Vinyl Records.

Gardner recalls:

> Gary always knew the right direction to go in—he could see the potential in the Internet. Yet he didn't really know the best way to proceed; he knew where he was going, but not necessarily how to get there. I offered to fly out and set up their site for them, but he was sure he could make his way through it on his own.

Gary was particularly taken, says Gardner, with the relatively new development of animated GIF files as, on top of everything else, he plugged away developing Black Vinyl's website (which in 2011 moved from blackvinyl.com to shoeswire.com).

BUT ALL THESE COMPONENTS—the studio, the label, the website—were eating up time Shoes wanted to spend making music. "The business made it difficult to get things done," Gary stresses. Jeff adds:

> Despite the fact that we kept putting more and more things on our plate (studio, label, band, manufacturing, distribution, songwriting, touring, etc.), we longed for some relief, to have *someone* take the busywork off of our shoulders so we could concentrate on being a band. *Just* a band.

Klebe and the Murphys had built this framework to support Shoes, but the framework threatened to engulf the creative part of their partnership. "It causes a lot of stress that most bands don't have to deal with," Jeff states—even though they had figured out a way to use their skills to keep their band afloat (and by the Short Order/Black Vinyl era, they'd been doing it for twenty years). "We did well, better than most bands," Gary confirms, "but any partnership is a delicate balance that can be thrown off by external stuff." And the external stuff was becoming harder to work around.

For a while, the expanded Black Vinyl Records functioned fairly well. "We sold tens of thousands of records," Gary estimates. When things started to implode, in the mid-nineties, it was the result of outside factors—not mismanagement of the company. The entire independent music industry was in flux, and the fate of this small label was inextricably entangled in the turmoil: a minor player in the larger scheme of things.

THE PROBLEMS WITH INDEPENDENT distribution arose, perhaps not so surprisingly, from the success of independent music. By the early nineties, the indie scene was flourishing. But as major labels had done in the late seventies, independent labels let their exuberance over strong sales inflate a bubble of overproduction and overspending that inevitably burst, leaving the labels in financial crisis. This complicated process took several years to play out, roughly from 1990 to 1994—almost exactly the gap between Shoes' two new releases of the period, *Stolen Wishes* and *Propeller*.

The first victims of independent music's success were independent record stores. Since the sixties, small record retailers had been the source of new music for the cognoscenti. Often run by enthusiasts who supported local acts and lavished recommendations on their customers, these stores were known as "mom-and-pops" (though they were usually more like pop-and-pops, male-dominated enclaves where guys went to talk to guys about music made by other guys).

The members of Shoes speak fondly of Strawberry Fields in Waukegan, a record store that opened in 1970, while they were still in high school. It was run by an ex-soldier called Bots, who knew all the coolest new music—and just maybe, if he was having a good day, would tell them what to buy. John remembers that buying a record from Strawberry Fields meant taking the smell of the store home—incense? Hashish? He wouldn't have known the difference—an aroma that would linger on the album jacket for days, sometimes. Strawberry Fields was the only store ever to stock *One in Versailles*. When it was pressed up and they'd taken the platter to Bots to see if he'd sell it, he had listened to Shoes' pride and joy with approval. (Indeed, Bots kept John's handmade poster advertising *OIV* on his wall for years.) And when they played *Black Vinyl Shoes* for Bots, gaining his approval, "We thought, 'This is Bots! He likes our record! And he works in a record store, so he really knows!'" Gary recounts with a grin. Bots is thanked on the original liner notes for *Black Vinyl Shoes*.

Most small towns had a Bots, but the presence of such fixtures did not mean their respective record shops were financially secure. In order to buy groceries, meet rent and utilities, maybe even pay their employees, independent stores would primarily purchase product from independent distributors and one-stops, who stocked records from independent labels. This interdependent system was similar to that of the majors, only on a smaller scale: distributors sold units to the record-store owners at a fixed rate, the owners added a little to the price to cover their costs and make a modest profit, and then the consumer paid the end price. Discounts were unusual; no one frequented independent record stores for deals. They went there to find music they couldn't find anyplace else.

The complete collapse of the independent record-store system had been prophesied for so long that by the mid-nineties, it was tempting to dismiss even obvious signs of its erosion. One clear moment of decline occurred in the seventies with the ever-broadening spread of mall-based record-store chains—Musicland/Sam Goody and Listening Booth and Camelot (who had snatched Barry Shumaker from Shoes), for example—which could undercut the prices of independent stores because they could buy in volume. The trend only got worse with the rapid expansion of the deeply discounted "big-box" stores like Target, Best Buy, and Wal-Mart, which started in the 1980s and accelerated during the 1990s. Another disruptive force was the massive independent chain Tower Records, whose rapid expansion in the nineties directly challenged mom-and-pops on their own turf: independent music. (This rapid expansion would eventually drive Tower itself to bankruptcy.) These factors combined to put smaller independent chains and stand-alone record retailers out of business.

Tom Braam managed just such an independent record store in Lake Geneva, Wisconsin. Braam recollects:

> It seems to me we ran out of money about '94. We were typical, and just one of many that had to pack up due to the increase in cost of CDs—from around $8 to about $11—and the chains were pricing them at $9. ... Shipping prices rose around the same time, and the system was being rearranged for a new way of record selling, one in which low cost was the deciding factor in purchasing.
>
> Independent music was where my heart was, but there was no money in it.

Eventually, the carnage would spread upward, but in the mid-nineties, the little guys got it worst. As synthesizer innovator Robert Moog commented in Ben Kettlewell's 2003 book *Electronic Music Pioneers*, when such chains were in financial trouble, "I'm sorry if Tower Records' and [former video rental goliath] Blockbuster's sales plummet. On the other hand, it wasn't that long ago that those megastore chains drove a lot of neighborhood record stores out of business."

With the big-box stores' entrance into the music business, the math of music distribution changed completely. Bill Nowlin, co-founder of Cambridge, Massachusetts-based Rounder Records, a highly-regarded independent roots-music label and regional distributor in this period, emphasizes that the big-box stores were never looking to make money off compact discs:

> Places like Best Buy used CDs as loss leaders. They could afford to lose money on every CD they sold, because the point was never the CD. But if you could pull people in to buy one for $9.99 [as opposed to the typical $14.99 or $15.99 [and some CDs fetched as much as $19.99], they'd stop to look at electronics, which is where the real money was. There was no way for indie record stores, the places with clerks that knew music well, to sell below cost—they simply couldn't afford to.

Though this development would further weaken dedicated record retailers, it generally had little effect on distributors or labels, initially; they merely began shifting their sales from the shrinking pool of specialty record retailers to the big-box stores. One 1990 press release from Black Vinyl Records reports that both Musicland (the national record chain) and Best Buy had started carrying *Stolen Wishes*. For Black Vinyl Records, entrée into the big-box world represented both opportunity and risk. "There was a huge bump in sales," Gary recalls. "Best Buy was ordering a lot of CDs, yet there were a lot of returns, too. They ordered a larger quantity than independent distributors, but gave the discs less of a chance to sell before they returned them."

Still, the indie labels' exuberance over the expanded distribution was understandable: going from a little local store to a national chain meant getting your product to a lot more people. Rounder Records' Nowlin points out that that one good chain deal could buoy a whole company: "Tower [Records] was twenty-five percent of Rounder's business at one point."

With this radical increase in potential sales, Black Vinyl and hundreds of other labels like them overproduced units, just as the majors had done in 1979. Also like the majors in '79, independent labels generally expected payment only after a record was sold; if it just sat on store shelves, it could ultimately be returned for full credit. The distributors had the same deal with the retailers.

Often there was some cap on how long payment could be delayed—thirty days, or sixty, or ninety—but no distributor ever paid Black Vinyl Records on time, according to Gary, and even if a wholesaler did promise to pay up, there was no way of knowing whether Black Vinyl would receive a check or returned product.

Gary tells of Black Vinyl once trying to take a distributor to small-claims court—the threat alone was enough to produce payment. But if threats didn't work, there were very few options available. With another deadbeat wholesaler, Shoes offered to pick up their unsold product themselves in lieu of payment; the distributor in question threatened to have them arrested. He may have owed them money, but as long as he was in possession of the discs, they were his property until he relinquished them. Back in the *Stolen Wishes* days, Jay Whitehouse's vivid threats to get distributors to rectify their debts may have sounded over-the-top, but getting paid or taking returns was the only way to keep going.

Only within the retail record business were CDs an alternate currency, with labels accepting them in lieu of cash. But that currency only held value as long as it had the potential to be sold: that is, turned into *actual* cash. The utility company wasn't about to accept a box of CDs in payment for an electric bill. Therefore, any CD that had been shipped was always a potential loss.

After a brief honeymoon, big-box stores started to sour on independent music. Major labels were busy spiriting away from independent labels any act with money-making potential: why re-ink a contract with Sub Pop when you could sign with David Geffen? (Nirvana had made just this leap.) And Gary thinks there was probably some pushback on the part of major labels against the independents' invasion of mainstream retail space:

> Major labels wanted to get into the big-box stores, and *we* were in the way. ... I assumed the major labels weren't taking too kindly to these independent labels coming into these major chains. Why would you let that happen when you could undercut an independent anytime you want and push them out? We thought all along that major labels were forcing the little guys out.

Because independent labels did not sell to the big-box stores directly, this challenge to their shelf space wasn't clearly seen by the indies right away.

The pressure was felt first by the distributors, who found that at the same time their clients on the label side were ramping up the number of units produced to feed this new big-box market, the new market itself was beginning to withdraw its interest in independents. Best Buy, for example, started stocking fewer CDs across the board, and the ones they did stock tended to be from reliable sellers—established acts from major labels. In-store real estate was precious: taking up shelf space to stock an artist appealing only to a small segment of your customer base was wasteful. As Gary recalls, "Having a bin divider with our name on it at Best Buy was amazing, but that was brief and then it was gone, just like it was for anyone else with less than mega sales."

Given the sweeping demise of small independent record stores, there was no fallback option in this not-quite-Internet era. If the big national chains didn't want independent product, there was no place else for it to go.

So the indie wholesalers started to go under, slowly at first. Jeff remembers it wasn't evident right away that the problem was serious, even though "the landscape seemed to be constantly changing. Distributors were constantly disappearing, or declaring bankruptcy and merging." As long as there was another wholesaler waiting to take their place, labels like Black Vinyl figured they were safe.

In the face of these new economic realities, it appeared to indie distributors as though joining forces might be the only way to survive. To play with the big boys, to get back into the big stores that were increasingly the only game in town, independent wholesalers had to get bigger themselves. "During the nineties, independent distribution changed from primarily a regionally-based network of distributors, that were separate businesses from each other, to a system of very few national distributors competing with one another for labels to distribute," explains former Rounder Records general manager Duncan Browne, who also served as president of Rounder's eventual wholesale operation, Distribution North America.

DNA was formed when Rounder's original distribution arm (REP) started assimilating troubled former competitors in order to survive; its growth was largely unplanned. "Suddenly, we had an office in Kansas City," Bill Nowlin offers as example. "We didn't expect that." The other major national distributor of indie labels was Independent National Distributors, Inc. [INDI], and between them these two companies absorbed financially-troubled regional distributors at a rapid rate. Soon, such mergers became more deliberate, and more widespread: in a March 13, 1993 *Billboard* article, "Changing Boundaries: Indie Distribution Playing by New Rules," Deborah Russell writes, "The past few years have seen an ongoing transition in what was once a territorial industry, defined by geographic boundaries and a set of specific (albeit unwritten) rules [in which] a number of industry leaders push to create a national playing field." Russell uses both DNA and INDI as exemplars of this push.

Shoes were aware of these developments, though it wasn't clear, at this point, what they meant for labels like Black Vinyl. "More and more we started to see distribution become national instead of regional," says Jeff. "But we didn't expect the type of contraction that occurred later in 1994 and beyond," when retailers drastically cut orders to the independent distributors. Gary asserts, "We knew there was a problem. We didn't know what it was."

And as small regional distributors disappeared, the CDs piled in their warehouses met uncertain fates. Some were returned, certainly. But in other cases, the piles would be sold—for pennies per unit—to *another* distributor who would then return them to Black Vinyl for full credit. "We began to see people returning a thousand CDs for credit," Gary recalls, "and then when we checked our database we'd see that they had only ordered five hundred." Shoes ended up, then, essentially spending dollars to buy their pennies back. "We got burned so many times," says Gary.

Being bigger companies, INDI and DNA *did* have more negotiating power with retailers. One important innovation was limiting returns, for example. But the law of unintended consequences kicked in, just as it had in the Crash of '79: if distributors were going to limit returns, retailers were going to order considerably fewer CDs so that they would not get stuck with unsold product.

Despite the complexities of the system, it could, theoretically, have worked for Shoes. In some ways, having one distributor—Shoes had signed on with DNA—made things a lot simpler. It lessened the chances of getting left in the lurch financially—as a larger company, theoretically DNA was more secure—and instead of shipping individual packages to twenty companies, they only had to ship to one (though Black Vinyl Records was still selling directly to consumers as well). "We thought DNA was basically honest," Gary says. "We don't have any hard feelings about them." But now the health of DNA, and the willingness to gamble of that one company, could make or break Black Vinyl Records. It was just like being on a major label, except that Shoes themselves bore all the financial risk.

It was into this all-bets-off landscape that *Propeller* was released.

Stolen Wishes-level sales would validate everything Shoes had done, shoring up both the studio and the label, and allowing them to go on. They were confident about *Propeller*, sure that its grittier aesthetic matched the times, happy with their songwriting and performances.

But it had been so long in production—almost four full years after the completion of *Stolen Wishes*—that the band members were in tough straits financially. Gary, who had been living off irregular freelance gigs and his credit cards, finally decided in desperation that he had to pay himself a salary just before *Propeller* came out. Jeff, who had long been concerned about the unsteady influx of his own income—which depended solely on the ebb and flow of recording clients—went on salary, too. And they gave themselves health insurance.

The band members were reasonably sure everything would be fine. Black Vinyl's most dependable product was Shoes, and they had a new Shoes album to release. Everything hovered, waiting for the cash infusion sure to follow that release.

But when *Propeller* came out in early 1994, the anticipated demand didn't materialize. Retailers were ordering fewer discs, and some were locking out independents altogether, says Gary:

> I remember when *Propeller* was released it was like, "Wait, that's all you want?" And it was apparent, suddenly, that we couldn't get into a lot of retailers; I don't think we got into Best Buy, for example. It very well may be that there were so many independent records coming out that they just didn't have shelf space. They might have had only so many slots for independents, and then they were done.

"And after *Propeller*," Gary says, "things really got tough."

CHAPTER 12

SLIPPING THROUGH YOUR FINGERS (1994-2009)

BUT *PROPELLER* WAS RELEASED—IN early '94—to now-customary near-universal acclaim, with reviewers across the country, primed by the success of *Stolen Wishes* and the alternative-rock movement, lavishing praise on Shoes' new album.

As had happened with *Stolen Wishes*, many write-ups included a précis of the band's history, and nearly all pointed approvingly to the melodies, the harmonies, and the songwriting. Most reviewers acknowledged the apropos fit of Ric Menck and Mike Zelenko as guest drummers (though one reviewer gratuitously identified Zelenko as "the only positive aspect of the vile Material Issue"). Claudia Perry, writing in *The Houston Post*, remarked on *Propeller*'s refreshing maturity:

> Both [Velvet Crush and Material Issue] owe a huge debt to Shoes, who singlehandedly made pop safe for thoughtful adults. ... This record is a must for anyone who's convinced that melody and lyrical coherence have completely headed south during this momentary devotion to grunge and soundbite phrasing. *Propeller* is laden with masterly hooks, breathtaking modulations and adult lyrical content.

Or, as *Goldmine*'s John Borack succinctly (and facetiously) summed it up: "Ho-hum, another incredible Shoes album."

But *Propeller* lacked one bit of press that had measurably altered the landscape for *Stolen Wishes* four years earlier: *Rolling Stone* did not review the record.

It was a blow, without question. Still, plenty of other publications did, and Shoes tried not to be impatient while they anticipated record sales heating up through the spring and summer. But as Gary relates, "We kept waiting for things to kick in—and nothing was happening." They kept busy nevertheless —pushing forward on building the studio and the label—and eventually decided to go on tour late in the year.

THE DRUMMERS SHOES HAD toured with before were not available this time out, so they turned to someone who had been recommended to them repeatedly by their old sound man and friend, Billy "Beet" Richardson: his younger sibling, John. Beet had first mentioned John to Shoes when Skip left for good a decade earlier; John Richardson was still in his teens at that point. John Murphy says that Shoes didn't take Beet's suggestion seriously: "Ah, c'mon. That's your little brother!"

The Richardsons, like Shoes, were native Illinois boys; they'd grown up downstate in Champaign, where John and Gary had gone to college. The younger Richardson had honed his skills as a drummer-for-hire, playing regularly with a number of different acts. By the early nineties, he was working steadily with acclaimed major-label-turned-indie pop-rocker Tommy Keene, and had settled in Keene's home base of North Carolina.

Shoes had first met their future stickman when Richardson and Keene came to see their 1990 show in Washington, D.C. Not long after, when Keene played Chicago's premier showcase club, Metro, the Murphys and Klebe returned the favor. Both Richardson brothers took part in the Keene gig, Beet at the mixing board and John on drums. The members of Shoes, who'd been invited by their old friend, were genuinely impressed by John's drumming; Jeff remembers their group response as, "Wow! That guy can *really* play!"

So when Shoes were planning the *Propeller* shows four years later, they called Richardson. The young drummer was psyched; after all, this gig was something he'd had his eye on for years. However, he didn't say yes right away, according to Gary; the geographic distance between Shoes and Richardson was understandably giving the latter pause. But finally, according to Gary, "He said, 'I'll *make* it work.'"

THE '94 TOUR WAS EVEN MORE stripped-down than the '90 run; in pursuit of a simpler, harder sound, Shoes went back to being a four-piece. The tour was comprised of nine shows over three weeks in December, including a break for Christmas. Booking was handled by the William Morris Agency's Brad Gelfond, who'd been a friend of the band for several years. They began with three dates in the Midwest—kicking off in St. Louis on December 7, then on to Champaign (their old college stomping ground and Richardson's hometown), and last of all Iowa City—before heading out to do five nights on the East Coast: Boston, New York City, Washington, Philadelphia, and Hoboken, New Jersey. Then it was back home to Chicago for the tour's final date, on December 30.

As noted, Shoes had long been aware that what worked best live were their full-on rock tracks, and a revved-up mode of live performance was by now their habit. Since their new disc was a comparative bruiser of an album to begin with, the *Propeller* concerts were particularly headbanging—but in hindsight, the band has some regrets. "It tended to make the shows bombastic," Jeff acknowledges. "It would have been nice to mix it up a bit and do some acoustic or slower tunes, too."

This was, after all, the year that Nirvana's largely acoustic *MTV Unplugged* performance had been a huge hit in the wake of Kurt Cobain's suicide: playing acoustic did not necessarily mean sacrificing rock credibility.

John recalls that in Philadelphia, several fans told him that they'd missed hearing Shoes' more contemplative songs in concert. "They said, 'Next time you come through, play "Karen!" We can take it!'" He muses on the band's scrupulous avoidance of such songs in concert:

> It's a little scary playing acoustic, because you're naked. Shoes is nervous not hiding behind the noise and the distortion: we don't feel comfortable unless all pistons are firing.

Given the band-imposed ban on live ballads—and even some of their midtempo songs were sidelined for the *Propeller* tour, according to John—the role of the drummer as driving force in concert took on special heft. And John Richardson was an excellent fit.

Klebe and the Murphys all credit Richardson with helping them improve their live performance by driving them a little harder than they were accustomed to be driven. "A good drummer is seventy percent of playing live," John Murphy asserts, "and Johnny is a *great* drummer." Richardson dealt with Shoes' ever-present discomfort with stage banter by powering on to the next song without a break (much as their idols Cheap Trick had always done). "Johnny just plowed away, which we liked," Gary observes. "A good drummer will put a band at ease, and he did."

They'd never really experienced that ease while performing live, so Shoes felt positive about the *Propeller* concerts once they got past the beginning of the run; Richardson recollects the band being stiff at first, and easily thrown off by minor issues like monitor levels and feedback, which are common on the road. After over four years away from the road, Shoes seemed to have forgotten how to push through those issues in performance. "Technical difficulty rattled them," the drummer says. "If you don't play for a long time, that's what happens." Indeed, Richardson adds, as the tour progressed, Shoes became smoother, sharper, more confident: "By the time they got to Chicago, they were *smoking*. They had done ten shows in a row, and they were in a groove." And it was that Chicago show, at Metro's compact, grittier sister club Double Door, which ended up immortalized on Shoes' first full-length live CD, 1995's *Fret Buzz*.

THEY HAD DECIDED, BEFORE the *Propeller* tour started, to record the performances with an eye toward a possible live disc. Jeff explains part of Shoes' rationale: "We thought it would be a bit novel for 'the band that rarely tours' to release a live album." As part of their tour prep, Jeff continues, Shoes assembled a digital recording unit to capture their shows:

> We decided to rent two machines—a mic splitter and a small 16-track mixer—and mount it all into a rack case, to take out and record shows on tour. All of the drums were on eight channels on one machine; three vocal mics, bass, two guitars, and two room mics were on the other.

Jeff notes that, in order for the two decks to sync later, they had to be formatted before each show, something for which there was scant time on the road. (Shoes usually arrived at the club just in time for sound check.) Gary adds that any small mistake in the setup process would make the recording unusable: "And the odds were, any night, that there would be *something* wrong."

So Shoes weren't absolutely counting on a stellar live disc, seeing as they were leaving everything to luck and imperfect technology. It was "just a possibility," Gary says.

And eight gigs in, they still didn't have a usable live recording; none of the shows leading up to Double Door "took." What made the difference at the closing performance in Chicago, Shoes agree, was simply time.

"When we performed at the Double Door, we had the luxury of its being close to home," Jeff points out, "so we could set everything up well in advance of the show." Shoes even had time to record a new song—Gary's brooding "In Harm's Way," written at the tail end of the *Propeller* sessions—during sound check. In addition, the room was bigger, and the ambient P.A. system much better, than they had been dealing with during the tour's earlier dates. "That surprised me a little," Gary remarks. "I would have thought that the East Coast would have the best P.A.'s, but Chicago's blew them out of the water."

So Shoes hit the right night, and the right venue, and even their own exacting technical standards, to make their first full concert CD. Barring the employment of a professional recording crew with a mobile studio, this was about as good as they were going to get it.

The band members were happy with the rough mixes of *Fret Buzz*, but didn't rush to release it. Black Vinyl Records was busy enough: *Propeller* had dropped the previous spring, and June had seen the release of the Spongetones' *Beat & Torn*, a CD combining their early releases ('82's *Beat Music* and '84's *Torn Apart*).

By the time *Fret Buzz* was mixed in early '95, Black Vinyl Records was ready to release the Spongetones' first album of original material in four years, *Textural Drone Thing*. Jeff was producing the Critics and 92 Degrees, Chicago bands that had been Short Order clients since the early nineties—both artists had appeared on the *Yuletunes* compilation—and the fruit of those sessions, the Critics' *Braintree* and 92 Degrees' self-titled album, were also issued by Black Vinyl in 1995. So there was no real hurry about getting *Fret Buzz* out; as Gary drolly remarks, "It wasn't going to be *Frampton Comes Alive*."

STILL, WHEN *FRET BUZZ* WAS released in the summer of '95, the live disc received wide-ranging praise for the aggro edge it revealed on Shoes' sound, each song functioning not just as a re-creation, but as a re-interpretation. The reviewer from *New York Press* approvingly stated that "every Shoes song here gains renewed value, sounding like its own deadly flipside." Brett Milano, writing in the *Boston Phoenix*, observed:

> [*Fret Buzz*] shows that Shoes aren't just sensitive, lovelorn pop types; they're bad-ass rockers as well, and their textured guitar sound is as close to Smashing Pumpkins as it is to Badfinger. Not really a greatest-hits set, these twelve songs (including a new one) draw from the band's more aggressive side, and it matters little that they were originally released over [a period of] fifteen-odd years. ... The live Shoes are just as polished as the studio Shoes, but with a harder kick to match the emotive tunes.

Shoes welcomed both the redefinition of their sound and the reviewers' recognition of the contemporary nature of their music.

But the summer release of *Fret Buzz* had a strictly practical purpose, too: it continued the steady flow of Black Vinyl product to record stores. As Jeff details, "It helped beef up our catalog and push things through the distribution pipeline."

Said pipeline was, of course, as leaky as ever. At that time, the only recourse an indie label had with a slow-paying distributor was refusing to ship new product until the last round had been paid for or returned; without new product to withhold, that leverage disappeared. Gary says Shoes saw *Fret Buzz* as "something to put out to fill the new-release space between *Propeller* and the next studio record."

Like *Shoes Best*, *Fret Buzz* didn't just round up some of the band's most-beloved songs; it also gave a taste of their new music to come, a promise for the future. "In Harm's Way" filled the same transitional role for *Fret Buzz* as "Love Is Like a Bullet" had done on *Shoes Best*, pointing toward what was in the offing.

IN JANUARY 1996, SHOES HEADLINED a Black Vinyl Records showcase at Chicago's Metro. Pulling together a handful of bands they were working with at the studio and the label, they presented Black Vinyl Records for the first time as a cohesive, multi-artist entity. "Black Vinyl Records Night" featured effervescent popsters 92 Degrees and the Critics, along with the soulful Nicholas Tremulis Band, opening for Shoes.

They did some press interviews as the show loomed, focusing on the label as a path to keeping the band alive. Speaking to Rick Reger of the *Chicago Tribune*, Gary said:

> The fact that we have our own studio and label has a lot to with our survival. ... It's been difficult to survive on our own, but we've diversified and become self-sufficient.

Jeff, speaking to Dan Kening of the suburban *Daily Herald*, had a slightly grimmer perspective:

> According to Jeff Murphy, the band constantly worries about finding enough time for Shoes.

"Every day we think about that," he said. "Shoes is obviously why we started all this, and it's what we truly love. ... With us it all came out of necessity. We needed to have a record label to get our own records out. Then we built a studio because we needed one to record our music in. Both eventually became their own businesses and are full-time jobs in themselves.

"Actually, I hate the music *business*. I hate the business end of the music industry. But I love making music and creating a song out of nothing. It's like having a child: you're creating something that is exclusively yours and that no one else can create. That's the joy of writing a song."

In a *Chicago Tribune* review of the Black Vinyl Records showcase, Mark Caro pointed favorably to the influence of John Richardson, "who knocks the bejesus out of his instrument, thus emboldening a relatively refined studio outfit. ... His hammering on the syncopated rhythms of 'Feel the Way That I Do' was so hard and precise that you wanted to dance around like a hyperactive robot."

Caro commented, too, on Shoes' "unassuming stage presence" and their "powerhouse guitar riffs." In a shift from the shows a year earlier, however, the band did not depend solely on their high-octane material. They also included some ballads; Caro described "welcome changes in dynamics with a shift to acoustic guitars for several songs and a violin accompaniment [by string player Jenny Scarlato] for 'In My Mind.'"

IN EARLY 1996, AROUND THE SAME time as the Black Vinyl showcase, Shoes were interviewed by their old friend John Borack, who was profiling Black Vinyl Records for *Goldmine*'s annual indie-label issue. In the article, Shoes are upbeat about their label's path, remarking on the upswing in new releases and envisioning a meaningful role for themselves within the alt-pop community; Gary is quoted saying, "We figure that there's a genuine need to have a home for good pop bands."

But the article points out that Black Vinyl was defining "pop" pretty broadly, releasing, for example, Nick Tremulis's collaboration with Beat poet Gregory Corso, *Bloody Show:* one reviewer called the record, "an earthy, unusual integration of spoken word and rock 'n' roll. ... Think Chicago power pop (not surprising, considering that the album was mixed by Jeff Murphy of Shoes), with some Nick Cave and Kim Fowley thrown in. ... The result ... integrates poetry, musical interludes, pop numbers and hard-edged guitar-driven songs in a unique fashion."

Still, according to *Goldmine*, Black Vinyl and Short Order were primarily focused on their own genre: Fun w/Atoms and Swingset Police, both of whom Borack mentions as having projects in progress, were artists much closer to Shoes' own style. And as always, the focus came back to Shoes. "'It inspires me to hear what groups like the Critics and 92 Degrees are doing,' says Gary Klebe. 'It makes *me* want to keep doing it.'"

Nevertheless, the complications of running Black Vinyl Records were already having a zero-sum effect—though Shoes were, at that point, playing it off to Borack as a wryly humorous inconvenience:

> "It's ironic," laughs Gary. "We originally came up with this endeavor to help Shoes, but now it's more difficult to make *our* records!" "That's the main reason why there's so much time between Shoes releases," agrees Jeff. "We spend so much time on the business end that we're left with very little time to write and record."

Shoes put up a brave front in the *Goldmine* feature, focusing on the benefits of being independent—as Gary remarks, "We don't have to deal with the trends of the [Top 40] chart; we've already established what it is we're doing, and we're very focused."

But in order for their system to work, pop—Shoes' kind of pop—would need a commercial resurgence, and soon. As Gary tells Borack, "We know that pop music is not in the public eye right now, but we're hoping things are going to change."

Behind their hope for a pop renaissance was a very real gamble: Shoes had staked their livelihoods upon one *Stolen Wishes*-sized record a year. Without that level of sales, the shaky foundation of their overextended businesses—which they took such pains to conceal in the Borack interview—would crumble.

Good creative partners, they all agree, do not necessarily make good business partners, but the band members were caught in this high-stakes game together. Within six months, out of funds and stretched to the limit, Shoes had reached the breaking point.

FOR THE PAST YEAR OR SO, Jeff had been performing extracurricular live gigs. He and longtime Shoes compatriot Herb Eimerman played acoustic sets pretty regularly in Waukegan at Madison Avenue, a bar owned by a friend of theirs. Originally, they billed themselves as Two White Guys Strummin', but the pair soon adopted another moniker, one a teenaged, pre-Beatles Lennon and McCartney had used when performing a raft of acoustic gigs as a duo: the Nerk Twins.

Eimerman's first band, Hot Mama Silver—a sturdy Chicago blues-rock group that supported the likes of metal gods Rush in the early seventies—had opened for Shoes at the Zion Leisure Center in 1981. Another Eimerman band, Roc Sinatra, had been an early Short Order client, and as a solo act he'd cut two records at the studio; he'd also appeared on the *Yuletunes* compilation. All the members of Shoes were friendly with Eimerman, who'd lent them several instruments during the *Propeller* sessions.

The Nerk Twins started, Jeff says, as a pleasant diversion, "a way to do some acoustic stuff and a chance to play out without the complications of amps and a big P.A." The focus was on wood-bodied axes and tight harmonies, and as Jeff describes:

> Those gigs were baptism by fire; nothing but you and an acoustic guitar, with no drums or distorted electric wash to hide behind. I think it made me a better player; it ended up helping my confidence a lot.

Murphy and Eimerman started out performing mostly covers—the Beatles, Tom Petty, the Everly Brothers—and then began bringing songs they'd written separately to the project. Before too long, Jeff and Herb were composing together for their new band, and their first collaboration became the title track from the Nerk Twins' 1997 album, *Either Way*.

The Nerk Twins' tunes tended to be more lighthearted and playful in tone than Shoes' songs. Eimerman brought in five of them ("In the Middle of the Night," "Stay Away," "I Love Jamaica," "Cast in Stone," and "What Does It Take?"), and Jeff contributed an equal amount ("I'm Broke," "Dream for Love," "On & On & On," "2 Women," and "Ugly"). Plus, there were three collaborations ("Either Way," "I Still Don't Love You Anymore," and "She Said"). By spring '96, the Nerk Twins were recording at Short Order.

Nerk sessions were fast-paced, compared to Shoes' usual meticulous recording process. Coming in with more-or-less finished songs (as opposed to writing in the studio, as Shoes had long done) saved time for the Nerk Twins at the outset. Their sessions were guided as much by gut instinct as craft, partly as a result of Eimerman's outside-job-constrained schedule: he would drop in for a few hours and lay down some tracks, leaving Jeff to work his magic alone. But the comparative haste was a conscious artistic choice, too. Jeff says that they intentionally tried to limit each song to three recording sessions, though some were done more quickly and others more slowly:

> It was all accomplished very efficiently and without a lot of discussion or debating. We generally accepted whatever idea the other guy brought in and simply reacted to it. It was a low-pressure, fun project, top to bottom.

As for Eimerman, he pronounces *Either Way* "the most fun I've ever had doing a recording project."

And the Nerk Twins went beyond a working relationship: as both Herb and Jeff were married, the Murphys and the Eimermans socialized frequently. Their wives became good friends, forming an a cappella group called The Kracker Jack Pearls; they dressed in vintage clothing and performed forties standards at nursing homes and senior centers, eventually meriting a *Chicago Tribune* write-up.

JOHN AND GARY WATCHED THE development of the Nerk Twins first with mild amusement, then with increasing alarm.

For one thing, both of them had new Shoes songs ready to record, hoping to get moving quickly on a new album. Each had finished the *Propeller* sessions with unfinished demos—Gary's "In Harm's Way," and John's "Rugged Terrain" and "What Never Was." ("2 Women," a song of Jeff's about a comically mercurial romantic partner, was also left over from the *Propeller* sessions; it ended up on the Nerk Twins album.) These "extras" meant that, at least in theory, Shoes had a head start on their next record—but now the studio, financially squeezed anyway, was being used gratis for the Nerk Twins. It was hard not to see this as Jeff cutting John and Gary out, stepping off on his own in this new direction without having consulted them (though of course, they acknowledged he didn't need their permission). And all these individual elements—even more troubling in the aggregate—made it look as if Shoes itself was in peril.

For his part, Jeff understood the side project made his bandmates nervous. He tried to ameliorate the situation, he says, by inviting them into the process: during the recording of *Either Way,* Jeff asked Gary and John to sing background on a jangly, infectious paean to off-again, on-again relationships entitled, "I Still Don't Love You Anymore":

> I wanted to include them because I value them and didn't want them to feel left out, or that it was any threat to them. [The Nerk Twins] was fun and I, perhaps foolishly, hoped that everyone could get along and encourage each other in our little musical world.

John and Gary did agree to supply background vocals, largely keeping their concerns to themselves. But while Nerk recording continued through the spring of '96, tensions rose. Sure, the three Shoes had sung backup together for some other groups—like the Sneetches and Swingset Police—but those projects never threatened Shoes itself. This was palpably different.

Still, both John and Gary attended Nerk Twins gigs, despite their reservations. "As fans of Jeff's music—which we definitely are—we thought the Nerk Twins were great," John stresses. "But in terms of what it meant for Shoes, well, that really wasn't clear." John expressed his concerns to Jeff several times, all the while catching nearly every Nerk Twins show. Gary went to fewer performances, and refused to offer a critical opinion beyond his belief that this time-consuming side project was a distraction from the new record that Shoes Inc. sorely needed, and that Jeff was "wasting his songs" on his outside concern.

THE FRICTION AMONG THEM WAS exacerbated by Short Order Recorder's and Black Vinyl Records' significant financial difficulties. As with any marriage, money problems were a constant stressor.

Short Order's woes were largely driven by the recording industry's technological developments.

During the first decade or so of the transition from vinyl LP to the compact disc, analog studios were stretched, but as long as they could digitally master the analog music they produced, they could stay in business. Astutely, Shoes had purchased digital mastering equipment as part of their 1990 studio upgrade.

The larger problem was what followed the 1991 advent of ADAT (Alesis Digital Audio Tape) technology; the digital tape easily allowed for as many as eight channels of information (twice what Shoes had available for *Black Vinyl Shoes*). Throughout the early nineties, the subsequent rapid development of digital recording equipment and techniques meant that more and more artists began to regard the technical act of recording as something they could do entirely for themselves, without leaving the comfort of their home. Major recording studios lost business not to each other, and not to fully digital studios, but to ADAT-equipped bedrooms and basements. The scathingly articulate, blazingly furious Alanis Morissette's monster 1993 album *Jagged Little Pill*, for example—the nineties' top-selling album—was recorded at home, exclusively on ADAT.

Shoes' long-past conquest of the humble TEAC-3340S in Jeff's living room, and the lengthy learning curve that had taken up so much of their lives since—the punching-in and overdubbing and ping-ponging and mixing down, on an increasingly sophisticated phalanx of recording equipment—was now moot.

Primordial fidelity and clarity were literally just a click away—and the result was a rapid amateurization of recording. Professional studio engineers found themselves in the once-unthinkable position of having to argue for their own usefulness. Jeff himself proffers the compelling analogy, "You can go and buy a dentist's drill, but do you really want to work on your own teeth?"--and indeed, when bands booked time at Short Order, they were there not for a generic recording space, but specifically to work with Jeff. And if they arrived and found a second engineer instead of Jeff Murphy himself, they'd be disappointed. This, however, placed a burden on Jeff, who was still trying to live something like a normal life as a family man.

While small studios like Short Order felt the ADAT fallout first, the loss of business to home recordists has only increased. Even bigger-ticket, more-established recording facilities have closed their doors: 2010 saw the end both of London's fabled Olympic Studios (the Rolling Stones, the Beatles, Cream, and the Yardbirds all recorded there) and the Butch Vig-founded Smart Studios in Madison, Wisconsin.

Short Order's business had always come partly from artists seeking Jeff, and partly from locals looking to make a bargain demo. Zion-based post-grunge duo Local H, for example—whose Island Records releases made some noise in the late nineties—did their first demos at Short Order. But as Shoes' studio business slowed in the wake of ADAT, so did their label business, again due largely to factors outside their control.

Independent distribution now rested in the hands of two large companies: INDI and DNA. But almost immediately after the September '94 formation of Distribution North America—now Shoes' only distributor—the problems began. "There wasn't really a 'golden age' with DNA," Gary recalls. "We knew there was trouble from the beginning." Personnel frequently shuffled between sales and marketing, as well as among DNA's scattered corporate centers. Some offices, like the one in Kansas City that Bill Nowlin had never expected, were closed altogether, as *Billboard* writer Chris Morris noted in his March 11, 1995 "Declaration of Independents" column. The slow-moving crisis took a couple of years to unfold: DNA president Duncan Browne stepped down at the end of 1996, a year during which majority-stakeholder status in DNA had turned over three times. DNA righted itself—temporarily—under the hand of business-manager-turned-general-manager Jim Colson, and by 1998, the whole independent distribution industry had recovered a little. Morris's *Billboard* cover story from February 14, 1998 stated that the "worst is over": "The U.S. independent record industry is apparently beginning to see some light at the end of the tunnel after nearly two years of harsh fortunes." Not everyone survived, though; the once-formidable INDI, for example, had filed Chapter 11 the previous July.

For Black Vinyl Records, too, the recovery was not fast enough.

Repercussions from the independent-distribution crisis were becoming harder to evade, even for small labels; maybe *especially* for small labels like Black Vinyl, which had almost no financial cushion. "The returns started coming in droves," Gary says simply. A larger operation might have been able to shrug off the fact that expected payments were coming in not as cash, but as returned product—but every cent counted at Black Vinyl.

Back in the summer of '96, Shoes—who couldn't foresee the end of the crisis—knew that the only way to stay afloat was to release something, pronto. They kicked around ideas—release some of their old demos? John thought that was a good idea. An album of friends doing Shoes covers? No, wouldn't that seem arrogant?—but they couldn't agree on any course of action. Clearly, there *had* to be another Shoes album.

IN A PAINED MEETING, Jeff announced, "This thing is going *down*—I don't know when, but it's going down." He reminded his bandmates the studio was $25,000 in debt at that point, and there was no sign of that situation improving in the short term.

But Jeff went on to inform them he'd found a solution to their seemingly intractable fiscal woes: he had arranged for a couple of Short Order clients to buy out John and Gary. With an influx of cash, the studio could stay active; what they had built together could go on. It would only be a couple thousand dollars each, Jeff cautioned, but Shoes would be out from under that crushing weight. However, Gary and John inferred that under the new management, Shoes wouldn't be able to use the studio anymore, except as paying customers.

Gary and John reacted angrily, stunned that Jeff would go so far as to negotiate with specific people for specific amounts without even consulting them. Jeff seemed shocked at *their* shock, according to John and Gary, but they point out that, while Jeff was primarily in charge of running the show in the upstairs studio, the whole operation was legally owned jointly by all three. Jeff counters:

> It makes sense to me now that they were upset by the offer, but frankly, Shoes never recorded in Short Order Recorder after mixing *Fret Buzz*, and didn't use the studio again after we did the compiling for *As Is* in mid-1996. It seemed like the studio was going to waste.

Jeff may have thought that he was doing the band a favor in removing the financial albatross from their necks, but from John and Gary's perspective, an offer to buy them out—especially under these conditions—seemed a clear indication that Jeff thought Shoes was over.

Besides which, Gary stresses, though Shoes were not actively recording as a group, he, at least, was using the studio to write, much as he had always done. He wasn't necessarily happy with what he was writing—the band's difficulties were having a decided impact on his creative process—but Gary *was* working on new Shoes material.

He was dealing with profound issues outside the band as well: his father—whose health had never really bounced back from his 1979 illness that had brought Gary back early from England—was dying. The two sources of distress compounded each other, and months after Jerry Klebe's October 1996 death, Gary would accept a part-time role in the specialty-retail business his father and brother had co-founded.

But back in the summer of '96, that transition had not yet occurred. He was still working at Black Vinyl Records full-time; even his freelance architecture work had fallen by the wayside.

On the evening of the band conference, though, it was the crisis in Shoes that took the forefront. John remembers the meeting going on for hours, until finally he looked at Gary and said, "So, I guess you and I just have to decide what *we're* going to do now."

Jeff protested that they were intentionally misunderstanding him, that he was only trying to separate the band—which would go on—from the businesses, which would (of necessity) change. But neither of his bandmates believed him.

Gary went to his parents' house after the meeting, sat by his father's bed, and told the dying man that Shoes had broken up.

Jeff realized almost immediately that reducing everything Shoes had done to a simple financial transaction was a grievous mistake. He still believed that while his offer may have been naïve, and possibly autocratic, it was not intentionally mean-spirited. And according to his bandmates, when Jeff saw how it pained them—his older brother and his close friend—he did not bring up the deal again. Neither did Gary or John. The buyout never came to pass.

Shoes continued to seek answers to their dilemma, but one decision was obvious: Even the regular paychecks they'd allowed themselves to draw had to stop at this point (though Jeff continued to get paid, irregularly, for engineering at Short Order).

By the time Shoes' rarities compilation *As Is* was released in the fall of 1996, Jeff and Gary had each taken outside jobs to make ends meet, though both were only employed part-time—continuing to spend the majority of their working hours keeping Shoes' adjunct businesses going as best they could.

As Is WAS A FUNDRAISER AIMED squarely at diehard Shoes fans. It combined the band's two fledgling albums—*One in Versailles* and *Bazooka*, often mentioned in interviews, yet never heard by any but the most tenacious Shoes collectors—along with a second disc of outtakes, demos, and even studio shenanigans from the madcap, Dashut-directed *Tongue Twister* sessions.

Jeff observes that in releasing *As Is*, Shoes were inspired, as they so often had been before, by the Beatles:

> My recollection was that, following *The Beatles Anthology* [an exhaustive three-volume compilation released on CD and vinyl in 1995 and 1996], we realized that outtakes and rare tracks might be of interest to some of our ardent fans.

John notes that *The Beatles Anthology* pointed up a change in the music-loving zeitgeist. "It seemed like people were more interested in alternate versions of well-known songs, and so were willing to accept rougher mixes," he says. "Certainly that was true on *Anthology*." Volume 1 (released in November 1995) and Volume 2 (released in March '96) contained a variety of fascinating outtakes, from false starts on "One after 909" and "Eight Days a Week," to three separate versions of "Strawberry Fields Forever." John describes having been particularly struck by an alternate take on "Tomorrow Never Knows" ("It had a different riff," he recalls) and demos for the *White Album* done at George Harrison's house. These displayed previously unknown facets of their idols.

Jeff asserts that they were trying to loosen up Shoes' serious-artists image with this double disc, as well:

> *As Is* helped to show a lighter, more humorous side of Shoes. Because I was free at the studio on days that I didn't have a session, I was able to choose from hours and hours and hours of tapes. I listened to most everything we ever did.

From that substantial trove, Jeff culled a couple dozen songs to bring back to his bandmates. Some were never-heard gems that had unfortunately slipped through the cracks; others they'd never *meant* anyone to hear. Unveiling these more primitive tracks on *As Is* ran counter to every instinct Shoes had, but they tried to adjust to letting the ragged edges show.

The winnowed collection of final tracks spanned over twenty years, from the embryonic *Heads or Tails* to the tail end of the *Propeller* sessions; there were tentative early experiments and comical tape loops. Gary's "Jet Set," buried since August 1979, finally saw the light of day (albeit as a demo; the Mike Stone-produced version was and is still lost), as did a practically prehistoric eight-track attempt ("Ever Again") and three songs from the aborted soundtrack to *The Dirt-Bike Kid* ("Lickety-Split," "Lucky Tail," and "Victorious"). Also making the cut were selections from outside compilations and tribute albums, including "I Miss You" from *Yellow Pills: Best of American Pop! Volume 1*, a 1993 CD compiled by St. Louis writer Jordan Oakes' celebrated pop fanzine *Yellow Pills*; and Shoes' cover of "Words of Love" from the 1989 Buddy Holly tribute, *Every Day Is a Holly Day*, both previously unreleased by Shoes. Rounding out *As Is* are alternate and demo versions of John's "Feel the Way That I Do" (with an additional guitar intro by John), "Too Late," "Karen" (an acoustic take, with preliminary lyrics), "Tomorrow Night," and Gary's scuffed-up interpretation of John's "A Thing of the Past."

The band members gathered at Short Order late that summer and drank in Shoes' recorded history, reliving the moments, laughing uproariously, and debating each other about the validity of certain tracks' inclusion. Jeff says that the particular Shoe who wrote a particular song tended to be the one most hesitant about its inclusion; he remarks that the authors of "Black and Blue from You," "My Husband's Home," and "I Wanna Hide" each had to be reassured by his bandmates that these tracks should join the party.

There were also times when one band member would put his foot down over something he absolutely did not want to see on *As Is*. John was Gibraltar-like with regard to the "screwing around on tape" from 1973 called "Lovely Angie": "It's *not* a song." (And John prevailed; "Lovely Angie," discussed in chapter one, is *not* among the fifty-two tracks on *As Is*.)

It was a healing process.

All songs on the outtakes release were framed, as previously noted, by non-musical *vérité* snippets from the *Tongue Twister* sessions. These include lots of laughter and horsing around, as well as fiddling with tape speeds, looping verbal glitches, and other playful aural snapshots of the recording process.

Originally, the band had considered punctuating *Tongue Twister*'s tracks with these bits and pieces; in fact, they'd been collected for that purpose, though the concept was ultimately scrapped. Still, Shoes got a kick out of the fun-fragments reel, and had kept it around for possible future use.

Gary says that the band members "were really happy and excited to be putting the outtakes disc together," and that "selecting them as a group was the best part of the project." The inclusion of *One in Versailles* and *Bazooka*, he says, was more specifically for hardcore fans: "Over the years, so many people had asked us about those records that we knew they'd be disappointed if we left them out." Jeff points out that these two albums appear on *As Is* in reverse chronological order, "because we wanted to ease people into the primitive nature of those recordings, and we knew that *Bazooka* was a little closer to what people would think of as our sound than *One in Versailles*."

Once the musical decisions had been made, the production process turned to graphics. Shoes ransacked their cabinets of band slides, their parents' houses, and their baby books to find pictures for the CD booklet. John wrote the liner notes, requesting input from his bandmates—but their contributions, he says, tended to be terse and factual rather than descriptive. Thus, the text illuminating individual songs varies widely; some notes merely state the rough time frame of the composition and recording—Gary's "Black and Blue from You," for example, notes only that it was "written just after the completion of *Silhouette* (1984), it got set aside and, unfortunately, overlooked when preparing for *Stolen Wishes* in 1988"—while others relate full background stories and divulge inspirations (John explains that "I Wanna Hide" owes its genesis to Cheap Trick's "Ballad of Richard Speck" (the disturbing original title of "The Ballad of TV Violence") from Trick's eponymous debut album.

Shoes wanted to make *As Is* an impressive package, and *The Beatles Anthology* was again their model. Even the double-sided jewel box and insert booklet mimicked the Beatles album's presentation. Each individual copy of the 1,200-unit limited run was numbered, and the booklet for each disc was signed by John, Jeff, and Gary. At $45, *As Is* bore a relatively hefty price tag, but Shoes had gone to great lengths to make sure fans got their money's worth.

When *As Is* was finished, Shoes did not market it in the usual way; they didn't send the disc to reviewers, nor did they solicit media features. Instead, says Jeff, "We sent out postcards to our mailing list and posted the release information on our website. That was the extent of its promotion." *As Is* sold at a reasonable clip, given these constraints, and did raise a little bit of cash to keep Shoes' operation afloat temporarily.

BUT THEIR ECONOMIC SITUATION in general was not getting any better. With fewer recording clients at Short Order, and with Distribution North America in trouble, the legs were cut out from under the businesses Shoes had built themselves. However, accustomed to making things work through sheer grit, they resisted acknowledging that reality for as long as possible. "Anyone from the outside could see what was happening, but we couldn't at the time," admits John.

When Shoes' first proprietary legal arrangement, Black Vinyl's manufacturing and distribution deal with the Spongetones, expired in 1996, they simply let it go—shipping the Spongetones all their remaining CD booklets, graphics, and marketing materials, just as Elektra had once done with them.

Shoes also started extricating themselves from the other acts whose records they were selling: artists like 20/20 (their fellow veterans of the Crash of '79); alt-country-pop wizard Bill Lloyd; and Short Order client and friend Leroy Bocchieri, who had accompanied Shoes on their '90 tour. Black Vinyl Records wasn't releasing anything new, but the label continued to sell and market the discs on other imprints for which it had taken responsibility.

There were still some recording clients, of course. Tommy Keene, for example—encouraged by their mutual friend John Richardson—recorded the majority of his Matador Records album *Isolation Party* at Short Order in late 1997. Black Vinyl Records had ongoing business arrangements, too, though the label was only administering the remainder of those contracts over the last half of the nineties.

In the summer of 1997, death touched Shoes from a completely unexpected corner. Jeff took a call at the studio one day from an insurance company looking for John. Their mother was listed as the beneficiary on the life insurance policy of John Michael Murphy, who had died of sepsis—twenty-five years earlier. "I never developed that close of a bond with him, so I'm kinda cold in my feelings about him," John says. "I mean, he left her, and us, in quite a state."

The Nerk Twins' album, *Either Way*, was released on Leroy Bocchieri's Broken Records imprint in 1997 as well. It sold out two pressings, "and when they were gone, they were gone," says Jeff. (Sealed copies of the CD were fetching as much as $150 on eBay in 2011.) The duo continued to perform irregularly through the rest of the nineties. John played out too, with friends as well as Black Vinyl and Short Order clients: he did a show with Swingset Police and sat in a few times with the 45s, a cover band assembled by the Critics' Marty Winer. Gary stayed out of the spotlight.

But it would be naïve to think that the wounds of '96 had lost their sting for all concerned.

IT HAD BEEN A LONG DECADE. By 1999, Shoes were profoundly mired in the stresses of daily living, unable to see past their own provincial boundaries, their personal scars. But then they were reminded that another world was still out there, a cosmopolitan realm in which they had respect and stature.

The alternative-pop underground was still thriving, and there, Shoes were nigh-legendary elder statesmen. And at the turn of the millennium, two important entities—the creations of two longtime supporters of the band—confirmed Shoes' stature.

One was the International Pop Overthrow Festival, at which they performed in 1999. The other was the multi-band tribute CD *Shoe Fetish*, compiled during 2000 and released on the independent Parasol label in 2001. And the recognition afforded by both IPO and *Shoe Fetish* helped Shoes move past their sundry predicaments. It offered them some perspective on their experiences, helping them remember that what Shoes had done was important, and had a measurable impact on a generation of music fans.

IN 1998, CALIFORNIAN DAVID BASH inaugurated his International Pop Overthrow Festival in Los Angeles. An outgrowth of the strictly L.A.-based Poptopia festival, IPO was intended to extend Poptopia's geographic reach: Bash says he "wanted to bring the worldwide pop scene under one umbrella." In a 2000 interview with the *Los Angeles Times*, Bash stated, "I had an epiphany. ... It was *Field of Dreams* thinking—if you hold it, bands will come." He has succeeded; the festival has expanded rapidly since its inception, adding new venues almost annually: in 2012, IPO was staged in fifteen cities.

International Pop Overthrow has played a pivotal role in establishing the underground pop movement as a recognized community. "Besides uniting a bunch of pop bands, I wanted to unite a bunch of pop *fans*," says Bash. "The people who were coming were people who were really, really into it, but they didn't necessarily know a whole lot of other people were into it, too." One participant, speaking to the *Los Angeles Times*, called it "a family reunion of a family that had never met before."

For his second festival, in 1999, Bash convinced Shoes to travel to Los Angeles to perform at IPO. And in a sold-out show at venerable Hollywood rock club The Troubadour on July 30, Shoes closed the night. Though IPO sets are customarily limited to thirty minutes, Bash bestowed exceptional status on Shoes, who played a blistering hour-plus. They were introduced by Bash, who called Shoes "the greatest band walking the face of the earth today." The crowd, one attendee recalls, was high-spirited and loud, and many had brought records for the band members to sign afterward.

Bash describes booking Shoes as a triumph for his then-year-old festival. "It really showed me what IPO could be—we'd gotten a *legend* of the power-pop scene," Bash enthuses.

And for the band, International Pop Overthrow was a reminder that, outside of Zion, away from the frustrations of the studio and the label and the barely-eking-out-a-living, Shoes mattered. One reviewer related how "Der Bashmeister called them back for encore after encore, to the delight of the assembled pop enthusiasts."

Shoes played IPO again in Chicago in 2003.

THE 2001 TRIBUTE ALBUM *SHOE FETISH* was the second encouraging development at this stage of Shoes' saga. The brainchild of John Borack, the album gathered together pop luminaries, longtime friends of Shoes, and relative unknowns to interpret twenty-one Shoes songs: some as dead-on recreations, some as radical retoolings.

Ironically, Borack had joked with the band—about the unlikelihood of just such a project—years earlier. In 1992, interviewing Shoes for *Yellow Pills*, Borack had brought up the subject of extant covers of Shoes songs—specifically, British mod trio Squire's upbeat interpretation of "Boys Don't Lie" from their 1984 EP *September Gurls*, Silent Movies' straightforward 1985 reading of "She Satisfies," and perhaps most oddly, a rumored cover of "Love Is Like a Bullet" by Peter Noone (aka Herman of British Invasion combo Herman's Hermits). In his article, Borack somewhat facetiously ventures, "Maybe someday you guys will have your own tribute album!" To which Jeff replies, "Count me a skeptic!"

Tribute albums were still relatively rare in 1992, though not unheard-of: (Shoes, of course, had covered "Words of Love" for the Holly tribute in 1989.) But as the nineties wore on, such compilations were on the rise, says Borack—Badfinger, the Hollies, and the Raspberries all had their work reinterpreted by contemporary artists in that decade—and Borack continued to cogitate on the idea. "Tribute albums shine a spotlight on the artist again; they make it possible to listen with fresh ears," he says. Borack's conviction never wavered that Shoes' sterling songwriting would make them prime candidates for the treatment. The band members had discussed it among themselves, as well. (John recalls that Jim Ellison wanted to redo "Too Late" as a piano ballad.) So when Borack formally approached Shoes about soliciting tracks for their own tribute disc, they were ready to forge ahead.

Borack knew quite a few artists through his work with various pop fanzines—*Goldmine*, of course, as well as *Yellow Pills*, *Audities* (a publication "dedicated to lesser-known 'insanely great pop'," according to its website), and the indie-rock review *Amplifier*—and solicited numerous contributions. Some participants were assigned songs: for example, Borack specifically asked Bobby Sutliff (late of the respected Mississippi duo Windbreakers) to cover John's "Turnaround." "'Turnaround' always reminded me of one of

Bobby's gentle, jangly-guitar-dominated songs, so I immediately thought of the pairing," Borack says now.

Other contributing artists were suggested by Shoes themselves. Old friends astroPuppees were brought on for "The Tube": their spare version emphasizes lead singer Kelley Ryan's voice, equal parts mellow contralto and rock & roll rasp. "She was a friend of ours and we loved her song on *Yuletunes*," John remarks. Some contributors, once on board, specifically requested certain tunes. For example, Borack waited an hour to catch Matthew Sweet after a show in Orange County, and when he corralled him, Sweet agreed immediately—but told Borack that he'd insist on tackling John's romantic reminiscence, "Karen." Borack was present for several recording sessions, and even drummed on the sparklejets*uk's slamming version of "Cruel You." Shoes themselves did not hear any of the covers until the album was complete.

Longtime Shoes supporter Chris Morris reviewed *Shoe Fetish* in *Billboard*, and fell prey to the irresistible lure of the pun in his write-up: "The material is so superlative that even the lesser-known groups on this collection positively shine. We suggest that you shoehorn *Shoe Fetish* into your bins, and your personal record collections, at the first opportunity or risk being called a heel. (Ouch!).”

But most reviews of *Shoe Fetish* appeared in the pop press, primarily online. David Fufkin at *PopMatters* referenced one of the album's song titles, saying, "You really *can't go wrong* on this CD: this is an all-star lineup of pop bands paying tribute to one of the great power pop bands of the late '70s, early '80s. ... The director of this compilation, John M. Borack, and Parasol should take a bow here. The band deserved the tribute."

Klebe and the Murphys only heard *Shoe Fetish* for the first time after Borack sent them a cassette of the final mix; John describes driving to his brother's house, pulling up in the driveway, and listening—before calling Jeff out to join him:

> It was a bit like looking in a funhouse mirror. Other singers had different emphases, little alterations. I thought it was especially interesting when women were singing; that on its own is a radical

interpretation. ... It was an emotional thing for me; I got all choked up.

Shoes themselves wrote liner notes for the finished product. In them, they own up to being nervous about the new versions, for "after all, these were our fragile little babies in strange, albeit friendly hands." The band members detailed their pleased surprise at the results:

> Our paternal instincts were instantly calmed while listening to the completed tracks. ... we had the utterly unique experience of hearing our own music with fresh ears. It's kinda like overhearing a conversation in the next room where someone is complimenting you over and over.

BOTH THE INTERNATIONAL POP OVERTHROW appearance and the release of *Shoe Fetish* seemed to mark a transition for the band, one both inevitable and tough to accept: no longer earnest aspirants, they now perused their considerable legacy.

The transition to elder statesmen was accompanied by a reluctant but necessary decision: though Short Order Recorder had stayed active as a part-time business through the late nineties, there was no turning back the clock on the demise of analog recording studios. By the new millennium, Shoes had accepted this reality and put the building up for sale.

They would have liked, they all say, to have sold Short Order as a going concern—"We wanted it to go to someone like us," Gary says—but if they could not make a go of it under the existing circumstances, there was no reason to believe anyone else could, either. When the building finally sold in 2004, it was to another business entirely, a construction company.

The members of Shoes had often asserted that their studio was the band, and the band was the studio. But with Short Order consigned to the past, they rediscovered home recording—which had, of course, catalyzed the industry-wide shift that had doomed Short Order. But the tide had turned again: now the progenitors of DIY could use home-recording to save themselves.

These days, Shoes have returned to their roots. Both Jeff and Gary installed analog/digital recording setups in their houses. Shoes' piecemeal recording habits and DIY ethic make their return to home recording a peculiarly well-suited one: indeed, they were doing it long before it was the industry standard.

By 2000, THE MUSIC BUSINESS WAS reeling across the board. The problem started, of course, with MP3, CDA, and WAV files. The industry had embraced these digital-audio-encoding formats as an efficient method of music delivery: they were cheap, portable, easily replicated—and reduced the cost of production by a significant margin.

And the formats' beneficiaries were not limited to labels; consumers, too, could replicate and share high-quality digital files. As the digital generation matured, they simply assumed that they could copy the tracks onto their computers with no loss of fidelity; though most CDs were comprised of the higher-quality WAV files, they could easily be rendered to MP3s that—at that time—had no copy protection whatsoever. But the industry that had squawked loudly over home taping on cassette in the 1970s was largely silent on the digital issue—at least at first.

Three developments changed the industry's perception of digital music files. One was the advent of broadband technology, making these unwieldy files almost instantaneously transferable from machine to machine on upstart peer-to-peer sharing networks like Napster and LimeWire. Another was the increasing inclusion—as part of standard computer packages—of inexpensive, user-friendly CD burners, which allowed music lovers to take these computer files, transfer them to recordable discs, and play them on standard CD players. But rock & roll fans loading their own previously-purchased CDs onto their own computers was one thing; fans copying and burning songs they'd downloaded from Napster free of charge for themselves—music files that could then be made available to countless others—was something else altogether. And the third innovation was the paradigm-shifting advent of portable digital music players like the iPod, which had the effect of rendering CDs themselves obsolete.

Together, these forces combined to make copyright law all but unenforceable, and labels scrambled to find a way to stop the unrestricted reproduction of their pre-recorded music.

THE POWER OF THE MAJOR LABELS, the one thing they controlled most successfully, was the production and distribution not of music, but of the physical objects upon which music could be inscribed and transported—first vinyl records, then 8-tracks, then cassettes, and finally CDs. With music largely liberated from those physical media, the music becomes its own vehicle; its sale separate from production and shipping and up-front investment in units that may or may not move off store shelves. When there are no concrete units, distribution is a moot point. With downloads, there are no returns.

The labels got slapped hard in 2000 when forty-one states brought a successful anti-trust lawsuit, accusing them of price-fixing. According to *Billboard*, "[T]he states charged that the companies from 1995-2000 had conspired to inflate the price of CDs, costing consumers millions of dollars." Consumers who burned their own CDs knew perfectly well that the cost to make the physical unit had dropped to almost nothing, yet they routinely paid up to twenty dollars for pre-recorded CDs. They justifiably felt bilked.

However, as Greg Kot notes in *Ripped: How the Wired Generation Revolutionized Music*, his 2009 study of the social and economic changes wrought by the new technology, it wasn't that consumers weren't willing to pay for digital music. Though some embraced piracy as resistance (or just as piracy), others merely wanted an easier, less costly way to buy and organize their music without paying the huge overhead demanded by record labels, an overhead now officially designated as criminal. All that was needed was a method to make that possible. (Radiohead's radical experiment—the indie-electronic Brits' hugely successful 2007 album release *In Rainbows*, an Internet-only, pay-as-you-will gift to their fans—was still years away.)

The infrastructure was already in place. Apple's iTunes had premiered in January 2001; one of its early print ads had pictured a raucous group of road-trippers: "Take any tunes you like, put them in any order, and burn a CD. The new iMac with iTunes. After all, it's your music. Think different." In the lower-left corner is a custom CD—"Road Trip"—with nine songs: "Running Wild—Shoes" is number seven.

By spring 2003, the online iTunes Store had opened, selling music virtually; no brick-and-mortar stores, no physical product. Soon after, iTunes expanded to the Windows platform, exponentially increasing the number of users who could access the service. Apple was not alone: online retailers Rhapsody, eMusic, MusicMatch, and CD Baby were all inventing similar wheels at roughly the same time.

Shoes had signed up the Black Vinyl catalog with CD Baby, the Portland, Oregon-based online music-distribution service founded by Internet entrepreneur Derek Sivers (whom *Esquire* called "one of the last music-business folk heroes"). CD Baby was more closely tied to the independent labels than were some other online services, and in late 2003, the company offered its subscribers an opportunity: instead of selling downloads and physical CDs solely through their own site, CD Baby would act as agent and administrator for any of their acts who wanted to sign up with other download services, especially the juggernaut iTunes. It was a benefit to all parties; artists would get more exposure on larger sites, iTunes would have fewer administrators to deal with, and CD Baby would get a small cut for their services.

In a 2003 interview with the Future of Music Coalition—a nonprofit organization that, according to its mission statement, "has provided an important forum for discussion about issues at the intersection of music, technology, policy and law"—CD Baby's Sivers described the path from online store to distributor as a natural progression for his company:

> I realized that CD Baby was already doing most of what was needed by these download retailers. We were already encoding every CD that came in the door. Already paying the artists every week. Already keeping a database of all the details of all of their albums.

So delivering [the music] to Apple, then dispersing the payments, is no big change for us. I think that's why we're able to do it so cheaply.

Shoes were one of the earliest artists to take the deal and make CD Baby their conduit to the larger online retailers.

The level playing field of iTunes, Spotify, Pandora, and Amazon has already benefited independent artists in innumerable ways, and the potential for still greater benefit continues to offer the promise of access, affordability, and convenience for artists and fans alike.

For artists like Shoes, the knowledge that their music has a market, coupled with the ease of tracking who is buying what and when—and the simple lift from knowing, to paraphrase Gary Klebe, that "people still give a damn"—are inarguable boons. And while these rewards are not extravagant, they're steady, and measurable, and affirming.

SHOES NEVER REALLY STOPPED creating music. Jeff in particular had continued tinkering in the studio as long as there was one, and in the early part of the new millennium, he decided to make a true solo album, "like the first McCartney record, or Emitt Rhodes', or Todd Rundgren's. I think when an artist does all their own recording, plays all the instruments, it's kind of interesting." So he hammered out every part himself after his day job, when Short Order was empty of its now-infrequent clients.

Jeff continued to do irregular sessions some nights, as well, but only for "long-term clients, finishing things up." One of Short Order's last clients were Wisconsin guitar-pop band the Bradburys, who released the tracks recorded there as *Don't Pump the Swingset* in 2009. "We weren't taking on anything new," says Jeff.

He had four tracks of his solo project partially completed when the studio building sold in April 2004; it had languished nearly half a decade on the market, suffering from the post-9/11 economic downturn of 2001. Shoes did what they could to make it an attractive property, including taking advantage of civic beautification funds to repave the parking lot, and campaigning to lift Zion's then century-old ban on alcohol sales. "We thought it would be a good location for a restaurant," John explains.

But when the building did finally sell—abruptly—it was a surprise. Shoes hastily packed up decades' worth of tapes and business records and memorabilia and CDs, cramming the boxes wherever they'd fit, in their basements and attics and garages.

Jeff took his solo tapes home, assembled a studio in a spare bedroom, and continued to fine-tune the tracks that would become his 2007 solo record, *Cantilever*.

TWO-THOUSAND-SIX AND 2007 represented a relative flurry of activity for Shoes.

In summer 2006, they'd been approached by Oklahoma independent label FastLane Records to contribute to a planned Cheap Trick tribute album called *Tricked Out*. Using their two home recording setups—Jeff's new space, and a small digital complement Gary had placed in an extra bedroom—the band pieced out a cover of Cheap Trick's "If You Want My Love." "It seemed like a good project to shake off the cobwebs," says Jeff, "and try out the compatibility of the new digital gear we both had." The single was Shoes' first completely computerized recording. "It worked like a charm," Gary recollects. "That was our first experience with the ease of trading files."

It wasn't a lengthy project: once they had settled on the song, says John, the most contentious issue was deciding whether or not to include snippets from Cheap Trick's 1978 song "Oh Claire" (from *Heaven Tonight*) to frame Shoes' version of the later track ("If You Want My Love" had appeared on 1982's *One on One*.)

Much of the work was done at Jeff's, though Gary provided his own guitars and the lead vocal as completed pieces he'd done at home, in addition to programming all the drums. But the whole project was suddenly imperiled due to computer trouble, according to Jeff: "Unfortunately, just as we were preparing to mix it, the power supply that runs the automation in my machine died, and I had to rig something up to finish it." Computer crashes were a new recording problem for Shoes—as much as digital technology made things easier, it had also created new risks.

Long after they were done, *Tricked Out* had yet to materialize, and as of this writing still hasn't—though FastLane has posted four tracks, including Shoes', on the project's YouTube channel. Shoes were proud of their take on Trick's classic tune, and two years after recording it, they released "If You Want My Love" themselves—first on iTunes, and then as a bonus mini-CD for a boxed set of Shoes rarities released by independent Air Mail Recordings in Japan.

Around the same time as cutting the Cheap Trick single, Jeff did an on-camera interview for an indie documentary called *Player: A Rock and Roll Dream*, which examines the history of Chicago's scrappy rock scene. Filmmakers Greg Herriges and Tom Knoff, both faculty members at a Chicago-area community college, Harper College, taped Jeff's interview in his home studio. The documentary also features interviews with members of other Windy City rock & roll notables, including the Shadows of Knight, the Buckinghams, and the Mauds, as well as footage of an aspiring young band called the Redwalls.

Player, released in late '06, took gold in the 2007 Aurora Awards, an international competition focusing in part on special-interest entertainment.

Another project Jeff took on in 2006 was writing and publishing his memoir—*Shoes: Birth of a Band, the Record Deal, and the Making of <u>Present Tense</u>* (large sections of which have been invaluable source material for this book). In it, Jeff details the musical and professional evolution of Shoes. Plentifully illustrated with black-and-white and color photos spanning Shoes' career, the glossy volume offers a one-of-a-kind insider's view of this singular band.

BUT IT WAS WHILE SIFTING THROUGH photographs to use in the book that another idea struck Jeff. One image in particular got him thinking seriously about John's long back-burnered plan to release Shoes' early demos for *Present Tense* and *Tongue Twister* as an album. Jeff then suggested to his bandmates another retrospective Shoes disc—with said photograph as the cover—which would be called *Double Exposure*.

The photo itself was an intentional double exposure, a Randee St. Nicholas shot from 1979. They wouldn't have used the picture in those days, because it offended their sense of democracy: Skip is barely a shadow in the corner. But images of the three writing members of Shoes are all duplicated in their entirety: John, Jeff, and Gary along with their ghostly doppelgangers. "This one double-exposure shot of us jumped out at me and gave me the idea," says Jeff. "The title worked on a couple of different levels, at least for me, so I mocked up a cover and proposed it to the guys." John and Gary agreed at least to give it a try.

The demos for *Present Tense* and *Tongue Twister* had been done on reel-to-reel tape, a nigh-prehistoric technology. Jeff had not even included a reel-to-reel machine in his new state-of-the-art studio, but Gary had one; Jeff borrowed it to render the tracks in a workable format. Other than that, though, Jeff says they didn't do much else to the vintage tapes. "I dumped them into my digital recorder," Jeff relates, "and did the mastering at my house to match the levels and correct any extreme EQ differences between songs. Nothing was re-mixed, but we did change the sequencing a bit to group some songs together for each respective album." Jeff continues:

> I had originally proposed sequencing them in the same order as the finished *Present Tense* and *Tongue Twister* albums, but those guys opted to change it around a bit. I think it surprised us how good those demos actually sounded; Gary said he thought they might actually sound "too good," and people might not believe they were the original demos.

Double Exposure reveals some interesting details about Shoes' recording process: the guitar effects are often considerably heavier than on the professional studio versions, and the lyrics are incomplete—underlining the band's tendency to focus on musical performances while treating lyrics as afterthought. The album features two more versions of Gary's lost gem "Jet

Set," and a still-forming take of "Your Imagination," here called "Time to Make It."

Black Vinyl Records released the CD in the United States in 2007; the previously-mentioned Air Mail Recordings issued *Double Exposure*, complete with Shoes' Cheap Trick cover, in Japan two years later.

JEFF FINISHED HIS SOLO ALBUM, *Cantilever*, in early 2007. Some of its eleven tracks could have been lifted straight from one of the band's records: "Never Let You Go" and "It Happens All the Time" are swathed in Shoes-like luster; "I'm a Tool for You" features a string of double entendres worthy of John himself; "Won't Take Yes for an Answer," Jeff's cutting dismissal of then-president George W. Bush, has a positively Klebian bite. Other tracks are rife with Jeff's distinctive sweetness and optimism, including the gently swaying "Someday Soon" and "Unconditional Love"—while the minimalist pencil sketch of depression, "Havin' a Bad Day," is like nothing else in Jeff's personal catalog.

In a review on NPR's *Fresh Air*, pop critic Ken Tucker states that "whatever Jeff Murphy loses in not harmonizing in the uniquely breathy, intense way he did with his brother John, he gains in a certain independence." Singling out Jeff's stylistic flexibility, Tucker notes that *Cantilever* "adapts the Shoes sound to different sonic landscapes."

Tucker is especially taken with chiming album opener "I'm a Tool for You," which, he says, "can not only stand with the best of what Shoes ever did, but also the best of any current music out there." Pronouncing the song "pretty glorious," Tucker continues:

> Jeff Murphy is really nobody's tool. ... [He is] an inspiration who keeps on doing exactly what he wants, aiming for the mass audience in his head, willing us to listen.

In a September 1, 2007 interview, Jeff detailed his recording setup for *Electronic Musician* magazine, beginning with the fact that the center of his home system is a Korg D32XD personal digital studio. Interviewer Debbie Galante Block has Jeff enumerate the rest of his gear:

> For monitoring, Murphy has both Event ASP8 and Tannoy PBM 6.5 monitors. "I've got a Hiwatt guitar amp and a Vox AC30. I don't have many mics because I'm recording myself. I only use one or two mics at a time." On this CD, Murphy used his "trusted old friend," a Shure SM57, as well as an AKG C 451 and C 3000B, a Sennheiser MD 421, and a beyerdynamic M69.

Jeff's goal on *Cantilever*, he tells *Electronic Musician*, was to achieve a certain organic roughness:

> It's so tempting nowadays to make tracks perfect by quantizing, looping, and pitch-correcting them into a highly polished, finished song. But I really miss the blemishes and hiccups that come from actually playing.

THIS RELATIVELY BUSY PERIOD was capped by Shoes' headlining concert in Millennium Park, which opened Chicago's Great Performers of Illinois Festival in August '07.

Shoes' appearance came during the second year of the concert series, which according to one contemporary article was designed to celebrate "the arts unique to Illinois." Their co-headliner (and festival closer) was gospel legend Mavis Staples, who had gotten her start with her family in the hitmaking group Staple Singers. In his write-up, the *Tribune*'s Greg Kot declared Shoes and Staples "two Chicago-area treasures."

In preparation for the performance, Shoes did print press and even television, appearing on Chicago's ABC affiliate on Wednesday, August 5, and on WGN's midday news show on August 7. "We played the old Bozo room at WGN," John says of the brand-name Chicago TV station where Bozo the Clown got his start. Shoes were sequestered in the studio for several hours; every so often a staffer would cue them and they'd play. "We'd never done live TV before," John says, pointing out that they didn't know what to expect, and are still not quite sure how much of their performance made it onto the air. Shoes performed three songs, "Tomorrow Night," "Your Devotion" and "Don't Do This to Me." One was aired while the program credits rolled onscreen next to Shoes.

The concert in Millennium Park, a prime Chicago tourist attraction, went fairly well—though the August afternoon was brutally hot. "I was thinking we'd only drawn a light crowd," Jeff recalls, "but one of the girls that worked for the Chicago Park District said it was one of the best audiences they'd had so far for that event, which ran for two days. I guess it's a lot to ask folks to drive downtown and stand for ninety minutes in the sun during the hottest part of the day. But I do remember feeling good after the gig." And when Shoes headed back north that evening, they popped on the TV and saw, as John reports, that "we made the 10 o'clock news."

THINGS QUIETED DOWN FOR SHOES after Millennium Park, temporarily. There were reissues and European releases and other stray projects. But it wasn't until 2009, when Air Mail Recordings released a four-disc boxed set comprised of *Present Tense*, *Tongue Twister*, *Boomerang*, and *Shoes On Ice*—with lyrics printed in English and liner notes in Japanese, as along with a commemorative pin from the original Shoes on Ice show, plus eleven bonus tracks mostly culled from *As Is*—that Shoes got really moving again.

Just prior to the boxed set's release, Shoes traveled to Japan to play two nights at Shinjuku JAM (*Time Out Tokyo* says that the primary offering of the club, "located in a basement on the outskirts of Shinjuku's red-light district," is "1960s-70s music, with a bit of guitar pop thrown in.") Jeff took the lead in setting up the shows, after hearing from Al Chan of Berkeley, California's long-serving power-poppers the Rubinoos how much they had enjoyed their 2007 visit." Al suggested that I contact Hiroshi Kuse," Jeff relates, referring to Air Mail's proprietor. Kuse proceeded to book Shoes for his annual power-pop festival, the Greasy Rockers Party. (Other iterations have featured the Rubinoos, John Wicks, the Flashcubes, and 20/20.)

Before they left for the Far East, Shoes did a warm-up show on March 28, 2009, at McAuliffe's Pub, a bar in nearby Racine, Wisconsin, playing primarily to old friends and family. A freak springtime storm unloaded almost a foot of snow on Racine that night, but Chicago-area video company TMOVideo captured some quality footage of the band in action, performing John's "Rugged Terrain"—which had been previously released only on *As Is*—live for the first time. (In the video, Jeff apologetically attaches a list of chords to his mic stand, explaining, "This is a new song, so I have a cheat sheet.")

Then it was off to the Land of the Rising Sun—and Shoes all agree that the Japanese experience was extraordinary. They met John Richardson in San Francisco and flew across the Pacific on Tuesday, March 31. It took a few days to adjust to the dramatic time difference, Tokyo being fifteen hours ahead of Chicago.

Shoes loved Tokyo. "It was surprisingly quiet," John observes of one of the globe's most populous urban centers. "It did not feel like a big city at all." Since they didn't know any Japanese, Shoes relied heavily on their hosts, Air Mail Recordings owners Hiroshi and Yumi Kuse. They were also shown around by two members of one of their opening bands, Rock Bottom. "Koji and Tatsuya also took us around the day after the last show," says Jeff, "shopping and seeing the sights."

Shoes played two nights in front of the kind of crowds they hadn't seen in years: housefuls of exuberant Shoes fans. Gary recounts:

> I was shocked how knowledgeable they were about Western music—about *our* music. They were mouthing the lyrics to every song, even during the sound check. We're considered by many in America as a cult band, but people there knew *everything* about us.

Shoes were joined during sound check and encores by their longtime friend, Velvet Crush's Paul Chastain. In 2009, Chastain and his wife were living in Osaka, and a brief phone parley led to a plan: Chastain accompanied Shoes during "Hate to Run," a song not originally on the set list. The whole trip "was a lifetime event and made a huge impression on us," Jeff states. "*Oh*, yeah," John agrees. "Just a great, great experience."

CRITICS INTERESTED IN SERIOUS ANALYSIS of pop music routinely place Shoes among the finest practitioners of their genre. In 2009, *the Onion* A.V. Club—the humor publication's generally straight-faced arts and entertainment section—ran a feature on Shoes in its "Gateways to Geekery" series (some of which was quoted in chapter three). There, writer Noel Murray declared *Black Vinyl Shoes* the obvious starting point for any exploration of power pop as a genre:

> Power-pop was like bubblegum with balls, but as with the late-'60s bubblegum craze, power-pop quickly became the chosen genre for workmanlike musicians with sheaves of simplistic lyrics about cars and girls, and a storehouse of melodies so sweet that they could give Willy Wonka a bellyache. ... *Great* power-pop—and there's a lot of it out there—has to be more idiosyncratic and regionally flavored, with a touch of grit.

For Murray, Shoes are the exemplars of this movement. He elaborates:

> Through the tinny murk—sounding like it was "produced by elves," according to critic Robert Christgau—the songs' chiming guitars and fluid melodies remain unshakable ... the homemade quality of *Black Vinyl Shoes* draws more attention to the band's inventive arrangements and earnest performance. Too much of power-pop sounds slick and uniform, but *Black Vinyl Shoes* feels as personal as it is accomplished. It's like finding a love letter in the county dump, then discovering it was written by Wordsworth.

Glenn McDonald, in his web 'zine *The War Against Silence*, frames Shoes' importance somewhat differently:

> Shoes are the band that Devo would have been if they were shy and serious, the band the Knack would have been without the self-confident sneer, the band the Beatles could have been if they'd grown up in Zion, Illinois and never become stars or heard Stockhausen or a sitar. ... [Y]ou come across them only suddenly, through untraceable ways, and yet feel like every song they play you've heard inside your head a dozen times before.

Such an analysis argues for an understanding of Shoes' importance as something secret and personal. And for many Shoes fans, that is indeed their experience of the band and its music: as a private thing other people just don't *get*. Shoes' lack of commercial success, even of name recognition, seems to confirm this perspective.

From this vantage point, Shoes can best be understood as a cult band: either the most dreaded musical cul-de-sac, or a badge of honor. Maybe both. But in a 1985 interview, John Murphy declared, "There is a niche for us, and we think it's above cult status."

To the extent that Shoes escape such consignment, it must be due to their role as the standard-bearers of melodic guitar-based rock, tying past and future together by recognizing and acknowledging their debts on the one hand, and innovating and inspiring the bands who followed them on the other.

As Cary Baker argues:

> Shoes are one of the greatest indie bands ever to emerge from American rock. To me, they are as important as R.E.M., the Replacements, the dB's, Cheap Trick, or Big Star. Some of these bands made it, some didn't, but I hold them in that same esteem.

Baker theorizes that their relatively low profile may simply be a function of timing: "Too bad Shoes weren't coming out now. With all the indie stuff going on, they'd fit right in."

Yellow Pills founder Jordan Oakes has written:

> Shoes are an integral link in the American pop lineage that took flight with the Byrds and jangled on with Big Star. Their power lies in the fact that they're cynical about love but not, thankfully, about music. Whereas many bands obsess on lofty topics, Shoes focus on the politics of the heart.

David Bash declares Shoes to be "without question one of the most important bands in the history of pop music. They've had a profound influence on pop artists and regional pop scenes around the country."

Shoes cast a shadow over rock history all out of proportion to their moderate commercial success. Whether because of their modest beginnings, their adherence to the melodic standards of their predecessors, or their determination to plug on in the face of adversity—or all of the above—they strike a chord in fans, critics, and musicians alike, cementing their position as one of the most indelible American pop bands of the last half-century.

It is a legacy that the members of Shoes, who still live within a couple of miles of each other, just up the road from Zion, Illinois, welcome.

Epilogue

Sign of Life

But a funny thing happened on the way to Shoes' legacy status. They made a new album—2012's *Ignition*.

It was the summer of 2010 when the latest chapter in Shoes' saga took off.

Jeff demoed a new song and handed it off to John and Gary, just to see what they thought of it. A ballad addressed to a friend who had died suddenly, "Out of Round" began as a measured acoustic-guitar-and-piano-based reverie dealing with grief. "Brian was a big bear of a guy, so full of life," says Jeff. "Then he contracted Creutzfeldt-Jakob Disease, the degenerative brain disorder; it's the human form of Mad Cow." Brian declined rapidly, and in talking to his friend's wife after his death, Jeff was struck by the many little things she now did to fill the empty space her husband had left. "The coworker who inherited his phone at work hadn't changed the voicemail message," Jeff recalls, "so she could call it to hear his voice. She would stuff a sleeve of his coat with a towel and throw it over herself in their bed. Stuff like that." Deeply touched, Jeff composed the ballad and brought it to his bandmates.

Jeff had played songs for John and Gary before, including tracks from *Cantilever* he'd shared with them during that album's composition and recording. Initially, they thought Jeff didn't necessarily want them to intervene in "Out of Round." Ultimately, however, according to John, the two "'Your Imagination'ed it."

As always with Shoes, the process was driven by a technological intervention. It was October 2010, John recollects, when Gary took him to the basement of the house Gary had moved into the year before. The last time John had visited the utilitarian cellar, it was all wide-open, raw concrete. But in the ensuing year, Gary—without a word to anyone—had built a two-room recording studio in the space.

One room was "live," its concrete walls, ceiling, and floor left in their natural state to reflect sound. The other was "dead," with columns and walls carpeted, ceiling tiles wrapped in fabric, and a rug strategically positioned on the floor. John was stunned that Gary had accomplished all this in secret, but his bandmate had kept mum for a reason. "I *wanted* it to be a surprise," he says.

Gary's system is a hybrid of analog and digital tools, centered on Cubase software. And because all recording is digital, there is no set number of channels. "I might run into memory problems after a hundred or so," Gary surmises, "but we'll never need that many channels for anything we do." The goal "is to have digital flexibility while retaining analog warmth," Gary says.

"I have a pretty nice home setup," Jeff remarks, "but Gary's is really a professional-quality studio."

AND SO, IN THIS SOPHISTICATED surprise of a studio space, John and Gary took on Jeff's "Out of Round."

John says the first time he listened to the ballad, "I kept envisioning it picking up in the middle, maybe adding more drums, changing the mood." John told Jeff what he was thinking; his fraternal bandmate gave him carte blanche to mess with the song. And when John voiced his suggestions to Gary, the floodgates opened, as both the other Shoes began reconfiguring Jeff's track.

The three of them hadn't worked like this in literally decades, getting in each other's heads, making changes to each other's music. And at first, John and Gary were worried about Jeff's reaction. "We did an awful lot to it," Gary admits. "'Out of Round' went from being a relatively short ballad to becoming a much longer, fuller rock track." And the first time they played the transmuted tune for him in the basement, Jeff found it "initially a bit jarring. But I liked it." He goes on:

> What they did was to use a double-time drum pattern in the chorus and add an extended guitar break. ... Gary's guitar work reminded me of Lindsey Buckingham, and John had done two different bass lines. We used a hybrid version of them both, and extended the

instrumental section even more. ... The song's length went from 2:30 to 3:45. [The final mix is 3:58.] And most of the basic demo instrumentation—which was done at my house—remains in the track.

But since all this doctoring had been done on Jeff's original demo, an extra keyboard scrap remained on the track. Initially, Jeff had tried the song in a different key, but then decided to change the key and just record over the original piano part. "When I finished recording," Jeff says, "a little bit at the end popped on, because the song had ended. I liked the reprise feel, so I grabbed a vocal line and flipped it over backwards, and also grabbed a military-style snare drum part that I had tried in the body of the song and reversed that, too."

Even before "Out of Round," Gary had been tinkering—again without telling anyone—with a new song, "Nobody to Blame." He'd been working on it for some time: "We never really stop writing," he points out, "even if there's no recording going on." The general structure and words were taking shape, but were not yet complete. Gary had a rough demo in place by the end of summer 2010: the initial vocal track was laid down before he underwent thyroid surgery that September, sidelining him vocally for over six months. "I did do scratch vocals during my recovery," he says now, "but they were gravelly."

Once Gary revealed the new workspace to his bandmates, Shoes started recording in earnest, and the pace picked up, though none of them were ready to admit yet that they were working on a new record. "It was like being first-time parents before the first trimester is over, you know?" John described in a *Popdose* interview. "You don't want to jinx it." They treated each other cautiously, respectfully, ever-mindful of how wrong this process had gone before, unsure whether anything would come to fruition this time.

A chorus of John's that he called "Been in Remission" was next on the docket. He'd roughed it out on an instrument he'd been playing for about a decade, a baritone guitar (which has a slightly lower tone than a standard guitar, but higher than a bass).

John liked the instrument so much that he ended up doing most of his composition for what would become *Ignition* on the baritone guitar, using a capo when necessary to adjust the range. He raves about the guitar, a

Danelectro: "Back in the sixties, they made them from surplus parts. But Danelectro has brought them back in the last ten years. I love it; it makes me think differently. It has this lowish, almost piano-like tone. It feels like spaghetti-western music."

Gary had been roughing out another demo, despite the fact that his voice wasn't fully recovered: "Heaven Help Me." Musically, he had the soaring rocker framed out when he presented it to his bandmates, but he was still refining the lyrics through the holiday season:

> By the time I finished, I was proud of those words. Lyrically, we'd set ourselves a pretty high bar this time. We used to worry more about the sound of a word than what it meant. When I go back and listen to our old stuff, I think, "No wonder the lyrics came fast." Now we want them to be more substantial.

Gary says he keeps lists of individual words he wants to use, but notes that "it has to fit; you can't smash it in sideways."

At this point, they invited longtime stage drummer John Richardson to come in and record. "Johnny has *always* wanted to do a Shoes album," his brother Beet recounts. But with Richardson's arrival looming, Gary needed to get "Heaven Help Me" in shape quickly: "I put the scratch vocal down the night before John came, literally just before I went to bed."

CHRISTMAS DAY 2010, THE AREA north of Chicago got walloped by white. As the National Weather Service reported at the time, "[B]linding lake-effect snowfall has been pounding portions of Kenosha and Racine counties in far southeast Wisconsin all evening."

But it was a fortuitous storm. John Richardson was scheduled to come into town just after a New Year's Eve concert drumming with durable alt-rockers the Gin Blossoms (his steady gig for the past several years). "Been in Remission" wasn't panning out as John had hoped, so he needed something, quick, before the drummer's imminent arrival.

John turned to "In On You," a tune for which the melody had been percolating a long time. "I really wanted to return to a singer-songwriter kind of song, one you could just sing with a guitar, one that was led by the vocal," he says.

John had spent December 25th at Jeff's, but now he was stranded because of the storm—and the next day, still snowed in, the brothers began recording. "John asked if I had a baritone guitar he could play on," Jeff recalls. "I did, so I set him up with headphones and he played until he was ready to put down his new demo for 'In on You.'"

John's newly-minted song was ready for Richardson's arrival, and the visit was productive: there in Gary's basement, he laid down drums for all four of the tracks the Murphys and Klebe had at that point.

RICHARDSON'S WORK WITH SHOES on this record, beginning early in the process and continuing at regular intervals throughout—he made four visits total—had all the band members enthused. According to John Murphy, Richardson gives them "alternate readings" of songs, injecting even more juice into their creative process. As Jeff describes:

> Recording the initial stages of a song with a real live drummer, and one of Johnny's caliber, is truly inspirational. It makes it so much easier to relax and enjoy the process. He will always be his own worst critic, but his timing is spot-on. The most difficult thing to settle on was which pattern he should play; the subsequent overdubs come much easier and more naturally than they ever have.

"He's in tune with the way we're thinking," Gary declares—no surprise, given that Richardson has backed Shoes on the road for nearly eighteen years. "Johnny's extremely instinctive," continues Gary. "He'll listen to a song once, take notes the second time, and by the third time through we're recording." And, John Murphy adds, "He's got a great personality, just a really fun guy to have around."

SOON, KLEBE AND THE MURPHYS settled into a pattern of meeting several nights a week in the studio. "We were all there," John says, "even if we weren't directly involved in recording." That gave them the benefit of each other's regular input. John was struck with their air of generosity, of shared purpose. Jeff too was taking note of their sense of camaraderie: "We respect each other's musical opinions like nobody else's." When one of them was unsure whether what he had was working, he always had two more sets of ears to help make a determination. Gary recalls that, on "Heaven Help Me," his bandmates helped *him* trust his own writing. "They reacted well to it," he says, "and in our band, we take that seriously."

But if the members of Shoes expressed doubt about each other's songs, changes were in order. One example of the refinements they wrought was Jeff's second contribution: the tuneful-but-acerbic "The Joke's on You." The song's driving force, from its inception, was a descending riff (á la Todd Rundgren's "Couldn't I Just Tell You," according to Jeff) "to run through it in a jangly way," as he phrases it. Initially, working at home, he'd formulated a heavily-effected, vibrato guitar sound for the central motif: "I tend to like unique guitar riffs, like the opening of [Crosby, Stills & Nash's] 'Marrakesh Express' or the solo in [the Beatles'] 'Savoy Truffle,'" he discloses. His bandmates, however, were not enamored of the result, so Jeff stripped it back to a more traditional sound. But he took the recommendation of Chuck Fieldman and tried it on a twelve-string, and the result, Jeff says, is "a great compromise between a unique and a more traditional guitar sound."

That spring, Jeff brought another partially-completed song to the table, called "Say It Like You Mean It." He didn't have much, just a chorus and some chords—"a single riff as an intro and outro," Jeff recollects—and he'd intended the song to be a group composition from the beginning. Gary took the piece and used the riff to build his verses; John built his bridge over Jeff's chord structure.

John's own second track was the pensive "Diminishing Returns," which they'd begun that spring. It was a title he'd had rolling around in his head for years. "I think the first time I ever heard the phrase was when we were working with Hank Neuberger in 1982," he says. "But I always thought the words were a good mouthful, and wanted to use them in a song about recognizing the slow erosion of a relationship. You start to realize that you're putting in more than you're getting out of it." Still, turning the words into a song was as vexed a process as ever, and over time he over-thought the lyrics.

Shoes' piecemeal production style, John notes, sometimes results in a track being partly done for months. "It's like a big lazy Susan," he explains, referencing that rotating staple of food service. "You just wait for your song to come back around again." He'd put down a scratch vocal of "Diminishing Returns" at Jeff's in the spring, but by the time they got back to it in the fall, he'd completely rewritten it. "It took me a long time," John admits, "and then sometimes after all that work, you realize the lyrics on the scratch vocal fit better than the ones you labored over." The final result, he says, is "stitched together from those two different versions."

Also appearing in this set of tunes was another Gary composition, the reflective "Only We Remain." Like many—okay, most—Shoes songs, the surface tale is about a relationship: "We all go down wrong roads, but at the end, there's just the person you're with. It *is* about facing hardship and disappointment and dead ends, but it's also hopeful, about survival." Referencing an earlier statement regarding his lyrics being a pastiche of "five or six girls," Gary admits, "I guess in some cases, the band itself is one of the five or six relationships in the mix."

John Richardson came in again around Memorial Day and laid down drums on the next four tracks: "Only We Remain," "The Joke's on You," "Diminishing Returns," and the still-not-quite-complete "Say It Like You Mean It."

WITH FOUR SONGS OF HIS OWN IN THE CAN, Gary was slightly ahead of his bandmates in terms of composition. Thus, when he sheepishly presented them with a set of chords for yet another creation early in July 2011, he apologized. "I know I don't need any more songs, but I've got these chords," Jeff remembers him saying before he ripped through the blistering riff for "Hot Mess;" he then asked John and Jeff to help out on the track. Gary knew the request he was making of his colleagues was awkward. "You don't want your bandmates to feel pressured into collaborating," he says, "but it definitely takes the pressure off you when they agree." After he played the riff, he asked, "What do you think?" Jeff continues:

> Wow! It was literally an instant reaction by John and me. I said, "I know exactly what I want to play." And John said, "I've got a title and an idea for some lyrics."

And so "Hot Mess"—Shoes' homage to the Rolling Stones—was born. Jeff explains the process:

> I played Gary's Rocco Reverend [guitar] through his Matchless amp and recorded my part on the fly. As I played, John sat next to me in the control room and wrote lyrics. After I played my counter-rhythm guitar, I ran another track of a riffy guitar. Then John went out and did a scratch vocal. We loved it and really laughed our asses off, as John had some pretty risqué lyrics at first.

The song sketches out a night in the life of the daughter—or maybe granddaughter—of the faded vamp from "Tested Charms," but unlike her somewhat pitiful predecessor, this young woman is all bronzer, tramp stamp, and *Jersey Shore* insouciance. John wrote a number of verses for the song, only some of which made it to the final track.

Jeff took on the melody for the chorus, though John wrote the words for that too. Of his first pass at the chorus, Jeff frowns, "It was too safe and proper." John recalls his brother complaining, "I sound like a wimp!" especially in contrast to John's Jaggeresque growl. "I went back and redid the chorus with more aggression," Jeff says. "I think it works better."

Jeff's solo, recorded only a few days after the initial session for the song, was played through his trusty Hiwatt amp. Here, too, the raw edge of inspiration was a crucial component. "Jeff and Gary usually really think out their solos," John observes, "but this time, Jeff just let it rip. It felt like a Keith Richards solo," in keeping with the general character of the song.

DURING THE SAME PERIOD, JOHN was working on the words for "I Thought You Knew," his captivating saga of the misunderstandings and missed cues that can doom a relationship. The production of the track, John remembers, was relatively quick and painless. "We just knocked it out one night," he says, noting that he laid down not only the bass, but also the rhythm guitar track. "Things I thought were demos, just rough versions, we ended up keeping," he says. "I'd play a line, just to show them what I was thinking about, and they'd come back with, 'Great. That sounds fine. You do it.'"

That summer, Jeff came in with "Maybe Now," much of which he had already worked out in his home studio: "Virtually all the piano parts on the record were done here, as were the electric guitars and backwards stuff." The last of these—the backward-tracked guitars—is particularly prominent on "Maybe Now," a thoughtful consideration of opportunities lost and others still to come.

Gary's next offering was the rollicking "Sign of Life," which features heavily-flanged acoustic guitars, many of which came from the scratch demo. It's marked by an attention-grabbing instrumental passage in which Jeff and Gary trade off guitar licks in a call-and-response pattern. "The solo section is really a duet," says Gary, pointing out a similar guitar interlude on *Black Vinyl Shoes* track "If You'd Stay." "But there's a lot of air in between the guitars; the idea was to keep the rhythm going. I put mine on first—I was tracked to the left—and Jeff put his answers on, tracking to the right." The effect is almost conversational.

Similarly striking is Gary's "Head Versus Heart," which features a chorus that's "really more of an anti-chorus," as Gary puts it:

> You get to the chorus, and the song empties out, becomes fragile. The bass drops out, along with all the distortion and fire of the verses. It's kind of a flip of what we usually do, where the chorus swells above the verses.

Jeff's last contribution was "Where Will It End?" which he calls "part biographical, part political, part fictional." He says that he had trouble pinning the song down—"I had so many ideas for it that I kept apologizing for adding stuff," he recollects—and they rearranged it several times. Jeff's lyrics express his exhaustion with a lot of situations—"Tired of how difficult life can be. Tired of the national political battling and vitriol. Tired of intolerance and prejudice. Tired of how long we'd been working on the album." Still, he likes the song, particularly Gary's solo, which Jeff feels is his bandmate's best on the album.

Richardson's third trip Shoes-ward, around Labor Day, was a marathon, with the drum tracks for these six songs recorded in just a few days.

JOHN'S FINAL TRACK WAS THE UPTEMPO "Wrong Idea," which he was racing to finish even as John Richardson's last planned trip loomed at the close of 2011. As always, John says, "I was scrambling at the end."

John had again composed on the baritone guitar, capoing it to the third fret, resulting in "quite an unusual tone," says Jeff, who along with Gary tried to find chords to match it. When they started to lay the song down, Jeff recollects, "John used Gary's Papoose mini-acoustic tuned up three steps (to start on the A). He doubled that guitar (left and right), and then I played a normally-tuned acoustic guitar panned to the middle. Because of the weird key, I couldn't use open chords, so some of the voicings are not quite what John really wanted, but it's all that we could do." Gary notes that it was more the variance between the guitars that was the issue: "Each was a completely different configuration. If we were *good* guitarists," he adds, "it would have been easy." John admits ruefully that both Jeff and Gary came out of the sessions frustrated. "Jeff said it was the hardest song he'd ever worked on," John says. "And Gary agreed." In any case, "Wrong Idea" was basically in shape for Richardson's last visit.

All the new album's tracks came together by spring 2012, and aside from the usual DIY frustrations—the thousand-and-one extraneous production issues a record company would normally handle—Shoes are proud of the disc, which represents not only a triumph of long friendship and musicianship and goodwill, but also a significant step forward musically. "It won't take much for us to look at this record as a success," Gary says. "We're really happy with it."

BUT EVEN MORE THAN THE TRACKS themselves, making *Ignition* just seemed, well, *right*. "It felt very natural—like we'd never stopped recording," Jeff says.

"There's more community spirit now," reflects John, commenting on the high band morale during, and since, the recording of *Ignition*. "There's no overhead to cover; there's no time clock. In that respect, *Ignition* feels like *Black Vinyl Shoes*." Gary agrees: "All the restraints were taken away from us; we were doing it just because we like to."

Coda

IT'S AN APRIL NIGHT, AND I'M waiting in an emergency room somewhere in the Midwest alongside John Murphy—both of us muddy from the same fall down a treacherous hill—and Gary Klebe, who is grimly studying my x-rays and predicting surgery or worse. Amputation, maybe. John and I had gotten caught in a freak spring hailstorm after dinner—husky prairie iceballs the size of shooter marbles—with predictably slapstick results, and now my left arm is broken. Gary, responding to my post-plummet text message, has joined us here straight from work, despite the fact that it's ten o'clock at night.

The doctor comes in and wraps my wounded wing in a stabilizer for the night—it's just a minor break—making chipper small talk with me and my companions.

"She's a college professor, you know," Gary volunteers.

"Oh? Where do you teach?" the medic asks, not really listening. It's a measured dance of civil protocol, not worthy of full attention.

"Upstate New York," I reply. We establish where I teach, a school he's actually heard of.

Then comes the inevitable question, perkily posed: "So, what are you doing in the Midwest?"

"I'm working on a book," I answer.

"About what?" he says absently.

"About these guys." I gesture with my good arm toward my companions. That gets his attention. He stops what he's doing, sizes them up—John disheveled from our ass-over-teacup tumble, Gary rumpled from a day at the office.

The doctor delivers what he clearly considers to be a real knee-slapper. "What are you guys? *Rock stars?*"

The three of us exchange a brief, panicked look, wondering who's going to field it. "Kinda," Gary says almost sheepishly.

The E.R. doctor is as taken aback by the answer as we were by the question, but in small-town Midwestern style, everyone politely soldiers on with the small talk the situation demands, at least until my arm is set.

It's an illustrative incident for me. The members of Shoes have told me repeatedly that around here, they're nothing special—and I admit, it's hard to visualize a realm in which the idols of my youth are merely ordinary. What kind of Greek city-state of exceptional people must this place be where a Jeff Murphy just, you know, goes to the grocery store? Or a John Murphy does the laundry? Or a Gary Klebe shovels snow?

We know what rock stars look like. Right? No matter how ordinary they seem, they have an unmistakable aura; we'd certainly know if they were in the same room with us. But in a small town like this, no one expects rock stars in their midst. The fact that they're living here means they can't be rock stars: if they *were* special, they wouldn't be *here*. QED.

For almost four decades, Shoes have hovered—not always comfortably—between the rarefied world of rock respectability and the everyday exigencies of living in the parochial Midwest. Yet except for that one brief period in the summer of 1980, they never considered trading their string of smallish towns straddling the Illinois/Wisconsin border for the bright lights of Los Angeles, or even Chicago. "Hindsight is 20/20," Jeff muses, "but it would appear that we made the wise decision, even though you never know what *might* have happened if we had made the move to L.A."

It's a fascinating what if: what if, in the process of seeking big-time exposure and opportunity the way so many others did—the way they've been told for years they *should* have—Shoes had lost their particular purity of vision and, well, innocence?

It's an answer I'm glad I don't have.

INDEX

20/20... 110, 211, 248, 433, 448.
92 Degrees... 377, 381, 383, 418-19, 421.

ADAT technology... 425-26.
Ahlert, David... 236, 238.
Air Mail Records... 444, 446, 448-49.
Albini, Steve... 387-88.
American Airlines Flight 191... 157-58.
Ansani, Ted... 377, 384-85, 388-89.
Astor Tower... 220-24, 257.
Austermehle, Paul... 31-32, 36, 44, 59, 69, 74.
Azerrad, Michael, *Our Band Could Be Your Life* (2001)... 270, 307.

Badfinger... 110, 216, 373-74, 418, 436.
Baker, Cary... 93, 103, 105-07, 111, 115, 117-120, 216, 364, 369, 373, 451.
Baker, Roy Thomas... 156, 243.
Bash, David... 368, 435, 452.
Bazooka (1975), see Shoes.
Beatles... 21-23, 30, 33, 67, 88, 91, 95, 110, 119, 130, 141, 149, 151, 159, 182, 190-91, 206, 251-52, 316, 339, 345, 347, 373, 383, 394-95, 400, 422, 426, 430, 432, 450, 458.
Berg, Moe... 369.
Big Star... 30, 33-34, 83, 173, 329, 451.
Black Vinyl Records... 82, 220, 316, 331, 333, 344, 348, 351, 354-56, 361, 371, 376, 378-79, 382, 393, 399, 404, 407, 409, 411, 418-21, 425, 427-28, 433-34, 441, 446.
Bleecker Bob's... 137, 188.
Blondie... 155, 172, 184, 191, 237, 248, 297.
Blues Brothers, The... 195.

Bocchieri, Leroy... 320, 358-59, 383, 432, 434.
Bomp! (magazine)... 106-11, 118.
Bomp! Records... 23, 110, 112-15, 117, 121, 127-29, 134, 179, 189.
Borack, John... 172, 414, 420-22, 436-37.
"bouncing"... 87-88.
Bourgeoise, Dan... 114, 147, 150, 152, 154-56, 169, 178, 181, 191-92, 196, 198-200, 203-05, 208, 211-12, 222, 224, 226, 230, 235, 239, 241, 247, 249, 257-58, 261, 267, 275-77, 279-86, 289, 291, 296, 302, 304, 306, 308-11, 316, 369, 382.
Braam, Mike... 377.
Braam, Tom... 406.
Braga, David... 279-80.
Branson, Richard... 156, 161, 169-71.
Brat Stop... 68-69.
Browne, Duncan... 409, 426-27.
Buckingham, Lindsey... 227, 229, 233, 235, 239, 368, 454.
Bug Music... 114, 140, 145, 147, 226, 310-11.
Buttice, Ken... 137-38, 141-43, 145-46, 150-52, 176-78, 180, 184, 186-89, 195-97, 203, 209, 213-14, 216, 220-25, 230, 239, 252, 255-57, 267-68, 275-81, 288-91, 293-94, 297, 311, 334.

Cars, The... 138, 147-48, 156, 173, 195, 225, 242-43, 246, 248, 262.
Carter, Russell... 342-43.
CD Baby... 441-42.
The Cabin/*La Cabane*... 56, 59, 63, 67, 70, 82, 97, 113, 122, 124-26.
Camelot Music... 70, 403.
Cantilever (2007)... 443, 446-47, 453.

Capitol Records... 150-52, 173, 358, 364, 368-69, 373.

Caro, Mark... 420.
Carson, Tom... 211, 262.
Case, Ian... 265.
Cellar Studios... 46.
Champaign, Illinois... 30-32, 35, 40, 44, 50-51, 53, 55, 56, 61, 67-69, 73, 139, 263, 414.
Chapman, Michael... 184, 236-38, 389-90.
Charlie Daniels Band, The... 246.
Chastain, Paul... 133, 319, 357, 449.
Cheap Trick... 42, 68, 83-84, 108, 115-17, 119-20, 126, 128, 199, 303, 339-40, 416, 432, 443-44, 446, 451.
Chicago, Illinois... 9-11, 20-21, 25, 42, 69, 93, 95, 101-02, 105-08, 111, 114-15, 120-21, 126, 129-30, 132-34, 140, 143, 145, 153, 155, 158-60, 175-76, 179, 195, 203, 205, 220-21, 225, 228, 255-56, 263, 279, 281-82, 285, 299, 304, 308, 311, 319, 321, 323, 326, 331-32, 338, 355, 357, 360, 362, 371, 377, 380-81, 383, 387, 398, 414-22, 435, 444, 447-49, 456, 464.
Chicago Cubs... 25, 93.
Chicago Recording Company (CRC)... 281-82, 285, 351.
ChicagoFest... 130, 132-34, 265.
Chicago Reader... 106-07, 154, 228.124, 179, 267.
Christgau, Robert... 6, 82, 183, 210, 450.
Christian Catholic Apostolic Church... 10, 12-14.
College Music Journal (CMJ)... 260, 352.
Corso Gregory... 421.
Creem... 106, 262, 318.

Dahl, Steve... 299-300.
Dannen, Fredric, *Hit Men: Power Brokers and Fast Money Inside the Music Business* (1990)... 137, 147-48, 181-83, 208-09.
Dantzig, Jol... 126.
Dashut, Richard... 107, 116, 227-42, 244, 256-57, 389, 430.
de Vallance, Denis... 190-91.
Demon Records... 316-17.

Denisoff, R. Serge. *Tarnished Gold: The Record Industry Revisited* (1986)... 183-84, 251-52, 261, 269-70. *Inside MTV* (1988)... 270-73, 276-77.
Distribution North America (DNA)... 409-10, 426-27, 433.
Dixon, Don... 329, 381-82, 400.
Dowie, John Alexander... 9-14, 16, 18, 265.
Duncklau, Marlys... 168.
Dupree, Robbie... 222-23.
Dwight, Illinois... 74-75, 139, 197.

Eagles, The... 52, 246, 277, 297.
Easter, Mitch... 376, 400.
Eimerman, Herb... 265, 383, 422-23.
Elektra/Asylum Records... 38, 41, 103, 136-38, 140-43, 146-160, 166, 173, 177-81, 185-196, 203-10, 212-14, 220-26, 230, 239-40, 245-47, 252-53, 255, 257-61, 264-69, 271, 275-81, 284-87, 289-91, 293-94, 295-97, 299, 301-03, 304-06, 308-09, 311, 315, 321, 330, 339, 348-49, 355-58, 368, 372, 375, 378, 433.
Ellison, Jim... 319-21, 327, 368, 377, 384-89, 436.
Erickson, Ed... 22, 27, 32, 134, 240.
Erikson, Duke... 134, 249, 264, 279.

Fieger, Doug... 173.
Fieldman, Chuck... 201, 266, 279, 303-04, 308, 332, 347, 458.
Field's Dress Shop (BFD Studios)... 122-5, 138, 155, 196, 304, 357.
Fire Town... 134, 249-50, 360.
Fleetwood Mac... 57, 107, 116, 155, 178, 193, 195, 227-31, 233, 235, 239-40, 242, 244, 256, 297.
Fogerty, John... 149.
Fowley, Kim... 155, 421.
Freeman, Michael... 115, 312-13, 379.
The Future of Music Coalition... 441.

Galassini, Mike... 377.
Garbage... 134, 250.
Gardner, Steven... 402-03.

Garfield, Bruce... 151-52.
Gelfond, Brad... 358, 415.
Girling, Jim... 115-17.
Giuffria, Gregg... 334-35, 338.
Goldmann, Peter... 190-91.
Grin... 32-33, 69, 83.

Hamer Guitars... 126, 201, 234.
Hamer, Paul... 126.
Higgins, Joe... 27, 68, 96, 176, 198.
Hinkhouse, Lou... 321-22, 382.
Holverson, Garry... 37, 61, 96, 101, 198-99, 201, 204.
Hoover, Jamie... 382, 400-01.
Hunter, Jeff... 249, 262-63, 357, 359-60, 365, 367.
Hurd, Steve... 202-03, 263.

Independent National Distributors, Inc. (INDI)... 409-10, 427.
International Pop Overthrow Festival (IPO)... 368, 434-35, 438.
iTunes... 441-42, 444.
Inventory (2011)... 215, 313.

Jackson, Michael... 148, 298, 311.
Jagger, Mick... 93, 128, 162, 460.
Jam, The... 174.
Jay's Longhorn... 130-32.
Jem Imports/ PVC... 128-31, 136, 138, 140, 145, 160, 185, 189, 190, 401.
Jesperson, Peter... 130-32, 189.
Johnson, Neville... 147, 49-50, 247, 316..
Joseph, Andy... 26, 27, 29, 42, 47.

Keene, Tommy 414, 433.
Kelly, Bill... 321, 382.
Kings, The... 246.
Kiss... 182, 260, 303-04, 332-38, 343.
Korgis, The... 246.
Klebe, Arlie... 16-17, 38-39.
Klebe, Gary... 16-17, 22-23, 25-36, 38-41, 43-47, 49-51, 53-74, 78-81, 83-84, 87-90, 92-100, 103,108-09, 112-13, 115-16, 119-30, 133-35, 139-43, 146-53, 155-56, 158, 161-63, 165-70, 172, 174-76, 179, 186, 189-90, 192-97, 200-03, 206-07, 209-11, 214-15, 218-24, 226, 228-30, 232-36, 238, 240, 242-47, 249-52, 255 256 258 259 260 261 263 264 265 267, 268, 272-73, 275, 277-78, 280-87, 291-93, 304-05, 308-10, 312-15, 317-20, 322-27, 330-32, 333-37, 339-46, 348-52, 354-58, 360, 364-70, 373-74, 375-76, 379-80, 382, 387, 391-405, 407-08, 410-11, 414 415 416 417 418 419 420 421 424 425 426 427 428 429 431 432 434 438 439 442 443 445 449 453 454 455 456 457 458 459 460 461 462, 463-64.
Klebe, Jerry... 16-17, 22, 174-75, 428-29.
Klebe, Tim... 16, 57-58, 69, 186, 428.
Knack, The... 159, 172-74, 184, 191, 211, 237, 248, 450.
Kot, Greg... 352, 360-61, 385, 440, 447.
Krasnow, Bob... 301-02.
Kuse, Hiroshi... 448-49.

Leavens, Tom... 114, 130, 145, 147-48, 153, 189-90.
Lendt, C.K.... 336;. *Kiss and Sell: The Making of a Supergroup* (1997)... 303, 336, 343-44.
Lennon, John... 30, 41, 141, 251-52, 422.
Lime... 26-29, 47, 68, 73, 126, 134, 161, 176, 198, 240.
Line Records... 316-17.
Lloyd, Bill... 381-82, 401, 433.

Malboeuf, Mark... 361-63.
Mannequin 2: On the Move... 356-57, 437.
Manor, The... 156, 161-62, 164, 167-72, 174-75, 232, 236, 304, 329.
Material Issue... 319-20, 327, 367-68, 373, 376-77, 380-81, 383, 385-90, 413.
Marcus, Greil... 110-11, 262.
Marks, Howard... 303, 335-38, 343.
Martell, Dorn... 362-63, 371.
Mathé, Patrick... 344-45.

McCormick, Moira... 201, 204-05, 296, 318.
McDonald, Glenn... 450.
McLeese, Don... 106-07, 120-21, 132, 210, 229, 352.
Menck, Ric... 133-34, 312, 319, 346, 347, 357, 391, 413.
Meyer, Philip "Skip"... 71-72, 74, 78, 84-86, 89, 92, 96-98, 108, 116-17, 132, 146, 159-60, 162-65, 169-71, 175, 177, 180, 193, 196, 200-05, 217, 224, 226-27, 232, 235-36, 241. 247, 256, 261, 263-64, 267, 278-79, 283-85, 290-93, 301, 303, 305, 309, 314-15, 347, 414, 445.
Meyers, Steve... 115, 117.
Milgrim, Hale... 358, 364, 369, 373.
Millennium Park... 447-48.
Molland, Joey... 373-74.
Molloy, David... 152-53.
Morris, Chris... 198, 369-70, 426-27, 437.
Move, The... 32, 57, 340.
MTV... 191, 270-77, 279-80, 285, 295, 302, 361, 363, 372, 415.
Mulleman, Chip... 29, 40.
Murphy, Jeff... 17-21, 23-24, 29, 31-34, 37-43 47,49-50, 53-59, 61-65, 67, 69-70, 72-73, 77, 79-81, 84, 86-103, 106, 108, 111-13, 115, 117, 121-24, 126-30, 132-33, 135, 139, 141-43, 145, 148, 150, 152-55, 158, 160-72, 174-76, 179, 181, 190-91, 193-201, 204-07, 210, 212, 214-20, 226-27, 229, 236, 238-39, 241-43, 245-49, 259-60, 263, 265-68, 276, 278, 281, 283-87, 289-90, 293, 296, 300-05, 308-32, 333-34, 336-48, 350-55, 357-61, 364-67, 369-73, 375-76, 378-82, 384-99, 402-03, 409-11,414-19, 421-34, 436-37, 439, 442-49, 453-55, 457-62, 464. *Shoes: Birth of a Band, the Record Deal, and the Making of Present Tense (2006 memoir)*, 61-62, 143, 148, 152-53, 166, 172, 181, 193, 444; *Cantilever (2007)*,442-43, 446-47, 453.
Murphy, John... 17-21, 23-40, 42-48, 49, 50, 53-74, 78-81, 83, 85, 88-103, 106, 112-13, 117, 122-24, 126-28, 131, 134-35, 138-42, 145-46, 148, 150-53, 156, 158-71, 175-76, 177-79, 187-88, 192-96, 199-201, 204-05, 207, 210-11, 213-26, 228-37, 239-40, 242-47, 249-53, 255-56, 258-61, 263-66, 275, 280-83, 285-86, 288, 290-93, 302-03, 305-06, 308-10, 312-19, 321-24, 326-27, 330, 332, 333-36, 338-39, 341-45, 348-51, 353-54, 357-61, 363-70, 377-80, 383, 387-88, 392-99, 404-05, 414-16, 424-25, 427-34, 436-37, 443, 445-49, 451, 453-60, 462-64.
Murphy, John Michael "Mick"... 18-20, 433-34.
Murphy, Lorinda... 317-318, 323, 332, 382, 390.
Murray, Noel... 81, 450.
Murumets, Susan... 369.

Nerk Twins, The... 265, 422-25, 434.
Neuberger, Hank... 281-85, 351, 459.
Neville, Paul... 74-75, 139-40.
New Rose Records... 314, 316-17, 344-45.
Nicholas Tremulis Band... 419, 421.
Nicks, Stevie... 227, 239-40.
Night Gallery, The... 106, 120-21.
Nirvana... 250, 372, 380, 382, 387-89, 391-92, 399, 408, 415.
Nowlin, Bill ... 406-07, 409, 426.
Numero Group... 59, 67.

Oakes, Jordan... 431, 451.
Oar Folkjokeopus... 130-31, 189.
Olsen, Keith... 155, 227-28.

Paige, Bill... 102-03, 114-15, 117, 120, 210.
Pezband... 120-21.
Player: a Rock and Roll Dream (2006)... 444.
Popa, Lee... 299-301.
Posner, Mel... 267.
Power Pop (genre)... 81, 105, 108-10, 138, 171-72, 184, 192, 211, 331, 390, 421, 437, 450.
Public Image Ltd.... 162.

Pursuit of Happiness, The... 369.

Quatro, Suzi... 237.
Queen... 107, 156, 167, 190, 193, 242-43, 246, 277, 297-98.

R.E.M.... 261, 306-07, 376, 381, 400, 451.
"Radio Doctors"... 3268-70.
Ramones, The... 134-35, 155, 199.
Retinopathy of Prematurity (ROP)... 217.
Richardson, Billy "Beet"... 202-03, 263, 414, 456.
Richardson, John... 414-16, 420, 433, 449, 456-57, 459, 461-62.
Robbins, Ira... 81, 107, 118-19, 257, 295, 298, 307, 328-31, 390.
Rolling Stone... 32-33, 35, 111, 198, 211-12, 252, 262, 297-98, 331, 352-54, 356, 369, 383, 390, 400, 414.
Rojas, Hernan... 229, 231-34, 236-44.
Rounder Records... 406-07, 409.
Rudman, Kal (FMQB)... 256.
Rundgren, Todd... 32, 101, 369, 442, 458.
Ryan, Kelley... 381-83, 437.

Sachs, Bruce... 198-201, 203-04.
Sanden, Vern... 130-31.
Sartori, Maxanne... 138, 146, 232.
Schwartz, Marty... 136-38, 141-42, 146, 177-78, 181, 184-85, 187, 189, 195, 220, 222-23, 261, 277-78, 289-90, 302.
Scott, Leona Murphy... 19-21, 24, 36, 38, 44, 46-47, 54, 62, 153, 434.
Scott, Marty... 128-31, 136, 140 153, 160, 190, 401.
Scott, Tom... 20, 46.
Shannon, Del... 114, 149, 154, 198.
Shaw, Greg... 23, 107-12, 114, 118, 120-21, 127, 129-30, 140, 266,
Shinjuku JAM (Tokyo)... 448.
Shoe Fetish (2001)... 434, 436-38.
Shoes (albums)

Heads or Tails (1974)... 45-48, 50, 53, 54, 55, 58, 60, 64, 66, 78, 83, 431.
One in Versailles (1975)... 40, 49-50, 53-64, 67, 69, 72, 78, 83, 90, 103, 399, 405, 429, 432.
Bazooka (1975)... 60, 64-67, 69, 72, 77-78, 89-90, 93 98, 123, 350, 429, 432.
Black Vinyl Shoes (1977)... 6, 60, 66, 72, 75, 77-95, 97-103, 105-09, 111-12, 114, 118-21, 124-25, 127-31, 133, 136-39, 145, 155, 160, 185, 189-90, 210, 213-14, 223, 259, 264, 309, 330, 345, 351, 358, 368, 394, 405, 425, 450, 461-62.
Present Tense (1979)... 95, 125, 127, 142, 148, 158-59, 162-69, 172-76, 177-81, 185-86, 188-190, 194-95, 198, 206-08, 210-212, 213-16, 220-21, 223, 230, 232, 236, 241, 242-43, 245, 253, 256-62, 272, 275-76, 281, 296, 299, 345, 348, 351, 368, 386, 391, 400, 445, 448.
Tongue Twister (1981)... 125, 127, 213-16, 218-220, 225, 230, 233-36, 239-47, 250-53, 255-56, 258, 260-64, 266, 268, 275, 277, 280-81, 285-87, 295-96, 299, 306, 308, 348, 351, 389, 391, 400, 430-32, 445, 448.
Shoes on Ice (1981)... 266, 280, 296, 312, 351, 372, 400.
Boomerang (1982)... 91, 103, 218, 239, 268, 278-93, 295-98, 315, 351, 372, 396, 400, 448.
Silhouette (1984)... 91, 305, 312-18, 321, 328, 330, 332, 339, 344, 357-58, 392, 401, 432.
106, 360, 367, 368-73, 375, 378, 387, 389, 391, 400, 406, 407, 422, 423, 463, 474, 510.
Shoes Best (1987)... 330-332, 333, 337, 339, 344, 351, 400, 419.
Stolen Wishes (1989)... 91, 318, 332, 342, 344-54, 357-58, 368-70, 372-73, 375-76, 378-80, 391-93,

395-96, 399-400, 404, 407, 411, 413-14, 421, 432.
105, 106, 374, 391, 404, 406, 407-08, 409, 410-23, 435, 436, 439, 440, 443-44, 446, 447-49, 462, 463, 464, 465, 466, 468, 472, 478, 481, 482, 485, 487, 488, 497, 510.
Propeller (1994)... 91, 389, 391-99, 404, 411, 413-16, 417-419, 422, 424, 431.
106, 460, 462-72, 478, 485-86, 487-88, 489-91, 492, 493, 494, 498, 500, 508.
Fret Buzz (1995)... 416-19, 428.
As Is (1996)... 39, 46, 66-67, 175, 236-37, 345, 398, 428-33, 448-49.
Double Exposure (2007) ... 41, 220, 234, 445-46.
Ignition (2012)... 453-62.
Short Order Studios (La Cabane)... 82.
Short Order Recorder ... (Winthrop Harbor) 304-05, 308, 311-12, 319, 322-23, 325. (Zion) 95, 324-27, 331-32, 347-49, 351, 355, 358, 361-62, 376-80, 382, 386-88, 390, 393-94, 399-402, 404, 418, 421-23, 425-29, 431, 433, 438-39, 442-43.
Shumaker, Barry... 16, 55-56, 59, 62-63, 66, 68-70, 405.
Simmons, Gene ... 303, 332, 333-44, 346, 352-53, 379.
Sivers, Derek... 441-42.
Smashing Pumpkins... 250, 372, 380, 392, 418.
Smith, Joe... 188, 221, 276, 297-98.
Spongetones, The... 381-82, 400-02, 418, 433.
Spooner... 134, 249-50, 264, 360, 381-83.
St. Nicholas, Randee... 159, 256, 291, 315, 445.
Steele, George... 150.
Stein, Seymour... 134-36, 140, 143, 147.

Stone, Mike... 107, 156,159, 161-62, 165-68, 171-72, 175-76, 178, 207, 229-30,232, 235, 242, 431.
125, 181-82, 185, 188-89, 192-96, 199-200, 201, 204, 205, 208, 242, 268, 269, 272, 275, 283, 508.
Strawberry Fields (record store)... 33, 59, 404-05.
Summerfest... 132, 360.
Sweet, Matthew... 133, 349, 381, 437.
Swingset Police... 377, 421, 424, 434.
Szczepanek, Peter... 397-98.

TEAC 3340S... 37-38, 53-55, 63, 80, 123, 198, 214, 425.
Take Me... 249, 263, 37, 360.
Talking Heads, The... 134-35, 199, 386.
Thompson, Carol... 146, 157, 186, 188, 190, 224-25, 279, 288-89, 291.
Townsend, Sara Haack... 39, 43-44, 54, 56, 68, 73, 92, 101, 127, 259.
Townshend, Pete... 108.
Trident Studios... 169, 174-75.
Trouser Press... 38, 81, 93, 105, 107, 118-19, 131, 251-52, 298.
Twilley, Dwight... 83, 108, 110, 342.

United Western Studios... 226, 232, 234, 236-41, 243, 258.

Videos, Music... 190-91, 193-94, 209, 270-77, 279-80, 295, 321-22, 328, 356-57, 361-64, 371-72, 378, 406, 449, 447.
Vig, Butch... 134, 249-50, 264, 279, 293, 326, 360, 372-73, 380, 382, 387, 390, 426.
Village Recorder... 152-53, 231, 243-44.
Village Voice... 82, 210, 262.
Voliva, Wilbur... 13-14.

Wallace, Andy... 387-88.
Wax, Steve... 138, 187-88, 221.
Whitehouse, Jay... 322, 371, 379, 407.

Who, The... 52, 69, 118-19, 193, 200, 203, 251, 320.
Wild, David... 173, 352-54.
Wonder, Stevie... 217.

XTC... 208-09.

Yellow Pills... 431, 436, 451.
Yuletunes (1991)... 381-84, 401, 418, 422, 437.

Zelenko, Mike... 386-89, 391, 413.
Zion, Illinois... 10-14, 15-18, 21, 23, 27, 33, 39, 42, 45, 54-57, 61-63, 68, 70-74, 95-96, 99, 105-06, 108, 120-23, 126, 129-31, 133, 135, 141, 145, 150, 152, 155-57, 163, 64, 168, 184, 188, 197-98, 201, 205, 213, 225, 236, 240, 243, 247, 249-50, 265-66, 271, 277, 279, 285, 293-94, 304-05, 317, 321-22, 324-27, 345, 352, 355, 361, 370-71, 377, 381, 386-87, 390-91, 398, 400, 426, 435, 443, 451, 452.
Zion Leisure Center (Ice Arena)... 264-66, 319, 422.
Zonker...61-62, 198.

Chapter Heading Pictures

Prologue: Zion City Symbol, circa 1902

Chapter 1: Lime patch, Zion-Benton High School, 1970. (courtesy John Murphy)

Chapter 2: Original envelope, mailing One in Versailles to Gary. (Courtesy Gary Klebe)

Chapter 3: La Cabane, circa 1976. (Courtesy Jeff Murphy)

Chapter 4: Chicagofest. (Courtesy Shoes)

Chapter 5: The Manor

Chapter 6: Shoes display at Licorice Pizza, Santa Barbara, CA. (Courtesy Shoes)

Chapter 7: Shoes in control room at United Western Studios, summer 1980. (Courtesy Shoes)

Chapter 8: Shoes onstage at Zion Leisure Center. (Courtesy Shoes)

Chapter 9: Still shot from "When Push Comes to Shove," video. (Directed by Lou Hinkhouse)

Chapter 10: Still shot from "Never Had It Better" video. (Directed by Dorn Martell)

Chapter 11: Publicity shot, basement, Short Order Recorder/Black Vinyl Records (Todd Fedler photo)

Chapter 12: Corporate logo, Black Vinyl Records. (Courtesy Shoes)

AUTHORS

Mary E. Donnelly is a professor at SUNY Broome Community College in Binghamton, NY, the proprietor of the blog PowerPop, and the founder of PurePopPress, LLC. This is her first music book.

Moira McCormick is a freelance music journalist and editor based in Chicago. Her work has appeared in *The New York Times, Rolling Stone, Billboard, Vogue, USA Today, Chicago Sun-Times, Chicago Tribune*, and many other print and online publications.

www.ingramcontent.com/pod-product-compliance
Lightning Source LLC
Chambersburg PA
CBHW050117170426
43197CB00011B/1615